Mixed Relations

Asian–Aboriginal Contact in North Australia

Regina Ganter

with contributions from Julia Martinez and Gary Lee

UNIVERSITY OF WESTERN AUSTRALIA PRESS

THE AUTHORS AND PUBLISHER wish to respect Indigenous cultures and traditions and ethnic cultures and traditions in Australia. Indigenous readers are advised that this book contains references to and images of people who are now deceased.

Certain terms used by way of quoting or referring to legal terminology are no longer in public use. No offence is intended by the reproduction of such terms in their historical context.

This work has been produced with the financial assistance of the Australian Research Council; Australian Academy of the Humanities; Australian National University; and Griffith University, Queensland.

First published in 2006 by
University of Western Australia Press
Crawley, Western Australia 6009
www.uwapress.uwa.edu.au

Publication of this book was made possible with generous funding assistance from the Australia Council for the Arts, Australian Research Council, Australian Academy of the Humanities, Australian National University, and Griffith University, Queensland.

National Library of Australia
Cataloguing-in-Publication entry:

Ganter, Regina.
Mixed relations: Asian–Aboriginal contact in North Australia.

ISBN 1 920694 41 2.

1. Makasar (Indonesian people)—Australia, Northern—History. 2. Aboriginal Australians—Australia, Northern—Foreign influences. 3. Aboriginal Australians—History.4. Australia, Northern—Discovery and exploration. I. Martinez, Julia. II. Lee, Gary Mura , 1955–. III. Title.

303.482089915

Consultant editor: Diane Carlisle
Designed by Sandra Nobes
Typeset in 10½ point Berkeley Book
Printed by BPA Print Group

Unless otherwise stated, photographs were all taken by Regina Ganter.

Contents

Maps & Illustrations

MAPS

ILLUSTRATIONS

Author's note: the journey of writing

THIS book has many origins: a mixed lineage but a strong sense of identity, perhaps. In one sense, it is a direct descendant of my history of the pearl-shelling industry in Torres Strait, in which I started to talk about a certain 'camaraderie' between Asian and Aboriginal peoples in Australia, borrowing the term from one of my thesis supervisors, anthropologist Athol Chase. He had contributed to one of the earliest publications explicitly devoted to the topic of Asian–Aboriginal relations, a 1981 special issue of *Aboriginal History*. The topic appeared on the margins of Australian history, on the margins of Aboriginal studies, and not even remotely within the purview of Asian studies.

My thesis made an original argument about colonial industry and its attitudes to human and natural resources, and had worthwhile things to contribute to the history of government–industry relationships. But the examiners of the thesis, judges of the manuscript and reviewers of the book were most drawn to the curious arena of race relations that it explored, in which Japanese, Torres Strait Islanders and whites formed the fulcrum of a racially stratified hierarchy of labour. They might have sensed what I have come to conclude years later: that Asian–Aboriginal contact is not at the margin of anything but at the very core of the anxious nation.

'Asian–Aboriginal camaraderie' is now a term that has entered into scholarly discourse. It was this observed camaraderie, and the question of how to account for it, that launched me into a postdoctoral fellowship. I tentatively called the phenomenon 'triangular race relations'. It encompassed the idea that significant and consequential relationships existed not only between Aborigines and whites, and Asians and whites in colonial Australia, but also that these three groups stood in dynamic interaction with each other, and that neither Aboriginal policy nor policies towards Asians could be fully understood in isolation.

When I arrived from Griffith University to the Australian National University (ANU), at the History Programme of the Research School of Social Sciences (RSSS) in the middle of 1993, I knew exactly the scope of my topic. I already knew all that it was necessary to know about indigenous relationships with Japanese in Queensland and how to explain them. All that was required was to test my explanations against some different settings: different industries, different groups of Asians, different groups of indigenous people, different states (including the Northern Territory, which was to become a state within only a matter of years, it seemed). I needed only to look at Chinese miners in the Northern Territory, Malay trepangers in Arnhem Land, Filipinos in the Kimberley, and perhaps Afghan cameleers, and their various relationships with indigenous people to work out to what degree a shared experience of racism, and the legislative framework that cornered indigenous motivation, led to an affinity between them and to a symbiotic industrial relationship.

A small Griffith University research grant had already enabled me to gather much written material. With the generous financial assistance of the RSSS, and excellent facilities offered by the ANU's North Australia Research Unit (NARU) in Darwin, I now started fieldwork.

Within the shortest time my confidence was blown away. My interviews yielded a wild array of personal experiences amounting to a chequered history that refused to conform to the patterns that should have been dictated by the policies of each state. The notion of a shared history of oppression, which had seemed as solid as the desk on which I had put it to paper so well, revealed itself to be like a smog, clearly visible from a distance, but barely perceptible from up close. Expecting it to be somehow readily tangible, I hadn't developed a tool-kit to measure it. I had sincerely believed that historical methods would see me through: books, archives, oral history; research questions and evidence; cross-checking and substantiating.

The question of identity started to surface very strongly in these interviews: mixed descendants wondering about, searching for, defining, or defending their identity. Because my project was about Asian–Aboriginal contact, I was usually referred to people of Asian–Aboriginal descent. It might have been the neatness of my racial categories that spurned discussions about identity. On an intellectual level it is easy to understand that 'Aboriginal' has to be at least as Euro-centric a category as 'Asian', but the yearning for the quintessential, authentic, unadulterated-by-history, real Aboriginal is difficult to uproot, precisely because it belongs to the romantic and not the scientific.

In region after region that I visited in the north, I was assured that 'we all yella-fella here, plenty', that Asian men formed a significant part of the collective patrilineage of Aboriginal peoples. And that it was all right. That this was part of their history. That they were able to talk about it, and willing to recall it.

After my first fieldwork trip in the Northern Territory I returned to Canberra bewildered and excited. If I wanted to write about northern Australia, that's where I needed to be. Deborah Bird Rose, then the acting director of NARU, invited me for a visiting fellowship, and Paul Bourke as head of the History Programme graciously consented to my spending the remainder of my postdoctoral stint at the ANU's Darwin campus. I packed up all my belongings again, and moved to Darwin. Deborah has since reminded me how I steamed into town arriving with the Wet, and within a week rented a townhouse, bought a used car, and settled Yannick in a new school and after-school care. So the book started again, with another lineage: stories from northern Australia.

During our time in Darwin, Yannick and I visited communities along the Top End from Cobourg Peninsula to Yirrkala by single-engine Cessna piloted by my Darwin neighbour, Jo Shultz. The impression we generally made was that I had come with my daughter and son. I did not find this flattering, but then at precisely my age of thirty-six, Christine Camfoo, who became my sister in Bulman, was the grey-haired matriarch of a tribe of grandchildren. Jo made her time freely available because she wanted to get up flying hours for her commercial licence. I needed to pay only for the plane hire, calculated by flying time. When we returned the plane the air navigation company was unimpressed about how little flying time we had clocked up in three weeks. By air the communities are just fifteen to fifty minutes apart—but far enough for me to cast many an envious glance at the odd four-wheel-drive vehicle fighting its way through the dust below. By car I visited Oenpelli, Baringa and Bulman at the southern end of Arnhem Land, Daly River, Port Keats and Peppimenarti to the west, and the Kimberley.

The Northern Land Council, the Kimberley Land Council and the local land councils were extremely helpful. Still it was always a lot of writing, phoning and faxing to obtain prior permission to visit, to find out who to talk to and when, and to arrange accommodation and meetings. I twice drove from Darwin to Broome and back, visiting most townships and many communities along the way. I learned much that was useful for my project, and much more that is useful for knowing Australia. It is one thing to read about the poor condition of roads servicing indigenous communities, and quite another to try to navigate them, for instance.

In Wyndham I had my own lesson in the finely graded rules that underpin polyethnicity, or the close proximity of various ethnic groups. Wyndham is praised by many of its residents for its racial harmony. A retired police officer had come back for a final visit after many years away, and memories were relived in the lounge of the hotel where I was having dinner. I was cordially included in the discussions between several of the staff and patrons. From some of the stories it seemed to me that the indigenous man I had interviewed earlier must have been the offsider of this sergeant. I went to pick him up to meet the former sergeant. After engaging me in discussion for a while, he came with me reluctantly, protesting that he didn't drink, but I overruled his objections, saying we could have a soft drink. As we proceeded towards the lounge of the hotel, we passed the public bar where my companion was loudly greeted. The usual jokes were made, and he entered into the banter and seemed to have forgotten what we had come for. When I finally manoeuvred him past the public bar and into the lounge, the old sergeant had left, nobody addressed us with a single glance, and we spent more than ten minutes at the counter before it dawned on me that we were not going to be served. Anyone who had grown up in Australia, I'm afraid, would have known better.

When I returned to teaching at Griffith University in 1995 my book was not finished. As a matter of fact, it wasn't begun. I had done much travelling in the northern parts of Western Australia and the Northern Territory, much talking, much listening. I had piled case study upon case study, each more fascinating than the next, more tragic, more ponderous, and each with a long list of unanswered questions, pointers for further research, suggestions for further reading, addresses of further family members to contact. I had an impressive-sized manuscript, but it was not a book by any stretch of the imagination. It was a mountain of work to do. I had presented five papers, two overseas. I had done laborious translations for the Wik native title case useful for my work. I had also turned my thesis into a book, published an article in German, and met scores of interesting, important, intelligent, useful, resourceful, powerful and insightful people. But no book.

Teaching restored my analytic confidence. I started to write northern Australia into our Australian history subjects, not as an addition, but as a challenge to mainstream histories. I started to use materials from my research mountain in class, and began to teach history as work in progress, with problems attached, problems of ethics, method, interpretation, presentation.

In the 1996 grant round of the Australian Research Council (ARC) I gained what was called a 'Large Grant'—the academic's equivalent of drawing Carbine in the Melbourne Cup. I had already started another oral history project, on the Australian Allied soldiers who were surreptitiously assisted by the civilian population of Crete during the German occupation in 1941–42. This project put me in touch with many veterans and their associations, who tended to think of it as being about the Battle of Crete, the subject of an impressive number of books. The Battle of Crete meant strategies, manoeuvres, alliances, battalions, actions, enemies, heroes and males. It meant chance encounters, women and men, human interactions and misunderstandings, and taking big risks unheroically. It taught me that communities own their histories and do not particularly like to have them challenged and reinterpreted. Getting away from Aboriginal histories did not mean escaping that problem. Many will say that they could have told me so, but being told, or taught, can be such a long way from learning.

The ARC funding came through in 1997, and I cranked my mind back into Asian–Aboriginal relations. I took leave from teaching for a semester and conducted the Queensland fieldwork, by car from Brisbane to Bamaga, retracing my steps from two fieldwork periods of my first book, as well as venturing to the west coast of the Cape and into the Gulf to return through Mount Isa. This time I was accompanied by Ioannis Manousakis, who had never set foot in an Aboriginal community. Through his eyes I perceived again the disadvantage of people in remote Aboriginal communities, to which I had almost grown accustomed from much exposure, as well as the spark of cognition when one meets as individuals people from a group about whom one has much second-hand knowledge.

Jonathan Richards was engaged as a research assistant, and I negotiated access to restricted files in the Queensland State Archives on the basis of the permissions my interviewees had signed. We tried to be systematic, filling the gaps left open by the fieldwork. The result was that we doubled the research mountain. The book started again with another lineage: piles upon piles of departmental files.

The state government records on Aborigines in Queensland are more thorough, more systematic, more accessible and better indexed than those in either Western Australia or the Northern Territory. The Queensland State Archives (QSA), and the Department of Aboriginal and Torres Strait Islander Programmes and Development (DATSIPD, later DATSIP), which has control of some of these files, were very accommodating. And yet it was extremely difficult to find just what we were looking for.

We figured that at certain moments in their lives, the stories of interviewees ought to be reflected in departmental records, and so it must be possible to verify and date the stories gathered. If they were removed, if they needed permission to marry, if they applied for exemption from the Aboriginal *Protection Acts*, if their fathers arrived from overseas, or if someone went overseas—this must be somewhere in the files. In principle, this is true. In practice, it was a nightmare. There was a Register of Removals, but only from 1908 to 1971. There was a computerised index for public use, but without reference to restricted materials. The department's Community and Personal Histories section had another computerised index, the Heritage Database, but only for staff use because it contained sensitive material. There was yet another database, but the officer who compiled it had been so systematic in his encryptions that after his death the department staff were unable to interpret it well enough to lead back to the sources on which it was based. How would non-professional indigenous people fare if they needed to or wanted to research their histories without relying only on oral history? Providing access to such information to indigenous communities and individuals had been one of the strong recommendations of the Royal Commission on Aboriginal Deaths in Custody (1991). The *Bringing Them Home* (1997) report on the Stolen Generations showed how important the issue of forced removal was and how difficult it was to arrive at reliable estimates of the scale of removals. We partnered DATSIPD in a further ARC research project to commission a PhD candidate to prepare a public access database of forced removals of Aboriginal people in Queensland, and to identify the major periods and geographical movements of removals. This work was conducted by Mark Copland.

Jonathan continued to ferret through the QSA and the Western Australian archives, we took turns in the Australian Archives, and I had already done much work on the Northern Territory records. We unearthed some very good sets of documentation, and I started to write journal articles and to speak at conferences—conferences on history, Australian Studies, Queensland Studies, indigenous politics, postcoloniality, Chinese in Australia—addressing whoever would listen. The study of Chinese in Australian history was becoming a dynamic field, propelled in large measure by Henry Chan since his retirement from Newcastle University's history department. Henry continued to organise, and motivate others to organise, conferences and seminars in this area, and greatly encouraged me to speak about Chinese–Aboriginal families to largely Chinese audiences in Australia. He pulled me along to conferences in Newcastle, Dunedin, Sydney, Melbourne and Taipei.

As part of Henry's 'round the country' and 'round the region' series of events, I convened a two-day workshop in Brisbane in June 1999 on 'Asians in Australian history'. It had contributions on the polyethnic communities of Broome, Thursday Island and Darwin from Yuriko Nagata, Julia Martinez and Sarah Yu. Emeritus Professor John Mulvaney's keynote address considered the trepangers and cameleers as neglected factors in Australian history. Peter Read spoke about a sense of place among Asian, Aboriginal and white Australians; Christine Choo, about Chinese connections in the Kimberley; Anna Shnukal, about Asian–Aboriginal families in Torres Strait; and Guy Ramsay, about indigenous people of Chinese descent. Pauline Rule and Keiko Tamura addressed mixed marriages between Asians and Europeans. Don McMillen, Rachelle Allen, Karl Zhao, Zhigang Wei, Peta Stephenson and Shireen Stephen spoke about the contemporary identity of Chinese in Australia. Henry Chan, Michael Williams and Marian Diamond approached Chinese in Australian history, supported by Barry McGowan on the Chinese in the goldfields, Jonathan Richards on 'China Camp' in the Bloomfield, and Jan Hegarty on the 1913 census of aliens in Queensland. Eight of the twenty-three invited speakers were postgraduates, and most others were presenting work in progress. We gained a sense of an emerging field of interest.

In the course of all this conferencing, every year I met a few more members of Asian–Aboriginal families who were either published authors or capable researchers. Their presentations started to be grouped with mine on conference programs. And so, just as the ARC Large Grant was nearing its end, and still no book, the book reconfigured itself again, with another lineage: indigenous voices. Four members of such families and two young researchers with interests in northern and Asian histories agreed to write chapters.

The end of the grant roughly coincided with my first sabbatical, which I had saved up to make a full year. Little by little I had banked up commitments for this marvellous long twelve months I would have free from teaching. In the first seven months I submitted four papers for publication, addressed six conferences, and conducted fieldwork in Greece for my Cretan project. With five months to go, no prospect of further funding until this project was completed, and nobody else to blame, I did the inevitable: I sat down to write.

By this time, after so much writing and speaking about the topic, I found it easy to chat about. I chatted to John Milne, who had materialised at a Canberra workshop, and became a bouncing board of arguments on mixed identities, mixed-up identities and a case of alleged fraudulent identity reported in the press. I chatted also to Basia Meder, a Canberra-based freelance photographer who had visited much the same regions as I had, but whose attitude to text and story was quite different from mine. I told them some stories from my fieldwork and kept asking—myself more than anyone—how could I tell these stories as a historian? With all the gaps in the record, does one not need to be a creative writer to tell the truth? I thought it would help to be part of the story, to be able to give a personal slant, and encouraged my co-authors to write from their own perspectives, not as representatives of their families. As I faced these problems of representation, my co-authors encountered their own. When I had finished my share of the book, only two of the six had submitted a contribution.

So here we have this somewhat lopsided manuscript of many lineages, falling into a well-behaved historical narrative where it is based on documentary and secondary research, and exploding into a fireworks of stories from the north based on indigenous life experiences. According to the Kabbala, everything happens in divine time, and perhaps it is well that the book has not finished its project of including many indigenous voices. It might now be the prelude to and not the opus of mixed relations histories of Australia.

Solidly underpinning this book are the stories gathered from people in the north, and I thank them all. All of these stories were beautifully told, in their own style, with their own nuances. Many stories told to me with generous patience have not found inclusion in this book, and to those people, my apologies. Many others have become rigid and structured in the retelling, because as a historian I am starting at almost opposite ends to the narrators. The book is based on documentary and oral history, and it requires a two-tracked reading: the reader will gather story upon story along the narrative of the chapters that assemble themselves into an image of the polyethnic history of northern Australia. Like some economic indices, according to Joan Robinson, these stories are not 'well behaved': they follow their own patterns and meander towards and away from the point they are meant to illustrate. They are personal stories, and they are part of northern history. They are therefore about real persons, with real names as far as they could be ascertained. All interviewees have given their written consent to the use of this material, except where it is taken from published sources. This book has been several years in preparation and is intended as a long-lasting record and interpretation of northern histories. Regrettably it is not possible in such an undertaking to take account of restrictions that might temporarily append to certain names in indigenous communities.

In most instances I have retained the spelling of names in official records, even where they are unlikely renditions of a name, such as Doolah for Abdullah, or Ah Wang for Ahwang. The names of overseas Chinese are generally so distorted that it is in most cases impossible to recover them correctly. The 'Ah' prefixed to most Chinese names in Australia is an informal address useless for identification. In most cases the important clan name has dropped out of the name altogether, making it impossible to trace genealogies. Moreover, the pronunciation of Chinese characters varies according to language and dialect, so that the Latin spelling varies greatly. The names of many Japanese have in some cases been further anglicised by placing the family name after the personal name, and here the convention used by the respective families is followed.

ACKNOWLEDGEMENTS

My thanks are to all those who were interviewed for this book (named at the end of the book), and to those who facilitated my travels and work in various ways. During various excursions into unknown territory I had the supportive company of my son Yannick Vaughan, my partner Ioannis Manousakis, my friend Jerry Smith, pilot Jo Shultz and Dot Hunter. In Darwin Debbie Rose and Darrel Lewis, Patrick Sullivan, Marcia and Ruby Langton, and Jock Schmiechen and family made us feel at home, fulfilling a much-doubted prophesy of author Tim Jones: 'You'll like Darwin.' The then chairman of Galiwin'ku, Terry Yumbulul, and his wife Clellie took good care of us at Elcho Island. Their warm hospitality and undying humour were in themselves an experience. From the back seat of Terry's truck we watched silent discussions conducted by gesture only, with simultaneous interpretations from Clellie for our astounded entertainment. Warm hospitality was also extended by Nellie and Tex Camfoo and family at Barunga and Bulman, Helen Wilkes in Cairns and Peter Fischer at China Camp. In Broome Stephen Albert became my pillar of social support. Elsewhere I benefited from the introductions, discussions, ideas and advice of Murrandoo Yanner and his family and the staff of the Capricornia Land Council, including Tony Chong, Peter and Sarah Yu, the staff of the Kimberley Land Council, the Wilson family at Mornington Island, Martin and Vicky Nakata, John Ah Kit and the Jawoyn Land Council, Muriel Bin Dol, Chris Lee, Ricky Guivarra, Hagiga Bin Doraho, Maria Morgan, Reggie Birch and many others, some of whom are acknowledged as donors of photographs or tellers of stories.

To all those who affirmed the interest and worth of this research during fieldwork and at home I am very indebted. I had the constant encouragement of Mark Finnane, Wayne Hudson and Henry Chan. Valuable material contributions were made by Campbell Macknight, Peter Spillett, Gus Bottrill, Ted Egan and many others, especially Darrel Lewis and Jonathan Richards, who freely passed on pieces from their own extensive research. Research assistance and translations were also rendered by Andrish Saint-Clare, Niken Lim, Tsung Rong Edwin Yang, Christa Loos, Michel Zwartelé and members of Jack Sahanna's family. Many published authors have also made helpful contributions, and I will mention only those not already referred to: Richard Baker, Gordon Briscoe, Christine Chistophersen, Paul Clark, Gillian Cowlishaw, Mikki Dewar, Harry and Diana Giese, Dyiniyini Gondarra, Hubert Hofer, Annie Holden, Mary Ann Jebb, Jackie Katona, Keith Lapulung, Dhuwarrwarr Marika, Scott Mitchell, Yuriko Nagata, Lee Scott-Virtue, Anna Shnukal, Joy Rraying and Ray Wood.

Special thanks to the staff of the Queensland State Archives, especially Nola Fulwood and Margaret Reid, and the staff of the Northern Land Council, who facilitated visiting permissions and remote accommodation. I must also thank my former and current postgraduate students, Jonathan Richards, Mark Copland, Fiona Noble and Dale Kerwin, for leading me into many useful discussions. Underpinning all this work is the generous financial and institutional assistance of a number of institutions: Griffith University contributed a pilot research grant, the History Programme in the Research School of Social Sciences at ANU offered a postdoctoral appointment, the North Australia Research Unit of ANU lent its support for the fieldwork, the Australian Research Council approved a Discovery Grant, and the Australian Academy of the Humanities subsidised the publication. In the process I have gathered many debts to those who have persuaded the judges that this is a project worth supporting.

Brisbane, March 2003
Regina Ganter

Abbreviations

AA ACT	Australian Archives (ACT branch)
ABC	Australian-born Chinese
AFZ	Australian Fishing Zone
AIF	Australian Imperial Force
ANU	Australian National University
APB	Aboriginal Protection Board
ATSIC	Aboriginal and Torres Strait Islander Commission
AWM	Australian War Memorial
AWU	Australian Workers' Union
BEIC	British East India Company
BHP	Broken Hill Pty Ltd
CBD	Central Business District
CPA	Chief Protector of Aborigines
DAIA	Department of Aboriginal and Islander Affairs (Qld, 1965) and Department of Aboriginal and Islander Advancement (Qld)
DNA	Director of Native Affairs
FCAATSI	Federal Council for the Advancement of Aborigines and Torres Strait Islanders
GPS	Global Positioning System
HMS	Her/His Majesty's Steamship
MoU	Memorandum of Understanding
NAWU	North Australian Workers' Union
NLC	Northern Land Council
NSW	New South Wales
NTDB	*Northern Territory Dictionary of Biography*
NTWU	Northern Territory Workers' Union
QPP	Queensland Parliamentary Papers
QSA	Queensland State Archives
QVP	Queensland Votes and Proceedings
RAAF	Royal Australian Air Force
RSL	Returned Soldiers' League
SAA	South Australian Archives
UNCLOS	United Nations Convention on the Law of the Sea
VOC	Verenigde Oostindische Compagnie, the Dutch East India Company
WAPP (V & P)	Western Australian Parliamentary Papers (Votes and Proceedings)

Balanda the Yolngu Matha term for white people (or any foreigners), from the Indonesian *orang belanda*, for Hollanders (or any Westerners).

bondeng broad-beamed prau.

Bugis the people of the kingdom of Bone on Sulawesi.

Daeng (Dg) formerly a royal title in Sulawesi, still used as an address of respect. Occurs as *dayng* in indigenous names along the Arnhem Land coast.

Gowa a kingdom on the island of Sulawesi (Celebes); at its peak from the 1640s to the 1660s.

kampung Indonesian for village, or quarters in a town.

Karaeng a Makasar title, sometimes translated as 'king'. This term occurs in Yolngu Matha as Kara- or Garra-.

Kayu Jawa the Makasar name for the Kimberley coast from Cape Londonderry to Cape Leveque.

lambere a narrow-beamed prau.

lemba, lembana Makasar term for 'bay'.

Macassan used here to denote the people who traded from the port of Makassar, not an ethnic ascription. Macassans are a historical phenomenon and are referred to with this spelling in much previous literature.

Makasar a language of Sulawesi, centred on Makassar, sometimes referred to as Macassarese.

Makassar capital of Sulawesi, formerly (ca. 1974–2001) Ujung Pandang.

Mangatharra a Yolngu Matha term for Macassans, sometimes pronounced as Mangajarra, and rendered by Berndt and Berndt as 'Mankasaran'. Here the Yolngu Matha spelling from Milingimbi is adopted. It closely approximates the Makasar term *Mangkasara*.

Marege the Makasar term for the Top End coast, properly spelled with a glottal stop (Marege').

nakhoda Makasar word for 'captain'.

nihonjin-kai Japanese club.

oyakata leader of a group, from the Japanese *oyakata* system of industrial employment organised as groups of workers in the charge of a patriarchal employer.

padewakang a type of traditional prau from Sulawesi.

perahu the Indonesian word for 'boat', sometimes rendered in English as 'prau' or 'prow'. See also *padewakang*, *bondeng*, *lambere*.

Sama Bajo seafaring people, or sea gypsies of the Malay Archipelago.

serang commander in charge of crew, esp. of Indian sailors.

Top End the northern part of the Northern Territory, from the Timor Sea to the Gulf of Carpentaria.

trepang a holothurian, or sea cucumber, or sea slug, also called bêche-de-mer from the Portuguese *bicho di mar*. Trepang derives from the Malay *teripang*.

Yirritja Yolngu society is composed of two moieties, Yirritja and Dhuwa. The Yirritja are the seaside people who are the inheritors of the Macassan tradition.

Yolngu Matha the language of north-east Arnhem Land, consisting of more than forty dialects. The Yolngu region includes Milingimbi, Ramangining, Galiwin'ku (Elcho Island), Gupwiyak (Lake Evella) and Yirrkala.

zaibatsu a Japanese term for dynastic families who controlled large conglomerates of companies.

INTRODUCTION
Reconfiguring Australian history

All struggles begin by redefining something out of the private into the public. BENHABIB

THIS book approaches Australian history from the north, where it properly begins. Long before any British interest in Australia, its northern shores were enmeshed in a trading network that linked it to China. Drawing on new—and much old—exciting research, the chapter of Macassan contact has grown to take up a substantial portion of this book, as indeed it deserves. Not only is it an important and consequential era of Asian–Aboriginal contact but also it spans at least two centuries, roughly at least equalling the white presence on this continent. It is now too well researched and documented to be overlooked in Australian history.

Looking at Australian history from north to south, instead of the other way round, reconfigures much of what we think we know of the Australian past. It is easy to surmise the astonishment of the intrepid Arnhem Land explorers in 1875 when they chanced upon an Aborigine who had just returned from Singapore. But equally nonplussed were the Macassans habitually harvesting these coasts when in 1803 they came across a party led by Matthew Flinders, who claimed that a British outpost existed in some remote southern part of the same continent.

From their beginning, white Australians were besieged in the north and took steps to fortify their hegemony. The history of the north is the history of this fortification in the face of massive numbers of Asians having various interactions with Aborigines. Out of the trepang industry established by the Macassans emerged the pearling industry, which became the driving engine of northern development. It, too, became an Asian industry, involving Aborigines, and much vigilance was lavished on it for that reason. Add to that coastal activity the presence of Chinese in mining and public works and the lifelines of transport held by Afghan cameleers, and the image of a long and solid history of a white Australia founders under the weight of sheer population balance in the north. It would be more appropriate to say that in the north the moment of a white Australia has been brief.

Out of the Macassan contact emerged a Yolngu culture that was deeply influenced by its experience of culture contact in northeast Arnhem Land. And all across the far north, from the Kimberley to Torres Strait—the very regions considered the heartlands of indigenous culture today—are indigenous peoples whose physical features bear witness to the history of Asian contact. Personal stories of remembering and acting on that history are here interwoven into an account of Aboriginal management in the three northern states. What emerges is that Aboriginal management in the northern states must be understood against the backdrop of Asian contact because official race relations policy has been played out in a triangulated rather than binary black-and-white, or Asian-and-white, dynamic.

The stories gathered here are a collection of anecdotes of Asian–Aboriginal contact. They include stories of conflict with Asians, and of being friends; of people who have been abandoned by their Asian fathers, and of people who thought they had been abandoned and found out differently. There are stories of removals, and stories of staying together against all odds; stories of 'being coloured' and of 'becoming Aboriginal'. There are stories of Aborigines educated in China or Japan, and

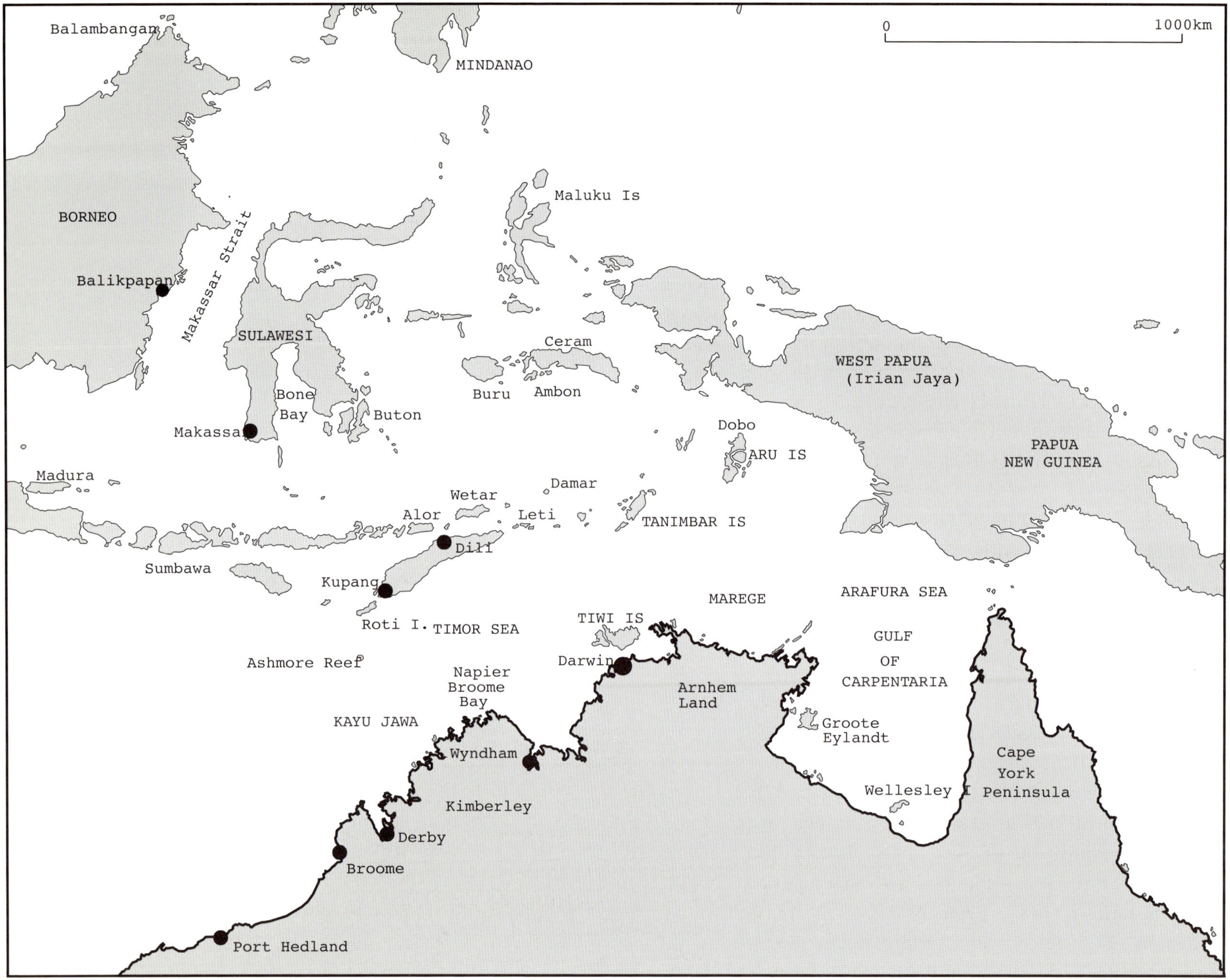
0
1000km
Balambangan
MINDANAO
BORNEO
Balikpapan
Makassar Strait
SULAWESI
Maluku Is
Ceram
Buru
Ambon
Bone
Bay
Buton
Makassar
WEST PAPUA
(Irian Jaya)
PAPUA
NEW GUINEA
Dobo
ARU IS
Madura
Damar
Wetar
Alor
Leti
TANIMBAR IS
Dili
Sumbawa
Kupang
Roti I.
TIMOR SEA
MAREGE
ARAFURA SEA
TIWI IS
GULF
OF
CARPENTARIA
Ashmore Reef
Darwin
Napier
Broome
Bay
Arnhem
Land
KAYU JAWA
Groote
Eylandt
Wyndham
Cape
York
Peninsula
Wellesley I
Kimberley
Derby
Broome
Port Hedland

even stories of indigenous people who moved from Australia to Asia and formed families there, one, two or more generations ago. Together these stories do not yield a formula by which we could judge that Asian contact has been good or bad for Australian indigenous people. But they do tell us that it has been important and consequential, and that Asia has long been solidly present in Australia.

This is the first study of Asian–Aboriginal contact in Australia as a phenomenon worthy of inquiry in itself, rather than as a characteristic of a particular area. It sweeps across the north, along the pearling belt and into adjacent pockets of contact that had little to do with pearling. It insists that northern histories are important for a national narrative, and in the process it yields sufficient surprises, and enough challenges, to spawn much further inquiry.

The identity politics of Asian, white and indigenous Australians are implicated by these northern histories. The population figures of northern Australia indicate that a white Australia was not achieved until World War II—unless we are content to say 'Australia' and mean its southern half. The 1970s were evidently not the first time anywhere in Australia that large numbers of Asians settled here, and at least in the north polyethnicity and its multifaith tolerance long predate the policy of multiculturalism. Australian Islamic societies have seized on the history of Afghans in Australia to point out what ought to be evident but is more often forgotten than remembered: that Asians—and Muslims—have long and proud histories in this country. Asians in Australian history are not mere colonial casualties, but are deeply entwined in the phenomenon of the Stolen Generation. Stories and cultural productions from the north suggest, moreover, that indigenous identity does not require the ahistorical chimera of a pristine people. It can embrace the creoleness conferred by the colonial past and engage it in a vibrant, living, contemporary culture.

The 2001 census reveals that 58 per cent of Australians now have parents born in two different countries. The trend is towards a mixed population with identity links to more than one country. It is a time for looking beyond the binaries. It all suggests that histories relevant for the future must pin themselves on a larger historical canvas, focus on the crossroads of culture contact and acknowledge the mixed relations that chequer Australian history.

OPPOSITE: The Indonesian Archipelago

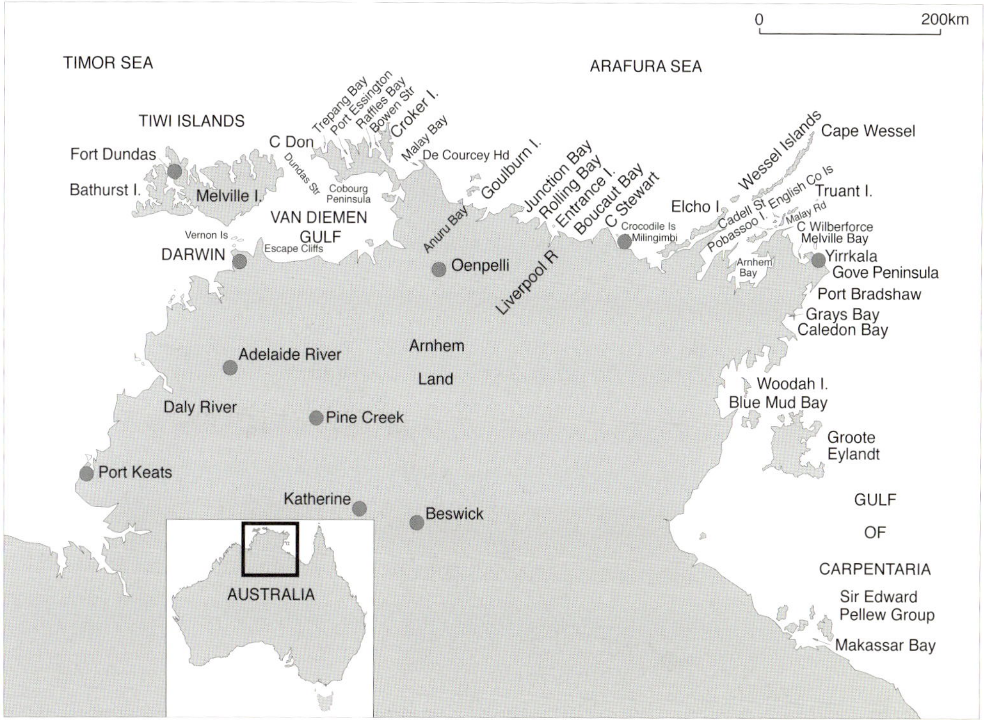

The Top End

CHAPTER 1

Trepang: Australia's Asian connection

THE PRECOLONIAL HISTORY OF THE NORTH

THE earliest regular contact between peoples from Asia and Australia took place well before the arrival of the British. Australian historians are well aware of this prior history, but what is not so well understood is that it is consequential: it changes the parameters of Australian history. That Chinese traders were in Australia before any British fleet is in itself worth noting. But this precolonial history has never been in the focus of national historical inquiry, and it is still hazy and riddled with mysteries. Here we will think about three types of consequences: how Matthew Flinders reacted when he discovered the trading armada for himself; how the trade spurned the British colonisers into northern settlement of the continent; and how the longstanding interaction with Muslim traders transformed the indigenous people of the north coast.

The Asian visitors came on annual trading voyages to a place they called Marege, the place of wild people. 'Marege' refers to the Top End coastline and islands. They referred to the Kimberley coast as Kayu Jawa, perhaps after the timber (*kayu*) they obtained there.[1] And because the place they visited was not yet Australia, I will continue to call it Marege. The Asians are known in Arnhem Land as Mangatharra[2] and in English as Malays or Indonesians, or more specifically as Macassans,[3] because they operated mainly out of the port of Makassar (known for a few decades as Ujung Pandang) in Sulawesi (formerly Celebes). Macassans are not an ethnic group; they are participants in a particular type of industry. I therefore retain the English spelling for this group of people because 'Macassan' refers to a far broader group of people than Makasar-speakers. Reference to Macassans in Australia usually includes, along with the inhabitants of the city of Makassar and the kingdom of Gowa, Bugis from the nearby kingdom of Bone (also referred to as Bugadji or Bugi' Mankasarau[4]), people from the islands of Aru and Timor (the latter sometimes referred to as Kupangers) and Sama Bajo, the 'sea gypsies' of Sulawesi. Strictly speaking it also includes the Chinese merchants who usually controlled and sometimes accompanied such trading voyages.

Makasar- and Bugismen had a vast reputation as seafarers and pirates. They took advantage of favourable monsoonal winds blowing them towards Marege in about December and back to Sulawesi in about April. Each year the Macassans set up camp on north Australian shores and islands, and gathered trepang. A fleet might consist of twenty or thirty vessels, of which at least one was equipped with a cannon and compass. On reaching the Australian coast the fleet split into smaller contingents and regrouped again before departure at the end of the season.[5] Trepang is a holothurian, or sea cucumber, or sea slug, also called bêche-de-mer (from the Portuguese *bicho di mar*). As soon as it is caught it must be gutted, boiled, spliced and dried for storage. When cooked it becomes quite rubbery, which is probably why it became known in English as 'swallo'. There are many different varieties, each fetching a different price, and China continues to be the main market for trepang.

This trepang trade locked the northern shores of Australia into a trading triangle with Makassar as the trading centre and southern China as the destination of the Australian trepang. Campbell Macknight, the foremost authority on its history, refers to it as Australia's first export industry. By 1820 trepang had become the largest export item from the Dutch East Indies to China next to pepper, and at Makassar at least thirty varieties of trepang were traded, most of them to southern China.[6] A comment from Macknight conveys some idea of the vitality of Australia's trepang industry: 'around the middle of the nineteenth century the North Australian coast was supplying . . . perhaps a quarter or more . . . of the total Chinese market for trepang'.[7] Today we consider trepang as insignificant as pepper, but sugar and spice and all kinds of food were powering world trade no less than precious metals and stones.

Trepanging became a major economic activity in the East Indies and had profound effects on the peoples engaged in it. People milled around the archipelago because of it. A sizeable Makasar population settled on Sumbawa Island to trade to the Kimberley region 500 miles away.[8] The maritime people of southern Sulawesi and nearby islands turned to trepanging as their major economic activity.[9] This means that they shifted from a subsistence economy—using a range of items for barter—to cash cropping: focusing on the production of a single commodity for sale. The region that was becoming the East Indies was still the southern periphery of a trading empire whose core was China, and Marege was one of its frontiers.

This lively and powerful trade to Marege was in full swing by about 1800. Matthew Flinders estimated the fleet in Marege at sixty vessels in 1803, and in 1818 Phillip Parker King understood it to involve 200 vessels. Neither the Dutch nor the British were to be very successful in dislodging the Chinese from their established dominance of this trade.[10]

Chinese probably entered the eastern archipelago in the early years of seventeenth century.[11] Resident Chinese were already participating in the intra-regional trade of the Indonesian archipelago before the Dutch ascendancy in the region. This trade gathered local produce and made it available for resale at local trading centres. Chinese merchants, known as *taukeh*, established themselves on many islands to participate in this regional trade. The British observed in 1665 that Chinese purchased 'putchcock' for the manufacture of incense and 'rassa', a civet cat, for its perfume along with more mundane objects.[12] Apart from grafting onto the traditional slave trade of the region, Chinese merchants supplied useful items and metals, and obtained luxury items in return. In the mid-nineteenth century several good descriptions of this trade appear. For example in 1841 a combined Makasar and Bugis fleet carrying 5,000 people traded to Dobo in the Aru Islands and left behind 'a few Dutch traders from Makassar, some dozen Chinese, and about 300 Bughis and Macassars'.[13] George Windsor Earl, writing in 1840, gained the impression that in the late eighteenth century Chinese merchants established a leading role in native trading and introduced new trades, such as trepang.[14] Indeed, we have an even earlier reliable reference for this instrumental role of Chinese traders, one that is also the earliest reliable reference to any trade to Marege.

In 1751 a Chinese trader set out from Timor 'to see if he could reach the large sand-plate beyond Roti, to search for turtle-horn' and that 'after five days sailing before the wind and two days and nights having drifted', he reached a southern coast whose people were 'very black', large and robust, unclothed, unarmed, with long woolly hair. The Dutch resident of Timor reported, 'Though said Chinese took it for a large island, we do not doubt or it will have been the mainland coast of the Southland.'[15] This news sparked great interest when it reached the Amsterdam headquarters of the Verenigde Oostindische Compagnie (VOC—the Dutch East India Company, established in 1601). But by the time the VOC directors requested more details, the Dutch resident at Timor had been replaced, and the new appointee could furnish no further news. The governor-general at Batavia (later Jakarta) added in 1754 that the journey to the Great South Land was 'made now and then from Timor and Makassar, but produces so far as we know nothing but trepang, being dried jelly fish, and wax'.[16]

Dried jellyfish, indeed. This response from Batavia suggests that the traffic to Marege was more long-standing, occasional rather than regular and more resource-diverse than the regular trepang trade that developed thereafter. And that the Dutch had little idea about trepang at this time.

A further expedition to the south land in February 1756 was to follow up on these reports but was unable to furnish any further detail on the trepang trade. Indeed any hint of Malay traders is conspicuously absent from the Dutch accounts of the Australian coasts from 1600 to the 1750s. Some of these voyages to New Holland took place during seasons when Macassan visitors could not be expected. But a number of journals of such voyages are lost, and they are a sore gap in the historical record.[17] British interest in the area awakened with the publication in English of Tasman's journal in 1694, and William Dampier was sent to reconnoitre with the northeast coast in January 1699. This caused the Dutch to reaffirm their interest with a 1705 survey of Van Diemen's Land (as Melville Island and Cobourg Peninsula were then known).[18]

The British became aware of a trade to Marege in about 1762. Alexander Dalrymple of the British East India Company sought to encourage such trading so as to defy the Dutch attempts to control it. He argued for a concerted effort to graft onto this trade by establishing a port to compete with the Dutch, within easy reach of Malay *perahu* and Chinese junks. Eventually Balambangan, between Palawan and North Borneo, was selected as a suitable site. Two attempts were made to establish a regular British trading post at Balambangan (1772–74 and 1803–05) at a time when the Macassan trade with Australian coasts was already thriving, but both attempts failed.[19]

THE COMMENCEMENT OF MACASSAN VOYAGES

That indigenous Australians had relationships with Macassans well before the British entered the scene has never been doubted. There is, however, some uncertainty over when this relationship commenced. Ian Crawford suggested that it must have commenced after 1669 and before 1763; that is, between the Dutch victory over the kingdom of Gowa and the time Alexander Dalrymple became aware of the Bugis trade to Marege.[20] Macknight's 1976 study accepts the 1751 source as the earliest reliable reference to the trepang trade to Marege, and largely agrees: 'The industry must have begun between about AD 1650 and 1750, and I believe that the most probable period within this century is the last quarter of the seventeenth century.'[21] He has since further refined his estimate and now doubts that the trade could have commenced before the 1720s.

This time frame credits the trade to Australia with greater antiquity than the historical record itself, strictly speaking, warrants at present. Using Dutch and British documentary sources, it has been traced no further back than the 1750s. From the 1750s British and Dutch sources make reference to this trade with increasing frequency. Still, a number of anthropologists and archaeologists have persistently challenged Macknight's estimate as being too conservative, and the question of the antiquity of contact continues to divide researchers. Anne Clark argues that anthropological and archaeological evidence suggests a more longstanding association.[22]

Some doubts remain also whether the trepang industry, that single-commodity export trade from Makassar to China, was indeed the earliest connection between the archipelago and the northern Australian coast. It seems far more reasonable to suspect that this industry itself grafted onto prior local knowledge. This is how Nicolas Baudin, leading a French expedition to New Holland in 1803, understood it: that the existence of the continent had been known for a long time, but that regular voyaging to it was of recent origin, stimulated by increasing Chinese demand for trepang.[23]

If there were earlier contacts, it is likely that they were not regular and not dedicated to a single product, such as trepang. It is also likely that they were not within the Macassan trading system but a more local connection, such as with Timor. Macknight, too, allowed for the possibility that contact 'may well have begun in a small, irregular and secretive way'.[24] It all means that there are other possible beginnings of voyages to Australia, but their base of historical evidence is far more brittle.

When the trade was in full swing, the travellers to Marege followed various routes. From Makassar they might proceed along Buton to the Kai and Aru islands, reaching the Australian shore near Elcho Island, or via East Timor arriving either near Melville Island or in the Kimberley, or via Flores, Kupang, Roti and Ashmore Reef towards the Kimberley. From Madura they trailed past Sumbawa, Sumba and Ashmore Reef to Rowley Shoals and returned via Makassar.

In a journey from the archipelago to Australia, using the trade winds, the most likely first point of contact would be either at the Tiwi Islands or in the Kimberley. Is it possible that the *taukeh* setting out from Timor in 1751 was following local advice on how to navigate and what to obtain from there? Is it possible that what he took to be a large island, and described in terms that well fit Australia, were the Tiwi Islands of Melville and Bathurst?

According to stories told to George Windsor Earl in Timor in 1840, Melville Island was a 'major reservoir of slaves for Portuguese slave traders', and in 1818 Phillip Parker King found a Melville Island woman repeating the words '*ven aca, ven aca*', Portuguese for 'come here'. In the 1880s Searcy understood Macassans to refer to Melville Islanders as *amba*, meaning slaves.[25] It is generally thought that Tiwi Islanders were less tolerant of strangers than other Aborigines because of a prior contact with Portuguese slave raiders.[26]

According to Marco Ramerini, the Portuguese first visited Timor in 1514–15 'on a Chinese junk', and thereafter conducted diverse *spedizioni commerciali* with Timor from their base in Malacca. They established a fort at Cupao (Kupang) in 1646 and a settlement in Dili in 1668, and did not leave the field to the Spanish, Dutch, Japanese or Indonesians until 1975. Their activities, if any, in Australia are surrounded by speculation. It has been suggested that Cristovao de Mendonca charted parts of the Australian coast in 1522–23, which later appeared in the Dieppe maps.[27] In the 1660s Portuguese trader Captain Francesco Vieira became prominent in the trade between China and Timor. As a result of this trade, Chinese settlers continued to have a noticeable presence on Timor (still at more than 3,000 in 1950). A connection between Timor and northern Australia did not require a Portuguese involvement. Until 1975 the official language of East Timor, Portuguese is most likely to have been used by East Timorese for interactions with foreigners. A pre-Macassan contact between Timor and the Tiwi Islands could have been conducted by Timorese or Portuguese, or by resident Chinese, or indeed by Sama Bajo.

SAMA BAJO

The Sama Bajo are sea gypsies who must be credited with a thorough knowledge of sea routes in the archipelago. They have traditionally been nomadic sea-dwelling people who reputedly get 'sea-sick' when they come on shore because they spend so much of their lives on boats. Sama Bajo have been in the southeastern part of the Malay Archipelago long enough to have a distinct dialect, spoken by Sama Bajo from the east coast of Kalimantan to Timor, Roti, Flores and Sumbawa. They belong to the Sama Bajau-speaking peoples who occur throughout the archipelago, with major groups in the southern Philippines and northern Kalimantan (Sabah).[28] Only about 5,000 of an estimated 900,000 Sama Bajau speakers in Malaysia, the Philippines and Indonesia are still permanent boat-dwellers. They are referred to as Bajau, Samal, Bajo, Bayo or Turije'ne'.[29]

Clifford Sather observes that for almost 200 years they have specialised on trepang fishing, operating as the sea-going dependants of Bugis or Makasar patrons. Their history is one of movement and dispersal, and of attaching themselves to a series of vibrant trading empires for which they rendered valuable services in return for protection. Sather argues that their folk myths, which claim origins in Johore or Bone, reflect the successive rise of such trading empires, and align the history of Sama Bajo with such powerful centres—they are in effect political myths.[30]

The Sama Bajo entered into their diaspora after Arab merchants opened direct trading links with southern China by way of the Sulu Archipelago in the late Sung period (960–1279), when Islam penetrated the Sulu region. The emergence of the Sulu sultanate was marked by ethnic stratification, with the seafaring Sama Bajo ranking at the bottom of the emerging social order.[31] Sather observes that 'slavery was a major social institution in eighteenth- and nineteenth-century Sulu'. Jim Warren estimates that slaves made up half of the population of the Sulu Archipelago and more than half the population of Solo in the period 1786–1898.[32] Active marauding was carried out under the patronage of Tausug aristocrats, sometimes by Sama Bajo subjects, especially the Balangingi' Samal.[33]

In such maritime trading empires the Sama Bajo

seafarers filled an important but subservient role. Under the influence of long-distance trade with China, India and the Middle East, they spread to Sulawesi, Kalimantan and other parts of eastern Indonesia 'some centuries before the first European [Portuguese] penetration of the region'.[34] They remained an ethnically distinct and politically marginal group, and some of the names for them are pejorative 'reflecting the pariah status generally ascribed to the Bajau Laut by those living ashore'.[35]

In Sulawesi the Sama Bajo appear to have been more independent, and somewhat less marginalised, than in the Sulu kingdom. They had their own leaders on whom special titles were sometimes bestowed, and the first ruler of the kingdom of Gowa is recorded as a woman who married a Bajo leader (the Karaeng Bajo).[36]

After the Dutch defeat of Makassar in 1669 the Sama Bajo further dispersed to other islands. It is known that by the early eighteenth century they were undertaking trepang voyages to Roti and Timor.[37] Here we have another possible link, perhaps via Timor, to the northern Australian coast: slave-raiding Sama Bajo. Indeed, the Sama Bajo have sometimes been linked to the Baijini myths of Arnhem Land.

THE BAIJINI

Considering the vast Macassan influence on the language, rituals and myths of Arnhem Land, anthropologists have generally tended to assert a more long-standing contact period than that supported by the historical record.[38] On the basis of extensive fieldwork in the 1940s, Ronald and Catherine Berndt theorised three contact phases: Macassan contact, commencing in the early sixteenth century and lasting until the arrival of the Europeans (which they dated at 1803 with Flinders' fleeting visit, rather than in the 1820s), Macassan contact influenced by the European presence to 1907—during which phase conflict and the consumption of alcohol increased—and a pre-Macassan phase of contact.[39]

The idea of a pre-Macassan phase was spawned by the myths and song cycles that refer to Baijini. It is as tempting as it is wrought with difficulty to match fragments of myth with historical data. The Berndts themselves cautioned that the Baijini stories appear to be superimposed with later Macassan stories. They understood the Baijini stories to refer to a period before historic times, to peoples who came not on the Macassan *perahu* but on *lolperu*, different sailing boats (*-peru* still suggests *perahu*). These people looked different from the Macassans, being paler, golden brown or copper coloured. They erected stone dwellings, speared fish and collected trepang, and the women wove and dyed cloth and cultivated gardens and rice.[40]

The Baijini stories make reference to women, and indeed the Berndts observe that on Buton and Salayar islands the words for 'woman' are *bawine* and *baini* respectively. Other words used by Yolngu to refer to Baijini women were *ngona*, derived from the Indonesian *nona* and *nonya* for 'woman' and 'girl', or *barambor*, possibly from the Malayan *perampuan* for 'woman'.[41] It seems most likely that all these terms were adopted during the Macassan phase.

The Berndts suggested that the Baijini figure refers to early traders to Australia. On the other hand, McIntosh, whose main informant was David Burrumarra, a Warramirri man and political and ritual leader of Elcho Island, distinguishes between Bayini, a white woman, ancestral mother for the Warramirri clan, and Birindji, her male equivalent, both of whom function as spirit beings who brought forth both the Macassans and the Yirritja moiety (see Glossary) Warramirri clan.[42]

The emphasis on the presence of women, and the suggestion that the Baijini myth has a historical origin, has led some researchers to speculate that reference is made to the Sama Bajo, who travelled as families. However, the totality of descriptors of the Baijini recorded by the Berndts clearly does not refer to any known peoples. Reference to women on Macassan boats is scant. The Berndts were told that Macassans very occasionally carried Indonesian prostitutes on board, though this is not supported by historical or oral references.[43] Ian Crawford was told of an incident that may have involved an Indonesian woman at Red Island in the Kimberley, though in this story it was not clear where the foreigners came from.[44] In 1967 five *perahus*, which Crawford believes came from Timor, called at the Ashmore Reef oilrig carrying at least one woman.[45] The only historical reference to Macassan women is by Earl, who said that in the 1829 season the Macassans brought their families with the intention of settling at Fort Wellington.

The problem with measuring the Baijini myth against historical data is that it is not the function of myth to record history. W. E. H. Stanner found that the historical composites of myths are merely incidental. The myths involving Macassans and Baijini might better be understood as a means of coming to terms with the presence of strangers. Donald Thomson observed in 1949 that, in myth, strangers must be accommodated. McIntosh developed this approach to myth with reference to the Baijini myths. He argues that Macassans are viewed as totemic beings, and Baijini are the spirit beings in which both they and the Warramirri originate. This body of myth aligns Macassans with the Warramirri, and therefore with all Yolngu. The Baijini myth creates a place for Macassans in the Yolngu imagination and allows them to see the seasonal presence of Macassans as part of traditional law, rather than as a rupture.[46]

McIntosh examined twenty variations of a story belonging to Yirritja, which all feature the central figure of a dog interacting with Macassans. They involve the Macassans offering novelties such as matches or rice, and the dog sometimes accepting, sometimes rejecting the offer. In this corpus McIntosh observed an equal number of references to conflict with Macassans as to a wish to build a relationship with them. The Yolngu wished to accommodate the Macassans just as the Macassans were interested in a continuing relationship that would safeguard their access to the trepang grounds. McIntosh found that the essential information contained in these myths was how links were forged between clans. Those stories where Macassan gifts were rejected also contain references to establishing links with clans on whose land are known trepang camps, and most links were forged in this corpus with the Warramirri, who had the best access to Macassans. The myths ascribe Yolngu agency to the presence and absence of direct links with Macassans.[47]

McIntosh agrees with a number of established anthropologists that mythology is constantly renewed and invented, essentially because 'change was an ongoing feature of Aboriginal life'. This means that myths are linked to political action, and their patterned variation emerges from the people who create them. They give an insight not into 'what actually happened in the fleeting encounters, but what significance it had in Aboriginal life'. Myths are records of how Aborigines see themselves, not of historical encounters.[48]

With this understanding of how myths function and produce meaning, the aggregation of presumed descriptors of Baijini gathered by the Berndts, in order to portray the Baijini themselves, renders these myths meaningless. This is because their mode of production and their politics are lost in the process. The giving of rice, matches, or the offer of technologies cannot be aggregated into a sum of descriptors, because these are symbolic instances occurring in separate versions of the story to fulfil the same function. They are various signifiers with a common signified. It must be concluded from McIntosh that far from echoing the distant past of a pre-Macassan period, the Macassans logically preceded the emergence of the Baijini myth. The problem with a wholesale dismissal of myth as historical reference is that it is often difficult to distinguish between myth and recollection, as we shall see in Chapter 2.

THE 'LONG HISTORY' VIEW OF MACASSAN CONTACT

On the Macassan side, too, there is some sense that contact may need to be dated before 1669, the year the Dutch conquered the kingdom of Gowa. A map that shows the northern part of Australia as part of the kingdom of Gowa prior to 1660 is exhibited in the Balla Lompoa, a reconstructed palace of the kings of Gowa. Its caption reads 'Map showing the Gowanese kingdom and areas that accepted Gowanese sovereignty until 1660', and the boundaries indicating the kingdom clearly include the Top End, from about Daly River in the east to Caledon Bay in the west.[49] The map almost certainly originates from a study of the history of Gowa by Abdul Razak Daeng Patunru in 1967. Patunru's map, indicating the same boundaries, and with the same caption, also includes the years in which various islands became part of the kingdom, ranging from 1512 (Makassar, the eastern coast of Celebes and the Salayar Islands) to 1640 (Buru, Ambon, Ceram, Timor and Australia). The history itself gives no hint why Australia appears in the map, how it became part of the kingdom, or with what justification it is claimed that this occurred around 1640. There are only general references to the frequent Macassan visits in this study, without an attempt to date their emergence. The kingdom of Gowa was at its peak from the 1640s to the 1660s, and thereafter Patunru's history becomes one of anti-colonial struggle.[50]

While the Top End was certainly within the realm of Macassan influence, industry and consciousness, it would be misleading to take the second part of the caption—'areas that accepted Gowanese sovereignty'—at face value with regard to Marege. When Spillett raised this issue in Arnhem Land, he was told that, according to Yolngu custom, if a Macassan man married an Aboriginal woman, he had the right to the use of the land belonging to her group, which would become his children's land.[51] This certainly does not amount to an acceptance of sovereignty.

It is the third part of the caption, 'until 1660', that is most puzzling. It makes good sense in terms of the history of Gowa to use the 1660s as a turning point. But Macknight's detailed research on the commencement of

The Gowanese kingdom including the Top End, according to Abdul Razak Daeng Patunru, former Governor of Makassar. A larger version of this map in the Palace of Gowa at Makassar bears the caption 'Map showing the Gowanese kingdom and areas that accepted Gowanese sovereignty until 1660'.

Source: Patunru, 1967.

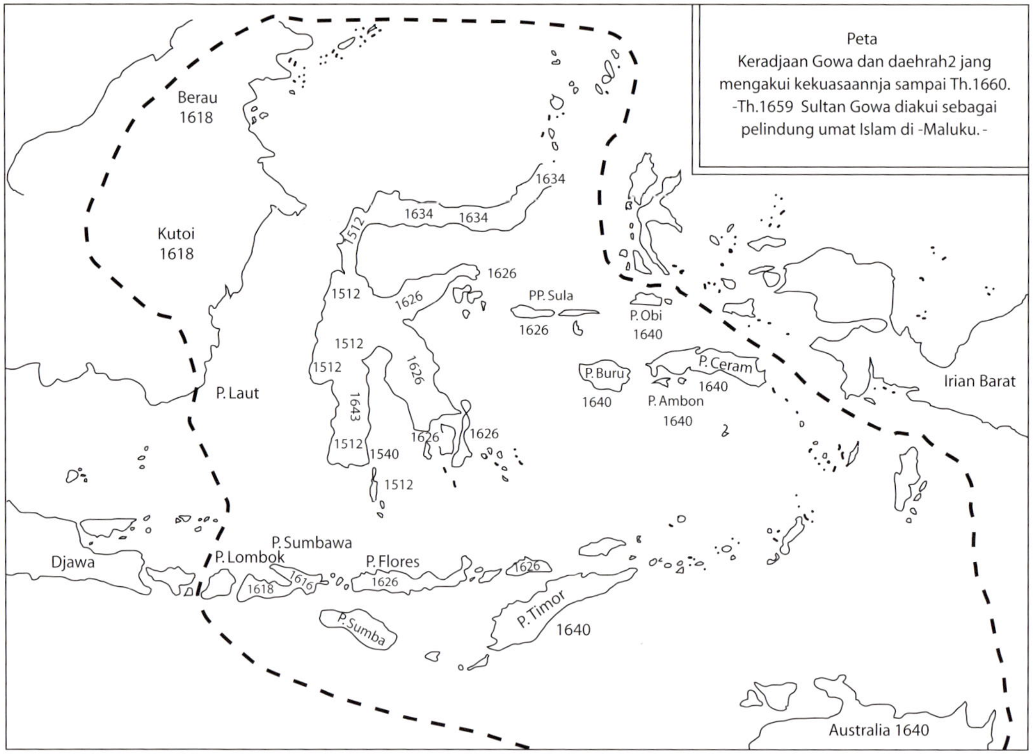

the trepang industry hardly encourages a view of the period before the 1660s as one of intensive contact with Marege.

Both Macknight and Ian Crawford have supplemented historical data with archaeological work, and neither they nor more recent scholars have offered a strong argument based on archaeological evidence to question the timeframe of contact suggested by the historical record. Macknight concluded from the remains he examined in eastern Arnhem Land that the industry was unified—much the same type of pottery was found across the sites—and well connected to world trade, with European and Chinese designs evident in the pottery. He dated the bulk of the pottery, coins and glassware in the eighteenth and nineteenth centuries. Macknight has expressed a strong distrust of his radiocarbon dates that indicated the age of wood extracted from Macassan fireplaces as 800 years (in the case of three samples) and 400 to 500 years (in the case of two samples). He believes these results were subject to a systematic source of error. A thermoluminescence test of pottery, although not entirely conclusive, was more in line with the historical data in suggesting an eighteenth-century origin.[52] Anne Clarke more recently questioned Macknight's inference of a systematic error. She argues that prima facie the 'long history' suggested by the archaeological results is as likely as the 'short history' supported by the historical record. Like Scott Mitchell's archaeological work on Cobourg Peninsula and Croker Island, Clarke's examination of indigenous midden sites on Groote Eylandt accepts the framework offered by historical evidence as a reference point. Clarke adds the interesting observation that the Macassan contact phase resulted in a shift towards coastal areas and marine resources, with larger groups and decreased seasonal mobility.[53] This work argues that the impact of Macassan contact has been profound and all-encompassing: much deeper than the observable material cultural and ritual practices.

There are still unsolved mysteries in this story. But what we do know reliably is already astounding. The earliest reliable documentary reference to a fishing voyage from the East Indies to Australia is a 1751 excursion commandeered by a Chinese merchant. It was well before Cook's venture into the Pacific, but when the map of Nieuw Holland was already dotted with Dutch names. If trepang fishing in Marege started no sooner than the 1720s, intensified in the 1750s, and was in full swing around 1800, it was an onslaught onto the north coast always just a few paces ahead of the British assault on the south.

THE BRITISH ARRIVE

Whatever the beginning of Asian–Australian contact, the British came late to the north of Australia. Its vigorous independent trading activities challenged their hegemonic ambitions. Matthew Flinders' encounter with a Macassan fleet has been described, repeated and elaborated, but never yet interpreted for the impact it had on his journey and its consequences.

'Pobassoo', 1803, drawing by William Westall. Pobassoo gave valuable information and advice to Matthew Flinders when the two captains met in 1803.
Source: NLA, ref. 4566030.

Phillip Parker King continued the task of charting the northern coast from 1818 to 1822. His father, a former lieutenant-governor on Norfolk Island and governor of New South Wales, was a friend of Flinders and Banks, and the end of the Napoleonic wars left many naval officers unemployed. It seemed an excellent time to resume the charting of Australia. King charted the entire north Australian coast from Darwin to Cambridge Gulf, though he bypassed the site of Darwin harbour, which was to become so important for British settlement.[54]

Flinders and Pobassoo: two captains meet

The trepang trade was in full swing by the time Matthew Flinders embarked on his circumnavigation of the Australian continent in 1802. The purpose of the *Investigator*'s journey was to survey the coasts and establish beyond all doubt that the continent was a single landmass. The journal of this voyage records with almost unrelieved boredom the measurements of distance, depth, and direction of surveying, suggesting unimaginative names for geographical features to assist orientation. But in the Gulf of Carpentaria, a sense of foreboding develops. Pieces of a wreck and seven skulls were found at Sweers Island in November and in the Sir Edward Pellew group of islands there were signs of boat-building activity: almost two acres of mangrove had been cut down or stripped of bark, with metal axes. Nearby were thirty-eight fireplaces supported by stone, arranged in rows close to the beach, as if perhaps for shipbuilding, since no other purpose was obvious. In fact these were trepang boiling sites. Pieces of bamboo, coconut shells, baskets and blue-striped calico in the fashion of 'moorman's trousers' and woven Chinese-style hats led Flinders to conclude that some Chinese had been in the area. Perhaps they had been shipwrecked and killed. Flinders had not expected to meet any strangers in these waters and appeared perplexed. The further he progressed the more distinctly he could read the signs of previous contact with visitors. At Caledon Bay the native inhabitants were evidently familiar with strangers and guns, though they seem to have been more impressed with the noise of a gun than with its power:

> The propensity shown by the natives to steal, especially our axes, so contrary to all I have known and heard of their countrymen, is not only a proof that they had been previously visited by people possessing iron implements, but from their audacity it would appear that the effect of firearms was either not very certain in the hands of the strangers, or had seldom been resorted to in the punishment of aggression.[55]

Flinders spent over three months in the Gulf before the puzzle was solved. On 17 February 1803 six Macassan vessels were spotted at one of the English Company Islands (subsequently called Pobassoo Island). Flinders strongly suspected them to be 'piratical ladrones' and had 'all hands at quarters'. However, to the hoisting of the military ensign the vessels responded with small white flags. Pobassoo,[56] the commander of this fleet, became a willing source of information, with the help of the Malay cook on board the *Investigator* who was able to translate.

They had come for trepang and explained how it was obtained and processed. Pobassoo said they sold their produce to Chinese merchants at Timor Laoet. Flinders observed that they were Muslims but did not abstain from alcohol, and were reasonably well armed with old Dutch brass guns and muskets. They had had some skirmishes with natives, and Pobassoo was still wearing the scars. They were anxious to learn everything about the wreckage found in the Gulf, because in the previous season one of their vessels had been lost. The six vessels commanded by Pobassoo were heading for the Gulf of Carpentaria.

Flinders found out that Pobassoo's wing was merely the spearhead of a vast fleet of sixty vessels belonging to the Rajah of Bone. With twenty to twenty-five men on a vessel, Flinders calculated that the whole fleet must be carrying more than 1,000 men; an armada was heading for the northern part of the continent.

The surprise of this meeting was mutual. The Bugis had never heard of a European settlement on this continent, and carefully noted down the name of Port Jackson. Pobassoo had the presence of mind to ask for a letter of introduction in case he should chance on other Europeans. Indeed, Nicolas Baudin's *Géographe* was also plying the northern waters and met Indonesians at Cassini Island off Admiralty Gulf.[57]

Flinders spent another three weeks in the area and then headed straight for Timor, though he was unsure of his reception there, as hostilities between England and Holland had not long ceased. On reaching the port, Flinders found that it contained 'no merchants', only a number of Chinese traders. The governor (presumably the Dutch resident at Kupang[58]) told him that it was well known that the Macassans had long been accustomed to fish for trepang around the islands and on the dry shoal south of Roti (presumably Ashmore Reef). Flinders understood that they had come from there to the Australian shore for about twenty years, after one of their vessels was driven there by the northwest monsoon.

The discovery of foreign contact changed the agenda of Flinders' journey. He decided that the foreign penetration of the northern coast merited further examination. The *Investigator* had been leaking in Torres Strait and was caulked at Sweers Island, when it was found that two planks were rotten. This did not hurry Flinders unduly, as he spent from November to March on the southern and eastern coastline of the Gulf, longer than the journey from Sydney had taken. It is on this coastline that evidence of foreign contact was noticed, first at Sweers and then at Bentinck Island. The reasons stated for visiting Kupang also appear somewhat facile. He knew that he would not be able to obtain salt in Kupang, but hoped to obtain the 'little comforts' of peas, rice and sugar, perhaps from another visiting vessel. He feared that without this his crew would be unable to

'Aotahi, a Chinese inhabitant of Makassar', drawn by Jean Baptiste Bayot, ca. 1839, on the *Astrolabe*. Chinese merchants were instrumental in organising the trade that sold trepang and other cargo to China and that required a high degree of expertise in judging the quality of produce. Colonial trepangers who tried to circumvent their involvement were unable to graft onto this lucrative trade. Every trading port worth the name had its resident Chinese merchants.
Source: NLA, ref. 20806541.

exert the work of pumping, which the approaching winter weather was sure to increase. Flinders thought he could continue his charting of the north and northwest coast during winter after Kupang, and proceed to the higher latitudes in the following summer. He also wanted to send word to the Admiralty to send a better ship.[59] As it turned out, the small port was barely able to provision his ship, and the water was of poor quality, making most of his crew sick. After Timor great haste was made to return to Port Jackson with little time for surveying during the three-month return journey, rapidly completing the circumnavigation on 9 June 1803, which had commenced on 22 July 1802. Five of the ten-and-a-half months had been spent in the area of Macassan activity, between Sweers Island and Kupang. Nothing in Flinders' edited journal confirms that he may have thought it advisable to head for Kupang for information on the Macassans, but his obtuse reasoning for that excursion does suggest it.

Flinders seems to come away from this experience with an idea that the Macassan visits were quite a recent phenomenon. Pobassoo stated that he had made six or seven excursions to this coast himself in the last twenty years 'and he was one of the first who came, but he had never seen any ship here before'. It is not clear from Flinders' account whether Pobassoo meant to say that he was one of the first to venture as far as the English Company Islands, or one of the first to come to New Holland. The naturalist Robert Brown's journal of the voyage reads: 'Tho' the old Commander has been employed in this trade for 20 years he never before met with any ship on the coast of New Holland. According to himself he was the first person sent from Macassar in this service.'[60] This may have been a statement to express that he was spearheading the fleet. Flinders' attempt to date the commencement of the Macassan visits to Australia is still the most conservative estimate, and is not generally thought to be reliable.

Flinders was a capable strategist. Cognisant of the very unwelcome interest shown by the French in exploring the coasts of New Holland, he used this leverage to solicit the financial support of Sir Joseph Banks for his circumnavigation.[61] Flinders thoroughly understood from his meeting with Pobassoo that a regular contact had already existed prior to the 1788 British arrival, involving Chinese in the Dutch East Indies. As such, Flinders must have found it expedient to date the emergence of this contact just after James Cook first staked out the British claim in 1770. Indeed, the new name he proposed for the continent was instrumental in erasing the prior reference to the Dutch claim on the continent. Henceforward, New Holland became Australia.

King also called at Kupang and was informed that the Macassan trepang fleet consisted of up to 200 vessels carrying 6,000 to 8,000 men. He understood this to mean the fleet fishing on Australian coasts, and thought the figure somewhat exaggerated. It is likely that this estimate included the fleets visiting Irian Jaya and perhaps the whole archipelago, but the vision must have caused some concern for British strategists eager to bring the whole continent under British ambit.[62]

FORT DUNDAS, MELVILLE ISLAND, 1824–29

Soon after King's return it was decided to establish a British military outpost in the far north with the objective to enter into intercourse with the Indian Archipelago. The British feared that unless some presence was established on the north coast, the area would fall to the influence of 'some other power'. King praised the harbour of Port Essington for its proximity to the Moluccas and New Guinea, and for being 'on the direct line of communication between Port Jackson and India'.[63] But the site chosen by Captain J. J. G. Bremer in 1824 was in Apsley Strait between Melville and Bathurst islands. It became known as Fort Dundas.

It was the very year in which a Dutch–British treaty ceded India, Malaya and Singapore to British influence and reserved the Indonesian Archipelago for the Dutch. Singapore, founded in 1819, had been a resounding success in attracting trade, already boasting a population of 10,000. A large part of the Macassan trade started to be diverted to this free trade port.

The idea that a port in northern Australia could play the same role is credited to William Barns, a former East India Company officer, who hoped that Macassans could be attracted to such a port and supply the vehicle for a 'trade with the Celebes, Moluccas and other eastern islands and ultimately with China'.[64]

John Barrow, second secretary to the Admiralty predicted that Fort Dundas 'will become another Singapore', and John Roe, who had been lieutenant to both King and Bremer expected that 'at some future time [this] must become a place of considerable consequence in the eastern world', being on the route from New South Wales to India, and 'admirably situated for the purposes of mercantile speculation'.[65]

Fort Dundas was established in September 1824 with a contingent of twenty-six royal marines—whatever could be spared at Moreton Bay—and forty-five convicts. None of them had any experience in the tropics. They erected a walled fort and awaited contact with passing traffic.

By 1827 the commander of Fort Dundas, Major John Campbell despaired that not a single trader of any nation had come near the establishment. Campbell had found that the Macassans were not willing to sell their trepang, which they said had been contracted to the owners of their vessels.[66] The only other trader ever to call at Fort Dundas was William Barns whose brainchild the settlement had been. He arrived in late 1824 to build a house and store, claiming land without anyone's permission. He sent a brig to Timor to obtain buffaloes, and like the *Lady Nelson*, the settlement's supply boat a few days before, it fell into the hands of pirates and the crew was killed. Alan Powell suggests that everyone at Fort Dundas longed to be somewhere else. They suffered from fevers, scurvy, dysentery, hepatitis, and from 'native attacks', which claimed several lives on both sides. Powell observes that while the successful trading stations at Penang and Singapore had been safeguarded through treaties with local rulers, no such attempt was ever made in northern Australia.[67]

Fort Dundas was nowhere near the 'direct trading route' either to India, or for the Macassan vessels, which tended to stay clear of Melville Island. What seemed conveniently close when viewed from London, Port Jackson or Moreton Bay, was in fact at a crucial distance in these difficult waters with strong tides and winds. Years later, the sub-collector of customs at Darwin found, to his despair, that it took five or six sailing days each time to cover the short distance between Darwin and Port Essington.[68]

RAFFLES BAY, COBOURG PENINSULA, 1827–29

A second attempt to move closer to those routes was made by setting up at Raffles Bay. Bowen Strait was known to be a Macassan meeting point, but because he could find no fresh water at adjacent Croker Island, Captain Stirling on the HMS *Success* chose Raffles Bay as the site for Fort Wellington in June 1827. The next year commander Captain Henry Smyth decided that to facilitate better relations with the surrounding locals, an indigenous person was to be captured. A reward was offered to the soldiers and convicts for 'procuring a native'. As a result, a six-year-old girl, 'Riveral', was wounded and captured. Four or five other children were wounded in the process,

'Singapore', 1839, lithograph by Eugene Ciceri on the *Astrolabe*. Founded by the Dutch in 1919, Singapore became a British possession in 1824 and soon after the paradigm of British trading success in the East Indies. It served as the role model for three attempted trading ports in north Australia: Fort Dundas in 1824, Raffles Bay in 1827, and Port Essington in 1838.
Source: NLA, ref. 20806695.

and a native man, a woman and a child were killed. In Britain it was considered an 'inexcusable transaction', but no action was taken against the officer in charge or any of his staff, and, at any rate, the rebuke came too late.[69]

Smyth was replaced by Collett Barker, who rolled out a completely different mode of race relations. He met the Iwaidja unarmed and visited their camps, even staying overnight. His positive reputation soon preceded him. In 1829 the languishing Fort Dundas was disbanded and its stores moved to Fort Wellington, which appears to have been rather more successful than the former in attracting traders. Earl asserts that the Macassans at first (1827) treated the new settlement at Raffles Bay with suspicion, but in the second season (1828) some of them remained at the settlement to fish from there. They were encouraged to bring trade goods to enter into exchanges, which they did in the following year, bringing also their families in order to settle. They came in thirty different *perahus*, carrying 1,056 men. By the time they arrived for the 1829 season, the European settlers had disappeared.[70] The slow-grinding wheels of the British Admiralty had responded to the earlier adverse reports by ordering the abandonment of Fort Wellington in August 1829.

When French navigator Dumont d'Urville visited ten years later, the scene that presented itself showed little trace of a former British presence. Instead, the French found thatched smokehouses, iron trepang boilers, *perahus*, tamarind trees, and some 150 Macassans at work together with Aborigines. This image, published in the account of the French journey, was a stark reminder that the British presence on the continent was still tenuous. The British convict settlements were nestled into Port Jackson with outreaches at Newcastle (1804–24), Port Macquarie (1821–33) and Moreton Bay (1824–39).[71] Two short-lived southern outposts were established in 1826, one at King George Sound (1826–28) and one at Westernport (1826–31), because the French had shown much interest in those parts of the coast. The northern outposts were motivated partly by the wish to head off any possible outreach from other colonial powers, and partly by the hope of emulating the Dutch to harness the existing trade. But neither of the colonial powers found it easy to graft onto the lively Macassan trade—the Dutch outpost of Fort du Bus (1828–36, West Papua), did not fare much better than the north Australian ones.

The notion prevailed that the abortion of Fort Wellington had been too hasty. John Dunmore Lang and George Windsor Earl became new advocates of a northern settlement in the 1830s. Earl had spent six years trading in the archipelago and was well acquainted with the Macassan trade.

Macassan trepang camp at Raffles Bay, observed in 1839 by the crew of the *Astrolabe*, under Dumont d'Urville. Ten years after the closure of the British outpost, Cobourg Peninsula had returned to business as usual between Macassans and Aborigines. Lithograph by Emile Lassalle.

Source: NLA, ref. 20806695.

PORT ESSINGTON, COBOURG PENINSULA, 1838–49

A third attempt to establish a British presence on the north coast was made in 1838 with the establishment of 'Victoria' at Port Essington, fifteen miles west of Raffles Bay. Port Essington had long been pointed out as a more suitable site than either the Tiwi Islands or Bowen Strait. The settlement was placed under the command of John McArthur and Earl was linguist and draftsman, accompanied by twelve marines, their wives, and a surgeon—but no convicts.

Dumont d'Urville's party paid a visit to the settlement in 1839 and noted that it had already attracted some Macassan trade, but they did not think there was much chance of success. The shipping route from Sydney to Singapore was still hundreds of miles to the north, but the real drawback was that there was nothing to be purchased or traded at Port Essington. Traders only arrived to sell livestock and supplies to the garrison.

Port Essington became the famous destination of Ludwig Leichhardt's overland journey from Queensland in 1844–45, which anticipated much of the route taken in the 1880s by many overlanders from Queensland. Leichhardt's party was returned to Sydney on the *Heroine*, which on its return voyage in July 1846 struck a reef in Torres Strait. Among those rescued was Father Angelo Confalonieri who settled at Port Essington and missionised Aborigines until his death from fever in 1848. During his two years at Black Point, near Smith Point, the Cobourg Iwaidja suffered from malaria, bronchitis and an influenza epidemic.[72]

Port Essington settlement, 1839, drawn by Emile Lassalle on Dumont d'Urville's expedition.
Source: NLA, ref. 20826282.

Relations between the military post and Aborigines were reasonably good—the latter being quite used to strangers camping on their land—and the station became a point of attraction. The Iwaidja brought bush tucker and assisted with building and on the vessels; some of them sailed to Sydney and to Indonesia.[73]

Whether it was considered a success in defending the northern coast from French interest, or a failure for not becoming a trading entrepot, this settlement was also abandoned in 1849, by which time it had become a Catholic bishoprice. The buffalo set free thrived so well in the bush that buffalo shooting became one of the Northern Territory's successful industries. In the 1880s 50,000 buffalo hides were exported within ten years, and Paddy Cahill is credited with shooting forty-five in one day.[74]

THE NORTHERN TERRITORY OF SOUTH AUSTRALIA, 1864–1911

Seven years after the British completely surrendered the north coast by withdrawing from Port Essington, South Australia became a self-governing colony in 1856, and in 1864 it more than doubled its size by annexing the Northern Territory. The colony started to advertise itself to prospective immigrants as 'the central state'. Like the New South Wales authorities beforehand, and the federal government afterwards, the South Australian parliament held great hopes for its northern territory and was keen to re-establish a settlement. There had been no British presence in the north for fifteen years, but the Macassans were conducting a lively trade.

After a short-lived settlement at Escape Cliffs at the mouth of the Adelaide River, which had been described by John Lort Stokes on the *Beagle* in 1839, the centre was moved in 1869 to Port Darwin, also named by Stokes after a friend and shipmate, Charles Darwin.

George Goyder as surveyor-general laid out the plan for Palmerston. Work soon commenced on a telegraph line linking it to Adelaide, and linking Adelaide to the world. Work on the line led to discoveries of gold and a rush to the Pine Creek area in 1872. This gold rush helped to put the Palmerston settlement permanently on the map after the failure of Fort Dundas, Fort Wellington, Port Essington and Escape Cliffs.

George Windsor Earl's 1835 proposal for a northern settlement had recommended the use of cheap Asian labour, and this indeed became the motor of northern development.[75] Chinese labourers were imported to work on pastoral stations and public works, and pearlers recruited in Kupang and Makassar from the early 1870s.

Soon after the settlement of Palmerston, its government resident, B. R. Douglas, proposed that the Macassan fishery could be harnessed as a revenue earner. He proposed the introduction of a £10 seasonal fishing licence to protect European pearl-shellers from foreign competition.[76] Nothing came of the idea; on the contrary, in 1875 Darwin became a 'free port' like Singapore, where no customs duties were levied. By the early 1880s the gold rush was in full swing and a substantial volume of goods was imported through the port to supply the large Chinese population, and quantities of gold were exported. In 1880 customs duties were reintroduced, but the volume of work exceeded the capacity of part-time sub-collector J. A. G. Little. Alfred Searcy from the customs office in Adelaide was appointed full-time sub-collector of customs at Palmerston in 1882.

Searcy and Robinson: policing the trepang trade

Alfred Searcy had his first spell in the tropics as sub-collector of customs at age twenty-eight, when he was neither too old nor too experienced for a little tomfoolery, as he himself admits in his biographical account of his fourteen years in Palmerston (1882–96). On his first contact with the Macassan fleet in March 1883, Searcy hoisted the customs flag, to which the Macassans responded merely by hoisting the Dutch flag. He was ready to have some shots fired across the bow of the *perahu* or perhaps a little closer, but the more experienced captain in charge of the *Flying Cloud* would hear nothing of it. Eventually the Macassans understood what was required, and Searcy was able to explain to them that from now on they needed to pay a licence fee as well as import duties on alcohol, tobacco and rice, payable in English currency. The Malay crew on the customs vessels greatly helped communication. Some of them had relatives on the Macassan boats, and they knew these waters well.

During his first tour of inspection Searcy located twelve *perahus*; much fewer than expected from earlier reports of the strength of the fleets.[77] In the following season only eight vessels were recorded. Two of them reported their presence to the new customs station at Port Essington, the others ignored the customs depot altogether. Arriving at Bowen Strait, Searcy found three and wanted to charge them £50 each, but negotiated to accept some stores in lieu of cash. Searcy and his two offsiders were able to display some heroism by pointing a gun at the head of the Macassan captain.[78]

Most of the Macassan vessels had proceeded further east than usual, probably to avoid the new customs regulations. Searcy seized the opportunity of the murder of two Chinese timber cutters at Mountnorris Bay (near Alligator River) to be put in charge of a search party on the government steamer, a much more capable vessel than the customs sailboat. His brief was to proceed as far as Goulburn Island on a ten-day trip. After a cursory search for the Alligator River Aborigines responsible for the murders, Searcy commandeered the vessel all the way to Melville Bay, inspecting Macassan camps at Liverpool River, Cadell Straits and Melville Bay, and 'acquiring' the cut timber that had evidently been stacked by Macassans at Entrance Island. He saw himself in the footsteps of Flinders, eighty-one years after that historic encounter at Malay Roads.

At Elcho Island Searcy met a Yolngu man who had been to Makassar. He found that the Yolngu were working with the Macassans to cut timber. On this extended voyage Searcy located five *perahus* and, in addition to the licence and duty fees, imposed fines of either £10 or £50, depending on the excuse given for ignoring customs regulations. At Melville Bay Searcy found two captains who had run out of rice, which Searcy was most happy to sell to them at an exorbitant price. Searcy is silent on the question of his welcome back at Port Darwin, where acting government resident, G. R. McMinn, was preparing to send out a search party for him after an absence of twenty-six days.

The vast numbers of vessels and men referred to by Flinders and the commander of *Victoria* were not to be repeated during Searcy's experience. The greatest number ever recorded during his time in customs was sixteen vessels in the 1885–86 season. He reflected: 'The sudden falling off of the number of proas visiting the coast must have been a great blow to the [indigenous people], and, there is little doubt, caused them to look upon the whites as greater enemies than ever.'[79]

During these voyages Searcy teamed up with E. O. Robinson, customs collector at Port Essington, who was able to show Searcy the ropes of the job. Robinson was a beachcomber on a grand scale and Searcy, as the new chum, had great regard for him. After the novelty of hunting down Macassan traders wore off, Searcy left them altogether in the care of Robinson.

Of all the colonial entrepreneurs trying to enter into the trepang industry, Edward Robinson is best known. He was entrusted with levying duties on the Macassan fleets (1881–99) and may have had some influence in the eventual decline of the Macassan visits, so it seems worthwhile to re-trace his involvement in the trepang industry. He credited himself with being the first to point out the large volume of dutiable goods imported by the Macassan fleets, in 1880.[80] We now know that the government resident had done so eight years earlier.

Robinson was a typical frontier fortune hunter who tried his hand at pearling, gold mining, trepanging, cattle, and buffalo shooting. He never married and had no known children. Born at Oxford in 1847, during his retirement in Melbourne 'he never tired of telling his adventures'.[81] From all accounts he knew how to trade on his experiences, at a time when experience was what was most wanting among the colonial officials from the south, for all of whom the territory was an unknown, unsettled quantity with vast promise.

He arrived in Australia in 1873 and claims to have sailed soon after to Makassar to recruit divers for a pearling syndicate. While pearling at King Sound he sustained a spear wound that brought him to Palmerston. In April 1874 he was already scouting out Port Essington by sailing boat. Shortly afterwards he joined a land exploration from Union Reefs to Port Essington with John Lewis, another well-known Territorian with a strong hand in Pine Creek mining, who had acquired a lease on Cobourg Peninsula in 1871. This expedition was equipped as a search party for two lost explorers. It resulted in the setting up of Lewis' Cobourg Peninsula buffalo station, and Robinson's trepang station, both at Port Essington. Robinson gave up after only six months of trying to compete with the Macassans at one of their favourite camps.

From September to November 1875 he led a party of prospectors to Blue Mud Bay, following the rumour that gold had been found there. The party met a Yolngu man who had just returned from Singapore, but no gold was found.[82] It appears that Robinson was at a loose end. He returned to the gold fields, and in 1877 he visited Melville Island.

In March 1878 he set up another trepang station at Croker Island in partnership with Thomas Wingfield. They built a substantial house on the site known as Whitecliffs,[83] on the western side of the island, facing Bowen Strait, and employed local Aborigines. In December 1879 Wingfield was killed and Robinson aborted the venture, now in debt. Success as a trepanger evaded him.

Robinson then settled as manager of Lewis' Cobourg cattle station at the old site of Victoria, where an old tamarind grove bore witness to a long association with Macassans. He drew a salary—most likely his first—of thirty shillings per week. In December 1881, having drawn the attention of the sub-collector of customs both to the income-earning potential of the Macassan fleets and to his own useful experience, Little appointed him 'provisional and temporary customs officer' with £20 per annum. Robinson held the job until 1899, increasing his salary to £100 on account of the substantial revenues collected from the Macassan fleets.

Neither Robinson nor his superiors acknowledged a conflict of interest in his appointment. In 1884 the customs station was returned to Robinson's Croker Island trepang station (west of De Courcey Head) and in the following season, Macassan fishing west of De Courcey Head was forbidden, so that Robinson now 'had a fair chance of doing well at his trepanging'.[84] Robinson was able to argue that his trepang station in Bowen Strait was more conveniently located as a customs station than the Port Essington site. His trepang camp was considerably improved with government funds—£100 in one season because it was a customs station. When government resident, J. L. Parsons, visited in 1888, he commended Robinson as 'the very man for the work, having a thorough knowledge of the coast and having a great influence over native races'.[85]

That he wielded a significant influence at Croker Island cannot be doubted. Searcy credits him with knowledge of the Makasar and Iwaidja languages, and he was locally known as Walparan.[86] In 1894 he and Joe Cooper kidnapped four Tiwi Islanders and brought them to Croker to teach some of the locals the Tiwi language. In the following year he sent Cooper to establish a buffalo shooting camp at Melville Island, accompanied by the Tiwi hostages and a group of Iwaidja. Buffalo shooting became a main source of income. Some 2,000 hides were sold in the first six months at Melville Island and around 1,000 per year thereafter until 1898.

Joe Cooper was also a trepanger and gold miner. In 1890 he married Alice Rose, an Iwaidja woman, and from 1905 to 1916 he was an honorary sub-protector of Aborigines at Melville Island. At Croker Island he was known as Djelkwar to the Iwaidja. The Macassans knew him as Djon, and his wife as Daeng Te'ne, 'the lovely one'. An Aboriginal–English child, remembered by Daeng Sarro as Roni, is probably a reference to Joe Cooper's eldest son, Reuben (see also Cubillo, viz.).[87]

As useful as his influence over Aborigines was, the way in which Robinson, who appears to have been well educated, was able to gain the confidence of men like Searcy, Little, Lewis and Paul Foelsche, the head of police, proved yet more useful.

It fell to Robinson to exact duties and licence fees from the visiting Macassans. In the first season of his appointment only the ship carrying his supplies from Makassar came to call, and Robinson now collected over £2 in duties from them.[88] This *perahu* also carried the survivors of a shipwreck at Melville Island, and Robinson's report on the incident augmented the importance of the new revenue station. Robinson soon argued that it was too difficult to estimate the dutiable cargo and proposed instead a hefty licence fee that would:

> ...hopefully mean that the Malays would go to New Guinea, Papua and other places in preference to paying the licence. The trepang would be profitably worked from Palmerston by men who would willingly pay the licence & for their own sakes would look after the Malays, hundreds of natives could be employed, which would add materially to the revenue.[89]

In other words, men such as he should be in charge, Malays should contribute their know-how, and Aborigines their cheap labour in order to place this industry on a 'proper' footing.

Robinson continued to lobby Foelsche, and both he and the sub-collector of customs, as well as the government resident who continued to argue for a better government steamer, were supportive. All manner of governmental concerns were rolled into the issue: quarantine and customs issues, coastal patrolling, alcohol and Aboriginal protection, environmental degradation, white settlement and industry.

In 1885 Robinson was issued with a revolver and a customs uniform to lend him greater presence, and he collected some £600 in gold from thirteen *perahus* that duly reported to him. In 1887 eleven vessels were charged £507, notwithstanding that they were carrying no alcohol (at least none could be found on them). Not counting any payments in kind, these figures average £46 per vessel for importing rice and tobacco, and must have been a considerable discouragement for the fleets.[90]

Robinson, on the other hand, was earning more than his wage for the government. He also looked after himself. He 'sometimes obtained rice and other supplies from the Macassans and, apart from feeding his own camp and employees, may have sold some rations to others'.[91] At any rate, by 1883, at the end of his second season as customs officer, his store contained twenty-four gallons of confiscated arrack.[92]

END OF AN ERA

At the turn of the twentieth century the trepang industry looked set to pass into European hands. Several beachcombers had started to interest themselves in this fishery, in the Kimberley as well as in Arnhem Land. The number of Macassan vessels in the Northern Territory known to customs had dropped to nine, and was falling. It is not completely certain that there ever were sixty vessels on the northern shores, because the figures given by Pobassoo in 1803 may have included the Kimberley and all of Marege, including Irian Jaya, but King's figure of 200 vessels suggests that it was certainly within the capacity of the Macassan trade to send sixty vessels. Thirty vessels were the largest fleet ever reliably recorded in 1829 at Port Essington. Under the influence of customs regulations this fleet shrank rapidly to a maximum of sixteen vessels in 1885–86, by which time the customs officers were confident that they had complete control over the traffic. The financial impositions on the Macassan trade were heavy compared to its profit, but most of all they were unpredictable, with yearly changes of instructions and practice, and they were onerous in disrupting the favoured routes.

The Macassans had never seen any fairness in the fees imposed on them. This had been their traditional fishery long before the British arrived—a sentiment that was expressed through the Dutch consul in 1883.[93] The effect of this constant interference was that some vessels started to visit the Kimberley instead, further decreasing the fleet to Marege.[94] They also cut down on the rice rations carried. The requirement to pay in gold sovereigns necessitated trade with Singapore, a difficult and expensive currency for Macassans. The average levy per vessel amounted to £50, while the gross income per *perahu* for its owner averaged less than £500. Despite strong fluctuations in the price of trepang, Macknight observed that the average financial return per vessel remained fairly constant. So did the quantities of trepang obtained per vessel. This means that neither market fluctuations nor resource exhaustion killed the industry. It was not a dying trade, it was a trade strangled by government regulation.[95]

In the 1903–04 season only four Macassan vessels arrived. Herbert, the government resident, proposed that licences should no longer be issued to Malays. Robinson's successor, Alfred Brown, owned four boats and wanted the area from Cape Don to De Courcey Head—his own closest fishing grounds—reserved for whites, effectively for himself. Brown's proposal for the 1904–05 season was a momentous tactical mistake. The income from the two Macassan boats in 1905 was barely above Brown's generous salary. Herbert seized the moment to suggest barring Macassans from the entire coast. The Bowen Strait customs station was closed in July 1906, and Brown's employment terminated. Deprived of his most reliable source of income in the form of a government salary, Brown continued trepanging but never did very well. In 1909 he married Mumuladj, an Iwaidja woman, at Port Essington.[96] The Macassans were informed that they were no longer entitled to visit Marege.

CONCLUSIONS

News of a lively and well-connected international trade on the northern shores rendered the British settlement of north Australia a more urgent project. The first three attempts at northern settlement, starting before even the western half of the continent was claimed for the British crown, were all motivated by the desire to harness the trepang trade. They failed to graft onto the trade but were successful inasmuch as other foreign powers were kept at a distance. British hopes for a second Singapore were dashed, but when the South Australian government took over control of the Northern Territory it revived the earlier visions. It hoped for Darwin to become a natural centre for trade with the Indonesian Archipelago, the gateway to Asia, and poured considerable resources into infrastructure. A state-of-the-art telegraph line was completed within only two years in 1872, and in 1889 the Darwin-to-Pine Creek railway was finished. But by 1895 South Australia was ready to return the indebted territory to British control. In an expansionist passion the potential of the Northern Territory was usually exaggerated.

Local enforcement of customs impositions was entrusted to persons who had a direct financial interest in the trade and who raised a log of objections about their competitors, including that they: were using Australian resources without returning a (sufficient) resource rent; were depleting resources; had a detrimental effect on Aborigines; used alcohol as payment for services; were introducing disease; and were unfairly competing with white entrepreneurs. This is the whole gamut of well-rehearsed, anti-Asian rhetoric, and, as in other occupational settings, they were strategically deployed. At the heart of the pious concern for Aborigines was the strongly felt competition for access to cheap Aboriginal labour. There is no doubt that, far from grafting onto the trade and turning Darwin into a gateway to Asia, government control choked the industry. Nor did a European-owned trepang industry take off after the departure of the Macassans. Lack of experience and a reluctance of Aborigines to make themselves available continued to beset the trepangers.

Tracing the emergence of the Macassan trepang trade with Marege takes us on a tour of Asian, European, Arabic and indigenous maritime histories converging in a part of the world that is marginal to all of them. Hints that cast shadows on the antiquity of contact add mystery to these partly known histories. The 'short history' view grates against the profound cultural impact of Macassan contact on eastern Arnhem Land and possibly in the Kimberley. This begs the question: How quickly can cultures change and how soon can the new become the traditional? Macknight concluded that two centuries were quite sufficient to cause the observed cultural changes.[97] Considering the aeroplane dance machines that feature next to luggers as ceremonial headdresses in Torres Strait, and the square-faced gin bottles found among ritual paraphernalia in Arnhem Land, one can be inclined to agree that the diffusion of culture can happen quite swiftly.

Whether it took two centuries or four, the effects of this contact are profound and interesting enough to be more than a footnote in Australian history. The earlier worlds of Arab, Indian and Chinese commerce in the region acquire a different salience when examined from the point of view of possible involvement with pre-British Australia.

Against the larger canvas of world history, Australian domestic histories which commence in the southeast and work their way up to the north appear entirely upside down. Australian documented history begins in the north, which was linked into an extensive trading network long before the arrival of the British. The north Australian coasts were connected via Makassar to the Indonesian archipelago, to the Dutch to China, and eventually to British Singapore. It was this trading network that interested the Dutch and the French and could have led them to establish competing claims had the British not hurried the extension of their tenuous presence to the northern coast.

The idea of an isolated continent does not stand up to historical interrogation, either in the north of Western Australia, or in the north of the Northern Territory, or in the north of Queensland, where the Torres Strait was a bridge of communication with Papua. On the contrary, for the Yolngu, who had been able to travel to Singapore, Papua and Makassar, a period of isolation commenced with the establishment of British sovereignty in the north, because it spelled the end of these international trading links. In Queensland, too, Torres Strait Islanders eventually became confined to their islands by law.

Because the ethnicity of the people involved is often uncertain and also mixed, I refer to them as Macassans—a phenomenon of Australian–Indonesian history rather than an ethnic group. Macknight points out several times the high level of sophistication of the merchants behind the trepang trade and of the *nakhodas* in charge of the fleets. However, if we examine more closely the people who made up the crews of the *perahus*, including Timorese and Sama Bajo, we may conclude that much of this Macassan–Aboriginal contact was a meeting of indigenous peoples. But distinctions between 'indigenous' and 'Asian' peoples are in themselves difficult and arbitrary.

Current thinking is that 'the pioneers who first settled in Australia and New Guinea were part of a great exodus from southern China, mainly through island Southeast Asia, long before Australia and Papua became separated 8,000 years ago'.[98] The Austronesian languages link regions from Hawaii to Madagascar, including Australia and Taiwan. In a sweeping *History of Australia, New Zealand and the Pacific*, Donald Denoon and Philippa Mein Smith argue: 'The conceptual separation of Pacific from Southeast Asian cultures and polities owes more to European classification than to historic connections and discontinuities. As on other cultural boundaries, there was no inhibition against the exchange of commodities, ideas and even people.'[99] This is history on a grand scale, history that requires us to examine the terms we use to refer to regions and peoples, boundaries and differences, for their historicity.

The non-British histories of Australia and New Zealand have never been unknown, but they have also never been privileged into the master narrative of domestic histories. Denoon argues with James Belich that their forgetting was convenient; because they did not extend British history, they were 'not remembered very hard'.[100] Compared with the histories of other regions of the world, it is not asking very much to extend the history of Australia another couple of centuries into the past to take account of a pre-British time. Hopefully the controversial Bicentennial celebration of 1988 will be the last time Australia tries to think of itself as beginning in 1788, and imagining that Asians came later.

DURING the struggle to establish a British presence on the northern shores of New Holland, early officials made some striking observations. They noticed that Aborigines there had a lingua franca with which they were able to communicate across vast distances and with strangers: they spoke Malay. And they understood that not only did Macassans come regularly and enter into trade relationships with Aborigines, Aborigines also travelled with them overseas. In 1875 the group of gold prospectors led by Robinson must have been fairly surprised to meet a Yolngu man at Arnhem Bay who had been to Singapore and spoke 'passable English'.[1] Stories of people travelling to Makassar also abound among Aborigines. Not only did Aborigines travel to and stay in Makassar, but Macassans were also occasionally left in charge of a shore station in Marege between seasons. The Macassans were linked into local families through trade and marriage arrangements; strangers had been turned into kin. These connections are especially strong with the Yolngu people of northeast Arnhem Land, and these are the connections that have been most extensively researched. We shall start with the Yolngu and then extend our vision across the northern coastline.

YOLNGU AND MANGATHARRA: ONE PEOPLE

Yolngu people today emphasise the exchange relationships arising out of Macassan contact. In traditional societies exchange goes far deeper than commodity exchange; it also involves trust, reciprocity and relationship. At Yirrkala, Bawurr Munyarryun told a story about *dharippa* (trepang) that was very much a story of Yolngu and Mangatharra people being together: travelling *selatang* (southeast), going all through the night, then going northwest. Macassans stayed for three, four, or even five months in one place, and Yolngu people worked with them in gathering trepang.[2] It was a story about contact in general. Later I realised it was a story about his father.

While Yolngu Matha is suffused with Makasar words, the speaking of Makasar is the realm of the highly educated. Elders at Galiwin'ku (Elcho Island) explained to me that Makasar words are far more common in ceremonial language than in everyday language, and that this level of language was reserved for important ceremonies.[3] Others also confirmed this ceremonial use of Makasar. For example, 'when they raise the flag from the ground on the pole they have to say a certain thing in Macassan before they look into the sea. You find it mostly in Yirritja ceremonies, that word.'[4] This speaker was not in a position to reveal the word, but it has been revealed elsewhere in publications, referring to possible Islamic influences.

There is a keen sense of intellectual property among Yolngu. If I roamed into issues that were not within my informants' ambit, I was often referred to someone else who would be able to give me 'full details'. This ownership of stories is linguistically expressed by the suffix '-wung' or '-wungu', which indicates authorship or ownership. Thus, Bopaniwung is the story told by Bopani, while Djäwawungu is the story told by Djäwa. These two, both held at Milingimbi Literacy Centre, have been told in different versions. Bopaniwung is a story of conflict with Macassans, and Djäwawungu is a story of relatedness.

Djäwawungu, recorded in the early 1970s at Milingimbi, is about the Macassan captain Gatjing taking leave for the last time. He came across from Gulmanngur (Elcho Island) to Walmungura (Howard Island) where Djäwa and his uncle were fishing. Gatjing explained that a Balanda man from Marege (white Australian) was continually chasing his boat, bringing trouble from the mainland. Gatjing asked whether Djäwa had a Makasar name, and gave him the name of 'Mangalay', with instructions to let his parents know that Gatjing had given him this Makasar name.[5]

Bopaniwung also makes reference to Gulmanngur on Elcho Island. It is the story of an Aboriginal attack on Macassans, Macassan retaliation, and the intermediary role played by two locals (who have both Yolngu and Macassan names, according to the version recorded by Spillett[6]):

> The Macassans, who used to visit the people living here before, went to many places for both Dhuwa and Yirritja, and left behind stones used for cooking trepang. They used to come for trepang, and sailed from their country on the Westerley wind and returned with the East wind.
>
> Once someone sold his *malka* (a Dhuwa ritual string) to the Macassans for tobacco and food. Gupiyawuy was upset when he heard this, and said 'this makes a war between us'. They ransacked the Macassan boat and set it on fire. Only one Macassan was saved by Gaya-Satiy and Gaya-Lambu. They went to go to the other side of the island called Gulmannuru. It was the time of the westerley winds, so they knew the Macassan boats would be coming. When the other Macassans came they found the Macassan and the two Yolngu at Gulman, and heard the story, and wanted to know where the other Yolngu were hiding. They wanted to find Gupiyawuy who had started the fighting. Two brothers told them that they were at a place called Derrpunu, but the Macassans called that place Segi-Nambuwathi (like they used to call Galiwin'ku Dakirrina).
>
> They kept asking Gaya-Satiy and Gaya-Lambu and said 'if we can't find them, we'll kill you two in their place'. The two said 'Yes, that's alright if you want to kill us. We're ready, because we don't know where they are hiding. Maybe they are over there at Nalumara near the creek.' Gaya-Satiy and Gaya-Lambu were taken prisoner and led the Macassans towards the creek and bushes. It's the same thing as the story of Jesus giving his life for us. Just as they were about to be killed, the young Macassan who was saved by them intervened and saved them. He offered them clothes and whatever they had in the boat. Then the Macassans sailed to the island Murrungga; it seemed a long distance away. When they were gone, the Yolngu people who had been hiding came out to the beach until it was covered by Yolngu people. When the Macassans were sailing back to their country they said they would never come back. That was the last trip they made, and the Macassan boat has never been here since.[7]

Bopaniwung has the local politics identified by Ian McIntosh as characteristic of myth, as well as a syncretic approach to lend it a more visible ethic. While it is very specific about places, it does not refer to any Macassans by name. Djäwawungu, on the other hand, is specific about Macassan names. It is difficult to ignore the historical content of such stories. To what degree are they history that belongs in the public domain, and to what degree are they stories that are owned and should not be taken away? Do they need to be read with all the strictures of myth, or are they stories that are not yet myth?

My understanding is that the Mangatharra stories are a corpus of knowledge about Macassan contact history, and that there are two historical types. The first type consists of stories about strangers, conflict and trade that belong to an older era of early contact and do not attempt to name the Macassans. Bopaniwung and the dog stories examined by McIntosh belong into this category. These stories are more in the nature of myth. The second type consists of stories of connectedness that name the Macassans and refer to the final phase—the departure of the Macassans—like Djäwawungu. These stories are more in the nature of family history.

The bestowal of names is an important token of connectedness. In these farewell stories it is like a refusal to allow the link to be severed. Despite Balanda interference, the connection is symbolically maintained; each telling of the story is then an act of resistance. The Macassan name of 'Mangalay' referred to in Djäwawungu functions as a personal as well as a place name. Mangalai is a Macassan trepang camp in Caledon Bay, more specifically Karaeng Mangnellai (King Mangellai), also known as Gray's Bay.[8]

The overarching effect of Macassan–Yolngu contact history is usually described as cultural borrowing: linguists will refer to loan words and anthropologists to adopted customs and fashions. This seems an objective enough way of seeing until we try it on ourselves. Neither German nor English speakers consider their occasional use of French terms as borrowing; they are a mark of distinction, a signpost of education and cosmopolitanism. So is a familiarity with foreign foods and implements, and the ability to blend exotic touches with local fashions. Of course, it is useful to understand the foreign origins of pipe smoking, the wearing of bandana scarves, the matches, pottery, *lipa-lipa* canoes, iron implements and the exotic plants like abrus (*Abrus precatorius*, or jequirity bean), the all-providing lontar palms, and the tamarinds that usually characterise former trepanging sites together with deeply dug wells. Equally interesting are local creative adaptations to contact, such as the ceremonial poles found on Elcho and the Tiwi Islands. At Elcho these are explained as representing the mast of a departing *perahu*, a time for farewell and mourning.

Oral histories tend to list the trade items that were received from the Macassans, such as matches and rice, and sometimes specify what was given in return, such as turtle shell and ochre. There is more a sense of exchange in such accounts than of borrowing. Joy Rraying told a story about the limits of borrowing, translated by Keith Lapulung:

> This is the story about the Macassan and the dog, who were trying to give each other matches. This story is told by Rraying. In that time the Macassans decided to sail by *balari* (sailboat). So on it he sailed till he got to the place called Bamalngur (Bamala). He then started putting up *bolo* (bamboo stands) to make a hut. He was starting to build a foundation with bamboo to build a shelter, so he started pouring *birrata* (rice). He poured the rice into a hole which is still there as evidence.

> That Macassan man offered a match and said 'here', handing it over, 'take this match', and offered the matches to the dog. The dog didn't accept it; he ignored it and didn't take it from the Macassan. He just shook his head, 'I don't have to touch that'. He said, 'that match is yours. I've got this firestick of my own.' It belongs to the dog itself and his people, the Yolngu.
>
> Then the Macassan man started to pull out the foundation of the bamboo house. After pulling out the foundation of the bamboo house, he then looked out into the horizon and saw a smoke that began burning out in the distance, towards a place called Gualilng'na (towards Makassar). The smoke was burning at a place called Dangarpura (the surrounding islands of Makassar). He said, 'It's about time that I leave back to my own country.'[9]

McIntosh recorded four other variations of the dog story. In three variations the dog refuses the gifts offered by Macassans, and in one story, which was restricted until 1978, it accepts.[10] Either way, it is up to the Yolngu to accept or decline what the strangers offer.

The Yolngu freely acknowledge cultural affinities with Macassans but they do not see this as borrowing. They assert common roots, they mythologise the exchange of technology and culture, and they claim their culture as their own. Presumably those on the other side of this culture contact take the same position.

Little effort has been made to discover Aboriginal influences on Macassan culture. Is it possible that culture contact might amount to a one-way process of 'borrowing' words and customs? Some Yolngu informants confirm this view by pointing to an overarching paternity, a genealogy where the Yolngu issue out of the Macassans. Mattjuwi Burruwanga argues that 'Macassan people came here and reared all the Yolngu people'. More specifically, Bawurr explained that of the two moieties, the Yirritja are the seaside people responsible for representing the shared history. Indeed, the difference between the two moieties arises out of the Macassan contact: 'When those Makasans came here, all those places that they camped, they were all Yirritja land, that's how it came to be Yirritja, that's how we are categorised, the Yirritja and the Dhuwa moiety, those two. Sometimes we call the Yirritja moiety Mangatharra, 'cause they supposed to be our, well, kins of Macassan people. Because they have similar names, place names, people's names, all that, they were adopted from there, inherit.'[11] Both Mattjuwi and Bawurr made it clear that they saw themselves as kin of Macassans.

Others, however, felt that parts of dances they had seen in Makassar were borrowed from Yolngu ceremonies. The final scene of the Macassan fire-dance, with a dancer carried away on a shield, looked to them like a boy being carried off after the circumcision ritual.[12] Bugis and Macassan spectators of Yolngu dances also noticed such similarities in 1994. While the meaning of the dances was different, the movements were the same.[13] It is not unusual for elements of ritual to acquire a completely different meaning when adopted into a new area.

Yolngu Matha today contains a host of words from Indonesia, reflecting the ideas or items introduced by Macassans: *Balanda* as a reference to whites (from the Indonesian word for Hollanders); *rrupyiah* for money; *dambako* for tobacco; *lipa-lipa* for canoe. Most surprisingly perhaps, the characteristic Yolngu expression *yo* appears in Makasar as *io*, with possibly a common Austronesian root.[14] Alan Walker and David Zorc found that Yolngu Matha faithfully reproduced the donor language syllable by syllable and sound for sound, with hard consonants becoming soft, and 's' becoming 'j' or 'c'.[15] However, it requires competence in several languages to decipher loan words. These become vernacular very quickly, particularly in oral cultures, so that it might be uncertain whether an informant is Charley Charley or Djalajari. Expecting to hear a vernacular name, Matthew can turn to Mattjuwi, and it can take some time to work out that the significant cultural event, Jubilipatti, took place in Brisbane city to mark the coronation of Queen Elizabeth II.

Through the filter of transliteration of words heard and written, expressions may be quite distorted. Thus, Berndt and Berndt render Lembana Panrea as 'Libabandria', and write 'Limbumitera' for Lemba Moutiara (Pearl Bay), the Makasar name for Port Essington. (*Mutiyara* is also the Yolngu word for pearl shell.)[16] Spillett, who speaks Indonesian, writes down 'Kayu Lompo' and 'Kayu Djati' for the Gaya-Lambu and Gaya-Satiy of the Bopaniwung. Different authors approach such names from different linguistic backgrounds and with different expectations of what they might find. Depending on whether we expect a story to be about a Muslim trader, or a man from the Dutch East Indies, or a Yolngu family member, we may be writing about Husain, Oesing or Yucing.

Indeed, a close reading of many different stories suggests that the Yolngu stories that do remember names of Macassans revolve centrally around the family of Husein Daeng Ranka.

WE ARE ONE SPIRIT

The arrival of the *Hati Marege* (Heart of Marege) in 1988 was celebrated in Arnhem Land as a family reunion. Captured on film by John Darling, we see Mattjuwi and other elders proudly walking with the Macassans, embracing them as kin.[17] This ship was captained by Husain Daeng Ranka (Jnr), a grandson of Husein's sister and Daeng Gassing. The *Hati Marege* was a Bicentennial project conducted by Peter Spillett, but for the Yolngu witnessing its arrival it was not a symbolic re-enactment of a historical episode, it was a personal joy and a resumption of history:

> Five years ago Makasan come here and anchor near Ski Beach [Kalupa Bay at Nhulunbuy] and tell that story from way back. They were travelling around, one of that captain bloke. He give us bag full of rice. They knew straightaway this country, like this is my place. Their culture, like their culture, our culture. Similar dreamings.[18]

The *Hati Marege* must be the singlemost successful event of the Bicentennial in connecting Australian people with their history: Yolngu people have broken the isolation that descended upon them in 1906.

Husein Daeng Ranka: a Macassan–Yolngu dynasty

Husein Daeng Ranka from Kampung Maluku in Makassar was the last of all the Macassan captains to visit the Yolngu. The year after the trade had been outlawed, he arrived on the *Bunga Ejaya* in the 1906–07 season to say farewell to his Aboriginal family and to convey a letter from the Macassan merchant Abdulrazak Puddu Daeng Tompo requesting to be properly informed how matters stood: 'When my proas were at your port, nothing was known about this new regulation. I cannot believe it is really true, but for prudential reasons, I now send only one prow, to see how matters lay and I will feel very much obliged to you for instructing my people how they are to act.'[19]

The letter came together with two sarongs as a token of friendship. Husein's appearance, reported casually by Brown, caused a flurry of communications between Darwin, Adelaide, Melbourne and Makassar, involving state, federal and Dutch authorities. Brown received another £10 for the information.

Husein did not find the *shabandar* at the customs station, because Brown had already been dismissed. He realised that the Marege trade had really come to an end. He undertook one more journey to Sumbawa and then retired completely from sea trading at age seventy-eight. Husein, also known as Jago, or Ayam Jantan (Fighting Cock), died in 1915 at the age of eighty-five. Customs records reveal that he had come almost every season since at least 1881, and he was not the first in his family to captain ships to Marege. His father, Samaila Daeng Bacan, the *punggawa* (headman) of Labbakkang, had also been a *PaMarege* (trepanger), as was his son Mangellai Daeng Maro (born 1889). His sister Hannaddah Daeng Ngai was married to Suleiman Daeng Gassing, also a frequent voyager to Marege. When his son Mangellai was born, Husein was living at Lembana Panrea (Melville Bay). Husein's Aboriginal daughter Gunanu was probably named after a woman at Matamata (on Elcho Island) who had been married to Husein's father Samaila.[20] Husein may have had children from six Aboriginal women[21] and since Marege was not his only trading destination, it is possible that he also had children in Sumbawa and elsewhere.

Husein suffered at least three shipwrecks in Marege, and perhaps he gained his nickname 'Fighting Cock' from this experience. The first time it was already late in the season when he arrived from Makassar in February 1882 and was wrecked at Aliyu, Melville Island. The Tiwi attacked them and killed two mainland Aborigines who were returning home, and one of the Macassan crew; several others were injured. Bapa Palu was able to pick up the survivors on the *Bondeng Katupa*. They proceeded to Lemba Moutiara (Port Essington), where there had been much Balanda activity. At first there had been Robinson in 1875, then Lake in 1876, and since 1879 Robinson again, buffalo shooting and trying to engage in trepanging. Husein had been carrying stores for them. Now Robinson had become a customs officer and charged them £2 off the price of the supplies.[22]

In the following season, 1882–83, another Balanda introduced himself to the captains as customs officer Searcy. He came to Tarrusanga (Bowen Strait), flying the British flag on the *Flying Cloud* and decorated with much gold braid to signify official status. He treated Bapa Palu, Daeng Matona, Saga and Daeng Remba to some gin and told them that in future they had to purchase a licence from Robinson at Lemba Moutiara. When they got home, the new regulations were relayed to them through the Dutch consul in Makassar. A duty was to be imposed on export cargo, and therefore the shipping manifests would now be divided between supplies carried as rations, and supplies carried for Aborigines.

In 1883–84 only two vessels reported to Robinson as instructed while the others gave wide berth to Lemba Moutiara. Husein, Bankasi and Aming Daeng Bali went straight to Tarrusanga, where customs eventually caught up with them and demanded £50 each. They argued that this much exceeded their cash reserves, and they also had a dispute over exchange rates between shillings, guilders and sovereigns. Aming Daeng Bali tried to get away and ended up having Robinson's revolver pointed at his head, while Searcy and Pinder each 'nailed a man to the mast'. The drama of this incident was amplified by the fact that the *serang* on the *Flying Cloud* had a brother on one of the *perahus*.[23]

Husein's shipping manifests for that season on the *Bondeng Patola* show that for £44 worth of stores he paid almost £20 in duty. Later in the season Husein and Daeng Matona went to Lembana Panrea (Melville Bay), while Unusu Daeng Remba and Pua Nando made a new camp at Goulburn Island. Searcy caught up with them again, this time on a faster boat, the *Fleetwing*. He also found Bapa Palu at Mallison Island in Arnhem Bay and relieved him of his entire stock of trepang and tortoise shell, as well as some pearl shell. It was to be Bapa Palu's last voyage as captain: he had been practically robbed and probably ended up in debt from this voyage. From now on, Husein captained the *Erang Poleang* (Returner).[24]

In 1884 the 'revenue station' was shifted from Lemba Moutiara (Port Essington) to Tarrusanga (Bowen Strait) and Robinson appeared in uniform and with a new revolver. There was no avoiding Robinson here: this is where the fleet regrouped before embarking together on the homeward journey. This year the fleet left £600 in taxes and fees at Lemba Moutiara—enough to persuade some captains to avoid Marege altogether.

Husein continued to come, as did his brother-in-law, Daeng Magassing. They had a disastrous season in 1886–87. First the *Erang Poleang* was wrecked near Ketampi at Melville Island and Husein's crew was attacked. Husein kept the Tiwi 'at bay with an old carbine', according to Robinson's report. They had crowded thirty-four crew into their four canoes, but one of these capsized as well. They were still travelling by canoe when they reached Bowen Strait three weeks later, having come by Lemba Binangaja at Trepang Bay, and Lemba Moutiara. Then the *Lasalasaya* was wrecked, also at Melville Island, and its twenty-seven-strong crew, crowded into two canoes, were close to starvation when they reached the revenue station eight days later.[25]

It became less and less attractive to visit Marege. In 1904–05 only Husein on the *Bunga Ejaya* (Red Flower) and Marika Uwa Madolangan on the *Lambere Ujung*

Tana are recorded in Marege, four vessels in the final year, and Husein on the *Bunga Ejaya* in 1906–07.

The Macassan story in Arnhem Land ends with Husein Daeng Ranka's last visit in 1906. And it picks up again with his children eighty years later. It was Husein's daughter, Ibu Saribanong Nganne (born 1904), who implored Peter Spillett during a 1985 visit in Makassar to piece the family together again: 'Please find my family for me, please find my brother and sister' in Marege.[26]

The Ibu remembered at least two of Husein's Aboriginal children by name, to whom she referred as Kunanong and Bacan (Bacan was also Husein's father's name). They are known at Elcho Island as Gunano and Bätjang. Bätjang died without descendants in the 1920s as a young man, and it seems certain that there have been at least two Gunanos. The Gunano stories do not make a single genealogy, perhaps because they have not yet been fully revealed. Mattjuwi described his grandmother Gunano as a powerful woman at Matamata outstation (Elcho Island). It is possible that this woman partnered Samaila Daeng Bacan, the father of Husein Daeng Ranka, because oral history refers to Gunano's husband as Djaymila. Mattjuwi explained that one of his grandmothers' grandchildren (from Gunano's second daughter Garnggar) was also called Gunano. According to Mattjuwi, Garnggar was abducted by 'Captain Maliwa' (presumably Daeng Mallewa of Barrang Lompo—a small island close to Makassar) and her daughter Gunano was born in Makassar.[27]

Ibu Saribanong also recalled that her father once brought two Aboriginal men back to Makassar. 'They lived in Unusu Daeng Remba's house in Jalan Ma'ip and were responsible for guarding the *empang* or fishponds at the back of the house, cleaning the *mushollah*... and pump water up bamboo ducts to the house and *mushollah*.' They died in Makassar in the 1930s.[28] Daeng Remba's impressively large house in Kampong Basi was later used as a school.[29] Daeng Remba, captain of the *Paduwakang Lakarinlong*, also belonged in the fleet travelling with Husein. Other captains in this fleet were Bapa Palu, Daeng Matona and Daeng Magassing. Their financier and merchant was Abdulrazak Pudu Daeng Tompo, an influential *bunggawa* at Kampung Maluku in Makassar.[30]

This network continues to recur in Top End stories that refer to Macassans by name. Possibly the earliest recorded of these is the account by Djaladjari Matullo (also referred to as Charley Charley Sitdown, or Sitdown Charley), rendered in Berndt and Berndt. He voyaged extensively with the Macassans from age nine, around the northern shores from his home at Cape Wilberforce as far as Groote Eylandt, then back along the coast calling in at the customs office in Bowen Strait on the way to Makassar. After almost a year away from home, they came back. Djaladjari and his Yolngu companions were wild with joy at seeing the Australian shore, and as a result of their antics the captain's cap was blown away by the wind. He was beaten in punishment for the loss of the cap and Djaladjari returned from this adventure permanently crippled.[31]

Djaladjari's account, though tinged with the romantic flavour of adventure, also contains glimpses about his status on the boat. Before departing from Port

Essington towards Makassar, Djaladjari's captain wanted to pay him off and presumably leave him there, however the captain of another boat in the same fleet decided to take him along to Makassar. The two captains had an argument and threatened each other with knives. Eventually Captain Jadjung who had recruited him, paid Djaladjari off with calico, rice, coconut, tobacco, and a knife, and accompanied him to Captain Wonabadi's vessel *Patti Jawaya*. On arrival in Makassar he and some other boys were handed over to Daeng Tompo, the *punggawa* who received the cargo.[32] (I am unable to identify Captain Wonabadi, but Jadjung most likely refers to Jago—or Husein—who was associated with the *Patti Jawaya* in the 1880s.)

> When we reached Kampung Maluku, the big *bunggawa* [boss] named *kareng* [King] Daeng Tompo came down to the wharf. He brought with him *djura*, *surat* [letter or paper] which had on it many *darabu* marks [writing], and on this he wrote down what my boss Wonabadi told him about our cargo. Then Wonabadi said to him 'I've got some boys here'—referring to my companions and to myself. 'All right,' Daeng Tompo replied. 'I'll take all these men, and they can come to my place to sleep and have food.' He gave us money, and we went with him. Near where I stayed several countrymen of mine [Aborigines] were living. There was Jamaduda from the English Company Islands, who had come to Macassar as a small boy. He had worked there, and never returned home. When I saw him he was a grown man: he had married a Macassan woman, and had four sons and four daughters. Then there was Gadari, a Wonguri-Mandigai man from Arnhem Bay; he had come as a young man, worked there, and married a Macassan woman. When I met him he was middle aged and had a lot of children there, but I heard afterwards that he had died. He had been married to an Aboriginal woman before he had left the Australian mainland, and Duda is his son; but he didn't return to his wife. I saw Brindjauwi, too; he was still unmarried when I left Macassar. I met a Ngeimil man, and many others as well. [Spelling of some Macassan names adjusted.][33]

'Macassans are the kin of Yirritja people', Mattjuwi at Elcho Island, June 1995.

This story, giving names and clan affiliations of some of the people observed, convincingly portrays the image of a fairly strong presence of Aborigines in

Makassar. Djaladjari also described the polyethnic port town of Makassar where each *kampung* (village, or quarters) was named after the ethnic group that dominated it, just as became the practice in north Australian port towns later on. The Malays and their headman lived at Kampung Malayu, the Chinese at Kampung Cina, Kupangers and Japanese lived along the creek and lily swamp at Kampung Dadi.

Djaladjari's son Bawurr Munyarryun added an important family dimension to this story. He told me that his father had worked with Macassans and learned their language. He accompanied them to Caledon Bay (Kartalala), and right up to Milingimbi, Goulburn Island, Croker Island, and to Makassar. Bawurr's father was young when he went to Makassar, and had a family there: Bawurr's older brother and two others who passed away. Then he came back and had a family here. After his return he became a *bunggawa*, a headman for the Yolngu, because he knew their

Bawurr, elder of Yirrkala, smoking a Makassan pipe, July 1995. His father Djaladjari had three children in Makassar.

language, Yolngu Matha and Makasar.[34]

Djaladjari's story makes an explicit connection with the fleet working for Puddu Daeng Tompo, at Kampung Maluku in Makassar. Other place names he mentioned were Lailai, Kodinggareng, 'Manggarei', 'Djamaluna' and Banda. These are also not merely incidental. Lailai Island, just outside Makassar, is one of the places where Willie Gundera received a cordial reception, and Mattjuwi named his son Lailai Latung after this place. Kodinggareng, a small island two hours boat-journey from the port, is one of the home islands of Sama Bajo people from where a number of sailors came to Marege, and this name is repeated in Gunyangarra (Ski Beach) at Yirrkala.

At Galiwin'ku (the main township on Elcho Island) Terry Yumbulul, Willie Danjati Gunderra and George Wulanybuma Pukulat'pi[35] emphasised that Macassan contact was not buried in the distant past, but close to them, a part of them. Terry acted as host and interpreter, rather than contributing his own story, but referred me to publications by McIntosh and Cawte for details about his father David Burrumarra.[36] He did, however, say that his personal name, Terichini, normally contracted as Terry, was the Sama Bajo word *Turije'ne*. (There is also a Yolngu myth about a turtle hunter, Dhurritjini.[37])

Willie Gundera received a cordial family welcome when some years ago he visited Kampung Maluku, Lailai Island and nearby Lumbu Kassati, because his father Wili Walalipa was the son of a Macassan: 'Oh, real happy, they called me the Makasan, "You don't go back to Elcho", they said to me, "Your family here, you stay here."' Willie's Macassan grandfather was separated from his Yolngu family when the entry of Macassans to Australia was prohibited.[38]

This farewell scene is remembered in manifold stories invoking family and kin. Peter Spillett was shown a tall post with a carved top at Elcho Island:

> It represents the mast of a *perahu* which Yucing had given to the people of Elcho Island for a ceremony on which a sail could be raised as a reminder of the sailors. It was recalled that Yucing sent a message to Dg. Mangu, in the English Company Islands, that he would send boats to protect Daymangu's family from the Balanda because he thought that they would soon come to Marege.[39]

We may take Yucing to mean Husein. But who is Daymangu or Daeng Mangu? Spillett does not refer to anyone by the name of Daeng Mangu in Makassar. Mangellai Daeng Maro at Makassar remembered Mangu as the 'rajah of Melville Bay'.[40] At Yirrkala Spillett said he was shown a *wuramu* figure depicting 'Daeng Mangung', a Macassan sea captain wearing a *hadji's songkok* (Islamic cap).[41] From Spillett it seems that in Makassar this figure is seen as a Yolngu person, and in Arnhem Land as a Macassan. George Wulanybuma Pukulat'pi demystified this figure. He said his father (great-uncle[42]) Dayngmangu was given the title of 'Daeng' by the Macassans. He died around 1925 and is buried at the top of Elcho Island, at a place called Gäwa, a former trepang camp. McIntosh also refers to this man, Ganimbirrngu, David Burrumarra's father. Burrumarra indicated that one of Ganimbirrngu's wives, a Djapu woman, had once been 'stolen' by Husein Daeng Ranka, and that her grandchildren and great-grandchildren lived at Elcho Island. He added that the name of Dayngmangu was given to his father by Husein Daeng Ranka, who on his last visit presented him with a mast and a white calico flag 'as a sign that each had an agreement and were friends and would remember each other'.[43]

So here are two stories linking Husein and Dayngmangu at a scene of farewell.[44] The second story is not unlike Djawawungu, where Gatjing bestows the name of Mangalay on Djawa and then takes leave for the last time. Mangellai is also the name of Husein's son. Gatjing may be read to refer to Husein's brother-in-law Daeng Gassing.

In another version of this story the historical figure of Pobassoo substitutes for the captain in question. (Not unlike many 'first-contact' stories referring to Captain Cook.) In this story Captain Pobassoo befriends the Gupapuyngu-speaking people of

Macassan contact history is not something of the distant past: it is here, now, us. Terry Yumbulul, George Wulanybuma, and Willie Danjati Gunderra at Galiwin'ku, Elcho Island, June 1995.

The *Hati Marege*.
This traditional *padewakang perahu* was reconstructed for the Bicentennial celebrations in 1988. It carried history as well as family.
Source: *Northern Territory News.*

Nikawungura, especially a man called Garrawarrpa, the father of Dhawa Danygululil and Djäwa. Pobassoo called Garrawarrpa 'brother', and before leaving for Karra-Mangalay (or Karaeng Mangnellai) he promised to bring his son with him on the next visit. Next year Pobassoo introduced his son: 'Here is the boy who I have told you about. This is our son, because you are my brother, and your sons will call him "younger brother".' His name was Mangellai Daeng Maro, and Djäwa and Dhawa Danygululil called him brother.[45]

In this story the names of the Macassans are not quite so reliable. But this version of the story makes the Macassan connection of Jawa Daeng Gululil's family more evident. Whether we see these stories as political myths making a claim, or as family history, we see the Djaladjari line claiming to have Aboriginal kin in Husein's home *kampung*, and both the Burrumarra line and the Djawa line making claims to belong to Husein's family.

The first resumption of contact took place when a group of Batchelor College students, working in association with Spillett, visited Makassar in June 1986. Michael Cooke recalls the emotional impact of that historic moment. For the Yolngu students their traditional stories, at the brink of entering into myth, came alive all around them—they saw real *perahus* which they recognised from paintings, real Macassan captains and sailors, speaking a strange language which was yet full of recognisable words.[46] Spillett recalls how surprised they were to hear what they thought of as Yolngu Matha words spoken all around them by Macassans. Sometimes their hosts were equally non-plussed. When meeting Dr Daud Nompo, the deputy governor of South Sulawesi, one of the Batchelor College students ventured to recall a Yolngu man by the same name.[47] They visited Sumpang Bita, some forty kilometres from Makassar, which contains a cave painting thought to be more than 5,000 years old. They felt that it had striking similarities to Aboriginal rock art, with hand silhouettes and footprints, and a large *lipa-lipa* (dugout canoe).[48]

There is an all-pervasive sense of connectedness between Macassans and all Yolngu people. Joe Mowandjil Garrawirtja, a Uniting Church minister at Milingimbi, spoke about the affinity between Macassans and Yolngu as indigenous peoples:

> They came here and explore the land and they found two things, one is trepang, and the second, they found Aboriginal people. And when they came together, they can feel similarities. They feel like we Aboriginal people, like Macassan. And when they saw artefacts and like what we're doing, they think, 'Oh, you're doing the same things'. And from there artefacts were exchanged. Macassan people gave their artefacts to Aboriginal people and from we to them, and that was the beginning of the relationship...
>
> The way I look at people like at Kupang in the village, like we people here we eat outside, sometimes we cook outside, sometimes we sleep outside, and we have a table, we have a chair, but we prefer to eat outside, more comfortable than sitting eating in a chair ... People like from Makassar we feel that we are one in spirit.[49]

Certain basic conceptions resonate very deeply across the Arafura Sea, but these are difficult to access and have not been subject to detailed study. Terry Yumbulul hinted at a synchronicity of concepts—including ideas of what defines secret knowledge—which point to a deeper common cultural stratum. He called it the 'Hindu flavour' of the Yirritja ways, but perhaps they express an indigeneity prior to all proselytising contact, of which the similarity in rock art is a visible expression.

Spillett had been told in Makassar that Sampara Daeng Ruppa was buried at Lembana Panrea in Melville Bay under a large banyan tree. This place appears in a drawing made for Berndt and Berndt, which they describe as a Baijini place.[50] He was subsequently shown a very large banyan tree at Melville Bay, believed to be the site of a Macassan grave which has a spirit: 'Whenever it sees a *perahu* sail into the bay it goes to a rock in the sea and cries for it, and when the *perahu* leaves, it cries for it again and returns to the tree.'[51] Macassan and Yolngu spirit stories merge.

Yolngu collective memory embraces the history of connectedness with Macassans. It belongs to the Yirritja moiety, and it must be largely due to the mediating role of David Burrumarra—who was able to speak for up to seven clans—that much of the once protected ritual knowledge has become more widely available. He was a leader of the 'adjustment movement' which resulted in the revelation of sacred *rranga* in 1957 and the suspension of ceremonies. When the Fraser and Hawke governments failed to deliver on the promise of a Treaty, Burrumarra revealed further symbols on the flag *rranga*, a flag incorporating British and Warramirri symbols to signify unity. Burrumarra has played a leading role in mediating knowledges between cultures and has been more willing than elders elsewhere to expose the ritual knowledges that harbour the relationships to Macassans. He was a chief informant to a long line of authors on Yolngu culture and contact, including the Berndts, McIntosh, Spillett, as well as anthropologists Cawte and Thomson, missionary Harold Sheperdson, and trepanger Fred Gray.

The Yolngu connection with Macassans is well recognised on all sides, but Macassan visits were not confined to Yolngu shores. Was the contact in Kayu Jawa and elsewhere in Marege qualitatively different? Were Aborigines elsewhere less accommodating, more hostile, or inaccessible? Non-Yolngu Aboriginal contact with Macassans is far less researched, so it seems that contact was less intensive. Of course, it could also mean that contact is further away in the distant past, or that the host culture was more resilient and less inclined to 'borrow', or that local politics have not brought forth a diplomat like Burrumarra.

TOP END CONTACT

Berndt and Berndt suggested that the formation of family links between Macassans and Yolngu might have been facilitated by the large polygynous families in northeast Arnhem Land.[52] This explanation is easily dispelled because polygyny was also practised in the other areas of Macassan contact. The Tiwi gained such a reputation for this form of marriage that in the 1960s anthropologists C. Hart and A. Pilling explained the whole social structure of these islands as being built on the 'currency' of women.[53] When Father Gsell established a Catholic mission at Bathurst Island in 1911, he could see no alternative but to pay for the girls whom he took into the mission dormitory. He became known among the Tiwi as 'the Bishop with the 150 wives'—a polygamist on a grand scale.

Why were the Tiwi Islanders less involved in the trepang trade than the Yolngu who were much further away for the Macassans? The Melville Islanders had a particularly fierce reputation for their dealings with strangers, and many authors have linked this to prior contact with slave raiders.[54] Of course, the record of contact is not all belligerent. During Martin van Delft's two-week sojourn in 1705, Tiwi were successfully invited on board.[55] In 1824, when Apsley Strait was chosen as the site for Fort Dundas, the British must not have been aware of a particular Tiwi hostility, but this settlement subsequently suffered from 'native attacks'. By the 1880s Alfred Searcy observed that the Macassans bypassed the Tiwi Islands and assumed that this was because of their hostility.[56] Yet in 1895 Edward Robinson and Joe Cooper set up a buffalo shooting camp at Melville Island that forged links between Tiwi and the Iwaidja. Daeng Sarro, too, described the Tiwi, whether from personal experience or from established reputation, as aggressive and unfriendly. He referred to Karaeng Mangngemba, a beautiful white beach stretching towards the east, with a row of casuarina trees, as a stretch known for its aggressive people fighting with clubs (*knotsen*).[57] Shipwrecked visitors certainly tended to fare badly at Melville Island, as Husein's experiences, reported by Robinson in the 1880s, attest. Michael McCarthy observes that a shipwreck places the survivors on an entirely different, and less advantageous, footing in their meeting with indigenous people, than a successful landing.[58]

But how do the Tiwi themselves recollect this contact phase? Two sources on Macassan contact are based on information from Tiwi Islanders. A small 1960s study by John Morris suggests that, despite documented incidents of violence, contact with Macassans is remembered positively and harmoniously, and there are some traceable family links. The Turupi say that they stole one of the Macassan canoes, and the Macassans in turn abducted a Turupula girl who later bore a son with a Macassan. This son, Mindaroli, returned from Makassar and married an Iwaidja woman from Cape Don, Yair-a-kart, and their son continued to live at Cobourg Peninsula. (In the excerpt below, Spillett also refers to a Tiwi woman who was taken to Makassar, but it is not clear whether this is Mindaroli's mother.[59])

Morris observed that Tiwi locals were not recruited to assist with harvesting or trepang processing. Some Makasar words entered into island language but it could not be said that the Tiwi spoke Makasar. Morris believes that the Macassans on their part had a small repertoire of Tiwi expressions, such as *pongki* as a greeting of peace.[60] This greeting also appears in a story told by Happy and Laurie Cook to Peter Spillett:

> My uncle Milangrapitjimi told me his grandfather Piadiringila saw many Mamangimpi [Macassans] landing and he hid in the bush while the Macassans cut wood, made fires and shelters. He killed one Macassan man—speared him here, in the chest. He was the first man to see Macassan people. The *perahu* ran into the rock at Aliyu, on the west of the bay.
>
> Then Pombiade, my father, said the Macassans put both arms straight up into the air and waved hands with fingers outstretched and called out '*pongki-pongki, nyawa-nyawa Mankatjara wila*'—peace, peace, we are from Makassar.
>
> Macassans showed gifts and then the Tiwi people dropped their spears and came out. The Macassans gave them *kanditawa* [flour], *birata* [rice], *gula* [sugar] and tea leaf . . . [They made damper and cooked it on hot coals, and cooked the rice in bamboo pieces.] . . . Then our people, the Turupula, looked after them. (They thought they were going to be picked up by the other Macassans, but eventually they left in their sampans.) '*Oh el-la, oh el-la sama ratana oh el-la, oh el-la*', these were the words used by the Macassans when they tried to pull the *mitjiang* [*biseang*, boat] off the rock.
>
> (When they left they gave our people tomahawks, knives and calico sarongs.)
>
> My grandfather's name was Piadirringila and my auntie's name was Tjipilatjimau. They think her name was given to her by the Macassan people and that she went to Makassar.[61]

Piadirringila is here given responsibility for the killing of a Macassan: the 'first Macassan' to come to the island. The part of the story involving Pombiade refers to a party who pleaded for their lives and eventually left in their small craft. It is hard not to think of the records kept by customs officers with regard to these stories. Husein Daeng Ranka was wrecked at Aliyu on the western part of Lethbridge Bay in February 1882. His party was attacked and Bapa Palu picked up the survivors. The *Erang Poleang* and the *Lasalasaya* were wrecked in the 1886–87 season and there were no casualties in these two incidents—in both cases the crew reached safety in their dinghies. Spillett also recorded another story about the wreck of the *Mitjian* at Aliyu, and the rescue of its crew by the *Buffalo*.[62] Clearly the shoals around the Tiwi Islands proved treacherous to a number of vessels.

It appears from these stories that Macassan activity in this area was focused on the smaller offshore islands, perhaps as a result of difficult waters, and contact was incidental, perhaps only resulting from accidents. Morris thinks that the Tiwi shores were not prolific with trepang, but Spillett's informants mentioned various sites of Macassan activity with old wells.[63] The waters at the former Macassan campsites at Wulintju (Wilintu) Island, and at Ulurangku on Karslake Island are reportedly prolific with trepang. Daeng Sarro, too, mentioned a number of sites, each occupying a day of fishing and sailing before proceeding to Cape Don, known as Lemba Peo (Mud Bay): Lembang Lantang (Deep Bay); Karaeng Mangngemba, Lembana I Ma'ne (Ma'ne Bay); and Lemba Kusissili (Sandfly Bay).

At Trepang Bay, known to Macassans as Lemba Binangaja (River Bay), on Cobourg Peninsula, the Iwaidja came on board to help with the trepang fishery in return for food and tobacco. From here they would sail to Lemba Moutiara, and then past Flagpole (Pa'banderanga), the beacon on Smith Point. Here too, a sense of relatedness still persists. At Black Point on Cobourg Peninsula, the Garik Gunak Barlu cultural centre exhibits the former Macassan links. Being shown through the museum by Brian Yambikbik (formerly of Cape Don) and Nelson Mulurinji, I gained a strong sense that the local community 'owned' this museum and the history it exhibited. Cliff Patlas, visiting from the Tiwi Islands, explained: 'They come here from Timor to here, so we all Mangijarra people. Mangijarra [Macassan]. That's our people, too, Timor, Malay people. They make all the half-caste people around there, Darwin, in here in Australia, in history, they made all the half-caste, coloured they made a family.'[64]

No significant distinction was made between Malay and Chinese in these discussions. When they were browsing through my collection of photographs from the Darwin and Daly River area, Cliff suddenly yelled, 'Ha! That's my mother.' He was looking at a woman of Chinese-Aboriginal parentage. Nelson explained to the others present that her father had been '*gulungulu*' (or *gurunguru*), meaning Asian. Cliff explained, 'We call that Chinese mate, *gulungulu*, come here from Timor, they married to Chinese and they come to Australia, they see us as *mangatharra* [*mangajarra*]. They see us in town, "Mangatharra, hello", they say "mate". They come here and they met a woman, cousin, *mo*, Chinese like the Asian people, Chinese, we all Asian people.'[65] In the evening an impromptu corroboree was held at Nelson's place, with 'all the old time, long time ago the people that married to Malay'.

Father Confalonieri, who lived at Black Point from 1846 to 1848, ended up with predominantly Macassan names for bays (recorded as 'Limba Piu', 'Limba Bina') and peoples (recorded as the 'Binanolombo', 'Limbaregio', 'Mancororota' and 'Monoba' tribes). Daeng Sarro in the 1950s called these places Lemba Peo (Mud Bay), near Cape Don, and Lemba Binangaja (River Bay), known as Trepang Bay.

From here the Macassans would pass a deserted settlement they called Old Englander (Anggarrisi' Toaja), probably Fort Wellington in Raffles Bay, and then to Tarrusanga (Sea Strait) also known as Bowen Strait. From there they went to Udjung Garnggong (Noisy Cape) called Point David at Croker Island, now the site of Tiwi Pearls, and to Lembana I Djawa (Mountnorris Bay), then to Lembana Siaolloa (One Day Bay, or Malay Bay) and then to Grant Island. Grant Island was uninhabited but had fresh water, and was used as a supply station where the Macassans could obtain water and vegetables. They called it Liukang Kangkonga (Spinach Island). They then went to Kampena I Pandjang (Pandjang Bight) at Aurari Bay, and to Waira (north Goulburn Island).

At Warruwi (Goulburn Island) Spillett interviewed six people who all remembered Macassan sites.[66] Four of them said that members of their family had worked with Macassans, three mentioned Daeng Remba by name, and two spoke of visits to Makassar. Peter Nangaraidt from Warruwi said that his great-grandfather, Nandal, worked for the fishermen at Wigu and sailed on a *biseang* to Makassar, where he married a Macassan woman. One informant mentioned the names of Daeng Remba, Daeng Gassing (Dayngatji), Husein (Yocing) and Mangellai. His (grand)father had been to Kampung Maluku, Kampung Dadi and Benteng (Fort Rotterdam).[67] These interviews suggest that contact with Macassans at the Goulburn Islands was more intensive, at least in the later period of contact, than further west. This sits well with the historical record, since Searcy found Pua Nando and Unusu Daeng Remba at a new camp on Goulburn Island in 1885, and reported one of the Iwaidja men had been diving in Papua.[68]

Between Goulburn Island and Elcho Island, Daeng Sarro mentions only two more places. From Pua Rengga for Braithwaite Point (about halfway between Warruwi and Maningrida) he remembered the name of the local 'chief' (*karaeng*), 'Mamborona', whose three grandsons he once took to Makassar. The next large camp was at Morongga, still known as Moorroongga Island (outside Milingimbi). In this area, too, there is a sense of connectedness with Macassans, reflected in the Djomi museum at Maningrida, and in the title *Lembana Mani Mani* released by the Sunrize Band from Maningrida.

Maningrida is the largest settlement on the north coast, supporting some 1,700 people from a number of language groups, including those in about thirty homelands surrounding it.[69] It was established in 1947 as a trading post to halt the migration into Darwin. Here I met Jimmie Bunggaru, who had travelled with the Macassans to Goulburn Island, Darwin and Timor, but he said his story came from his father, grandfather, brother and himself. It was delivered in the speech-making mode, which does not bear interruption. The areas of Macassan activity in this story overlap with those gathered by Spillett at Goulburn Island. Like some stories collected by Berndt and Berndt, this one refers to Macassan women and children. This is a summary of Bunggaru's story:

> The Macassans sailed from Kupang to a place outside of Maningrida (which was translated as 'Kupang outstation') where they dug a huge well. They then explored the Liverpool estuary and constructed further wells, but didn't like it. They stayed overnight at the site of the Maningrida barge landing, where they made another well, then they went to the opposite shore of the Liverpool River near West Point, where they stayed for four days, and cut down five trees for timber to take back with them. They went to Entrance Island and planted *cambak* (tamarind) and constructed another well. After two days they went to Samson Bay (in a northwesterly direction), where they planted more trees, and constructed another well. They were looking for trepang and pearl shell, and filled up many bags with trepang.
>
> They tapped the lontar palm and boiled the sap to make *aniji* or *tuak*. They brought bananas, flour, black sugar, sweets, and *aniji*, but also ate bush-tucker like yam, crab, and fish, and trepang. They wore a wrap around their heads; they had long hair and beards, and hairy chests, and wore wide shorts. They had brought their women and children.
>
> At Rolling Bay (on the other side of Hawkesbury Point) they made a camp with a big, long house to sleep in, and some of Bunggaru's relatives visited them there. They had run out of flour, sugar and tea, and asked for yams, 'big mob tucker for we'. But the reply was, 'tea, nothing, we drink water, we're travelling'. Then they went to Goulburn Island and back home.[70]

The story seemed to be about a single journey, but is more likely to represent a contracted account of contact over a longer period. A few days after my visit it was announced that Jimmie Bunggaru had received a fellowship from the Australia Council's Aboriginal and Torres Strait Islander Arts Board to produce a cultural map of Maningrida. It was to include a dug-out canoe with a woven pandanus sail, 'a skill taught to his people by Macassan traders over hundreds of years'.[71] He must have had this map on his mind when he explained the precise sites on which the Macassans landed, and the activities performed there.

Like Yolngu, Iwaidja and Tiwi claim family connections with Macassans, and have histories of visits to Makassar, but these are far less studied and lesser known than the Yolngu connections. Beyond the family connection, the history of Macassan contact, like myth, has a politics: it shows up the destructiveness of Balanda colonisation. Joe Mowandjil Garrawirtja explains:

> Macassan came not to take the land, not to take things, one thing they only came for, to take trepang. Not like the white people when they came and they took Australia, and they killed Aboriginal people and they put their flag, England flag, claiming that this is our land. They think they make the land, hey, they think they were like a God, hey.[72]

This was also the first thing Mattjuwi told me:

> They been here first, long long time. Makassar people come here for *dharippa* [trepang]. They don't want from here rock, anything, gravel, anything, bauxite, gold, no,

only that one, *dharippa*. But they here before, they come here all the Macassan people. They stay here for *dharippa*, for one thing. Get the *dharippa*, every year.

'Captain Cook people', on the other hand, were troublemakers, shooting at Yolngu people. While there was a mixing of Yolngu and Macassan people a long time ago, these people have become full Yolngu people, accepting Yolngu names and Yolngu culture, and people are alive and well, despite this admixture. Mattjuwi described the English people as 'really mad', shooting with bullet and gun. 'Yolngu people used the shovel-nosed spear to kill, but only if someone was stealing a promised wife. As for Macassans, they're friend. And Yolngu here, grandfather Macassan people.'

When I offered the consideration that the Macassans carried guns with them too, Mattjuwi knew that I still hadn't understood: 'No. These here Makasar people, very good start. Real good friend. All the Makasar bringit here friend, brother and sister, uncle, nephew, not they bringing trouble, not anything, because they looking for *dharippa* job [trepang], he working on the *dharippa*, ma.' Later he recapitulated again: 'This is the story from the beginning. True story. Different from there Captain Cook. Makasan people come here, they are friends. One group.'

They introduced clothing, *rupyiah* (money), and all manner of things; the Europeans didn't. Europeans came and uprooted the soil with bulldozers looking for minerals, rounded up Aboriginal women, and wanted to stay instead of going back home.[73] Using the comparison with Macassan contact to denounce European colonisation is not a recent mythologising of contact—it had already been observed by Worsley in the 1950s.[74]

THE KIMBERLEY

While the South Australian government attempted to earn revenue from the Macassan visits, the Western Australian government did not. As a result the Kimberley part of the industry is not as well documented. Ian Crawford has done most work on discovering traces of Macassan contact on the Kimberley coast. He concludes that this contact was not radically different from that in Arnhem Land. He believes that, like Marege, the Kayu Jawa coast was abandoned between the 1880s and 1900. There is some evidence that a trade Malay was spoken,[75] but no family or farewell stories have come to light from local Aboriginal people. There are myths about conflict, and, as for Arnhem Land, historical references to conflict.

At Cassini Island (Admiralty Gulf), Macassans warned the Baudin expedition of the fierceness of Aborigines, and at Kupang the same warning was given to Phillip Parker King in 1818. Vosmaer in 1839 referred to the need to construct earthworks around trepang camps in Kayu Jawa as defence from attacks, and R. J. Sholl in 1865 observed that the Macassans visiting Camden Harbour (between King Sound and Admiralty Gulf) were afraid of Aborigines, and had been attacked a year before.[76]

During the 1880s Searcy found several strands of old tamarind trees between Daly River and towards Port Keats (viz.) that he interpreted as evidence of long-standing Macassan visits, but no contact was within living memory.[77] Crawford drew similar conclusions in the 1960s. He conducted archaeological work at Tamarinda, an old Indonesian trepang camp in the 'mission beach' area of Napier Broome Bay, close to the former Pago Mission (viz.). The site takes its name from three very old tamarind trees found by Benedictine missionaries in 1908, but which no longer existed in the 1960s.

Crawford found the appearance of Tamarinda consistent with the historical references to conflict between Aborigines and Macassans. Though there was no evidence of earthworks to fortify the camp, it was in an easily defensible position, and contained two musket balls and a gunflint. No myths linked to the site were known, and it appeared that 'Aborigines have not shown any particular interest in this site, nor in the nearby Indonesian site of Ilanganana'.[78] The site contained no Aboriginal stone artefacts and only very small quantities of metals. Crawford concluded that the Macassans at Tamarinda had little to attract trade with Aborigines, and that there was no cooperation between Macassans and Aborigines on this site.

Oral histories of the area suggest that Aborigines did not welcome Macassans in their territory. The stealing of their canoes is a recurrent theme in stories and songs. A Wunambal man told Crawford that in his father's time the Macassans sailed as a fleet, and gathered at Cassini Island, then proceeded south to Wollaston harbour to camp. The Aborigines of Napier Broome Bay had driven them away by burning the bush. H. V. Howe, a pearler from before World War I, also recollected that in the early years of the twentieth century he and his crew were permitted to collect firewood and water on the shores of Napier Broome Bay, but were not allowed to penetrate inland.[79] The overall impression gained by Crawford from archaeological and historical evidence was that in the Kimberley, the Macassans stayed for short periods and frequently shifted camp, while their major activity was focused on the reefs off the coast.

There are strong indications of connections with foreigners, but Crawford was unable to determine whether such influences may have been Timorese, Portuguese or Macassan.[80] A cannon discovered on Carronade Island might point to Portuguese contact or might have been carried by Indonesian boats. Similarly, the Wandjina art—characteristic of the Kimberley coast area and strikingly different from Aboriginal art elsewhere—has sometimes been explained with reference to external influences, such as Timorese visitors.[81] He did, however, find evidence of a much larger European presence on the Kimberley trepang camps than anticipated.

In the Kimberley the Macassan fleets were supplanted by a motley collection of *perahus*, luggers and schooners operating out of Timor. These worked either under white skippers or were crewed entirely by Macassans, but in both cases they had gained a familiarity with the fishing grounds from previous engagement in the Western Australian pearling industry. According to Howe, this phase of the trepang fishery had commenced in the 1880s with captains Hart and Drysdale. In the 1890s, Langfelt, Hilliard, and later Robin Hilliard, Chamberlain and Smith joined the fishery. Dutch, Arab and Chinese merchants owned the vessels.[82]

Under the Western Australian fishery Acts, such Indonesian fishing in Australian territorial waters was prohibited, but there was virtually no enforcement in the Kimberley waters. As a result, this traffic did not come to the notice of authorities until 1911, when two Indonesian vessels were detained at Scott Reef. The

Western Australian press deployed the full range of anti-Asian rhetoric about 'hordes of . . . disease-laden Asiatics' pouring into the north.[83] The incident became highly embarrassing, because 'after the parties had been tried and fined it was discovered that Scott Reef was British, not Australian territory'.[84] The investigations revealed that about nine vessels, carrying 130 Macassans, were leaving annually from Kupang, under the command of Australian and British captains. They continued the practices of the earlier Indonesian fleets, both in the routes they took and the trepang processing methods employed, and frequently moving camps. Some of them subsequently used the leverage of anxieties about Asians to apply for monopoly fishing rights over certain reefs.[85] Ironically in Western Australia, the lack of official effort to profit from the Indonesian trepang industry with customs and import duties facilitated the success of white entrepreneurs in this trade.

By the 1920s fleets from Madura, home of another major Indonesian seafaring population, had joined the fishery. They operated out of a base near Makassar to proceed through Roti towards Ashmore Reef and Long Reef. Aru Islanders and Timorese were also found among the crews. They fished for trochus and tortoise shell. Also in the 1920s, Japanese motorised pearling vessels made their appearance off the Kimberley coast. In effect the area off the Kimberley coast had become an international fishing ground.[86]

The Ashmore Reef oil-drilling rig, established in 1965, was often visited by Indonesian fleets from Timor and Madura gathering clam shell, fish, and at least three varieties of trepang for sale to Chinese merchants in Makassar.[87]

The customary three-mile limit of territorial waters was increased in 1968 to twelve miles, and in 1979 an Australian Fishing Zone (AFZ) was declared extending to up to 200 miles off the coast. This gradual extension of Australia's territorial waters rendered the traditional fishing of Indonesian fleets illegal. It culminated in the early 1990s with a great media focus on what became known as 'Timorese poachers' making incursions into Australian waters around Ashmore Reef to fish for shark fin and trochus shell. In 1990 alone some 500 Indonesians were arrested, charged, fined and gaoled, and their vessels confiscated and burned, without offering the slightest deterrent to two further fleets detected early in 1991. Such fishing incursions continued to attract media interest throughout the 1990s, until interest shifted towards the phenomenon of 'people smuggling' at the end of the decade, and brought about a renewed federal government commitment towards northern defence and patrolling. Coastwatch, the Australian Customs surveillance service, added three new aircraft to its fleet in 1999, increasing its aerial surveillance capacity by 63 per cent, from 7,000 to 11,000 hours per year. The *Border Protection Amendment Act of 1999* gave powers of hot pursuit in international waters.[88]

TIMORESE POACHERS

The people referred to in this book as Macassans—Bugis, Bajau Laut, Butonese and Makasar speakers—still make up the majority of Indonesia's identifiable fishing populations.[89] Fishermen from Roti, Timor and Sulawesi have continued to engage in the fishing traditions which emerged during the rise of the kingdom of Gowa, and their right to do so has been nominally safeguarded by a 1974 Memorandum of Understanding (MoU) between the Australian and Indonesian governments. The MoU defined a 'boxed' area around a resource-rich area of 12,000 square nautical miles halfway between Indonesia and Australia within which traditional fishing is permitted to Indonesian vessels. During the negotiations with the Indonesian government in 1973, the Australian government claimed that the Rotinese fleets then fishing in that area were a 'recent commercial invasion'. Perhaps the Australian authorities had not kept a close watch on the area previously, since the visits reported by the oilrig crews belie the image of a 'new development'.[90]

From 1988 to about 1996 Indonesian incursions became a focus of public attention, fanned by hysterical media coverage that paid little attention to historical continuities.[91] By the mid-1990s some 2,000 fishermen from Sulawesi Tenggara had been detained in Broome, a considerable proportion of the male population.[92] Under the Justices Act prison terms were imposed for inability to pay a fine or for breaking a good-behaviour bond. But second offenders were always liable for a prison term. If they pleaded guilty they were usually dealt with quickly, but to contest the charge usually took two or three months, during which period they were confined either on their boats or in a prison.

Interviewing the fishing crews detained in Darwin and Broome in January 1991, James Fox and Anthony Reid discovered some interesting historical continuities. They came from tiny islands in a Butonese fishing network, and were of mixed Bugis and Bajau origin. They spoke both Bugis and the Sama language of Bajau Laut; they were Muslims, and a few still practised polygamy. Fox noted that one of the skippers had a wife in Wuring and one in Dobo, and that the young males might be almost described as a nomadic population, spending the fishing seasons away from home. The cost of fitting out for a voyage, and the proceeds, were shared between the crew and the vessel owner, the latter having a stake of three or two shares in a voyage, and the crew and skipper one share each. This meant that the considerable risk of a voyage was also shared, and if a vessel was lost the crew and skipper ended up in debt.[93] The dried shark fin was sold to the *taukeh* in Dobo (Aru Islands), who often helped to finance the acquisition of a vessel through credit arrangements. The produce was sold without value added, so that the largest margin of profit fell to the merchants who on-sold to Hong Kong and elsewhere.[94]

The push-factors for increasing the fishing terrain of Sulawesi fishers are enormous. In the late 1980s population pressures increased, and Sulawesi recorded one of Indonesia's highest rates of population increases (3.66 per cent per annum) boosted by transmigration.[95] By 1995 each kilometre of coastline in the Spermonde Archipelago supported 200 to 300 households, and the marine ecology was on the verge of collapse.[96] Until the 1970s the home reefs supported the island economies with trochus, giant clam, pearl shell, tortoise shell and trepang, but since then fishing voyages extended increasingly further afield, first to Flores in the 1970s, then to Tanimbar (Maluku), and to Irian, although the coastal people of Irian Jaya (West Papua) are reputed to ferociously defend their coastline. By the early 1990s the competition from between thirty and fifty Taiwanese vessels per season in the Indonesian part of the Arafura

Sea exerted further resource pressures. On the assumption that traditional Indonesian fisheries were 'ineffectual', the Indonesian government either permitted, or turned a blind eye to, well-equipped Taiwanese vessels using trawl nets, drift nets and long lines entering Indonesian fishing grounds in the 1980s.[97]

'These fishermen represent one of the poorer sectors of the economy of a poor Indonesian province', writes Reid of the people he interviewed in Broome. In the 1990s the per capita gross domestic product of Sulawesi Tenggara ranked twenty-second out of twenty-seven provinces in Indonesia, and until the 1970s they were out of reach of social services like health and education.

The Bugis and Sama Bajo of these islands were part of the traditional Macassan fishing empire. Their trail to Australian waters recommenced in 1988 under a Bugis skipper who had married into Roti Island. 'Roti fishermen were the ones who were first aware of the trochus beds of Australia, and who pointed the way to the Buton boats.'[98] Prices for trochus and shark fin soared in 1990, and news that King Sound was prolific with trochus spread fast. A complex fleet of vessels started to enter Australian waters, harvesting a range of produce including trepang, trochus, shark-fin and tuna. Examining the composition of the fleets in 1992, Bruce Campbell and Bu Wilson distinguished between five general types of fishery, ranging from traditional Rotinese fishing to industrial drop-liners. Among them were various quasi-traditional fleets with small, motorised vessels from Sulawesi, Roti and Kupang.[99] These have been among those confiscated for poaching in Australian waters. Traditional fishing became criminalised, largely due to the complexities of distinguishing traditional and legal from commercial and illegal operations. The problem with the idea of 'traditional' activity is that it essentially denies history and change.

For Rotinese, Ashmore Reef was part of their traditional fishing grounds. Ashmore Reef (Pulau Pasir) is only about eighty kilometres from Roti Island. Together with Scott Reef (Pulau Datu), Cartier Reef (Pulau Baru) and Rowley Shoals it forms a resource-rich area halfway between Indonesia and Australia. Traditional fishing permitted under the MoU means that vessels cannot be equipped with motors, radar, radio-communication or sonar. This is open-sea area prone to sudden cyclones and disturbances. The villagers of Papela on Roti Island estimate that 140 of their men drowned in this area within a decade.

More alarming almost than the tragedies themselves has been the lack of interest or concern shown by either the Australian or Indonesian governments. There are no search parties or rescue operations for these men and usually their fate becomes known to their families only after they fail to return to their village.[100]

Reid observes that the notion of 'traditional vessels' is difficult to maintain, since 'boat types have changed constantly over the last century'. In the 1970s boats became bigger, with a wider sailing range, and in the 1980s motors began to be fitted to them. They are known in Indonesia as *perahu layar motor*, while the Butonese vessels are still distinctly *perahu lambo*, based on nineteenth-century Dutch sailing boats. Vessels that have a motor or any modern navigational or communication equipment are considered not to be traditional vessels and, if found inside the MoU zone, are deemed to be in violation of the border.

A Fisheries Surveillance Enforcement Line defined in 1981 to protect the Australian Fishing Zone (AFZ) runs just south of Ashmore Reef and encloses that reef in a semicircle, which makes precise navigation difficult without the help of modern equipment. Often skippers state that they were not aware of having transgressed the boundaries. In mid-1994 a number of Macassan vessels were detected at Hibernia Reef, which lies almost on the AFZ dividing line. Some of the skippers produced maps they had purchased in Kupang that showed the reef to lie inside Indonesian waters. All were found guilty of border violations and their catch and equipment was confiscated. Those who could not produce these maps lost their vessels as well.[101] Complicating the border arrangements, Ashmore Reef National Nature Reserve was declared in 1983 and the area closed for collecting of sedentary species such as trochus and trepang, while allowing the gathering of non-sedentary species like shark fin and tuna.

Bu Wilson argues that the Australian government attitude has not fundamentally differed from colonial practices. Gradually expanding the territory over which it sought to claim sovereignty, the federal government excluded traditional Indonesian fishermen from the northwest coast. The reserve within which traditional fishing was permitted is not unlike the idea of a native reserve, and denying the prior presence of traditional fishers in the areas claimed amounts to a *terra nullius* (or *mare nullius*) argument. The 'traditional fishing' prescribed in the MoU denied development for these indigenous fishers. Wilson points out that the United Nations Convention on the Law of the Sea (UNCLOS III) does make provision for claiming traditional or historical rights for commercial fisheries within a territorial zone, if it can be demonstrated that the fishery existed before the fishing zone became territorial, and if the distribution of benefits from it remains essentially the same. Neither UNCLOS III nor the Australian Law Reform Commission recommendations on Aboriginal traditional hunting require that traditional activities need to be frozen in time by specifying the methods and equipment used.[102]

Those who have conducted research on the backgrounds of Indonesian fishermen imprisoned in Broome and Darwin all agree that the practice of confiscating and burning boats, and prison sentences, imposes undue injustice and hardship on the impoverished populations who rely on such fishing voyages. Several proposals have been put forward to stem the incursions without injustice. These have ranged from the nineteenth-century model of licences to earn revenue (Reid, Wilson), to education and information campaigns (Fox), to a technological fix with Global Positioning Systems (GPS) installed in the vessels (Sachse). A Maginti fisherman suggested the simplest solution, that a system of beacons and buoys be used to demarcate the boundary. Elliott adds that the volatile nature of the fishing area demands access to safety equipment and motors.

Elliott points out that the fishermen of Sulawesi are in a limbo of representation, ignored by the Australian and the Indonesian federal governments.[103] This was also the impression gained by a Western Australian journalist visiting Maginti and Jakarta in 1991.[104] She argues that the fishermen were the victims of a bilateral agreement which allowed Australia to claim sovereignty over 80 per cent of the seas between the two nations in return for a generous aid package of which nothing reached the islands who were most affected by the arrangement.

On the Australian side, it is not just the national government that sees its boundary violated by poachers. The Bardi people of One Arm Point, on Dampierland Peninsula, resented the infringements of their traditional fishing areas. They had been fighting to have their traditional fishing rights recognised in Australia, and had gained exclusive access to the trochus beds of King Sound and Buccaneer Archipelago, and were reporting sightings of Indonesian vessels to Coastwatch. Eventually they took matters into their own hands and sent a delegation led by Ernie Bridge, MLA of Western Australia, to Roti Island to protest against the incursions. When they reached Roti, their anger mellowed into pity for the poor people they saw. They returned asking the Western Australian government to assist these people so that they did not need to risk their lives to come into Bardi waters.[105]

Because the traditional populations involved in excursions to the Arafura Sea are well defined and local, small projects can make a big difference. Elliott notes that since a Western Australian citizen established small community projects for sustainable resource management at Kadatua, nobody from that island has been apprehended. At Masaloka, too, a cooperative trading venture was started, and these villagers also stopped coming to Australian waters. The Kimberley Indonesia Friendship Association, whose members include several staff from the Broome prison, started to collect funds to support a similar scheme in Maginti. There have been various plans to set up trochus hatcheries at One Arm Point and in Sulawesi to assist the trochus industry at both ends.

In 2000 Indonesia's new post-Suharto government appointed marine environmentalist Sarwone Kusumaatmadja as minister for a newly created portfolio of Marine Exploration and Fisheries. Illegal foreign fishing was identified as a priority problem.[106] Still, it seems unlikely at present that either the Indonesian or the Australian government will expend great energies to address the problem of traditional Indonesian fisheries in the AFZ in a way that is sympathetic to the villagers who rely on it. Since 1996 the 'poachers' have dropped out of media attention, and have been replaced by 'people smugglers' carrying illegal immigrants, mosty from the Middle East, to northern Australia. They use several Indonesian departure points to enter Australian waters, including Kupang, Lombok, Sumbawa, Flores and Roti, and have availed themselves of local knowledge of these waters. In 2002 they adopted the practice of stranding the migrants at Ashmore Reef for detection by the Australian patrols in order to avoid hefty fines. The *Tampa* incident brought these practices into heated national debate.

CONCLUSIONS

The documented history of the trepang trade suggests that the Indonesian visitors themselves were swept up in the maelstrom of mass production for a growing export market, thereby being transformed from traditional traders to industrial producers. As one Australian fisherman explained to me once, when this happens there is no such concept as 'enough', one always has to fish more, and if the resources are being fished out, then one does not reduce the fishing effort but has to re-tool to bigger and better vessels and go further afield. This has been the dynamic of the Australian fishing industry. It is tempting to speculate that the demise of the Macassans in Marege is a kind of happy ending to a many-sided story.

This is plainly not the Yolngu view of that history. All along the Top End coast Aborigines are familiar with a history of Macassan visits. From the work available it appears that in the northeast of Arnhem Land this contact was more intensive, because it has left stronger imprints on local culture. On the other hand, what we read as intensity of contact may reflect recency of contact. The customs reports of the 1880s suggest that there was an eastward movement of the trepang fleet to avoid policing. If under pressure from South Australian customs, the vessels participating in the industry increasingly focused their fishing efforts in the northeast, and became more dependent on the goodwill of Yolngu, then we would expect to find a more intensive social interaction, which would become more personalised as the number of vessels declined.

The visit of the *Hati Marege* has been a symbolic turning point in the approach to that history of contact in Arnhem Land. Ritual knowledges were wrested from elders under the questioning from indigenous and Balanda researchers and became popularised. Cultural connections and family links became celebrated through widely accessible songs, paintings, performances, visits and exhibitions.

Against this backdrop of celebration and reconnection, the Kimberley story of the same industry is astoundingly different. The Western Australian government made no impositions on the Macassan industry. Paradoxically, this resulted in a greater success of white Australians in grafting onto the trade, by becoming the owners of vessels running under foreign flags and using the crews, routines and routes of the fleets from Timor and Roti.

Kimberley cultures show far less evidence of Macassan or other Indonesian cultural impact, and no evidence of family connections has been located, perhaps because here the Indonesian fishers remained mostly offshore. The fishery did not suffer a rupture as at the Top End, but continued into the present while undergoing various changes in the composition of fleets and the resources harvested. Here, too, the year 1988 marked a turn-around, but for entirely different reasons. It was the year when Bugis re-joined the Sama Bajo fleets who had continued their traditional fishing excursions into what had become Australian waters. Under pressures of resource exhaustion and the mass production paradigm, commercial fleets joined the traditional ones and resulted in well-publicised Australian opposition and a renewed commitment to northern defence.

For the Yolngu people of northeast Arnhem Land,[107] the Macassan visits were not an industry, measurable by revenue or number of vessels. It is not important to know when the contact with Mangatharra started. Its ending is well remembered, not by its date but by its effect, because like so many government interventions on behalf of Aborigines, it ended in the separation of families.

The theme of Yolngu–Mangatharra connections runs so strongly through Yolngu culture that no account of Yolngu culture has been able to ignore it. Nor is it possible to give an historical account of this contact without entering into Yolngu culture. Neither the historical record nor the body of myth associated with Macassans leaves any doubt that there were incidents of violence and conflict in this relationship. However, Yolngu today use this history of contact to make significant distinctions between contact with strangers that is desirable, and contact that is harmful—between Macassan contact and European contact.

Many stories confirm that the connection with Macassans includes family links through the bestowal of names, the exchange of sacred objects, the sanctioned or unsanctioned taking of women. The forensic logic of research demands that these links be identified in order to be credible, so that individuals may be pinpointed who carry Macassan blood. The lines remain tangled and confused. In the Yolngu accounts, it is the community who is related to the Macassans. The children and grandchildren of Macassans are neither strangers, nor half or quarter of anything, but Yolngu. One group.

CHAPTER 3

Pearling: 'all kind of nation'

MORE than any other industry, pearling was responsible for attracting vast numbers of non-Europeans to Australia, with the pearlers coming for a longer period and from more diverse origins than even the goldminers. It was pearling that upheld the major outposts of the far north, and lent them their legendary character of polyglot communities. It was an industry for 'all kind of nation'.[1]

As the tide of trepangers receded from the Top End shores, the pearling industry filled its void. Pearling was a late arrival at the Top End, first attempted in 1884, having commenced in Torres Strait in 1870 as a result of trepang fishing there, and in Western Australia in 1866. While the take-off of the industry was rapid in Queensland, where the fleets were connected with the Pacific trade and imported their crews, in Western Australia it proceeded staccato for its first two decades, using local Aboriginal labour organised by beachcombing opportunists.

PEARLING IN WESTERN AUSTRALIA

In Western Australia the earliest trial at pearling was made in 1849 by Roebourne grazier W. F. Tays using local swimming divers at Shark Bay (later Denham), but it was not until the late 1860s that something approaching an industry commenced. By this time it was clear that the pearling grounds extended from Exmouth Gulf to Cape Leveque (Dampierland Peninsula), making them the largest in the world.[2] Along with some who had maritime experience from whaling or the navy, inexperienced men with an eye for opportunity rushed into pearling: pastoralists, adventurers, time-expired convicts, and prison escapees. The industry had a poor reputation for race relations from the start. Competition for cheap Aboriginal labour led to blackbirding, and the frontier conditions resulted in violations of Aboriginal women and children. The pearlers occasionally used Malay workers to recruit—or abduct—Aborigines. In many cases these Malays were recruited from the Indonesian trepang fleets. The resident magistrate at Roebourne, R. Sholl, made an attempt to blame Macassan trepangers for frontier violence when he wrote in 1869 that 'as far as Roebuck Bay the Malays make their kidnapping raids'. He further observed that such raids from Indonesian fleets led to a stand-off attitude towards strangers.[3]

Robert Towns, a Pacific trader from Sydney with a solid record in blackbirding, sent three vessels to Cossack (then called Mystery Landing) in 1868, including the *Kate Kearney* and *Melanie*, which had been in Torres Strait. They were crewed with Pacific Islanders and equipped with state-of-the-art diving apparatus from Siebe and Gorman in Germany. The strong tides and currents rendered them inefficient, and the equipment was withdrawn in 1871, and introduced in Torres Strait where it transformed the fishery.[4]

Still, the Western Australian fishery was considered an attractive investment, and in 1872 the Australian Fishery Company was formed, backed by English speculators, including the Prince of Wales (later Edward VII), on a capital base of £84,000. Its fine yachts, *Flower of Yarrow* and *Enchantress*, and Royal Navy lieutenant Ross in traditional yachting attire, cut an incongruous picture on the social landscape of Cossack. They only lasted one season, during which the *Enchantress* was wrecked and the fifty-strong Malay crew attacked by Aborigines.[5]

The Western Australian pearling fleet grew rapidly and by 1873 numbered forty-eight vessels. A *Pearl Shell*

Fisheries Act was passed in 1871, prohibiting the employment of Aboriginal women on vessels, and prescribing yearly agreements with Aboriginal men on the fleets, but the absence of a patrol boat meant that the Act was ineffectual. Policing improved somewhat when the *Northern Districts Special Revenue Act* of 1873 imposed an export duty on mother-of-pearl and a licence fee, and an inspector was appointed. One of these, Captain P. Walcott, died in the course of duty in 1882 while investigating the kidnapping of Aborigines at La Grange pastoral station. It was presumed that he had been poisoned by the station owners.[6]

Aborigines, being the cheapest available labour, were an important part of the pearl-shelling industry in Western Australia during its swimming diving phase, before diving equipment became widespread. Many pearlers during this period were also pastoralists, deploying their indigenous workforce seasonally. Some 500 Aborigines made up the largest part of the pearling workforce and remained at least nominally on the books until 1888 when their number dropped dramatically to sixteen, remaining low thereafter. Imported labour was found more conducive to the high-tech deep diving that replaced swimming diving with goggles.

The example was set by Captain Francis Cadell in the 1870 season with fifty experienced divers from Solor and Alor. Presumably these were experienced whaling crew, because the only two whaling villages in Indonesia are at Lamalerap on Lemata Island and on Alor, which was also an old Portuguese sandalwood headquarters, both to the east of Flores. Cadell's example was promptly followed in the following season when twenty-one pearlers recruited men from the Philippines, Timor, and the Sulu Archipelago in Singapore and Kupang. Again it is likely that these were men who had been participating in the Macassan voyages, and that those referred to as 'Filipinos' may have been Sama Bajo from the Sulu zone.[7]

Cadell, a Scot, after whom Cadell Strait and Cadell River are named, became known as 'the outstanding blackbirder', together with two pastoralists east of the de Grey River and the Shark Bay pearlers. Malay crews resorted to desperate measures in the face of abuse and neglect. In 1872 fourteen employed by Walter Hale in association with Cadell attempted to escape on a canoe from a makeshift camp at Condon Bay and were lost at sea. Eventually reports of food shortages, deaths from beri-beri, and the ill-treatment and abandonment of imported crew reached Batavia. This led to the introduction of recruiting licences and a security bond at Kupang in 1875—an imposition much resented by the Australian recruiters. The Western Australian government, cognisant of these practices, remained passive. The Dutch resident at Kupang was able to name Cadell among those running 'barracoons' or slave markets on de Lambre, Barrow, and Enderby islands. Sholl spoke to Cadell in 1874, but he was not prosecuted and instead moved to Torres Strait, where he soon became known to the resident magistrate at Somerset. Three government representatives could not protect Cadell's workers. He was massacred by his crew in the Aru Islands in 1879. His other associates were drowned in a cyclone off Western Australia in 1881.[8]

Sholl wrote excellent reports—being editor of the *Inquirer*—but does not appear as a bludgeon of justice in the north. When a group of Gascoyne River Aborigines were found captured in the hold of the *Ione*, imprisoned in heat and stench, Sholl set the fine at £2 per Aborigine

A Malay recruit in the pearling industry. The passport photo of Bargo bin Ahmat from Pontianak, Borneo.

Photo: courtesy of Clossom Nakata (née Ahmat), Thursday Island.

(the maximum fine was $100), and let the owner off with a caution.[9] To a report on a Malay attack on three white pearlers in 1872, the crew consisting of 'Makassarese, Batleens and Alorese', he responded hysterically with visions of 'fleets of Makassar prahus raiding the coast and attacking their new quarry, the pearlers and coastal pastoralists'.[10] The figure of the Bugis slave raider and pirate had become the bogeyman.

Two of Sholl's sons were owners of pearling boats, a situation much like that in Torres Strait where it was 'next to impossible to find on Thursday Island justices who are not more or less directly interested in pearl-shelling'.[11] All of the police magistrates, acting as government residents successively at Albany Island, Somerset and Thursday Island from 1868 to 1885, themselves took up pearl-shelling, the industry which they were appointed to police, sometimes using the government vessels. Indeed it was just the same with the customs officers patrolling the trepang industry at the Top End.

John Chi Lane, Broome. Pictured are Shima's Tornan Shokai shop, Habu house and Chi's shop and residence. Photo: courtesy of Pearl Hamaguchi, Broome.

Typically, staffing a frontier government was the search, not for disinterested parties, but for interested parties. Those with a knowledge of and interest in an industry, who were often already *in situ*, tended to recommend themselves for remote government appointments, such as shipping master, pearl shell inspector, or Aboriginal protector, often on fractional appointments with modest salaries to supplement a private income. They became the ones who wrote reports, which formed the knowledge base of governments and the platform on which policy was built. It is as well to be mindful of these local conditions of the production of knowledge, when weighing one type of evidence, such as the documentary record, against another, such as oral history.

Indonesians with experience in trepanging and swimming diving were evidently sought after. For a short while an even more attractive source of labour was Aborigines at Makassar. They had maritime experience and did not need to be repatriated. Six pearlers discovered this pool of much cheaper labour in 1873, and in 1875 McRae brought back eighteen Port Essington Aborigines from a 'slave market' in Makassar 'who had been captured by raiding parties' and who would 'probably be sold' if they were returned to Makassar.[12] It is evident here that the label 'slavery' lends itself to opportunistic use. McRae was making the case why Australian Aborigines should not be protected under the Dutch legislation of 1875 that required a surety bond for native recruits.

By the time the Dutch bonds were introduced, the number of Malays imported to Western Australian pearling had risen rapidly to an astounding 989, at which time the flow was dented by falling pearl shell prices and the recruiting fees introduced in Kupang.[13]

Theresa Chi: longing and belonging

Theresa and Gertrud Chi were among the few Australian-born Asian women who ever tried to return to their roots. For Theresa this set in train a series of personal calamities. Born in Broome in 1912, she was the youngest of four children of Yae Yamamoto from Amakusa in Kumamoto (Japan), and John Chi. This family has imprinted itself more than any other on Broome history. John Chi arrived in Australia from Swatow in 1872, aged around twenty-two, and settled in Western Australia two years later. He was naturalised in June 1887 yet in 1889 he was counted among one of five Asian 'aliens' to hold a pearling licence. In 1916 he owned freehold property in Broome and was a boarding house keeper in the lane that now bears his name.[14] In the early 1920s John Chi died, and Mrs Chi needed every support from her four children, working in the family's long soup shop. Yae spoke no English, nor was it necessary, since practically all her customers in the noodle shop were also Japanese.

Three of the Chi siblings found themselves in Japan during the war. Only the eldest brother Minoru (viz. Jimmie Chi) never left Broome. He was interned, presumably because his mother had been Japanese. Joe, who did not have a Japanese name, was the only sibling who ended up staying in Japan. He fell victim to the Kobe earthquake in 1995. Gertrud (Yoshi) and Theresa (Yukie) both returned to north Australia after long residence in Japan. They found it difficult to adapt to their mother's country and longed for the country of their birth, but in both places they were treated as foreigners.

At age eighteen, Theresa was sent to finishing school in Japan for two years to learn Japanese customs. She returned to Broome and married Shima-kan from Kushimoto in 1933. Shima worked in the Tornan Shoka shop in John Chi Lane, owned by Kitano and Inouye Sakai from Taiji, one of the leaders of the Japanese–Kupang riot in 1920. A branch was opened in Surabaya (Java) and Theresa stayed there for five years until they were evacuated to Japan at the commencement of World War II. Two of Theresa's children were born in Surabaya and one in Kobe, where her brother and sister lived. At first, while her husband was conscripted to serve in the Philippines, she tried to live with her mother-in-law in Kushimoto: 'I had a bad time with the mother-in-law, oh, I tell you. The father was very nice, because he's been overseas, but the mother has never been out of that place. They say, "People who come from overseas they're nothing but prostitutes", and things like that. I tell you. And coming from Australia, I'm not going to give in. I wasn't like Japanese, lady, I'd give it back to her. I wouldn't sit down and cry.'

After the war a friend from Broome helped her to move with her children to Nagasaki. She says she never looked back: 'No one objected to my divorce. My husband ended up marrying his brother's widow, Madame Shima's favourite daughter-in-law.'

Theresa worked as an interpreter for the US Navy in Japan for twenty years. Her sister Gertrud returned to Australia when a friend arranged her marriage to James Lee. (Their son Herb married Mary, the daughter of Jeannie and Edward Cubillo (viz.). Each of these families has produced an indigenous playwright, Jimmy Chi and Gary Lee.) At age fifty, Theresa followed Gertie to Darwin. She was accompanied by her now adult children, including her son's wife, all of whom considered Japan as their home. The children had difficulty adjusting to Darwin and her son's marriage broke up under the strain. These are personal stories, but they are also part of the history of migration.

Yae Yamamoto and Theresa Chi in John Chi Lane, Broome, 1920s. Photo: courtesy of Pearl Hamaguchi, Broome.

Singhalese jewellers

Ceylonese jewellers and pearl dealers played a pivotal role in the northern Australian pearling industry. In many ways they typify the polyethnic communities of the pearling centres. Saranealis and Mendis at Thursday Island and Ellies in Broome were all from the small area surrounding the city of Galle in southern Sri Lanka.

The Galle–Thursday Island chain of migration was boosted in June 1882, when James Burns visited Galle to recruit twenty-five workers for his pearl-fishery at Thursday Island. At this time twenty Singhalese were already employed at Thursday Island, but because there had been no significant emigration from Ceylon, the Singhalese were considered 'unadventurous stay-at-homes'.[15] Burns was tapping a new and unregulated labour pool for Australian employers. However, the recruitment of over 500 workers to Queensland sugar plantations later in 1882 took matters to a different level. The legislature shifted into gear to protect its subjects from conditions that were considered akin to slavery. Still, by the turn of the century there was a sizeable Sri Lankan population at Thursday Island, mostly from the Galle area.

Punchihewa Mendis (1883–1965) was a merchant, jeweller and pearler. He arrived at the invitation of his uncle at Thursday Island, Mendis de Silva, at age fourteen in 1896 and started work as a printer's apprentice on Alexander Corran's *Torres Strait Pilot*. He worked as a reporter while he opened a small retail business in 1904, at first as an agent for Hoffnung & Company, operating out of the See Kee building in Douglas Street. He became the local agent for a number of prominent Brisbane wholesalers including Thomas Brown, Chandlers, and Kodak, as well as conducting a photography studio and darkroom, a printery, and acting as licensed pearl trader and pearl cleaner. In 1913 he opened a branch store in Galle where a Punchi Hewa club acted as a friendly society for the clan. His brother Marshall opened a jewellery business in Yokohama (Japan). The Mendis brothers pioneered the first experimental consignment of trochus shell from Australia to Japan in 1915, which became a lucrative industry that buoyed the Australian pearl fishery through a number of upheavals.

In 1915 Mendis married Mercy de Silva, a member of the de Silva jewellery emporium based in Singapore. Mercy, of independent means, never came to Australia, where the migration of Asian women contravened official policy. They had two children, Siripala (born 1919) and Nissanka (1926–89) before Mercy died in childbirth in 1932. The two boys were brought to Australia, educated at All Souls in Charters Towers and then joined their father's business, which now also partnered J. C. Harman in a pearling fleet.

Mendis, a man of considerable wealth, became a prominent member of Thursday Island society with affectionate links to the white elite, including the Bishop of Carpentaria and Mayor Corran, as well as family links into the coloured population forged by clan members whose immigration Mendis had sponsored. Among these were Upatissa and Ariyapala Lorensu Hewa, H. Carolis, Sisira de Silva as well as Peter Warnakulasuriya who became part of the local Ahmat family, colloquially referred to as 'Peter Watercooler'.

In 1940 Mendis expanded his business to Darwin, which was thriving with preparations for war. He commenced construction of a large building at the corner of Bennett and Smith streets, which became the headquarters of General MacArthur's staff as soon as it was completed. It survived the repeated bombing to become a police station (now demolished). Mendis Road in Berrima, Darwin, is named after Punchihewa Mendis. Their properties at Thursday Island were demolished during the war, but Mendis, already in his sixties, rebuilt a house in Douglas Street. This shop was sold in 1974, but is still commonly known as the 'Mendis shop'. In 1946, when Mendis became a Justice of the Peace, he swore as a devout Buddhist on the Tripitaka instead of the Bible. He judiciously abstained from alcohol and spoke Singhalese to his sons. Both his sons also became JPs, and the jewellery business is now in the third generation.

Also on Thursday Island was Saranealis (ca. 1876–1919), who advertised his newly opened jewellery, watchmaking and pearl-dealing business in Normanby Street in 1897. His full name, Yahatowgoda Buddalegay de Costa Saranealis, contains reference to the village of Yahatowagodawatta in Galle, and to the name Baddlegay shared with the Ellies family in Broome. Saranealis married Irishwoman Alice Stewart (ca. 1876–1955) and had six children. The 'Sari Boys' featured in the musical scene of Thursday Island. One of the sons, Edward, a dentist, became a member of the local town council. The family spent the war years in Townsville, after helping to evacuate many others on their *Mitzi*. Their two-storey building in Douglas Street survived the war-time demolition of the Japanese end of Thursday Island's business district.

In Broome Thomas Bastian Ellies was a prominent jeweller, related to both the Saranealis and the Mendis families. Tudagala Badalge Ellies came from Bope near Galle and served his apprenticeship with the reputable de Silva jewellers in Singapore, also from Galle. He arrived in Cossack in 1888 and moved to Broome the following year, where he stayed for over thirty years. Bain observes that a number of other Buddhists lived in Broome at the time, but that they were not as closely united as the Muslims. Ellies had a house shrine where he intoned Sanskrit prayer, but never endeavoured to bring his sons to the faith. He financed a Buddhist temple in Bope in honour of his parents, and sent 307 kg of solid silver to be cast as a silver Buddha.[16] Reputedly T. B. became one of the wealthiest men in Broome. He had three Japanese wives in succession, and the first two bore him a son each, William and Charles.

T. B. was a humorous man and is much remembered in Broome. A journalist wrote that he 'chats as he works. He jests and laughs as he treats a pearl worth hundreds or even thousands of pounds'. He teased Theresa Chi, too, as Theresa recalled:

'The Ellies houses were further down the lane from us. One day Ellies called me in. He said, "I'm making a string of pearls for when you marry Charlie." He took me to the display window full of jewels, and said, "Which one do you want?" I said,
"I want nothing. I'm not marrying Charlie." I was only young. Charlie and I used to play together. He was like a brother to me. I didn't want to marry him! Charlie was going out with Agnes. She was from a comfortable background. They had a piano. At my home we always had to work. Ellies hated Agnes. When we used to go out together, I had to go to old Ellies and ask for the car so that Charlie and Agnes could go for a drive. They got married and had four children.'

PEARLING IN QUEENSLAND

As at the Top End, the Queensland government stretched itself into the far north in order to supervise the emerging maritime industry with hopes of another Singapore. Just three years after Queensland became a separate colony, a joint imperial and Queensland government outpost was established at Albany Island in 1862. This was also the home of the first trepang station in Torres Strait. In 1864 the outpost was moved to the Cape York mainland, at Somerset. 'As a free port and commercial depot it could become an important strategic position of British power, similar to Gibraltar, Aden and the Straits Settlement.'[17] It was a suitable place for police magistrate Frank Jardine's pastoral station, Bertiehaugh, and some private pearl-shelling on government vessels. As for the government's hopeful vision of development, only one in ten passing ships sailed within sight of Somerset. The harbour was poor, the weather unpredictable, and the shipping route much further north. In 1877 Thursday Island became the third, and permanent, northernmost government outpost.[18]

By this time the Torres Strait pearl fishery was growing exponentially, from five luggers in 1870 to fifty-seven vessels in 1875, and 109 in 1877. Imperial scrutiny was focused on the recruiting practices of pearlers and Pacific traders who formed a closely linked network of captains, vessels and companies, including household names like Burns Philp and Robert Towns. A *Pacific Islanders Protection Act*, the imperial kidnapping act, was passed in 1872 to protect natives 'not under the influence of any civilized power'. This included those north of 10th degree latitude, which meant half of Torres Strait. In the same year, Queensland's jurisdiction was extended to cover all islands within sixty miles from Cape York. In 1879 the border was moved further north to bring the whole Torres Strait under Queensland jurisdiction.[19]

PEARLING IN THE NORTHERN TERRITORY

The two yachts of the Australian Fishery Company attempted a season out of Port Darwin in 1876 but the company folded before anything came of it. Another attempt at pearling at the Top End was made by an Adelaide entrepreneur, Vaiben Solomon, editor of the *Northern Territory Times*. Starting out in 1882 with a small boat equipped with diving dress, he thought the prospects were promising. However, could not drum up investor confidence. Still, interest in the area had been awakened. Alfred Searcy relates how Streeter & Chippendale requested to accompany him on his tour of inspection of the Macassan fleet in 1883 in order to trade for pearls. Searcy found this proposal highly inappropriate and declined. In the following year the classy *Sree Pas Sair*, under command of E. C. Chippendale, also a former navy officer, explored the grounds with 'sixty experienced divers from Streeter's pearling stations in the Sulu Sea'.[20] They engaged in a little trepanging and eventually chanced on a rich pearl shell ground right in the Darwin harbour, where they reputedly gathered 107 pairs of shell in an hour.

It was hot news, broadcast by telegraph in the hope that it might stimulate a boom for the languishing Palmerston, which consisted of 517 whites, 3,725 Chinese and twenty Malays.[21] There followed a rush into pearling at Port Darwin. Vessels came from Cossack. Locals from

Palmerston, some of whom had helped to construct the telegraph line, formed the North Australian Pearl Fishing Company whose shares skyrocketed in March 1884. In 1885–86 more than a hundred boats from Thursday Island descended on Port Darwin, with Japanese, Filipinos and a few whites as crew. Searcy recollects that it was all over after one season. The beds were quickly depleted, the water was muddy and the harbour floor was uneven and perilous. The Queensland Pearling Company recalled its boats to Thursday Island and Streeter's *Sree Pas Sair* and *Flowerdale* went to the Aru Islands to work under Dutch concessions. The Palmerston-based company of Cloppenburg, Erickson and Wood went to Cygnet Bay in King Sound, and everyone else returned to their base.[22]

The pearling industry became divided between large and well-financed companies and small owners for many of whom pearling was a supplementary business. The largest pearling company in Broome was associated with E. Streeter, a London jeweller, and it was one of the first to recruit six Japanese divers to Australia, in 1875, heralding a new era for the industry.[23]

JAPANESE PEARLERS

The first recorded Japanese diver in Australia arrived in Torres Strait in 1876, and within eight years there were a hundred Japanese at Thursday Island. After lengthy negotiations the first ship-load of thirty-seven Japanese arrived at Port Darwin on the *Cattertun*, for the Australasian Pearl Company, in late 1883, just on time for the Palmerston rush. International concern about the treatment of imported crews was about to result in the expulsion of Australian recruiters from New Guinea, as the Royal Commission on the Recruiting of Polynesian Labour in New Guinea and Adjacent Islands submitted its report in 1885. For large and well-informed companies it was time to look for alternative sources of labour, and the initial scruples of the Japanese government were now overcome with the argument that the labour recruited for deep-sea pearling with diving apparatus was of a skilled type, not of a labouring type.

In 1884 Burns Philp's agents in Hong Kong, and Solomon's British representatives in Kobe, recruited Japanese for Australian pearlers. Complaints about their treatment promptly reached the Japanese consulate in Melbourne. There were no medical facilities for them, some recruits were unaware of the nature of their employment at the destination, and they were unscrupulously overcharged when drawing stores from the slop-chest on the luggers.[24]

Despite official concerns, the process of recruiting Japanese had been set in train. Japanese were sought after as divers, a prestigious and responsible figure in an industry that increasingly tended to dress diving to access greater depths. From head-diver, who also acted as skipper in charge of crewing, it was only a small step to taking full responsibility as vessel owner. In fact the arrangements were such that the owners bore hardly any risk. Japanese soon started to become interested in owning vessels.

ETHNIC RESTRICTIONS

In 1884 Western Australia's *Imported Labourers' Registry Act* was amended, both to improve the conditions of indentured workers, but significantly also to prevent aliens from obtaining a pearl-shelling licence. This was the colony's way of grafting onto the maritime industries, by safeguarding the entrepreneurial role for whites. It was before the Japanese became a significant population in Western Australia, and the Act at this time was aimed at Chinese and other non-Europeans.[25]

Eventually the Northern Territory followed suit in 1895 and Queensland in 1898. Meanwhile these colonies offered a window of opportunity that had been foreclosed in the west, and a number of Japanese became owners of vessels, usually under syndicate arrangements. Others rented or leased the vessels from their legal owners. This caused some alarm. At Thursday Island both the government resident, John Douglas, and the leading pearler, James Clark, claimed that the industry was passing into Japanese hands. In fact only eight of the 183 luggers had Japanese owners. A Japanese visiting observer of the pearling industry in 1893, K. Watanabe, concluded about Port Darwin, 'Here if you say "Japanese" you mean "diver" just as if you say "Chinese" you mean "miner".'[26] However, he also noticed that there was a strong fear of Japanese entrepreneurial competition fomenting among Thursday Island's European businessmen.

In 1895 the South Australian government, fearing a rush of Japanese-owned luggers from Thursday Island to Darwin, ceased issuing licences to Asians, and in 1897 Queensland appointed a commissioner to inquire into the pearling industry. Hamilton found that almost one-third of the Thursday Island pearling fleet was either owned or rented by Japanese. The Japanese population at Thursday Island had been increasing rapidly from less than 100 in 1892, to nearly 500 in 1893, and over 700 in 1894, overtaking the European population of some 500, and doubling it in 1897. The very businessmen who imported Japanese workers were also becoming concerned that these workers were stepping out of the servile relationship envisaged for them.

The entrepreneurial competition from Japanese at Thursday Island became a topical issue in a period of economic depression and unemployment. John Douglas thought that it was time for a 'radical cure' of the Japanese problem to 'secure the rightful ascendancy of our race'. At the least, 'coloured aliens' should not be allowed to recruit indigenous labour.[27]

Moves were being made to amend the *Aboriginals Protection and Restriction of the Sale of Opium Act 1897* so as to bar all Asians from employing Aborigines, but when the relevant amendment was finally successful in 1902, it only barred Chinese. Meanwhile Douglas implemented this colour-bar locally. As protector of Aborigines, under that 1897 Act he was empowered to issue permits to employ Aborigines, and he now required that non-British applicants had to submit a written request. It may safely be assumed that only whites, and those working for whites, were successful in obtaining a recruiting permit at Thursday Island from 1898 to 1902.

Access to cheap labour was absolutely crucial for this industry. It was why the industry became extremely inventive in tapping the labour pools of impoverished regions. Concerns over white dominance in the industry gelled well with the nationalist spirit of the 1890s. Pearlers were able to graft on to such national sentiments to defend what they saw as their entrepreneurial prerogative. But whereas the rest of the nation favoured the expulsion of coloured labour, such as employed in the sugar industry, pearlers insisted on continued access to

Japanese recruits. When questioned about their claims that the Japanese were essential for the success of the pearling industry, master pearlers revealed that they relied on Japanese skippers to recruit Aboriginal labour. They observed that Aborigines preferred to deal with Japanese captains, and to make their purchases in Asian-owned shops, and feared that Aborigines would abscond if Japanese captains were replaced by whites.[28] 'When a Japanese is recruiting boys in the north, a European has little or no show of getting any boys.'[29] This reliance on Japanese skippers was as threatening as it was convenient.

The ethnic stratification in the industry allocated the risky business of diving to Asians, the hard work of labouring to Aborigines, and the ownership of vessels with a 60 per cent share in the profits to whites. Asian ownership of luggers eroded this convenient stratification. More fundamentally still, lugger ownership was the only tenuous hold of white Australia on the industry: its crews were indigenous and Asian, buyers were from overseas, and the pearl beds were beyond Australia's territorial limits because by the 1890s those closer to shore had been fished out.

The Hamilton inquiry recommended restrictions on the operations of Japanese and resulted in a December 1889 amendment of the *Pearl-Shell and Bêche-de-mer Fishery Act 1881* so that aliens were prevented from renting boats or obtaining boat licences in Queensland as they had been in the Northern Territory since 1895. In addition to this legislation it was also agreed that Asians would be excluded from naturalisation so that they could not subvert the intention of this amendment, and Japanese were administratively prevented from entering Queensland until October 1900. This resulted in a decline in Japanese employment on pearling boats: from 576 in 1898 to 318 in 1901. Their places were taken by Filipinos and Torres Strait Islanders. The Japanese government had applied some pressure against this racist exclusion of Japanese nationals, and eventually, in 1900, it was agreed that replacements could be made to the level of 1898, but only if crew members were requested by white pearl-shellers.

When the Commonwealth of Australia was formed in 1901, Queensland already had a restrictive immigration policy, and all northern states had mechanisms to support white Australian dominance. Queensland had an administrative bar rather than a legislated one to control the number and economic position of Japanese that allowed it to discriminate between desirable and undesirable races of immigrants. Western Australia had imposed a dictation test in 1897 similar to the Natal Act, and in the Northern Territory there was a colour bar on lugger

Sheba Lane in Broome.

Photo: courtesy of M. Durack Miller.

ownership. It had always been clear that northern development rested solidly on the non-white population. The economic survival of whites in the north needed to be propped up by the state.

AFTER FEDERATION

The pearling industry gained an exemption from the provisions of the federal *Immigration Restriction Act*. It was agreed that the coloured workforce of 1902 formed a baseline that would be maintained by importing pearling workers under contract of indenture. The employer was responsible for the cost of passage and return, and was required to deposit a security bond with the state government to safeguard the repatriation of the workers. Indentured workers were thus prevented from entering into other employment sectors. This arrangement accommodated both the need of pearlers for imported crew and the federal priority for a White Australia.

The concession was hard-won and three subsequent inquiries into the industry, two of them royal commissions, sought to challenge the idea that the pearling industry could not be staffed entirely by whites, like the sugar industry.[30] Eventually they all reached the same conclusion, that it was in the interest of White Australia to permit Asians to perform the dangerous and arduous work in the industry. The large pearling companies had threatened to take their business offshore.

The pearling industry continued to be the exception that confirms the rule, and the far north continued to be the beaten path for generations of Japanese villagers and other Asians. Sister Albertus Bain wryly observes that the fiery speakers in Melbourne who argued about keeping coloureds out or else 'our race will become piebald', when it had to be kept 'pure and spotless', clearly had not set foot in the north, or they would have noticed that there had never been a White Australia.[31]

Preventing Asians from taking out boat or pearling licences placed them at a great disadvantage, but did not debar them from entrepreneurial participation in the industry. When Western Australia ceased to issue pearling licences to aliens in 1884, Jolly & Company started to buy up boats. By the turn of the century they held a monopoly of pearling licences in Western Australia, but in practice many boats were run by Japanese, some defiantly flying the Japanese flag. The practice of boat dummying became widespread, where European-owned companies were the nominal owners of boats permanently leased to aliens.[32] A Western Australian inquiry in 1902 determined that officially all owners, masters, and mates in the pearling industry in Western Australia were white, but only six out of 236 divers and two out of 237 tenders were not Asian. Aborigines were by this time only employed as crew (fifty-five Aborigines, 1,050 Asians).[33]

The ethnic composition of the Western Australian pearling workforce became a three-cornered contest between Japanese, Malays and Filipinos, with Malays making up the largest proportion. The Japanese dominance in the position of divers gradually slipped from 68 per cent in 1935 to 50 per cent in 1938, with Malay participation increasing from 22 to 40 per cent, and the remainder made up of Chinese divers.[34] The pearling workforce in Darwin was almost evenly divided between Japanese and Malays, and occasional clashes between them were widely publicised. At Thursday Island

Japanese gained a clear predominance in the industry at the expense of Malays and Filipinos. From 1925 to 1934 only one diver at Thursday Island was not Japanese, and from then until 1940, 90 per cent of divers were Japanese.[35]

A new industry was added to pearl-shelling with the development of a trochus shell fishery from 1912. Japan became the main importer of trochus shell, and by the 1930s all Australian trochus was exported to Japan. Japan now clearly had a very strong involvement in the Australian pearl shell fishery, and Mitsui used the Japanese mandated territory of Palau as a base for its own fishery. Japan's economy had become highly cartellised with *zaibatsu*, like Mitsui and Mitsubishi, closely linked to the state.

NATIONAL RIVALRY

In the 1930s Japanese fleets started to challenge Australia's implied claim to the pearl beds that lay, together with the Great Barrier Reef, outside the three-mile limit. The pearling industry now became a subject of national rivalry. Extra-territorial powers acquired by Queensland through the Federal Council's Queensland *Pearl-Shell and Bêche-de-mer (Extra Territorial) Act 1888* over Torres Strait and the Great Barrier Reef only pertained to British subjects and British vessels.

Australian pearlers had also exploited this void. When Queensland introduced an income tax in 1907, James Clark and Reginald Hockings successfully argued that it did not apply to them, since their income was earned outside of the territorial waters. Western Australia responded to the same argument by extending its extra-territorial powers in 1889 to Ashmore Reef, 180 miles off the coast, through the mechanism of the Federal Council. In 1933 the Clark fleet registered under the Dutch flag while continuing to fish in the grounds of the Northern Territory fleets. Poaching was part and parcel of the industry, and frequently Australian luggers entered the waters of New Caledonia and the Solomon Islands.[36]

Japanese vessels fished in New Guinea and the Arafura Sea, and in the 1930s were coming down along the Great Barrier Reef as far as the Swain Reefs, causing great concern. They were very well equipped and supported by research vessels surveying the sea floor and ichthyologists studying the growth of pearl shell to experiment with artificial cultivation. By 1938 the Japanese harvest of 3,495 tons of pearl shell from the Arafura Sea exceeded the Australian return of 2,543 tons, and Australia lost its position as the world's major supplier of shell. Mitsui took an aggressive marketing stance, selling below cost to the world's leading shell-importer, Otto Gerdau Company in the USA. International markets became glutted and the Australian pearlers fell into disarray. The frontier competition of practical men toppled before the sweep of a clever country.[37]

In this unhealthy state the industry entered into World War II, coming to a complete standstill with the evacuation of northern townships, the confiscation of vessels, and the internment and eventual repatriation of Japanese workers. Attempts to revive the industry after the war were short-lived. Today the industry consists entirely of the artificial cultivation of pearls on farms, a technology introduced, and in the main conducted, by Japanese.

The shelling industry collapsed in the 1960s under the weight of its own contradictions. It relied on the state to safeguard the ethnic stratification that reserved the entrepreneurial role for whites and confined Aborigines to the cheapest labour whose rates were set by the Aboriginal protection bureaucracies. But resource raiding continued to push it beyond the territorial boundaries of that state. Neither resource husbandry nor the production of surplus value through processing were taken seriously as practices that would have transformed a frontier industry into a mature economic activity. When challenged by the introduction of synthetic substitutes, like the wool and coal sectors, pearling had no muscle to rally for the support of the state. Staffed by a coloured workforce unable to unionise, conducted in extra-territorial waters and at the mercy of overseas markets, this Australian industry was considered barely worth rescuing.[38]

CONCLUSIONS

In the Northern Territory trepanging and pearl-shelling were conducted as two distinct industries, one associated with Macassans and those competing with them, and the other emerging out of pearling activities in Torres Strait and Western Australia. In Queensland the industry was an offshoot of South Pacific trading, a resource-raiding enterprise that had depleted successive fields of sandalwood and pearl shell and continually required the opening up of new fields of activity. In Western Australia it commenced from observing the pearl shell ornaments worn and traded by local Aborigines, but Pacific traders quickly joined in. In these two states the pearl shell and bêche-de-mer fisheries were administered as a single marine industry.

Commencing in the 1860s it may be thought that the industry arrived late in Australia, but in the far north, where white settlers trickled into the historical scene much later than in the south, it either preceded pastoral settlement (in Queensland), or followed close on its heels (in Western Australia). In every case, the marine industries served as the purpose for which territorial claims were gradually expanded northward.

With regard to trepang, white operators in Western Australia imitated the Macassans, working out of Timor and using the same vessels, crews, routes and methods, and selling to the same merchants, from the 1880s to about 1900. White entrepreneurs were able to usurp the role of Macassan skippers and enter into the trepang industry. As a result, no effort was made to debar the Macassans from the Western Australian fishery. Meanwhile the South Australian government sought to earn revenue from the Macassan activities in its Northern Territory. Both of these policies in effect respected traditional fisheries. Imperial policy in the 1820s encouraged them, and colonial policy in the 1880s taxed them, but the fundamental right of the alien fishers was not legislatively contested until 1906. The white trepangers in the Territory confined themselves to competing with the Macassans for Aboriginal crew and it was this entrepreneurial competition that led to the 1906 prohibition. Gradually the Macassan visits were replaced by pearling boats which started to recruit at the Top End among indigenous people who were already accustomed to maritime work and relationships with strangers.

Ethnic composition of the Northern Territory

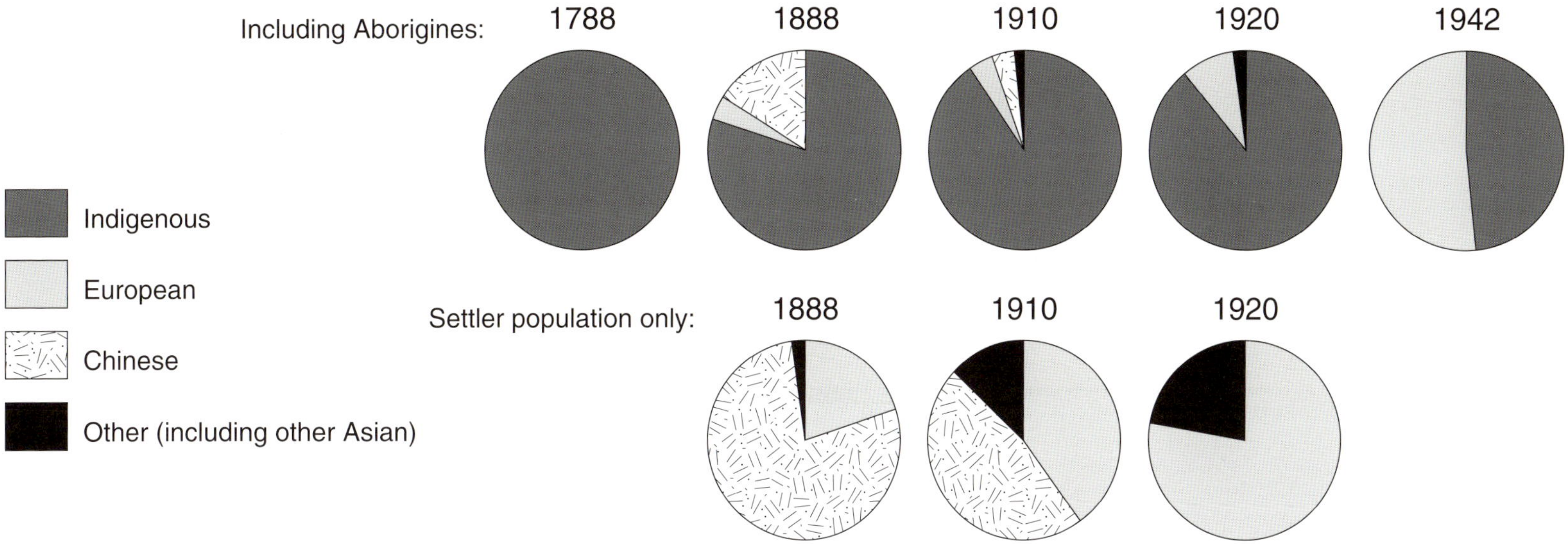

Ethnic composition of Thursday Island

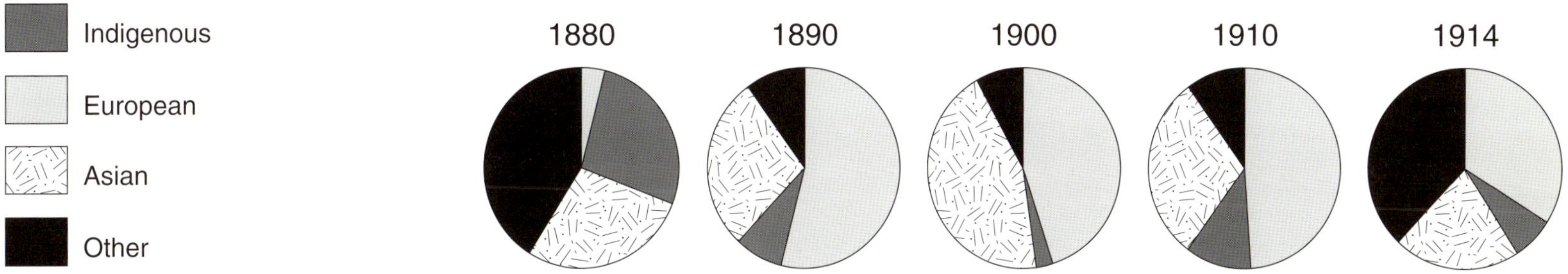

With regard to pearling, Western Australia was early in cementing the ethnic stratification in the pearl shell industry through law, when it barred aliens from obtaining pearl shell and boat licences in 1884. South Australia and Queensland also delimited the role of Asians in the pearling industry in 1895 and 1898 respectively to that of workers, not owners. By this time the pearling ports were polyethnic communities, composed of Filipino, Malay, Chinese, Ceylonese and many other ethnic groups, with a preponderance of Japanese, and linked by 'coloured' communities whose families spanned all of them, governed by a thin layer of whites. White hegemony in the north was as brittle as ever, thrown into sharp relief against the backdrop of economic depression and moves towards Federation.

The idea of White Australia had always been challenged by the polyethnicity of the pearling belt. As a frontier industry, perennially short of labour and requiring it to be cheap, pearling had pulled 'all kind of nation' into a vibrant industry and its remote ports. It had created a north Australian phenomenon, a paradigm of development that was the antithesis of a White Australia. Its polyethnicity was the success of the industry and also became the very reason why it could be allowed to whither.

WORK on the pearling boats meant working with Asians. Master pearlers took much trouble to convince successive governments and their commissions of inquiry that they needed Japanese and other Asians to conduct a pearling industry. That they also needed indigenous workers is less obvious from the evidence they gave, because their access to this labour was not seriously contested. While governments were cautious about the heightened potential for abuse of Aboriginal labour in remote areas, they agreed in principle that it should be made available. The result was the emergence of a protection bureaucracy that prevented Aborigines from operating in a free labour market and channelled them into a narrow range of employment sectors at prescribed wages. In 1902 about 580 Aborigines were employed in the pearling industry in Queensland, not counting Torres Strait Islanders who were not then under the Act, and in Western Australia about the same number participated until 1888.

But the Asian–Aboriginal contact engendered through this industry was not confined to direct employment. The presence of large numbers of Asians in the north meant that they had a wide range of interactions with Aboriginal men and women. Eventually Aboriginal protection policy in all three northern states was stimulated by indigenous participation in and proximity to the marine industries. It was the mixing with Asians that caused the greatest concern and the policy was to reduce contact between Asians and Aborigines.

ABORIGINES IN PEARLING

Both the state governments and the churches were involved in Aboriginal protection. Discrepancies in opinion about best practice often caused friction but there was a general agreement that indigenous peoples required management to protect them—from unscrupulous exploitation and, it was often felt, from themselves.

In Queensland Dr Walter Roth, as the first chief protector of Aborigines (CPA) (1897–1906), was cautious in his attitude towards commercial labour. He steered Aboriginal policy through a period when employers in the north were unused to the idea of Aboriginal protection and were often hostile towards attempts to regulate employment. When the first comprehensive legislation was introduced in Queensland with the *Aboriginals Protection and Restriction of the Sale of Opium Act 1897*, employers of indigenous pearling workers successfully argued that Torres Strait Islanders could be exempted from its provision, being ‘at a higher state of civilisation’, and ‘able to look after themselves’. Such arguments kept the intrusion of the protection bureaucracy at arm’s length in Torres Strait until 1904.

Roth’s successor, CPA Richard Howard (1906–13), strongly encouraged the participation of Aborigines in the marine industry and under his direction of Native Affairs a number of missions acquired their own boats. He also argued for a government recruiting station on the east coast of Cape York to facilitate and supervise commercial access to Aboriginal labour. Lockhart River Mission was established in 1924 to serve this function. Howard’s policy was to seek commercial employment of Aborigines and to control the wages they earned.

This commercial policy was at odds with the church-run missions. Missionaries preferred to engage Aboriginal labour on the missions, in farm work and other productive activities that could help support the missions, without relying on outside work and its temptations. Missionaries often protested about the abuse of Aboriginal labour in the pearling and trepang industries. Their main concern was over the sexual relations that accompanied contact with pearling crews. The 'chief trouble' was with polygamy that seemed to encourage prostitution.

This was the view voiced by an outspoken opponent of pearling, Father Nicholas Hey at Mapoon. This mission site, too, had been selected in 1891 because it was already an established recruiting camp and a traditional meeting ground of up to 400 Aborigines. Hey's views became widely known. He was closely associated with government resident Douglas at Thursday Island and wrote occasional reports to the colonial secretary. He was also a key informant for two official reports in 1896 that led to the 1897 legislation and gave evidence to a royal commission on the pearling industry in 1908, and to ethnographers Roth and R. H. Mathews. His observations reverberate through many accounts of the pearling industry.[1] Hey felt that polygamous marriages meant that 'the old men become the possessors of a plurality of wives and do not hesitate to lend their superfluous spouses to unprincipled men of various nationalities for a small compensation'.[2] He also supplied alarming figures on the death rate of recruits, observing that two-thirds of recruits died of consumption within six months of their return from the luggers.[3] As a result of these protests, he became recruiting inspector at Mapoon in 1899, and assumed control of all wages earned on the luggers at Mapoon. Hey was still unsuccessful in preventing mission residents from signing on with 'Japanese, Malays, Manila men, South Sea Islanders and a few Europeans'. He felt that 'a risk is run by bringing the natives into settled places like Thursday Island and Cooktown, without any medical inspection . . . and allowing them to go to the stores and mix with Europeans' since syphilis and other 'blood diseases' were widespread and there had been isolated cases of leprosy.[4] This was certainly the right language to prick the ears of the state government. However, Hey's agenda was far more holistic than that of a protective state—he aimed to revolutionise traditional society. By the time he gave evidence to a 1906 inquiry the mission ran four boats of its own, and he was also sending mission girls into marriage in Torres Strait. Hey had wrested from the elder males the power to allocate workers, distribute the material benefits of their labour, and regulate marriages. In his fight against polygamy he had 'prayed the devil out of Mapoon' and was well on the way of replacing the traditional society based on polygamous gerontocracy with monogamous patriarchy.

Most accounts of the marine industries in north Queensland refer to the 'habitual abduction' of Aboriginal women to serve the sexual needs of the foreign pearling crews. Whenever the recruiting frontier was extended over areas where Aborigines were unused to contact, misunderstanding and ruthless practices led to 'kidnap and decoy'. Usually the trepangers, who paid lower wages, extended these recruiting frontiers, and in Queensland the trepang industry had a much worse reputation than pearl-shelling.

Just as in the case of the Macassan trepang industry, the documentary references to violence and abuse pale into insignificance in oral histories. Where luggers continued to call season after season, a *modus operandi* was evidently reached. Camp Aborigines lit fires to guide the luggers in at the beginning of the season, and maintained personal trading relationships with particular Japanese captains. Alick Naiga at Lockhart told Athol Chase:

> My father took me down to Cape Sidmouth where my mother's country is because he heard a Japanese lugger was there. We went down and we signed up for crew. My father looked after me on the boat and that Japanese skipper taught me about boat work. The skipper made a camp at Cape Sidmouth, gave people a lot of flour, tobacco and other things. He was like a friend to that mob. If another skipper came to get a crew, he would say: 'Go away! This is my mob here, I look after them.'

Chase dated this encounter in the 1890s. He concluded that any long-standing relationship like that formed between many captains and Aboriginal camps must have been substantially founded on accommodation and acceptance with a degree of mutual benefit.[5]

Lugger work opened a vast horizon of opportunity to travel and learn. Often it became a family tradition and defined a sense of self. Sandy Yiela at Lockhart made a corroborree-style song about lugger-work. He used to work for Kono Tesaburo on the *Mildred*, and saw lugger-work as an essential part of his identity, something that set him and a number of compatriots apart from the rest: 'After next year, we still go. We can't work on dry land, you know, we go out in port all the time, everytime on the lugger. Diving, you know. I never learn horse. I learn boat. I don't learn station. I never been learned it. I been learned in a boat till today. Cause we diver, you know, special, you know. . . Doctor, Michael, me, some older ones, they died now. I always boat. Work on the boat, Japanee, every year.'[6]

Yiela told how this work forged friendships with Torres Strait Islanders. As a young man he visited Darnley, Murray, Yorke, Yam, Mabuiag, Dauan, Badu, and Moa islands, joining in their dances. He retained a repertoire of island-style songs to remember these days.

Being confined to mission luggers was sometimes seen as a lack of opportunity. Bob Flinders at Hopevale said: 'As soon as I left school [in 1928] I worked on the mission boat. . . No one from here worked on TI luggers . . .We only worked for the mission. Only lately are we allowed to work anywhere. We were segregated. Only during the war did the DAIA break that habit. We didn't know much about the outside world until we went to Woorabinda.'[7]

Before World War II Ambidjambi at Minjilang in Arnhem Land worked as a shell-opener with a Japanese crew, consisting of two divers, a cook, a tender and one holding the lifeline. Asked about his relationship with them, he said that they called their Aboriginal workers *binggay*.[8] *Binghi* became a popular name for Aborigines in the north, eventually taking on the same derogatory flavour as other euphemisms for natives. Yet *binggay*, meaning elder brother, appears in Aboriginal languages as far south as the Awabakal language around Sydney and has evident resonances with the Indonesian *abang* for elder brother, sometimes abbreviated to *bung*, as in Bungkarno, the popular name for Indonesia's first president.

Mapoon girls

The Moravian missions on the west coast of Cape York Peninsula were strongly encouraged by the Queensland government in an effort to exercise some control over recruiting there. The first of these was Mapoon, commenced in early 1892, followed by Weipa in Albatross Bay on the Embley River in 1896, and Aurukun on the Archer River in 1904. They were struggling to attract a steady population until the government started to assign mixed-descent children to the mission schools in 1905. These were classified as 'neglected children' and became the means by which the state government subsidised the missions. The girls often remained from early childhood until they were married.

The missionaries, engaged in battle against the tradition of polygamy, generally took it upon themselves to approve or arrange marriages. Police commissioner William Parry-Okeden, reporting on a tour of inspection of Mapoon in the charge of Reverend Nicholas Hey, approvingly observed that 'No young man can get a wife till he has, by his behaviour, proved to Mr Hay [*sic*] he is deserving.'[9] This meant that the missionaries were often approached by men who sought a wife and they therefore needed to decide whether the union was desirable. The problem of the eugenic management of a mixed population was prominently on the mind of missionaries and administrators, and sometimes the missions collaborated in organising suitable matches.

> The problem of what shall become of our grown-up half-caste girls is solved inasfar as the government has burdened me with the job of finding young men outside the station, a peculiar role. In the Torres Strait Islands where the London Missionary Society works there is a shortage of women and I have already had several requests from there. Even requests from Europeans are occasionally received. By this means we expect to lose three of our best baptized girls this year.[10]

Word went out that the Mapoon missionary was marrying the girls off to Islanders. It was just when the new church building at Mapoon was to be consecrated in late 1906, and the Aurukun missionaries planned to take their dormitory girls along for the celebration. When they heard that they were to be taken to Mapoon, the Aurukun girls were gripped by panic. They were sure that they were to be married off. They dug a hole under the wall of the dormitory and all the girls fled from the mission. Father Arthur Richter reported at the end of the following year from Aurukun: 'For several months all children, boys and girls, avoided us . . . We still have no girls and will build a more secure girls' house like the older stations.'[11]

Richter's is a rare glimpse into the bewilderment of the mission children. All of them had already experienced the traumatic displacement from their families. In the official record the administration of these children takes place in a rational and ordered world, but how differently the oral histories from these children read.

Gloria Guivarra told me how her mother, Mabel Clarke, ended up at Mapoon. Mabel was the Aboriginal daughter of Jimmie Clarke, a European. Her family was split up when they were removed from Lawn Hill and sent to Mapoon.

'Mum said she can just remember the police coming along with the buggy and "Little kid, want to come for a ride", and she said they were all excited, you know, a buggy ride, and they all jump in, she said, only with the clothes they had on, and she said, what a long ride it was, she said. . . Mum and the two boys were sent there, the older sister stayed on, and she's still alive, too, Aunt Gis. Gregory Clarke, that's my mother's brother, he preaches in the Catholic Church there at Palm Island. They never seen one another until last year'. By chance they were reunited, through a mutual acquaintance who picked up the shards of memory and pieced them together.

In 1928 Mabel married Sam Boota, a bêche-de-mer fisher, at Aurukun. Sam, born around 1903, was the third of eleven children of Maria, a Mabuiag woman (born around 1882) and Thomas Boota, a Solomon Islander (born around 1877) and also a bêche-de-mer fisher. It must have been a 'suitable match' in the eyes of the missionaries, who were content to marry 'half-caste' with 'half-caste', forming increasingly mobile families where attachment to land became more and more remote. But by the same token the Queensland administration was finding it increasingly difficult to rein in this growing mixed population under its umbrella of powers. Between 1926 and 1936 Mabel and Sam Boota had four children, Malcolm, Donald, Gloria and Henry. Gloria, too, married a Thursday Island boy, but after the war, away from the mission, and in the full splendour that she retained into old age.

Gloria Guivarra's wedding. The wedding of Pedro Guivarra and Gloria (née Boota), 1950s, with Mary Guivarra as bridesmaid. Photo: courtesy of Pedro and Gloria Guivarra.

Incidents of conflict between Aborigines and Asians are well known and extensively documented. My intention is not to deny these, but rather, to read them against the history of long and intensive contact in which they are embedded, and to probe into the vested interests that helped to publicise them. What follows is a review of Aboriginal protection policies in the three northern states paying special attention to the impact of Asian–Aboriginal contact on the management of Aborigines.

ASIANS AND ABORIGINAL POLICY IN QUEENSLAND

Queensland's *Aboriginals Protection and Restriction of the Sale of Opium Act 1897* carries a concern with Chinese–Aboriginal contact in its title. Seven of its thirty-three sections were exclusively devoted to curtailing the trade in opium, for which Chinese were mainly held responsible. The 1897 Act had been initiated with the 1896 reports from protector Archibald Meston and police commissioner Parry-Okeden that had commented at length on vast numbers of Aborigines addicted to charcoal opium, observing it as a typically Chinese means of payment to Aborigines. In areas where addiction was widespread, white employers had complained that they were unable to recruit Aborigines, who preferred to work for Chinese in return for charcoal opium. The disbursement of opium to Aborigines had in fact already been outlawed with the *Sale and Use of Poisons Act 1891*. Now the possession of opium was restricted to doctors, chemists and wholesale druggists, and to stocking a maximum of 900 grams ('two pounds avoirdupois') if they were more than 100 miles from the major cities of Brisbane, Rockhampton and Townsville. This Act was the first opium prohibition in Australia, and resulted, predictably, in a 'dramatic increase' in opium-related convictions against Chinese, most of them not involving Aborigines. Desmond Manderson observed that 'opium smuggling began in earnest' as a result of this Act.[12] The Act did not confine itself to the supply of opium to Aborigines and was clearly intended as a strike against the Chinese with a view to curbing the employment of Aborigines by Chinese.

Its impact on Aborigines was far more fundamental. It was the first comprehensive Aboriginal legislation in Queensland, and became the model of a holistic approach to Aboriginal management in other states. The state's entire indigenous population was constructed as a complex problem and this Act germinated what was to become a massive bureaucracy dedicated to the management of Aboriginal employment, health, education and morality. Previous legislation had been piecemeal, addressing particular issues. The *Poisons Act 1891* and the *Sale of Intoxicating Liquor Amendment Act 1895* disallowed the supply of opium and alcohol to Aborigines. The *Native Labourers Protection Act 1884* regulated the employment of Australian and Papua New Guinean natives in the marine industries. And the *Industrial and Reformatory Schools Act 1865* (not superseded by the *Protection Act 1897*) permitted the removal of indigenous children to special institutions after having defined 'any child of an Aboriginal or half-caste mother' as a 'neglected child' for purposes of the Act.

The 1897 Act defined the idea of 'half-caste' as a precise legal category which survived on the Queensland statutes, in one form or another, until 1971. It provided for the appointment of protectors of Aborigines and for the creation of reserves to which any Aboriginal could be removed unless in lawful employment. Aborigines and 'female half-castes' required a protector's revokable twelve-month permit to work, and their employers also required the permission of the protector to employ them. Anyone who permitted Aborigines or female half-castes into their premises except under the regulations of the Act, was liable to prosecution for 'harbouring'. Penalties were also imposed on non-Aborigines possessing blankets issued to Aborigines, or causing Aborigines and female half-castes to leave a district without the protector's permission, or supplying Aborigines or half-castes with alcohol or opium. In any prosecution under the Act, the onus was on the defendant to prove that the person involved was not Aboriginal or half-caste. Such provisions engendered resistance from white employers of Aboriginal labour.

Exemptions from the Act could be granted to Aborigines for whom 'satisfactory provision is otherwise made', and for half-castes. However, from 1902 these exemptions became revokable at the discretion of the CPA. Apart from the power to remove not only children, but also adults to reserves, some portentous provisions of the Act were inscribed in Section 31. It provided that regulations could be made from time to time about how wages earned by reserve residents would be apportioned, about the 'care, custody, and education of the children of Aboriginals', and about the 'transfer of any half-caste child, being an orphan, or deserted by its parents, to an orphanage'.

The Act laid the foundation for an increasingly restrictive management regime. Underpinning the idea of protection was the view that Aborigines had no rights to their own land, children, labour or property. The Act was amended in 1901 (entering into force in 1902), 1927, 1928 and 1934. Three of these amendments arose directly from issues in the far north.

At first Aboriginal women who were married to and living with non-Aborigines could be exempted from the Act, and the Act did not provide for 'half-castes' to be removed to or confined on reserves. But the state's protective gaze became increasingly fixed on mixed families.

The 1896 reports had devoted much attention to the lugger industries, and in 1901 the new CPA of Aborigines, Roth, stated: 'A large proportion of my time is devoted to the interests of aboriginals on boats.'[13] Roth was concerned about the increase in mixed Aboriginal populations, and sought to fine-tune the Act to gain greater powers over Aboriginal family formation. He urged that 'some check should be placed' on this development, 'especially in the case of Asiatics and Kanakas'.[14]

An amendment bill to the 1897 Act, granting the protector powers to prevent mixed marriages, was extensively debated in parliament in 1901, and it was made clear that it was to apply to Asians, not to 'respectable men'. Parliament was also keen to use this amendment to bar Asians from employing Aborigines. But because this had led to the failure of the amendment in 1899, this time the Home Secretary introducing the bill, and Roth, who was called to give evidence to the Legislative Council, strenuously opposed any clause that would jeopardise Royal Assent. The lower house insisted on inserting a clause to exclude Chinese from employing Aborigines, because, so the Hansard records, 'China was on its knees and would not lodge a protest'.[15] Section 5, clause 2 of the 1901 bill now read that 'a permit to employ an aboriginal or half-caste shall not be granted to any alien of the Chinese race'.

Roth did not share the members' concern over

economic competition from Asian employers and placed it on record that the anti-Chinese clause had been inserted against his advice. He had been lobbied by the Barron Valley Farmers' Association in the Atherton Tablelands who insisted that Chinese, Pacific Islanders and other Asians were 'the only people who supply opium' to Aborigines, and that they themselves could obtain no Aboriginal labour as a result. 'I have shot thirteen or fourteen niggers in this District and this is all the Government has done for me:—I can't get a _______ nigger when I want one. They all go to the Chinaman.'[16]

This offensive statement says much about the mood of the times when many white employers found the new government interference unhelpful and unwelcome. Roth made it a point to state in his report to parliament that to his knowledge the Chinese farmers treated Aborigines much better than most whites, offered them better wages, housed and fed them well, and 'what is more, pay the aboriginal their wages when due'. Under examination in parliament he moderated this view, stating that 'personally I am averse to the Chinaman employing them unless they are reputable'.[17]

Roth's agenda was the maintenance of racial boundaries. He referred to mixed marriages with Asians as promiscuous, even when the couples concerned had undergone a church wedding and obtained a marriage certificate. He tendered the following report from Mossman as evidence of 'the promiscuous marriage of Aboriginal women with coloured aliens': 'There are nine aboriginal women in this district at present who either live with Kanakas or Chinamen but they mostly all hold a marriage certificate as most of them went through a form of marriage with the Kanakas in the English and Methodist churches here about last January.'[18]

Pending the proclamation of the 1901 Amendment Act, and acting on Roth's insistence, a memorandum was sent to all ministers and marrying Justices enjoining them to 'use every endeavour to prevent the marriage ceremony becoming the harbour of refuge for those men who (under the *Aboriginal Protection Act 1897*) are deemed unfit to employ natives'.[19] It was as specific as the Registrar General's Office dared to be to prevent mixed marriages without exceeding the power of the law.

In 1902 Roth was vested with the sole authority to legalise all marriages of Aboriginal women with non-Aboriginal men, and the Aboriginal bureaucracy came under a barrage of requests. Missionaries and local protectors generally supported Roth's policy of disallowing marriages with Asians. The policy was not usually explicitly stated, but references to it are scattered in case files. In 1913 Roth informed a Murray Island woman wishing to marry a Japanese resident of Thursday Island that 'such marriages are much deprecated and it is not considered advisable to allow Japanese to inter-marry with aboriginals'. The task of local protectors was to record what they felt to be the relevant details of a case and to make a recommendation to the CPA. The Normanton protector wrote in 1906 that he was 'personally opposed to all such unions especially aliens to gins', and the Cairns protector wrote in 1905 that he had 'received applications from Kanakas for leave to marry aboriginal gins but in all cases I have refused to recommend such marriages'. Reverend E. R. Gribble revealed his attitude to Chinese when requesting to consult with Roth on 'the numerous waifs and strays in the Chinese-infested districts around Redlynche and Kuranda'. He was referring to Aboriginal–Chinese children.[20]

Doomadgee and Ali Hoosen

Doomadgee Mission owed its founding to an Arab whose Aboriginal children became a target for intervention. The mission was named after Doomadji (Many Sand Ridges), a native well forming an ecological island in the vast saltpan between Burketown and 'Hell's Gate' (beyond which the safety of white miners could not be guaranteed).

In January 1901 Ali Hoosen, an Arab stockman at Westmoreland Station, married Topsy, the mixed descendant of Rosie, a Gangalida woman from the Point Parker area. He is remembered in the family as Joe Hoosen and referred to in official correspondence as Ali Hoosan or Husen or Ali Usam. The couple moved to George Douglas' run at Doomadji and remained there after Douglas' departure. Their children are recorded as the boys Mahomet, Marikin, Arthur and Alex, and the girls Vadamoi (or Patima), Jessie and Alice. They had cattle, horses, goats, chickens and a garden. Ali Hoosen died in 1932.

Also in that year, the Brethren missionaries Mr and Mrs Akenhurst and Will Sharpe arrived at Burketown from Sydney to form an Aboriginal school. They obtained permission to set up on the Aboriginal reserve that included Doomadji, and endeavoured to have Hoosen's children declared wards of the state. Hearing this, the family fled with their stock to Westmoreland Station. The eldest son, Mahomet (or Hommed), aged seventeen, took up work there, while the remainder of the family fled across the border into the Northern Territory. Mahomet formed a business relationship with Tom Norris whose station was at nearby Seigal Creek (or Moondibarina waterhole), and the family later reunited there. Alice Hoosen married Tom Norris.

The missionaries set up near Hoosen's abandoned camp at Doomadji with sixteen Aboriginal children from Burketown. In 1934 Mahomet and Topsy Hoosen were sighted at Turn-Off Lagoons and Doomadji, and in the following year some of the children were taken to Doomadgee Mission.[21]

The children of Aboriginal–Asian marriages became a target of intervention. Having ruled out the option of legal marriage, the state defined these children as being 'abandoned' by their fathers. It became the practice to institutionalise such children and to proceed against their fathers for maintenance to be paid to the department. (See stories on Pan Quee and Sianna Sindhi.)

Indeed, many were the offspring of casual liaisons. Allegations of bribery and prostitution are rife, reflecting to a large degree a willingness on the part of Asians to enter into traditional expectations of exchange.

In 1927 the 1897 Act was further amended to permit the declaration of marine reserves for Aboriginal and Torres Strait Islander swimming divers to obtain pearl shell, bêche-de-mer and trochus shell. The Papuan Industries Limited had organised a lugger scheme enabling island communities to acquire community boats on hire purchase. Torres Strait Islanders enthusiastically embraced the scheme for 'swimming diving', harvesting shallow reefs by diving with goggles, and for visits, barter and transport. The department became increasingly intrusive into the working of the scheme, and after Cornelius O'Leary was appointed local protector at Thursday Island in 1922, the scheme became the department's showcase of successful business. A Thursday Island boat slip was acquired in 1927 to produce dinghies underselling the Japanese-owned boat slips, and in 1930 the department took full control of the scheme.

By the 1920s it became clear that the label of 'half-caste', defined under the 1897 Act as the offspring of an Aboriginal mother and a non-Aboriginal father, was no longer able to contain the mixed Aboriginal population in the second and third generations. New administrative labels like 'quadroon' and 'octoroon' were adopted, though never developed to quite the same sophistication as in the United States, where an elaborate system of nomenclature could label persons according to 'particles of blood' to the seventh generation. The French in the southern states referred to 'mulatto', 'quadroon', 'métif' or 'octoroon', 'meamelonc' or 'mustifé', 'quarteron' or 'mustifino', and in the seventh generation 'sang-mêlé' if one of the parents was white in each instance, and other labels if the parentage was different: 'lascos' for the offspring of two mulattoes, 'sambo' or 'griffe' for the offspring of a 'mulatto' and a negro, and so on.[22]

In the face of a growing population no longer within the four corners of the Act, local protectors in polyethnic communities were waging a battle to contain mixed-descent girls under the Act. This was done by 'deeming' their 'half-caste' mothers as 'Aboriginal', permissible under Section 4 of the 1897 Act if they had lived with an Aboriginal spouse in 1897, or if they 'habitually associated with Aborigines', or if they were in the protector's opinion under seventeen years old. This principle allowed endless generations of mixed descendants to be reined in under the Act, provided the mothers 'habitually associated' with Aborigines. Significantly, it was only applied to female descendants.

The Queensland bureaucracy had no intention of allowing the defined Aboriginal population to shrink by 'breeding the colour out', or permitting mixed descendants to leave their Aboriginal identity behind. Exemptions from the Act, granted mostly to mixed-descent males, were at the discretion of the protector and could be revoked at any time. They were not emancipations, and did not necessarily hold for the children of exempted parents. 'Coloured' women were drawn in under the Act. 'Half-caste' children became the foundation of success for missions, who would accept such children allocated by the bureaucracy and whose public funding depended on such children. The dormitory children, removed from their land and families, became the nuclei of sedentary communities, and missionaries tended to sanction marriages with the dormitory children from other missions. The population that ensured the survival and growth of the Aboriginal management bureaucracy was sustained by drawing in mixed-descent children and 'coloured' women.

In 1934 the battle to rein in coloured populations under the authority of the bureaucracy looked set. A further amendment to the 1897 Act specifically targeted the coloured population of north Queensland. Section 4 (b) of the new Act widened the definition of 'half-caste'. It now included anyone who was the child or grandchild of an Aboriginal, or who was the child or grandchild of two 'half-castes', and anyone of Pacific Island extraction, if they lived as an Aboriginal or habitually associated with Aboriginals, or if 'in the opinion of the CPA [they were] in need of the control or protection of this Act'. Under section 4 (d) they were deemed Aboriginal until they were twenty-one (instead of seventeen) years old.

All exemptions from the Act were revoked in order to be reconsidered in the light of the new legislation. A storm of protest followed. A public campaign at Thursday Island led by the Coloured People's Progressive Association rallied the support of unions, business-people, journalists and war veterans. Twenty-two per cent of registered voters on the Thursday Island electoral roll had been disenfranchised by the Amendment. All over Queensland associations were formed demanding citizenship. The State Public Service Commissioner was required to conduct an inquiry into arbitrary powers conferred by the Act to the 'opinion of the Protector'. At the zenith of its powers, it was brought home to the Aboriginal management bureaucracy that it was not a law unto itself.

In the ebullient mood of protest, Torres Strait Islanders went on a protracted 'lugger strike' in 1936 to gain control over their passbooks and wages and shake off the department's paternalistic grip over their lugger business. Thirty Badu Islanders were gaoled for the removal of the school bell, a symbol of time-management and regimentation. The lasting result of the strike was the formation of a regional identity as 'Torres Strait Islanders' replacing the older sense of island-based community identity.[23]

Daisy Green, age eighty-one, holds vigil at the Georgetown bus stop, 1997. She knows little of her own background.

Daisy Green: a relic of history

In the dying township of Georgetown Daisy Green holds a daily vigil at the local bus stop. Georgetown, in Queensland's gulf savannah, was once among the service centres for the Etheridge goldfields. Now Daisy is perhaps the only tourist attraction in Georgetown as she comes to meet the coach, chatting to the driver and passengers.

Daisy grew up with a notable family of the area. Edward T. Green, one of the local pioneers, is remembered for introducing grapes and date trees. His son Carl Einasleigh Green was chair of the local council from 1942 to 1964, and part-owner of Green and Clark's Motors, a company formed in 1919 to supply truck transport from Forsayth to the train line in Cairns. Daisy's own background, however, is less well remembered. She only knows that her mother Judy worked at Strathmore Station. Her father must have been one of the Chinese storekeepers, carriers, herbalists, poultry farmers, butchers, bakers or miners who used to inhabit the area. At age nine or ten she was identified as a 'coloured girl', not suitable for sending to the local school, and taken to the Green family. She worked for Tom Green and looked after the Green children, and moved with this family to Prestwood Station near Georgetown. Since then she has taken in many children, just as she herself was once taken in, and perhaps this is what compels her to her daily watch at the bus stop.

Atima Ahwang: a bureaucracy under siege

The pearling industry in Torres Strait relied on Pacific Island labour until the anti-slavery movement had drawn sufficient attention to the blackbirding trade for Britain to impose some measure of protection with the *Pacific Islanders Protection Act 1872*, followed in Queensland with the *Pacific Islanders Protection Act 1880*. Asians now started to be recruited in Singapore and Hong Kong. Among them was Ahwang Dai, a Dayak, arriving in Torres Strait in the 1880s. He was born the son of a boat builder in the Singapore Straits settlement around 1860, and lived until 1935. Presumably Ahwang was at least the second generation in his family pulled away from a tribal background by colonial opportunities and pressures.

In 1891 he married Annie, a Badu Island girl thirteen years his junior. At this time, the legal distinctions between Malays, Pacific Islanders and Torres Strait Islanders were weak, and there were no regulations preventing their marriage. Malays, as British subjects, were able to lease land and become naturalised while Torres Strait Islanders were exempted from the *Aborigines Protection Act 1897*.[24] Annie and Ahwang lived on Badu Island speaking the Kriol, or 'Sandalwood-English', that had developed through the Pacific trade. They inhabited a cosmopolitan world at the edge of international opportunity, participating in a modern industry that used diving apparatus to access depths of the sea never before seen. The industry was a lifeline into the future, in a dynamic state of growth, using colonial connections to assemble teams of fit and daring young men from Asia and the Pacific to staff the diving boats, and marketing its produce to the Continent, the United States, and Asia. The Ahwangs' life on Badu was worlds away from that of camp Aborigines.

Annie and Ahwang had seven of their eleven children before 1904. In that year all inhabited Torres Strait Islands were declared government reserves and Torres Strait Islanders were classed as Aborigines. This meant that their mixed descendants were to be classed as 'half-caste' if they lived with or 'habitually associated with' Aborigines and Torres Strait Islanders. All of Ahwang's children and his wife were threatened by this new policy. The whole family moved to Thursday Island some time around 1904 or 1905 to escape the new regulations. One of his sons explained: 'That's why my father brought the children from Badu. They left from Badu to TI. You had to be certain miles away so you don't come under the Act. Badu was in the limits. My father had to take the children to Thursday Island. But we not supposed to be under the Act, my father come from a different country. Shouldn't be under the Act.'[25]

At Thursday Island they became part of a growing coloured population that was causing official concern. This population had family links into indigenous and Asian families and yet was largely outside reach of the restrictive and protective legislation extended over aliens and Aborigines. To what degree it was outside this legislative reach was a matter of constant contestation. Just as the bureaucracy was determined to assert itself, coloured people were determined to extricate themselves from its grip. One of Ahwang's daughters was to become the focus of a test case of the hegemony of White Australia at Thursday Island.

In 1914 Ahwang's seventeen-year-old daughter Atima was to be married to a Malay pearling worker. The protector of Aborigines at Thursday Island, William Lee-Bryce, informed Ahwang that official permission was required for this marriage. Keen on his daughter's marriage to a compatriot, and intent on asserting his family's independence from the department, Ahwang ignored this instruction, and proceeded with a 'Malay fashion' wedding for his daughter.

Relying on official records, it is not easy to determine what a 'Malay fashion' wedding was, but it was clearly not an officially sanctioned wedlock. The protector used the term as a euphemism for an immoral practice, speculating 'I strongly suspect she has been married "Malay fashion" on more than one occasion.'[26] Atima's 'Malay' wedding was backed by Reg Hockings, the spouse's pearling master who was also the honorary Dutch consul with experience in Dutch New Guinea. It is reasonable to assume that Hockings was familiar with Malay customs, whereas Lee-Bryce's familiarity with other cultures is far less evident.

Atima and her spouse had undermined the protector's authority. Lee-Bryce brought to bear the powers of the state he represented to ensure that the marriage would not be sanctioned but rather that the couple would be torn apart. He was fighting a number of similar cases at the same time and felt he needed to put his foot down. He knew that Atima was not actually within his domain of powers, but recommended:

> the Minister will strain the interpretations of the Act and order the removal of Atima to a southern settlement—it will be for the girl's good and serve as an example to others…
>
> Unless some strong stand is taken with girls like [name withheld] and Atima, numerous other cases of similar description will occur: the consent to the marriage would be accepted by the coloured population as a sign of weakness, and immorality would become a lever to procure the necessary permission to marry.[27]

The protector was referring to two other cases and it is needful to mention these, since Atima's case became constructed as part of a phenomenon, of a complex of problems of morality in this coloured population. One was the part-Aboriginal wife of a Filipino bêche-de-mer fisher who 'frequently lives for long periods with men engaged in the bêche-de-mer fishery'. The protector recommended her return to Mapoon with her baby, and the sending of the other children to separate boys and girls missions at Thursday Island. The other was a sixteen-year-old Asian–Aboriginal girl who was pregnant from her white employer, and whose father approved of her marriage with an Asian to whom she had been promised long ago. In this case Lee-Bryce speculated that the father 'probably received some valuable consideration for his consent'. Both the promise system of marriage and a bride price were practices widely recognised in the cultures converging in this family (Aboriginal, Filipino, and either Muslim Indian or Malay), but these customs were no longer part of the British legal–moral universe, and were therefore condemnable. The protector prevented this marriage with the result that the baby was born out of wedlock, and he was able to pronounce on the girl's 'immoral habits'.

Recording the removal of this girl and Atima to

Barambah (later Cherbourg, in southern Queensland), the Removals Register reads: 'For their own protection. Living immoral lives.'[28] These two young women were sent into exile for several years because they wanted to marry men who met with the approval of their fathers. The key indictments of their immorality were by way of speculation ('probably received some valuable consideration', 'suspect she has been married "Malay fashion" many times before'). The CPA supported Lee-Bryce, knowing that the removals were, strictly speaking, *ultra vires*.

Atima's substantial Native Affairs file unravels the scenario of an illegal removal. It contains, inexplicably, a personal love letter from her Malay spouse addressed to her at Barambah, and no less than seven pleas for her release—including those from her employers, her father, herself, and John Douglas MP—all of which fell on deaf ears as the department closed ranks.

Atima's employer, Clara Riley, wrote that Atima was a highly regarded and well-protected domestic, 'the best servant I have ever had including white and black'. 'I have not one black mark against her. She was industrious, faithful and most trustworthy.' She lived with her parents, and was usually walked home by one of her family. Mrs Riley describes how on the afternoon of 16 June 1914, Atima had taken the Riley children for a walk to her parents' house when at four o'clock two plain-clothes policemen appeared to arrest her. They took her to the watchhouse by a back way, kept her locked up all night, and placed her next morning on the ship to Brisbane. She had been given no warning of her arrest, no opportunity to pack a suitcase or to 'purchase one solitary warm stitch of clothing, consequently she has been freezing ever since she left'. Mrs Riley added that previous employers of Atima, including 'Mrs K. O. Mackenzie, Mrs Allan (shipping master) and others like ourselves [are] very incensed at the action' which she referred to as extreme and difficult to comprehend.[29] Mr Riley protested against the removal arguing that Atima was under legal agreement until October and her removal was 'unjustifiable and drastic'. He promptly telexed the Home Secretary, A. G. Appel, before the close of business on the same day.

He was under the clear impression that Appel had signed the removal order, as he should have in the proper course of administration. However, the Minister's order for the removal of the two girls was signed only on 28 September, more than three months later. CPA Bleakley later claimed that an order for Atima's removal was earlier issued by the Acting Home Secretary on 2 May.[30] But if that were so, a second and retrospective order appears entirely unnecessary.

Riley's protest was well framed. According to Section 10 (a) of the 1897 Act, being under legal agreement to an employer placed Atima outside the ambit of the protector's powers to remove her. That is, if she was under the ambit of the *Aboriginal Protection Act* at all. The department considered that 'the matter can best be adjusted by allowing Mr Riley to engage another girl'. However the Rileys did not want another domestic. They had close links with the Ahwang family and wished Atima to be returned to their service. Mrs Riley maintained a correspondence with Atima.[31]

To stifle possible embarrassment in the face of the inquiries instigated by Riley, the entire administration closed ranks. Lee-Bryce argued that 'the removal of Atima and [name withheld] had a great moral effect, but if they are not detained for a few years my influence with the coloured population will be seriously affected'. The CPA was called to the Home Department for a personal interview when he admitted that the removal had been *ultra vires*:

> From the facts that the girl was a quadroon Malay and legally under agreement at the time she was really exempt from removal, but the Protector apparently acted in the interests of discipline and morality and it is certainly expedient that this action, though perhaps not entirely correct, should be upheld.[32]

When John Douglas' plea for Atima's release arrived, the local protector turned against Riley:

> It is quite evident Mr Riley has decided to ignore me and endeavour to obtain what he desires through other channels . . . It has been well known here for some time that Mr Riley was using every influence at his command to secure the object he has in view and if his request is granted my position will be considerably weakened in the eyes of both the white and the coloured population.[33]

Lee-Bryce's language was conveniently equivocal, but in the entire voluminous documentation of the case no doubt was cast on Riley's good character. The 'object he had in view' was Atima's return to his wife's employment.

Despite all efforts on her behalf, and the CPA's admission that the removal was 'not entirely correct', Atima was now fully in the grip of the Act. Just what that meant is amply illustrated by the fact that when she asked for ten shillings out of her earnings (not an advance) to send to her ailing father (she had to state reasons, in writing) the protectress in Brisbane passed the request to the CPA. The CPA, equally unable to reach such a momentous decision alone, consulted the Thursday Island protector. The latter carefully weighed his response in the light of the local knowledge he possessed, and concluded, but without going so far as to consult medical expertise, that 'the father is not in need and could probably do light work if he cared to'. He referred at length to Ahwang's gambling habit and supplied an unflattering character reference. His two surviving sons also remember how he indulged in the popular Thursday Island pastimes like *gee far* (a lottery) and *luk-luk bat* (meaning '6–6–8', in Chinese). He amassed the wealth to buy a house through gambling and lost it in the same manner.[34] He may in times of need have leaned on his children. The poignancy of this anecdote is, however, that the whole family came under the purview of paternalistic rhetoric because one of its members was deemed to be under the Act.

After Lee-Bryce's death in December 1916, Mrs Riley resumed her lobbying. She gained the support of the acting local protector, but CPA Bleakley now insisted that Atima must serve out her current contract as Mrs Cameron's domestic in Toowong, Brisbane. He personally interviewed Atima and reported that 'the girl appears very happy and well looked after in her present place'. He felt Mrs Riley was placing 'undue pressure' on the girl and gives the impression that Atima felt neither an urgency nor a wish to return home: 'Atima informs me she wishes to visit Thursday Island, but only for a holiday, in about six months time, after the wet season, and when she has saved sufficient to pay for her trip.'[35]

Her own letter to the CPA only a month afterwards, in November 1917, suggests that the CPA's recorded impression merely projected his own wishes:

> Dear Mr Bleakly,
>
> just a few lines to let you know that I made up my mind to go back to Mrs Riley again when my times up. I think she done her best to get me back since I been away from her place and I like her very much. I was quite happy with her. Also Mrs Cameroon. So I would like to know if you let me go back to Mrs Riley for good. I rote to her and told her that I was going to ask you to let me go back.
>
> So I have nothing more to say.
>
> Your faithfull
>
> Atima Ahwang[36]

How more determined might a nineteen-year-old dare to be with the CPA? No response to this letter is recorded. After more than three-and-a-half years of exile Atima returned to Thursday Island. Her Malay spouse had long given up waiting for her.

The bureaucracy continued to keep a watchful eye over Atima's personal affairs. In 1919 she had a baby and came under some pressure to enter into a marriage. In June 1919 and in March 1920 applications for marriage were made by different 'suitable' men of mixed descent, and both were approved, but neither took place. Atima was keen to escape the purview of the department.[37] In September 1920 the local protector questioned Atima about her marriage plans, and within a few weeks she submitted an application for exemption from the Act. Her elder brother had already gained an exemption. Though the department had always been of the opinion that 'strictly speaking' she was not under the Act, her application was denied.

Walter Filewood, the Australian Workers Union representative at Thursday Island, pulled all possible strings to support Atima's application. He wrote a personal letter to the Home Secretary McCormack 'trusting this finds the labour party a successful term of office', to Chief Protector Bleakley sending 'regards to you and your brother Charles', and to the local member Ryan mindful that 'I conduct his election business'.[38] He went completely over the head of the local protector. The department responded by proceeding against Filewood for having an affair with Atima, for 'harbouring a female half-caste'. Atima was subjected to police interrogation to give evidence against Filewood. But in order for charges to be brought, it needed to be ascertained that Atima was indeed a 'half-caste' under the Act.

What followed was an elaborate process of determining Atima's status under the Act. This was not initiated by Atima's application for exemption, already denied, but by the department's intention to proceed against Filewood. According to Section 3 of the 1897 Act a 'half-caste' was the offspring of an Aboriginal mother and a father who was not Aboriginal. This definition excluded much of the mixed population by now, consisting of the children and grandchildren of 'half-caste' mothers. But there was a possible loophole. Section 4 made three provisions by which 'half-castes' could be deemed to be Aboriginal: if they had been living with an Aboriginal spouse at the passing of the

Act (Clause 4 (b)), if they otherwise habitually associated with Aborigines (Clause 4 (c)), or if in the protector's opinion their age did not exceed sixteen years (Clause 4 (d)). Ingeniously, if it could be argued that Atima's mother Annie was not a 'half-caste' but an Aboriginal, then Atima would, as the daughter of an Aborigine, be a 'half-caste' under the Act. Referring this question to the Home Secretary for deliberation, Bleakley clearly indicated what he would like the Home Secretary to conclude: 'A question has arisen in regard to the position of a crossbreed girl. . . It is extremely important that the Protector should, if possible, have the power to deal with this case to maintain discipline amongst the numerous crossbreeds under his charge.'[39]

The crown solicitor was now asked for the first time to consider the status of 'quadroons' under the Act. His determination accepted the advice of the CPA and was sent to all protectors as Circular No. 21/6: 'A female quadroon comes within Section 14 of the AP Acts of 1897 if it can be established that the mother is the offspring of an aboriginal mother and other than an aboriginal father and that she (the mother) otherwise than as wife, habitually lived or associated with aboriginals.'

It meant that if Annie 'habitually associated' then she was an Aborigine under the Act, and under Section 14, which referred to the 'harbouring of half-caste females', her daughter Atima could not be harboured by Filewood without penalty. But this still did not answer the purpose, because Annie lived at Thursday Island, and was not currently 'habitually associating'. The local protector now formulated five fine-tuned questions about Atima's case for consideration by the crown solicitor.

First, Annie's mother was a full-blood native of Badu and her father a native of Madagascar. (Actually some uncertainty pertains to his origin. He may have been from Madagascar—as Atima claimed under police interrogation—or from Barbados as another document on the file claims, or as is most likely, from Niue.) Annie had married a Malay and lived at Badu Island at the passing of the 1897 Act until 1904 or 1905. Since then she had not habitually lived or associated with Aborigines. Was Annie an Aboriginal under Clause 4(c)? Second, would Annie remain an Aborigine within the meaning of the Act after she left Badu, or would she automatically become a 'half-caste' on ceasing to 'habitually associate'? It was determined that Annie was an Aborigine from the time of her birth until she left Badu. Upon ceasing to habitually associate, Annie ceased to be Aboriginal and became a 'half-caste'.

The third question, whether Annie's children born at Badu were 'half-caste', was also answered in the affirmative, because their mother was retrospectively classed as having been an Aborigine until 1905. The fourth question was effectively whether Section 4 was able to place succeeding mixed generations into a time-warp: could the offspring of a 'half-caste' mother also be deemed Aboriginal? If the 'half-caste' mother were 'deemed' Aboriginal, could her offspring also be 'deemed' Aboriginal under the same provision because they habitually associated? (Blissfully nobody thought to point out that they must be habitually associating with their Aboriginal mother.) The crown solicitor determined that while they were under sixteen or habitually associating, such children were Aborigines, and afterwards

The Ahwang family, ca. 1915. L-R standing: Nealum, Jeffa, Raima, Abosman, Noranee (Rocky). Sitting: Ahwang, Abdulla (born 1915), Saia, Annie (née Savage, age ca. forty-two). Not in this photograph are the older children: Anima, Saptu and Atima and Ahboo (Starchy). This 1891 marriage produced twelve children, who continued to show a preference for Malay spouses. Anima's first husband was Ahmat Ahmat from Borneo, her second Mathias Rumakato from Timor. Raima married Bargo bin Ahmat from Borneo. Saia married Hassan bin Awel from Ambon. Their daughter married Saleh bin Doraho from Tanjong Kling, Malacca.

Photo: courtesy of Ahwang family, Mackay, Hervey Bay, Thursday Island.

they became half-castes. But if they continued to habitually associate, then they remained Aborigines.

Finally the protector inquired about the status of the last two children born at Thursday Island. It was determined that these were 'neither half-caste nor Aboriginal'.[40] This meant that some of the eleven children of Annie and Ahwang might be Aboriginal (if they habitually associated or were under sixteen), some were 'half-caste', and some were 'neither Aboriginal nor half-caste', because their mother 'had been an Aborigine' only until 1905.

The whole case was built on the assumption that while Annie lived on Badu she 'must of necessity have habitually associated with aboriginals'.[41] However, on further inquiry, Protector Holmes realised in August 1921 that this did not necessarily hold:

> When at Badu I inquired fully into the question of Atima Ah Wang and found that she did not at any time, nor did her mother, habitually live or associate with aboriginals. It appears that the girl's grandmother lived with her husband, a native of Madagascar, at the South Sea Settlement, so that her daughter Annin Savage, Atima's mother, did not from the time of her birth or at any time habitually live or

The Ahwang family in the second generation.
The men are: Ali Ahmat, son of Anima Ahwang and Ahmat Ahmat, and Richard Ahmat, son of Raima Ahwang and Bargo bin Ahmat. Sitting: Matilda, wife of Richard, Richard (Jnr), Raymond, Sona, Debbie, Gwen (wife of Richard) and Sandra.
Photo: courtesy of Clossom Nakata, Thursday Island.

> associate with aboriginals. Her mother is a half-caste female within the meaning of the Act, so that her children are all exempt from its provisions.[42]

It does not appear that Filewood was proceeded against, because the department could not reliably establish that Atima was a half-caste. But neither did Atima gain her exemption from the Act.

Not long afterwards, in November 1922 an ambitious young protector was appointed to Thursday Island, who would later rise to the office of CPA for twenty years: Cornelius O'Leary. After only half a year in office, he gingerly raised the question of the female quadroons, referring again to Atima's case in order to gain an extension of his authority. Although not mentioning Atima by name, O'Leary's letter landed in her personal file. It claims that 'an outstanding phase of aboriginal life' at Thursday Island was 'the prevalence of temptation to halfcaste or aboriginal girls, who are domestically employed, to go the wrong road'. He had come 'to the definite opinion that the temptation is accentuated by the example of many quadroon females who see fit to lead an unhindered and immoral life'. He realised that 'this phase of the question is officially no concern of mine in that I have no jurisdiction over these females or interests in their welfare'. However, one of them, who had been signed on as half-caste under Mr Holmes, 'refused to recognise this office after the expiry of the agreement, and she now preaches her doctrine of defiance and immorality to her associates'. O'Leary had had to call several Aborigines before him 'for associating with those avowed immoralists'.[43]

Lee-Bryce's prediction, that the local protector's authority was tested by Atima Ahwang, had come true—but it was because the department had tried its best, and failed, to assert its powers over her. We learn from O'Leary's letter that Atima had the support of her employer to make a stand and refused to recognise the protector's authority over her. O'Leary was lobbying for an amendment of the Act to rein in the coloured population, and Bleakley had to inform him that as matters stood, 'the only hope at present of exercising official control of such women' was by deeming their mothers Aboriginal.[44] It was not until 1934 that the desired amendment was passed. (See 'Asians and Aboriginal policy in Queensland'.)

In an effort to split the protest movement of its most vocal base in Torres Strait, the 1897 Act was repealed in 1939 and replaced with two separate Acts, one for mainland Aborigines and one for Torres Strait Islanders. The latter granted a degree of self-government to the island communities with the recognition of indigenous courts and the formation of island councils performing local government functions. Separate legislation for Torres Strait Islanders has remained a feature of Aboriginal policy in Queensland with the exception of a brief interregnum from 1965 to 1971. Different management practices have both helped to cement a regional identity and sharpened the cultural differences between Torres Strait Islanders and mainland Aborigines, with the result that practically all federal and Queensland government initiatives concerning Australia's indigenous people now refer to two indigenous groups, Aborigines and Torres Strait Islanders. The Federal Council for the Advancement of Aborigines and Torres Strait Islanders (FCAATSI), an organisation lobbying for citizen rights and social service benefits in the 1950s, in which many of the mixed descendants in the Torres Strait region became active, pioneered this practice. Torres Strait Islanders have continued to set keynotes in Aboriginal politics, of which the *Mabo* case is the best known.

The far northern experience, characterised by the marine industries and contact with Asians, has had a profound impact on Aboriginal management in Queensland. The *Protection Act* carried reference to Chinese in its title, and three of its four amendments were imprinted by the contact with Asians in the north (1902, 1927, 1934). The 1934 renovation came because the large mixed population in the north could no longer be accommodated in the 1897 definition of 'Aboriginal' and 'half-caste'. By the same token, the replacement of the Act in 1939 was a damage control measure to break the spearhead of rebellion from the mixed and cosmopolitan populations of the north.

ASIANS AND ABORIGINAL POLICY IN WESTERN AUSTRALIA

In Western Australia, pearling became a major area of Aboriginal employment next to pastoral work in the 1870s and 1880s. In 1871 the employment of Aboriginal women in the fishery was prohibited by an Act that was soon replaced with the *Pearl Shell Fishery Regulation Act 1873*. From then on, the inspectors of fisheries acted as *de facto* protectors of Aborigines in the pearling industry. The Act set a maximum of 150 working days for the season, though the season usually lasted only four months. When diving apparatus was successfully introduced in 1888 the many cheap swimming divers on each vessel were replaced with a few hard-working dress divers. Asians were imported for this job and the number of Aborigines employed in swimming diving fell off quickly.

Aboriginal protection in Western Australia was caught up in debates over responsible government in the 1880s. Amidst international attention on statements by the Reverend J. B. Gribble that the Western Australian Parliament was dominated by squatters hostile to natives, and that 'there are men in the Council now who have been charged with murder, and who have been acquitted',[45] an *Aborigines Protection Act* was passed in 1886 for those not employed in pearl-shelling.

The parliamentary select committee considering the bill, chaired by E. H. Wittenoom (owner of Boolardy Station), was intent on minimising its protective effect. Wittenoom suggested reducing the age from which Aborigines could be employed under contract from sixteen to ten, since 'Aboriginal children mature so much more quickly than civilized ones'. The Act settled on fourteen as the age for employment. The committee did not see a need to have employment agreements witnessed by a Justice of the Peace (as the pearling agreements were). Such a person 'may not at times be procurable' and the resultant inconvenience would dispose employers towards Asian labour, in which case natives would either have to be 'provided for at Government expense' or would 'become a source of great mischief'. Although the bill did not require wages to be paid, the committee felt that fines for absconding from a work agreement ought to be increased, and the protector need not be empowered to enter any dwelling-house to enforce the law.

It was a hard lesson to learn for white employers of Aboriginal labour that the state might act in a watchdog function over them. The squatters claimed to know best how to deal with Aborigines, and resented interference into what they felt were their affairs. As one honourable member put it: 'We all know—those of us who have had any experience amongst natives—that there is only one way of keeping them in order, and that is by instilling them with fear.'[46]

Squatting was deemed a handsome qualification for administration and government in Western Australia. In 1892 Sholl, as member for Gascoyne, regretted 'that the Police Department should have at its head a Commissioner who really has no experience in squatting, and it is unfortunate that the police department should be under the control of a Minister who has no sympathy with these Northern settlers, and who certainly has had no experience'.[47] It did not escape the notice of those charged with the protection of Aborigines that in 1892 'The members of the present Ministry are, to a man, directly or indirectly connected with sheep farming.'[48] Of thirty-two members of the lower house in 1895, ten appear on a list of station-owners visited by a travelling inspector of Aborigines that year, two of them connected with Attorney-General Burt and Premier Forrest. Needless to say, the inspector raised no hint of criticism about the treatment of natives at the hands of squatters.

The 1886 Act also set up an Aborigines Protection Board (APB) responsible to the governor as the Queen's representative. It merely oversaw the distribution of blankets and the reimbursement of station owners for relief doled out to station Aborigines. The board was a paper tiger with neither the powers nor the will to enforce any protection. For its first three years it was unable to spend its budget allocation of £2,700. Still, the APB became a point of contestation when Section 70 of the *Constitution Act 1889*, conferring responsible government on Western Australia, increased its annual vote to £5,000 or 10 per cent of the colony's budget, whichever was the larger amount. Premier Forrest successfully promoted the view that it was a 'question of honour' to gain 'full independence from the purview of the crown', and launched a sustained attack of vilification against the board.

In 1897 the board was simply abolished by the Western Australian Parliament, repealing Section 70. The *Aborigines Act 1897* that replaced the board was a machinery-of-government Act to claw back responsibility for Aboriginal affairs to the state government. It never received the Royal Assent necessary to legalise it. In this legislative limbo, an Aborigines Department was set up and Henry Prinsep appointed as CPA (1898–1908). Consistently unable to spend its budget vote, the board had accumulated a reserve fund of over £7,000. This money did not appear in the budget of the new department. Ironically, only after the board, and the minimum expenditure allocated to it, had been abolished, did spending on Aboriginal affairs begin to exceed £10,000. But it never lived up to the crown's formula of 10 per cent of state revenue contained in Section 70.

In his first report to Parliament in 1899 Prinsep noted the 'considerable increase of half-castes' that ought to 'receive consideration by the legislature'.[49] He also noted that the Forrest River Mission had been disbanded, and that two of its members had established a 'private mission' among the sixty or seventy residents of Sunday Island, engaged in trepang fishing. Prinsep welcomed this move because they did not ask for financial assistance. Syd Hadley and Harry Hunter were granted a 100,000-acre reserve on Sunday Island. In the following year, they complained of 'frequent visits of Asiatic pearlers whose influence is much against the improvement in the habits and lives of the natives'. Broome was also afflicted with a 'large number of Mongolians and other Asiatics', and Prinsep was 'considering measures to prevent the natives from being mixed with these people'.[50] He commenced a policy of removing indigenous children to the few institutions then operating.

By 1902 Prinsep reiterated that 'one of the special points that has engaged my attention during the past year was the condition of the half-castes . . . becoming not only a disgrace but a menace to our civilization'. He requested legal powers to deal with the 'immorality at the centres of population', despite his observation that 'the immorality is rarely ever accompanied with any cruelty or injustice, when we consider that the native is generally a consenting party for the personal benefits which temporarily accrue'. Fathers White and Walter at Beagle Bay Mission also complained about the 'influences of the Asiatics working with the pearling fleets during the lay-up season'. They wanted constables stationed in the creeks during lay-up, and punishments meted out to Aborigines who frequented the creeks. To illustrate the good civilising influences of the Beagle Bay Fathers, Prinsep praised the prizes of tobacco and sweets given during the Christmas festivities, and the magic lantern show in the evening 'with some comic character sketches by the boys'. It looks like the local adolescents voted with their feet, preferring the attractions at the creeks to the tame amusements offered by the Fathers.

With a view to Aboriginal contact with pearling crews, the CPA pleaded for legislation similar to that enacted in Queensland in 1897. Meanwhile steps were taken to prevent the intercourse between natives and Asians. Those who were 'not legitimately employed' were expelled from Derby in 1902 because in town they were 'coming in contact with the coloured crews on the various pearling boats'. Furthermore, constables were stationed at La Grange Bay and Beagle Bay to watch over Aborigines during the lay-up season, 'keeping them apart from the pearlers'.[51] In the attempt to stem a rising tide of mixed-descent children it was clearly easier to impose controls on Aborigines than on the Asian workforce. Aboriginal protection became the flipside of Asian exclusion.

The Beagle Bay constable reported intercepting seventeen coloured men in one night who were heading for the native camps with bags of flour, rice, sugar and tea. He ordered them back to the luggers and then patrolled the beach until midnight. He suggested 'that the best way to prevent any disturbance between the coloured men and the natives was to clear the natives away, and not allow them to camp near any of the luggers'.[52]

Constable Kuhlmann at Whistler's Creek in La Grange Bay was particularly officious, and not to be outdone by a lack of legal powers:

> I camp at the creek during the spring tides and sleep down at the bank of the creek, and keep the coloured men on their boats at night and by day. I do not let them go beyond the wells where they get water, which is one mile from the boats. At night time is the worst, as they can go up the creek in the dinghys, and I then have to walk perhaps six miles to prevent them from getting to the natives' camps.
>
> There have been about 60 of the Whistler's Creek tribe of natives carrying water for the boats, and these natives were quite willing to work for their food, so I tried the experiment, not once but twice, to see how it would work, and found that it worked admirably. As the boats come in I put them in four or five tubs, and let them fill the boats with water, and in return they receive either flour or bag-rice or tinned meats or tobacco, and their food whilst carrying. I take care of what they receive, and have it taken over to my camp when they finish the boats; and when they are all gone from the creek the natives come to my camp for food, etc. as they require it . . . I make the natives camp two miles from the creek, and I then camp on the beach and prevent any crews from landing at night; and during the day they are under my eye all the day, and I am certain then that there are no connections between the coloured men and the native women. I have to use a great deal of bluff in dealing with these men. I have chained some of them up all night at times—illegally, I think, but the only way to deal with them is by main force.

Kuhlmann observed that from Saturday afternoon until Monday morning the luggers anchored close to shore, and 'the natives are on the lookout for them, and there are great goings on whilst the coloured men are on shore'. The travelling inspector reported about Kuhlmann 'that on the 15th January he swam off to the luggers in Cape Bossute Creek, seven miles off his camp, and found a native woman on each boat with the crews'. Two men were eventually fined £9 and £5 respectively. On another occasion Kuhlmann ordered twelve coloured men back to their boats, intimidating them with his revolver, but sometimes this failed because they were armed. Once a coloured man stabbed him in the arm and was subsequently sentenced to six months hard labour.[53]

The travelling inspector also observed that a Japanese named Kimura had started a garden at Whistler's Creek. Being Asian, this man was under immediate suspicion:

> I think there can be little doubt this man intends to run a garden only as a blind. He will probably go in for illicit pearl buying, wood-cutting, etc., and I consider it inadvisable that he should be allowed to start operations on these creeks; it can only mean a harbour for natives and Asiatics, and will go far to undo any good that has been done by the constable.[54]

Dot Hunter: woman stories

I do not know whether I met Dot Hunter by accident or by fate. On my arrival in Broome I made an appointment to see ATSIC commissioner Glynis Sibosado as part of my usual introductions, and as was so often the case, the first person I spoke to had a personal story of Asian–Aboriginal contact. Glynis mentioned her Timorese father and Broome resident, Simon Poelina, but most of all she spoke about her mother who had arrived here on the run from a previous violent husband with five children, and started a curio shop and a laundry to see the family through. From Glynis I gained the impression that I needed to meet this woman.

When I finally caught up with Dot Hunter she was preparing to leave for Perth the next morning. And like Glynis, she omitted to mention her own achievements, but was full of praise for her own mother.

> My mother was a brilliant woman, her name was Emily Edgar. That was her maiden name. She not only ran the household, she had chooks, and wild birds as pets, she had a garden that provided all the greenery that we needed. She came from Noonkambah, Bunaba country up around Fitzroy.

Emily was young when she left Noonkambah forever. Her first two children, from a white man, were taken from her.

> They used to tell you who you could marry. These wolves, the men. My mother had two children, and they sent her with the children with the bosses' wife down south. They took the children, kept her [as] a housemaid, put the children in Sister Kate's [home] and she never ever seen them again. That was a home for quarter-caste children, they had to be very fair.

Emily had another eight children. With her husband William Watson she worked at Lower Liveringa and later at Mt Anderson, in the kitchen of the big house, both owned by the Rose family. All of these homesteads—Liveringa, Mt Anderson, Noonkambah and Quanbun—looked 'very grand', according to Dot's brother Harry. Dot is very critical of the way in which Aboriginal labour was used on the stations:

> They ran the properties for the white Europeans. They did all the work, they did all the mustering . . . The Aboriginals carried the cattle and sheep industry on their backs. They did all the work, no pay, long hours.

Dot Hunter with friends. Isobel D'Antoine (née Sariago), Dot Hunter (née Watson) and Katherine D'Antoine (née Omira) at Katherine, 1995. Dot and Isobel are childhood friends who both married men descended from the Sunday Island private mission. Isobel's mother May Richards was raised in the Broome convent and married Dorotio Zuriega, who arrived from the Philippines in 1911, at age thirty-six on the SS *Sultan*. They lived in Broome's Sheba Lane.

Emily Edgar at Mt Anderson. Emily Edgar from Noonkambah married William Watson, a mixed descendant of the Rose family of Lower Liveringa and Mt Anderson stations. Her children came 'under the Act' in Western Australia. Photo: courtesy of Dot Hunter, Broome.

Emily's husband William Watson was the overseer at Lower Liveringa, an outcamp of Mt Anderson Station. His mother was a Nyikina woman from the Yeeda area, and she and her husband Dick worked for the white station owner George Rose who was William's father. George's brother Jeff also had an Aboriginal son, but, reminiscent of Xavier Herbert's novel *Capricornia*, these children were not officially acknowledged, although their parentage was well known. Still, Canny Rose, the patriarch, made sure that William's younger children were allowed into the Derby school instead of Beagle Bay Mission.

Two other coloured families were sending their children to the Derby school at the time, the Buckles and the Ah Chees. One of the Watson children married an Ah Chee, and one married a Buckle.

Dot believes that old Mrs Ah Chee was one of Emily's cousins, because their fathers were brothers. She had married a Chinese baker in Derby and escaped from the reach of the *Protection Acts*. This led Dot to some interesting comparisons.

> Because she was married to a Chinaman, get this one, her children were automatically free. And because my mother was married to my father, we were all under the Act. And my father was providing for us, we had motor transport, and motorbikes in them days, he had all that. . . Years later my other sister—her marriage more or less broke up—and she was drinking with a girlfriend. To drink they used to have to hide, and the police used to harass them all the time. And my sister is in tears, speaking to this sergeant, and I listened for a while. And I'd never thought of this before, but I said, 'Excuse me, the Ah Chees are descendants from a Chinaman. They are free in Australia and they're free in China. We are descendants from the likes of you'—and I touched him on the chest, and I said—'and we're all under the Act. Aren't you classing the Chinaman a better man than yourself?' And he scratched his head, and he said, 'that's what it amounts to'. He hadn't thought of that himself.

Dot is almost certainly wrong to think that being Chinese–Aboriginal in Western Australia 'automatically exempted' anyone from the Act. The Western Australian *Aborigines Act Amendment Act 1936* exempted quadroons under the age of twenty-one who did not live with natives, all quadroons over age twenty-one, and persons of less than quadroon blood born before 1936. It should not have made a difference whether they were of Chinese or European descent. The significant difference between Emily's children and those of Mrs Ah Chee must have been that Emily's husband was classed as Aboriginal, since his white paternity was denied. But in practice the reach of the *Protection Acts* depended largely on the discretion of the local protectors, and was evidently difficult to decipher.

Dot Hunter did not go to Perth the next morning. Instead, she bundled up a few essentials and came with me all the way back to Darwin. Her stories along the way brought the landscape alive with memories and people and histories. During a journey that took almost two weeks she introduced me to many more women—family, friends, childhood acquaintances, sharing sad and happy memories and many hilarious anecdotes. She told me about her two marriages, but preferred not to make these available for a formal interview.

The North Australia Research Unit had equipped me with every possible implement—camping gear, spare fuel jerry cans, an extra sturdy jack, tow rope, winch. It was not until I did run low on fuel that I found what was missing—a funnel to push down the inside lid of the unleaded fuel tank while refilling. So as not to alarm Dot, I hadn't mentioned the sinking needle on the petrol gauge, but recommended the hot driving breeze over the air-conditioned comfort of closed windows, and eventually announced that it was time for an extended smoko. At length, a truck full of young men came by, their family relationship with Dot was established, and I finally admitted our dilemma. They cut an empty plastic bottle into a makeshift funnel, but still its neck was too short to push the lid. Finally Dot produced a long bread knife from her bundle, just narrow enough to enter the neck of the fuel tank and long enough to hold safely, and the problem was solved. As soon as she saw it in her bundle, Dot knew she had no other use for it. I still have the knife for any further emergencies.

Mrs Ah Chee of Derby. Opinion among descendants is divided whether she may have been a Maori woman, or an Aboriginal woman from Noonkambah. She married Owen Ah Chee, baker, of Derby. Her children were exempt from Western Australia's *Protection Acts.* Photo: courtesy of Norma Ah Chee, Derby.

The inspector suggested that instead, the department might follow the splendid example of Kuhlmann's labour experiment and

> might place a man at Cape Bossute Creek as caretaker of this water supply, with power to cut, stack, and supply firewood to the boats at a reasonable and fixed rate, he would be able to employ the natives in obtaining this wood, and also in pumping water for the boats, for which, also, a small charge might be made. . . I feel sure the majority of the pearlers would be delighted to see some such scheme adopted.[55]

This would not only have pleased the pearlers. It was also designed to ensure that natives were working for whites, not for Asians. The tone of this report suggests that any white man was more trustworthy than any Asian man.

How different was the attitude to F. S. Hadley at Sunday Island. He had the blessing and praise of the department for running a 'private mission' that amounted to a work camp where natives were engaged without wages and 'without any departmental interference'. In 1902 Hadley was asking the department for tobacco seeds, and the CPA, far from having qualms about abetting the consumption of addictive substances, felt that this 'shows he is performing good work and should be encouraged'. Having lost his two assistants in that year, Hadley claimed to be single-handedly educating twenty pupils in the school, next to running a pearl shell and bêche-de-mer business. In the following year the CPA himself suggested that this private mission should receive some public funding, because 'the inroads from Asiatics' were giving Hadley financial trouble. The department's annual reports, which had so glowingly reported on Sunday Island, fail to explain why in 1906 the Church of England took over the mission. Hunter established himself at Boolgin homestead with a cattle property and issued in a sizeable Aboriginal family. He was later convicted of 'harbouring' Aboriginal women.

Another pearling company, at Monte Bello Islands, applied to the CPA for 'some old natives to do light work' on their pearl-culture farm. The idea was to take them 'off the hands' of the CPA if they were receiving relief, and the CPA expressed himself fond of the idea, but could not find anyone suitable on the relief lists. He was hoping that 'If in the future natives are collected in large reserves, as some have suggested, we may possibly be able to do something in this way.'[56]

Like Roth in Queensland, Prinsep continued to channel information to parliament to underline the need for comprehensive legislation. In 1902 he informed parliament that after requesting all resident magistrates to compile lists of mixed-descent children who might be induced to enter into institutions, only a few parents were found who were willing to institutionalise their children for education. He clearly outlined a problem complex of Asian–Aboriginal contact, immorality and mixed-descent children who required firmer powers:

> One of the principal questions which has exercised my mind during the year is the condition and proper government of half-castes . . . The returns show that there are more than 850 known half-castes throughout the State. . . I have several times, upon urging legislation, referred to this branch as one of the most important. A section proposed by me would make me the official guardian of all these children, and by tactful action, I believe that if power were given me, I should be able in

> a comparatively short time to have most of these children placed under proper care, and brought up in useful knowledge . . . I trust that during this session the Aborigines laws will be made more perfect. At present they are very vague, and the department has really no power at all to make regulations for properly controlling the intercourse between Asiatics, who are so numerous and ubiquitous, and the natives, who are always ready for the benefits it brings by pandering to their lusts.[57]

Prinsep's objective was achieved with the *Aborigines Act 1905*, modelled on the Queensland legislation with a strong bent towards preventing 'miscegenation'. As in Queensland, the CPA was empowered to manage the property of Aborigines, to remove Aborigines from one place to another, and to permit or forbid the marriage of female Aborigines with non-Aborigines. The Act included wide regulatory powers and employment provisions (feeding and clothing of Aboriginal employees), the establishment of government reserves, and the provision for exemptions from the Act. It prohibited the supply of liquor to Aborigines and 'cohabiting'—the living together of non-Aboriginal men with Aboriginal women.

As a local flavour, the Act also specifically provided for the removal of camps from townships, and the declaration of 'prohibited areas' where Aborigines were not permitted to go. Unlike the Queensland Act, it did not require employers of Aborigines to pay wages, and made no provision for the department to administer such wages. The Aborigines Department was established again—legally this time—with an annual budget of £10,000, a vote that was immediately overdrawn. The CPA became the legal guardian of all Aboriginal and half-caste children under sixteen.

The definition of persons deemed to be included under the Act was much wider than in Queensland. It included Aboriginal inhabitants of Australia, as well as half-castes, and their children. At this time the CPA in Queensland was already frustrated with the narrow definition of Aborigines in the 1897 Act, which defined half-castes as the children of Aboriginal mothers, therefore excluding the children of mixed descendants who were later to be referred to as quadroons and octoroons.

The new Act was a boon to the missions in Western Australia. It had always been difficult to maintain a large enough population to justify the expense of any mission. Beagle Bay immediately offered to take in 'all the half-caste children of Broome'. By accepting such children referred by the CPA, the missions could secure a source of income. In fact, the protector not only sent the Broome children, but endeavoured to send 'all half-caste children in the Kimberley to Beagle Bay', although 'a little difficulty is experienced in getting the parents to part with these children'. The CPA was confident that 'every persuasion will be used' because the 'mission is ready to receive any number'. Father Bischofs hoped that the Beagle Bay Mission would eventually have charge of all children over age seven born on Dampier Peninsula. The main trouble, he felt, was with Asiatics.

Two new missions appeared on the peninsula in 1906. The Church of England took control of Sunday Island and Trappist Father Nicholas Emo established a mission at Cygnet Bay in King Sound. The assistance of Filipinos in these Catholic mission endeavours is generally played down. It starkly contradicts the images of 'Asiatics' reverberating through the archival memory.

Nicholas Emo and Pago Mission (Kalumburu)

Father Nicholas Mario Emo helped to extend the reach of Catholic missions in the far north of Western Australia with the help of Filipino Catholics who had been attracted to this part of the world by the pearling industry. Emo was sent to help entrench the Catholic mission founded at Beagle Bay in 1890. His special assignment was to minister to the Filipino community in Broome where a hospital and school were established in 1895. In 1906 Emo and two Cygnet Bay men undertook an excursion with the Benedictine Abbot of New Norcia, Fulgentius Torres, to determine the site for Pago Mission. It opened in 1908 staffed with Emo, the Filipino Leandro and Leandro's Timorese wife. They established a thriving garden but remained isolated from the local Aborigines. Perez observes that Pago was a meeting place and neutral territory for several groups of Aborigines, and the missionaries witnessed much fighting between Kwini and Kulari groups. The locals had much contact with luggers and were 'addicted to chewing tobacco'. The mission history records an indigenous society in turmoil with widespread syphilis rising to epidemic proportion in 1917.

In 1909 Emo took in nine 'half-caste' boys from Derby to form the nucleus of a mission. None of these nine boys is named in Perez' mission history and two are entirely unaccounted for, but Perez mentions that Emo decided to return to Broome in 1910.[58] Mary Durack suggests that this episode was crucial for Emo's relationship with the Benedictines. She candidly states that the 'half-caste boys' were required to justify the mission, and thinks that this caused a deep rift between Emo and the missionaries:

> Relations between Father Nicholas and the Benedictines were becoming strained over the Dampierland boys, who with three or four half-caste youths sent there from station properties, had helped to justify the isolated Kalumburu mission in the eyes of a sceptical government. The youths . . . had long since grown homesick and their relatives had protested bitterly at their being kept away for so long among alien tribespeople. Father Nicholas's proposal to return them had been seen by the monks as an attempt to sabotage their struggling mission, and it was only when one of the boys became dangerously ill that the priest decided he could delay no longer. . . At all events he knew, when he sailed off with the Dampierland youths about May 1910, that he had burned his boats with the Benedictines.[59]

The extent of Filipino presence at Pago is also veiled in Perez who only occasionally supplies their names. He mentions that after Emo returned to Broome in 1910, another Filipino family was sent to Pago to look after the schooner *Dickie*, but when this was wrecked in August 1912, this family returned with Leandro to Broome. There is reference to Toribio and Sylvester who remained at Pago until 1915, but no hint to their date of arrival on the site.

Clearly the Kalumburu story is not one of a meeting of white missionaries and savage natives in the untouched jungle. It is a story of the importance of an intermediate layer of coloured people: mixed-descent children and Filipino Catholics were the formula of success of Catholic influence here.

Puertollano and the Kimberley missions

The family of Thomas Puertollano has been closely linked with the missionary efforts of the Catholic Church on Dampierland Peninsula. The family memory of that involvement differs significantly from the way it is recorded by the Church. In the written histories the missionaries are the pioneering agents on the peninsula, but according to Puertollano's daughter Theresa, the missionaries merely followed in the wake of Puertollano's pioneering, taking advantage of the contacts he established with Aborigines.

My father, he was one of the Filipinos who came to Australia when all these countrymen came on a boat, a big schooner or something, and they came to Broome. It must have been in the last [nineteenth] century. My father came from Mindanao; he was well educated in his country and spoke English well.

That Fishermen's Bend outside of Broome just across Roebuck Bay was leased to my father and all those Filipino people for ninety-nine years, so I was told, so they all lived there. They were all tradesmen, carpenters, and that first church that was built in Broome, that's what my father now, he was the—what would you say—the headman, and he helped to build that church with all his Filipino people. They built houses and they had fish traps all around Broome there, and some of them had shops in Broome, barber shops and, oh, everything.

And so my father stayed there and he thought, oh well, he'd like a look around the country. So him and a few others went overland along the coast to Disaster Bay. He wanted to start a new station. He met a lot of Aboriginal people on the way, in those days they used to just live in little humpies. So he took them with him and they knew the country, and he brought some of the old men and some of their wives, and they showed him this place, what they call Disaster Bay. He liked the place and that's where he started to make a station. He had all these Aboriginal people working for him. At that time my mother was only a young one, fourteen or fifteen years old, she was with them, with her mob—my grandparents, I suppose—travelling around in the bush. That's how he met my mother.

They were all carpenters and they built a house for themselves and they lived there for about two or three years. And then there were a lot of other priests, French priests, the Trappist Fathers, they wanted to make a mission. So they came across my father and his Filipino people. So what did he do, he gave up his home, his house, and moved further along the coast. He gave that house up to the priests. He was well established. He had gardens and everything going. He just left it there for them. That's what was told to me. By this time my mother and him were married.

And then he went further up north and he found this place, I don't know what they called it then, it was only bush and he cleared it up with his Filipino people. And that's where he started Lombadina. And my mother was with them, and she had her child but it died. No doctors or anyone was there. That was the second one I think she had. Another Pallottine priest came, another Fathers wanted to start a mission around that place. They came across my father again. Then he had to give up his place. There already was a lot of people there, Aboriginal people bilong that place in the bush and their community, and they all came to the place where my father was, to work for him. They made gardens and he had goats and cattle, he was well off. It was going already, then he had to give it up to the Fathers

Theresa Puertollano, Derby, 1995.

> and the Sisters and nuns, and he went to Broome. He already had three sons, three brothers I had, they were all born there except me, and another sister of mine, she died. Two girls and three boys were born there. So he had to take them all to Broome and he started a bakery.[60]

According to Theresa her father smoothed the path for the missions at Disaster Bay and Lombadina, having already established gardens and a workforce in both places. One might expect this important role to be reflected and acknowledged in the history of Catholic missions in the Kimberley commissioned by the Bishop of Broome. But Margaret Zucker's *From Patrons to Partners* assigns a very marginal role to Puertollano, making only four brief references to him. Mary Durack, drawing on local knowledge, adds a little more detail, but still Thomas Puertollano appears simply a helpmeet for the initiative of the Trappist missionaries. A closer reading of sources lends credence, however, to Theresa's view.

Filipino Catholics were prominent at the interface between missions and Kimberley Aborigines from the beginning. A short-lived Catholic mission commenced by Duncan McNab at Disaster Bay in King Sound failed in 1886. McNab wrote that the Aborigines he worked with at Disaster Bay had been employed by pearlers, and welcomed the idea of a mission. 'With the help of men from Manila I tried to teach the Blacks the use of tools, how to work, to dig and plough, to build houses of bark, of brushwood and of slabs, to fish with nets, and so to catch and cure fish by salting and pressing it for a night and then drying it in the sun.'[61] It is possible then, that a Filipino community was at Disaster Bay as early as 1884. Regrettably McNab does not mention by name any of the Filipinos who assisted him in the 1880s. The building, fishing and processing techniques described suggest that the Filipino fishermen contributed valuable experience to the experiment.

French Trappists from New Caledonia established Beagle Bay in 1890. Trappist reinforcements for Beagle Bay arrived in 1895, including Father Nicholas Emo. Durack writes that Beagle Bay Mission became so successful that the cultivable land became insufficient and a new site was selected on Nimanboor land at Disaster Bay for which Bishop Gibney had already obtained a grant of reserve land in 1888:

> In this enterprise the monks had a staunch friend and helper in Thomas Puertollano, a young Manilaman who had come to Broome as a diver. He had recently married a half-caste girl named Agnes O'Bryan whose Irish father had placed her with the missionaries at Beagle Bay, and the couple now wished to settle down on the land and raise a family. Although small in stature Thomas brought to the task all the enthusiastic faith of his Filipino heritage and worked with tremendous energy under Trappist direction.[62]

Contrary to Durack, Theresa believes that her mother was with her own people when she met Puertollano. As far as Theresa knows, her parents met at Bungadok, outside the ambit of missions and protectors, and were later married by the French Fathers at Disaster Bay. Durack places Beagle Bay five miles from the inland camp of the Bungadok, so perhaps these two places are collapsed into one in her account. Durack's account leaves uncertain whether Puertollano came to Disaster Bay with the missionaries, or was already well established there.

Zucker does not refer to Thomas Puertollano at

Disaster Bay at all. She writes that Father Jean Marie Janny moved there in 1896, and by 1898 this grange housed six children, while Beagle Bay housed thirty children. Zucker only mentions that Agnes Puertollano acted as godmother for twelve catechumens in 1899 and was to become an 'outstanding member of the Catholic laity in the Kimberley', without specifying whether Agnes was at Beagle Bay or Disaster Bay.[63] Durack is explicit though, that Thomas Puertollano was the only assistant for Father Jean Marie in mustering, and that Agnes Puertollano hand-sewed the bridal dress for Marie Parambor at Disaster Bay.[64] Neither of these sources makes it clear that Puertollano and other Filipinos were already at Disaster Bay before Jean Marie Janny arrived, but neither do they contradict Theresa's recollection.

In 1900 the Trappists suddenly wound down their operations in Australia, and a hasty retreat was underway at Beagle Bay. Much of the livestock and machinery was sold, Father Emo was placed in charge of Beagle Bay, and only he, Father Jean Marie, and two lay brothers, John and Xavier, stayed on in Australia, according to Zucker. Durack writes that when the Trappists were recalled from Beagle Bay, Puertollano was left in charge of the grange and took a job with the pearling fleet to help maintain the mission.[65] Presumably the grange referred to is Disaster Bay, since Beagle Bay was under the charge of Emo.

Bishop Gibney had not been consulted and was angered by the Trappist retreat. Just at this time the 10,000-acre lease for Beagle Bay came up for freehold tenure, and the Church had to demonstrate that the conditions of the lease, improvements amounting to £5,000, had been fulfilled. The bishop, his assistant Father Dean Martelli and the resolute Irishwoman Daisy Bates who had befriended Martelli on the journey to Australia, set off to the north to prepare the site for the land valuer in August 1900.

Bates adds another brief glimpse into the mission story. She recorded that they were joined in Broome by Father Emo, and taken to Beagle Bay by skipper Filomeno Rodriguez on the *Sree Pas Sair*, no longer a luxury yacht, but marked by many years of service in the pearling industry. At Beagle Bay they met Brother Daly (Xavier), Brother Jean (Father Jean Marie Janny) and Brother John as well as Brother Sebastian, a Filipino lay brother omitted by Zucker. From Bates' account, the Beagle Bay gardens were overgrown and the wells in a state of disrepair. Bates worked with the 'native women', among whom she mentioned Domcilla, Philomena, Agnes, Ernestine, Josephine and Mathilde.

After putting the site in order, the party visited Disaster Bay for which a 2,000-acre lease had also been secured, and which had been without a priest for some months. Bates observed that the stores there had been left 'unguarded' for six months, but had not been touched. Unlike the Beagle Bay gardens, the Disaster Bay gardens were thriving with sugar cane, tomatoes, cucumbers, sorghum, rice and arrowroot. They needed no clearing, and were supplied from a 'splendid well'. There was a house and chapel of corrugated iron.[66] For the three days spent there Bates makes no reference to Puertollano, but does mention that Father Emo had been performing marriages between Aboriginal women and Filipino men here, a practice that earned him much criticism. The healthy state of the gardens, stores and buildings at Disaster Bay strongly suggests that someone was in charge of this out-station, and it was not quite as abandoned as it may have appeared to Bates. It may have been unguarded by whites, but Durack's reference to Puertollano in charge of the grange would support Theresa's statement that her father was well established at Disaster Bay.

The party, including the sixty-five-year-old Bishop Gibney, worked themselves to exhaustion with the result that the Beagle Bay improvements were valued at £10,000, and the title deed was secured. Zucker notes that this news was greeted with protests, because 'the monks had performed marriages of Manilamen to Aboriginal women'. Suspicions were raised that the freehold of such a large territory was being granted merely to provide 'a place of refuge for Manilamen' and 'to found a mixed settlement of Manilamen and Native women'. This prospect was condemned as 'a horrible travesty on 20th century civilisation'.[67] Zucker's consistent obfuscation of the role of Filipinos on the missions suggests that the Church might have shared such sentiments and preferred not to record their names and roles.

It is not clear from the written histories when Disaster Bay was abandoned, much less when Puertollano left there. However, we find him again at Lombadina when it became a mission, just as Theresa recalls.

The German Pallottines took over from the French Trappists in 1901. Father Emo stayed on in Broome but left the Trappists and became naturalised in 1905. For reasons not well explained by Zucker, Father Emo's relationship with the Pallottines had become untenable in 1904. It seems most likely that they had very different views about Asian–Aboriginal relationships.

Pallottine relations with the various pearlers and trepangers on the Dampierland Peninsula also deteriorated. Harry Hunter and Frenchy d'Antoine had a camp at Lombadina, Syd Hadley ran a 'private mission' at Sunday Island, there was a Malay camp at Garamal, also near One Arm Point, and Filipinos in the Disaster Bay area. Durack observes that around 1904 relations between the Beagle Bay Mission and Harry Hunter and Frenchy d'Antoine soured because Hunter had moved his camp from Lombadina to Pender Bay, close to Beagle Bay, taking many Aborigines with him, and pearling became a greater attraction than mission life. When a Royal Commission of Inquiry was conducted into native affairs in Western Australia, chaired by Queensland Chief Protector Roth in 1905, the question of contact with the marine industries ranked prominently. The Kimberley missionaries were keen to keep pearlers and trepangers separate from Aborigines. In 1910 the Pallottines established Lombadina Mission 'at the request of the Government to take charge of the Natives who were removed from Harry Hunter's place when he was found guilty of immorality and imprisoned'.[68]

Durack's understanding of Puertollano's role at Lombadina contradicts both Theresa Puertollano and Zucker. Durack writes that Father Jean Marie helped the Puertollano family move to a place called Lumbingun near Lombadina, 'which property they took over on some arrangement from the mission'. It is possible that Jean Marie assisted in Puertollano's move, because Zucker mentions that for some years he 'had lived almost as a hermit on the coast near Broome'.[69] But Durack believes that the Pallottines sold the title deeds and whatever stock was still running on Lombadina to Thomas Puertollano. This is highly unlikely, since according to Zucker, Puertollano's house served as a chapel for the new mission until a new one was built in 1912.[70] The mission was in establishment, not in retreat. Moreover, Chief Protector Neville raised objections to Lombadina Mission arguing that the 20,000-acre property 'belonged to a Manilaman' who 'was technically employing the Aborigines in breach of regulations, as Asiatics are not allowed to employ Aborigines'. To overcome Neville's objection, the brother of Pallottine missionary Father Creagh bought the land for £1,100 'and transferred the lease from Thomas Puertollano to Fr. Creagh'.[71] Theresa's recollection appears far more reliable than Durack's on the question of the lease: it was Puertollano's property that was being devolved to the church, not the other way round. However, the transfer of property did not take place until 1917.

Apart from observing that Puertollano's house was turned into a makeshift church, Zucker is vague on the emergence of Lombadina Mission. There is no mention that a station was already established and thriving under the care of Puertollano when the Pallottines arrived. Durack writes that Puertollano ran a herd of 500 head of cattle as well as goats, pigs and poultry at Lombadina. He built a garden, and sold produce to the lugger crews. 'Since he demanded after all no more than a modest living for his family, he shared what he had with the community in a prudent, but truly Christian spirit.'

Durack also fleshes in why Lombadina was a useful location. It was the site of a traditional camping ground of Bardi people, not sheltered enough to become a lay-up base for luggers. The Filipino families and their Aboriginal families camped in the little coves and along the tidal creeks in the area. Theresa was unable to remember the names of other Filipinos, or how many were in the community led by her father, but from Durack we glean some of the names associated with Lombadina. She mentions Joseph Marcelina from Chile, John Andriasin from Manado in Kupang, Severo Acosta (possibly Seveiro da Costa) a Broome diver, and the Filipino Damasco Maagina—most likely Don Damasco Maagna Trinidad, a Trappist novice who had accompanied Abbot Torres in 1906 when finding a site for the Benedictine mission.[72] The descendant families adopted the names of Marcello, Damaso and Manado. Martin Sibosado, of Filipino–Japanese parentage and raised at Beagle Bay, also joined the Lombadina community soon after the mission opened.[73]

Durack, too, recalls official resentment against Puertollano's leadership of Lombadina, even before the mission commenced in 1910.

> Because he was classed as an 'Asiatic', he could not obtain a permission to employ Aborigines, and could not employ even those willing to work for their keep. This meant that Puertollano's Lombadina station was neither a mission nor a pearling base.
>
> A sympathetic policeman advised the Department of Aborigines to declare Lombadina a government feeding depot. This was done, the depot being put in charge of Syd Hadley to run in conjunction with his Sunday Island mission. More natives than ever flocked to the site and Puertollano found that despite the free rations, his vegetables were constantly raided and his stock speared, while Hadley refused to impose any discipline whatever. For a time ill-feeling ran high, those in sympathy with Puertollano

> contending that a good family man, no matter what his nationality, had more right to control a government depot on his property than a white man who was known to cohabit with Aboriginal women. Hadley was soon afterwards convicted of this charge and relieved of his supervision of the Lombadina depot, though not of his mission. This move did no one any good, as the ration station was thereafter closed down and the natives grew more and more resentful of Puertollano for failing to provide for them on the government scale. This was the dilemma in which Father Nicholas [Nicholas Mario Emo] found his Filipino friend when on his way to Broome early in 1910.[74]

Emo was departing from Pago in 1910 when he called in at Puertollano's Lombadina Station. It is likely that Durack confuses Hadley and Hunter who were both associated with Sunday Island. According to the CPA it was Hunter, at the Boolgin homestead, who was found guilty of immorality. Hadley remained at Sunday Island, which was in financial trouble when Hunter and d'Antoine left in 1902. These two moved to Lombadina, and in 1904 relocated to Pender Bay, much to the chagrin of the Pallottines. At any rate, Puertollano must have been at Lombadina well before the Pallottines came in 1910. Quite possibly he was displaced from Disaster Bay when the lease was granted in 1900 to the Catholic Church. Durack's story must refer to the period from 1902 to 1904 when Hunter and d'Antoine were at Lombadina. She may be correct in stating that they acted in association with the Sunday Island Mission, because in 1902 Hadley asked for government assistance, and granting the supervision of a ration depot at Lombadina may have been the CPA's gesture of support.

According to the CPA the government requested that the Pallottines take over Lombadina in 1910 to take charge of the Aborigines left behind by Hunter's conviction. Although Zucker thought that Emo's relationship with the Pallottines was untenable, he became the priest at Lombadina, having just broken his ties with the Benedictines at Pago. Emo was on very good terms with Puertollano, and his assignment signals the commencement of the mission. Puertollano made over his house for a church from 1910 to 1912, and when three St John of God Sisters arrived at Lombadina in 1913, 'the Puertollano family vacated their little home for the sisters until a convent was built for them'.[75] Surely this signals a deep commitment to the Catholic mission on Puertollano's part, and the Church could scarcely hope for a more solid ally.

Puertollano continued to stay on at the mission and play a supportive role. Durack recollects that in March 1915 the schooner *Alice*, belonging to James Clarke, was wrecked in the Lacepede Islands, and Puertollano rescued the Kupang crew and captain James MacKenzie. Theresa remembers that afterwards the Kupangers came to her father's place every season with presents and supplies of salted fish, pearl shell mussel, and whatever they had. Emo died in 1915, leaving his boat to the Sisters at Lombadina and his diving gear to Puertollano.[76] Zucker cites Father Creagh that Puertollano 'for years kept the mission there going' until the Chief Protector raised the spectre of prosecution and he sold his property to the Pallottines around 1917.[77]

Having assisted the establishment of a mission at Lombadina, it appears that Puertollano lost his property because of it. He became embroiled in the rivalry between the Church and a Chief Protector who was generally hostile to missions, and under whose administration practically all children's missions in Western Australia were wound down.[78] The gaze of the department made it impossible to continue to run his property, and he was forced to sell 20,000 acres with established gardens to the only bidder for £1,100.

Agnes and Thomas Puertollano left for Broome in 1918 with their three sons and two daughters, and opened a bakery. Here Thomas remained until the wartime evacuation of 1942 and died two weeks later.

The Puertollano family is mentioned frequently in written histories of the Kimberley, sadly not for its pioneering role for missions but because it was struck by leprosy from which only Thomas and two sons escaped. Theresa, the youngest of six children, born in Broome in 1920, was institutionalised at age thirteen, and has never left Aboriginal institutions since then. At age eleven she was sent to New Norcia, but became ill, and was sent home. She and her sister were diagnosed with leprosy and taken to Channel Island, an asylum for Aboriginal lepers near Darwin, because there was no local institution. After seven years Theresa was transferred to the Derby leprosarium opened in 1936. She was discharged in 1958 and worked at the native hospital for three years. Her mother and three siblings died in leprosaria. When I met her she was seventy-four, completely blind, and living at Nungula Nunga, the former native hospital in Derby where her exile as a leper commenced in 1933.

Theresa's account of her father's role amounts to substantial pioneering by the Filipinos on the Dampierland Peninsula—a role which is entirely absent from the written histories. Zucker all but ignores Puertollano as well as other Filipinos involved in the Kimberley missions, while Durack acknowledges his valuable role without going so far as conceding that Puertollano was at Disaster Bay and Lombadina before the missionaries arrived. Still, a close reading of both accounts tends to give credibility to Theresa's story. What appears from the three accounts is a close working relationship of the Catholic Church with Filipinos, starting with the building of a church in Broome. It is possible that Puertollano's moves around the Peninsula were initiated by missionaries, but it seems certain that his family links and those of other Filipinos into the Aboriginal community cemented the Church's success on the peninsula.

Disapproval of mixed marriages was endemic among white administrators, and indeed, this was the trump card played by Protector Neville in 1917, when the Lombadina Mission subsidy was withdrawn. This may be why the Church played down the Filipino–Aboriginal presence on their missions. Zucker's history of the Catholic Church in the Kimberley might have turned out quite differently had the Church records been supplemented with oral histories from former mission residents. The racial blinkers of the book are aptly illustrated through the photographs, whose captions name all whites and none of the non-whites depicted there. Named individuals contrast with anonymous community members across a racial divide. If we take for granted that the Church records may have had political reason to construct a racial divide in what is recorded and acknowledged and what is omitted, then Theresa's history of the Kimberley missions is a reminder that the shift from patronage to partnership requires a shift in historical method.

The question of 'half-castes' had appeared immediately on the agenda of the new Aborigines Department and continued to gain in prominence as the non-indigenous population increased. By 1907, 181 children were educated in institutions, but the CPA's 'plan to draw in all the half-castes to civilisation has been foiled by a decrease in the budget vote'.[79]

Anti-Asian sentiments had been festering in Western Australia since the early 1890s when Asians had become dominant in pearling, but were more pronounced in the south of the colony. In 1892 over 2,000 Fremantle residents petitioned for immigration restrictions on Chinese who were being imported for public works. In 1894 the immigration of Chinese, Afghans and other aliens became an election issue, and restrictions were imposed with the *Imported Labour Registry Act Amendment Act 1894*. A 1904 commission appointed to inquire into aliens in the state's mining industry, with a view to turning the mining industry white, carefully sidestepped the question of aliens in pearl-shelling, because it was known that Asians were vital for the survival of this industry. At this time the non-indigenous population in the Kimberley had reached 4,400, mostly due to workers imported from Singapore and Kupang for the pearling industry.

Aboriginal interactions with Asians remained high on the department's agenda. During his last year in office in 1908, Prinsep introduced a new regulation, that Afghan camel drivers were not permitted to employ natives under the age of twenty, and hoped to extend this provision to all Asians. (See also Sianna Sindhi and Afghan cameleers.) C. F. Gale, who succeeded Prinsep in office (1908–14), implemented this suggestion in 1908. Gale had been Chief Inspector of Fisheries, including pearl shell fisheries, and therefore had a good grasp of the activities of Asians.

Gale used the 'prohibited zone' provisions of the *Protection Act* to clear natives out of Broome and Fitzroy Crossing in 1908, followed by Halls Creek, Derby and Beagle Bay in 1910, and declared further prohibited areas in the north. 'The creation of these reserves has been found necessary in order to keep the bush natives away from the watering places frequented by the pearling fleet, mostly manned by Asiatics, to whom the necessity for these restrictions principally applies.'[80] After the imposition of such restrictions it was claimed that the supply of liquor to Aborigines at Fitzroy Crossing practically ceased, only 'one case happened last year, and that was the usual Asiatic'.[81]

Because of the rising incidence of venereal disease among Aborigines, which was increasingly seen as threatening the 'community at large', two lock hospitals were established to confine infected Aborigines at Bernier and Dorre islands. Gale felt that steps should also be taken to 'stamp out the disease in the men of other nationalities' but did not go so far as to propose measures dealing with whites.[82]

According to the travelling inspector,

> The worst feature of West Kimberley, and I may say of the whole State, is the coast-line within the sphere of the pearling luggers and Asiatic crews . . . Nearly all the coastal half-castes are half-bred Asiatics . . . About Broome and along the coast there are a number of full-grown half-castes married to Asiatics, and most of them have children . . . I would not hesitate for one moment to separate any half-caste from its aboriginal mother no

matter how frantic her momentary grief might be at the time. They soon forget their offspring.

The powers of guardianship were strengthened with a 1911 amendment, and by 1913, 320 children had been institutionalised. New missions, such as Pago, and Lombadina, established by Father Emo in 1913, dealt with the increased demand. Because the pearling industry, with its Asian population, centred on the Kimberley coast, the institutions concerned with Asian–Aboriginal children also focused on this area. In 1935 the Kimberley had three government stations and six missions, while the remainder of the state had only one government settlement and four missions. Gale argued that it was not fruitful to send mixed descendants into service. He felt they should be able to remain in each other's company on industrial missions.[83]

Cattle killing continued to compete with the 'half-caste question' as the major administrative preoccupation. In 1910 three adjoining cattle stations were acquired in the Kimberley to create Moola Bulla, an Aboriginal cattle reserve intended as the eventual home for all Kimberley natives. Violet Valley near Turkey Creek was added in 1913 as a 'native feeding depot'. The Moola Bulla Cattle Station became Gale's showpiece of achievement, 'the pulse of the native situation in the East Kimberley' for years to come.[84]

In 1915 Gale was sacked as pragmatism won out over humanitarian concerns under the Scanlan Labor government's new Minister in charge of Aboriginal Affairs, Rufus Underwood. He drastically reduced mission funding and appointed in Gale's place A. O. Neville, a permanent officer of the Immigration Department that had become rather redundant since Federation. Neville, a personal friend of Underwood, considered the native reserves 'an interesting sociological experiment'. The nickname given by his 'wards' to this inept officer was 'The Devil'.[85]

Like Prinsep, Neville became preoccupied with the mixed population. By 1919 he reported that only 327 'half-castes' were administered under the Act, and 826 remained outside its provisions. He particularly felt that mixed-descent women ought to be drawn under the Act and prevented from drifting into the urban centres. Any non-Aboriginal man wishing to marry an Aboriginal woman had to deposit a bond with the department. Neville formulated an amendment bill for the greater control of the mixed population in 1929, however no great changes in policy occurred until the 1930s, when the killing of Japanese at Caledon Bay stimulated wide-ranging discussions. An amendment to the *Protection Act* was again underway in 1933 to extend the definition of 'half-castes', but was postponed to await the report of a royal commission. Neville had little support in the bureaucracy, most of whom had been alienated by what Anna Haebich calls his 'increasingly tyrannical' administration.[86]

In an atmosphere of wide public debate and criticism of Aboriginal administration, police magistrate H. D. Moseley was appointed in February 1934 to head a Royal Commission of inquiry into the condition of Aborigines. Moseley had no experience in Aboriginal Affairs and his report by and large concurred with the opinion expressed by Neville.[87] He seemed to somewhat misunderstand his brief when he ventured to recommend on the removal of particular individuals. Nevertheless, the biggest changes in Aboriginal policy are credited to his report. He declared that 'the great problem confronting the community today is that of the half-caste' whose population in the state had reached 3,891, heavily concentrated in the Kimberley. 'Broome has, and for some time past has had, greater police protection than any other Northern or North-West town, and yet we find in the Broome Police District, according to latest returns, 417 half-castes—more than half the total half-caste population of the North.'[88] Moseley felt that Broome presented 'peculiar difficulties' because 'one great disadvantage to the native population is the contact which takes place with Asiatics' who 'associate with the half-caste native women in the town' enabling these 'to live a life of ease, if not of virtue'. They ought to be evicted from the town 'only allowed in on permit and the greatest supervision exercised over their reserve to prevent contact with white men and, of course, Asiatics'.[89]

Moseley was pleased that Asians were not permitted to employ Aborigines. He felt that the 'young half-caste men' could profitably be employed on luggers so long as they were under the supervision of 'a white man in charge of each boat'. For 'those who have definitely adopted a life of indolence' and became troublesome, he recommended a 'Palm Island scheme'. He expressed himself confident that 'with proper management as much success can be achieved here as has been done in Queensland'.[90] Acknowledging the differences of the Aboriginal situation between the northern and southern parts of the state, Moseley suggested the establishment of districts with divisional protectors to replace the central control of the CPA. Health was also a prominent concern in the report because 'the danger of contracting disease from the native is always prevalent'. He suggested to declare Sunday Island near Derby as a leprosarium and to prepare a 'temporary holding ground' for lepers in Derby. The report recommended a definition of 'half-caste' 'to include persons of aboriginal origin in a remote degree'.[91] To the indigenous people who had presented evidence, some by smuggling notes out of the reserves where they were detained against their wishes, and many of whom complained that they were falsely treated as falling under the Act, the report must have been a great disappointment.[92]

Neville's following annual report again raised the question about the management of mixed-descent children, suggesting that they should be segregated from their parents on the missions, and that a far more inclusive definition of 'half-castes' was required. 'Since 1915 the character of our work has gradually changed; the half-caste question, then in its infancy, has now assumed formidable proportions and the activities of the Department have had to be considerably extended to meet ever-increasing needs.'[93]

Neville reported that Queensland's CPA Bleakley, who had tried to achieve legislative amendments for sixteen years, had visited the state in March 'to secure all the information he could regarding the half-caste question here'. With its 1934 amendment Queensland was now able to exercise 'greater control of half-castes', and the Northern Territory had also achieved a 'clearer definition of half-caste and aboriginal, and clause protecting female aboriginals and half-castes' that was now 'as in Queensland a most drastic provision'.

Leprosy in the Kimberley

Leprosy was first reported in Darwin in 1894 and gradually gained momentum. In Western Australia sporadic cases had occurred since 1908, and in 1912 there were a number of cases in Broome. A leper station was opened near Cossack in 1923, and Cecil Cook as CPA in the Northern Territory advised a systematic investigation. Still, the Western Australian Chief Protector felt there was no cause for alarm.

In the 1930s leprosy became a serious public health concern. Several members of the Board of Health in Derby resigned in protest over inaction in 1933, after thirty confirmed cases and eighty-five suspected cases were found in the Dampierland port areas. The number of new cases peaked in 1935 at fifty-eight, and the St John of God nuns lobbied the Health Department to open a leprosarium near Derby. The Moseley Report supported these calls for a local institution. The Derby leprosarium opened in 1936 with ninety patients managed by five Sisters, of whom four were siblings from the Greene family.[94]

Until that time, because quarantine was a federal responsibility, the Western Australian patients were sent to the Channel Island leprosarium near Darwin. This exile magnified their suffering. Mary Durack describes the departure of such a group from Beagle Bay:

> The 13-ton lugger *W. S. Rolland* was then hired and the captain instructed to take as many cases as possible from Beagle Bay. The leave-taking of the twelve who were packed on board was one of the most pathetic incidents in the mission's history. The more advanced half-caste and part-Filipinos among them, hoping to encourage the terrified full-blood victims, made brave attempts to be merry as though setting off on a holiday cruise. One had an accordion and played a jaunty air, but as the lugger pushed out to sea a high-pitched keening of tribal lament went up from both the ship and the shore, and even the captain, a hardened old sea-dog, could not restrain his emotion.[95]

Theresa Puertollano remembers this incident. She said that it was Gregory Howard playing the accordion. This ship departed in April, and Theresa and her sister were sent in June 1933, on the *Miriam*, under Captain Pentheny. Their pilot was Uncle Jacky Hunter (one of Harry Hunter's daughters had married Alfons Puertollano and Jacky was their son). The captain refused to take any lepers from the native hospital (now Nungula Nunga in Derby) until they were released from their big ankle chains. Patients were begging to be allowed to stay in their own country. Theresa remembers that thirty or forty Aboriginal men and women were chained up together.[96] Their spokesmen in the native hospital in Derby demanded to see the local protector.

The Aboriginal protection bureaucracy viewed leprosy as an 'Asian problem', outside its ambit of responsibility. Though no leprosy cases were reported from Thursday Island or Darwin, Neville concluded that leprosy was 'most common in pearling districts', and that the disease was 'common in all Asiatic countries from which the crews have been drawn'.[97]

Bowing to the pressure of opinion expressed by Neville, Moseley and Bleakley, a 1936 Amendment Act replaced the distinction between 'Aborigines' and 'half-caste' with the collective 'native' to rein these populations in under the Act. The Act was intended to include the 'whole coloured population', with the exception of 'quadroons over the age of twenty-one and octoroons'.[98] Introducing the bill, W. H. Kitson reiterated the argument Neville had made before the Moseley inquiry, that coloured people would not object to their new status under the law because they were to be referred to as 'natives', not 'Aborigines'. This semantic diplomacy did not cut with those who were affected. It was the year when strikes spearheaded by the coloured populations of Queensland and protest movements in every state were already shifting the territory of Aboriginal affairs.

The effect of this law was that families were torn apart, because those who were not defined as 'natives' were not permitted on reserves, and were not permitted to cohabit. The CPA—now the Commissioner of Native Affairs—became the guardian of all native children, had extensive powers of removal and control of native wages and property, could enforce medical examinations and treatment, and was empowered to authorise all native marriages.

In 1938, shortly before his retirement in 1940, Neville undertook his first inspection of Aboriginal institutions in other states. He was hopeful that the recent conference on Aboriginal welfare would result in policies hastening the eventual absorption of the mixed population in the white community. The mixed Aboriginal population in Western Australia was now well over 4,000. The introduction of 'quadroon' and 'octoroon' in official nomenclature represents the high point of discrimination according to blood. Still, the Australian nomenclature never developed into the meticulous lexicon that had been inherited and developed in the United States from the Spanish and French, because blood or descent were merely acronyms for cultural identity.

ASIANS AND ABORIGINAL POLICY IN THE NORTHERN TERRITORY

In the Northern Territory Aboriginal policy developed later than in the other two northern states. Because it was able to draw on the Queensland and Western Australian models of administration, the considerations leading to administrative or legal amendments are less explicitly documented. Still, the impact of the Asian presence on such laws and policies is apparent.

In the spirit of the Letters Patent issued for the colony of South Australia in 1836, the administration of Aborigines was unobtrusive until 1910–11. Until then, Acts affecting Aborigines were mostly in the criminal justice area, with a few exceptions: the *Northern Territory Crown Lands Act 1890* (No. 501 of 1890) empowered the governor to grant land to Aborigines, and also specified that 'no Asiatic alien shall be entitled to acquire the fee simple of any land in the Northern Territory'. The *Opium Act 1895* forbade the supply of opium to Aborigines, and an amendment in 1905 outlawed opium altogether. The supply of liquor to Aborigines was prohibited in 1908.

When the Commonwealth took over the administration of the Territory, it swept with a new broom. Just a year before bowing out of the Northern Territory, and preparing the way for a hand-over, the South Australian

Parliament passed its first comprehensive Aboriginal legislation, the *Northern Territory Aborigines Act 1910*. This was followed by an *Aborigines Act 1911* that no longer affected the Northern Territory. The 1910 Act largely followed the Queensland model, with a system of reserves, and a CPA whose duty was to protect Aborigines against immorality, injustice, imposition and fraud. As in the 1901 amendment in Queensland, the CPA's permission was required for marriages between Aboriginal women and non-Aboriginal men, and the CPA assumed curatorship of Aboriginal property.

Like the Western Australian Act, it specified that the CPA was the legal guardian of all Aborigines and 'all half-caste children'. It also specifically forbade Aboriginal camping in townships and made provision for the declaration of prohibited areas into which Aborigines were not allowed. It had no anti-Chinese or anti-Asian clause (until 1928), and it made no provision for exemptions from the Act until 1936 (revokable exemptions for 'half-castes'). This became incorporated with the federal government's *Aboriginals Ordinance 1911*, which enlarged the group for whom the CPA was responsible by including 'half-castes' among those whom he could control if in his opinion it was desirable to do so.

These powers were reiterated in the *Aboriginals Ordinance 1918*. 'Half-castes' were generally not under the Ordinance, but were deemed to be Aboriginal if they were living with Aboriginal spouses, or habitually associated with Aborigines, or were under nineteen, or were 'female half-castes' living with European spouses without being legally married. In 1927 the definition of Aboriginal was further extended to include 'half-caste males above 21 years who in the opinion of the protector were incapable of managing their own affairs'. During the twenty-nine years that it was in force, the *Aboriginals Ordinance* was amended fifteen times, sometimes twice in a year. It is not likely that the people who were governed by it could have kept up with the changes in law.

Anti-Asian provisions were added to the Ordinance in 1928. It now excluded 'any person of any Asiatic or Negro race' from employing female Aborigines. Sexual intercourse with Aboriginal females outside marriage became an offence for all non-Aborigines in 1936. The vast Arnhem Land Aboriginal reserve was declared in 1931 in an attempt to prevent the landing of unauthorised luggers and the mixing with Asian crews.

In the 1930s Japanese recruited heavily in Arnhem Land, and the distinctions between foreign fleets and Australian ones staffed by Japanese became blurred. The number of Japanese sampans rose steadily from two in 1931 to a peak of 175 in 1938. Their fleets were staffed by crews 'of adventurous types from Formosa and the outer islands of the Japanese empire'. In the early 1930s a number of reports of misbehaviour of Japanese crews concerned the Japanese authorities.[99] The foreign fleets were held responsible for many instances of conflict with Aborigines, though the demonstrated cases reaching the authorities tended to be perpetrated by Darwin luggers.

Aborigines often complained about Japanese displaying an instrumental attitude to women that violated indigenous ethics. An elder at Minjilang, whose father had made several journeys to Makassar, candidly admitted that in the lugger days they used to have 'girlfriends all over the place' but the *Nagasaki* carried Japanese prostitutes, shamelessly exhibited and traded as wares.[100] David Burrumarra recalled an incident at Rrunhawu, where Japanese had demanded access to women, and were about to be killed by Djingulul and his nephew Nyambi, when Nyambi's father Ganimbirrngu intervened and spoke to them in Makasar language which they seemed to understand. The Japanese, whose canoe had already been taken off them, were thankful for their rescue and left gifts of cloth and tinned tobacco.[101] He said that by the time the Japanese started to recruit in Arnhem Land he was already so used to Asians that he had no hesitation to go with them.[102]

A number of well-publicised attacks on Japanese crews occurred, and it was generally agreed that these were occasioned by Japanese demands on Aboriginal women. Nemarluk, a well-known Murinbata man famous as a bushranger, was held responsible for the killing of three Japanese crew of the *Ouida* in Treachery Bay at Fitzmaurice River in August 1931. 'The predilection of the Japanese crew for Aboriginal women—used in this instance to gain the strangers' confidence—was motive enough.'[103] In June 1932 a group of Japanese were killed at Port Keats (viz.).[104]

In September 1932 five Japanese on the *Myrtle Olga* and *Raff* under the charge of Kamishima were killed at Caledon Bay. Only one of the six Japanese crew members was able to escape, and the eight Tiwi and Gumatji crew were unharmed. Again the attack was presumed to result from an argument over women. Ted Egan, who has researched this incident most exhaustively, somewhat mediates this explanation with the observation that it appeared to be a dispute over how long the Japanese were to be granted access to certain women. He believes the attack was a direct result of the demeaning treatment doled out by the Japanese to Wonggu, a tribal elder, in this dispute.

The Japanese victims received little sympathy from the white community, but to fulfil their obligations, the police undertook an investigation. During this expedition one of the police officers was killed at Woodah Island, and it was this incident that brought the Caledon 'massacre' to wide attention. To head off a police revenge party, a 'peace expedition' of missionaries was organised. It appears that Fred Gray, a trepanger at Caledon Bay, was the only person showing an interest in bringing the attackers of the Japanese to Darwin. He seemed to have an idea that some kind of *makarrta* (treaty) could be struck between Balanda and Yolngu justice. If that was the intention, as Egan suggests, it was a bad miscalculation. Three sons of Wonggu presented themselves for 'talk longa big boss' and were sentenced to twenty years prison each, but provided good behaviour by themselves and their tribe, they were to be released after four years.[105] For killing police constable McColl, who was found to have also interfered with Aboriginal women, Dhakiyara Wirrpanda (Tuckiar) was sentenced to death. He was later pardoned and released from prison but disappeared shortly after his release. Egan presumes that vengeful police officers were responsible for his death.[106]

Fred Gray at age ninety-four in Darwin recalled that Aki Kinju, the survivor of the Caledon Bay killings, came to say goodbye to him in 1956. The Japanese involved had been in Australia for quite a long time and spoke passable English. They had already had an affray at Port Bradshaw, firing at Aborigines to keep them out of their camp. He said they had good relations with the people of

Melville Island and the north coast, but were not used to dealing with the 'Caledons' who were 'notorious for cleaning up many boats'. Gray had met skipper Kamishima in Darwin, while working for jeweller Charles Ellies (viz.). It was the Darwin Japanese who taught Gray where and how to fish for trepang. This explains why Gray felt it important that the Japanese deaths came to trial.[107]

During the proceedings over the Caledon Bay and Woodah Island killings, Lt-Col. R. H. Weddell, the Territory's administrator, referred to the 'Caledon Bay Aboriginals of Japanese and Macassar strain of superior mentality'.[108] Several attacks on vessels had occurred within a few years in that area. In one of these incidents Clara Dilyera, a Mara woman from Borroloola, was captured by the Djapu of Caledon Bay from a Japanese crew. Clara's son, also on the vessel, was killed. This woman warned Gray on the day of the killing of impending trouble. She later became the first wife of David Burrumarra.[109]

The Caledon Bay and Woodah Island incident had long reverberations. Charles Rowley notes that government support for Ted Strehlow and Donald Thomson, who were both to play prominent advisory roles for the Northern Territory administration Aborigines, 'came largely as the result of the events surrounding the Tuckiar case'.[110] Thomson reported extensively on the impact of pearling, 'which was very different, he thought, from the long-established contacts with the Arafura world through the Malays' and on 'Japanese policy of giving large presents to Aborigines at a particular spot so that they would continue to assemble there with their women'. Rowley recognises that the lugger industries moved Aboriginal affairs along: 'It is significant that the disorders with which the government was mainly concerned occurred at the points of contact with industrial economy, mainly at the re-fuelling and watering points along the coast.'[111] Rowley also links the case to changes in Western Australia, where inquiries by Moseley and Bleakley initiated legislative change in 1936.[112]

The Northern Territory *Welfare Ordinance 1953* replaced the *Aboriginals Ordinance*. It repealed all exemptions that had been made under the old Ordinance and established instead a 'Register of Wards' to list all 'full-blood Aborigines' and those deemed to require protection. The register was never completed and caused much confusion (viz. Tex Camfoo). The administration's strong emphasis on 'full-bloods' continues to predominate in the minds of older Aborigines today, who tend to relegate mixed descendants to the realm of non-Aborigines (viz. Larry Ahlin).

As in the other two northern states, Northern Territory Aboriginal policy was influenced by the presence of Asians. This is further explored with reference to Darwin in Chapter 5. On the whole, Northern Territory Aborigines fared better than those of the two other northern states. White settlement was delayed and much sparser, and caused less displacement, and the long-distance style of government afforded a buffer from squatter interests. Aborigines in adjacent parts of the other two states often sheltered from the more rigorous administrations through border crossings (viz. Doomadgee). It was in the Territory that the veil of dispossession was first lifted with the *Aboriginal Land Rights (Northern Territory) Act 1976*, enacted before 'responsible government' for a new state could turn back the clock.

Fred Gray, latter-day trepanger and Aboriginal protector. Gray was for many years in charge of Umbakumba Station at Groote Eylandt. He played a key role in the Caledon Bay inquiry. Photographed shortly before his death, at age ninety-four, Darwin, 1995.

Tex Camfoo: confusion

The story of Tex and Nellie Camfoo is a love story entrapped in identity politics. Tex was born around 1922 at Roper Bar as Harry Kamfu, the son of Chinese Jimmy Jenkins Kamfu. His early childhood was divided between time spent with his Aboriginal mother Florida and her older Aboriginal husband Powerjack (Nanyengaluk) in a semi-nomadic lifestyle, and staying at Roper Valley with his Chinese father and stepmother Lily, a Malakan woman from Hodson Downs. At age eight, Tex was taken to the CMS mission school at Roper River, and from there to the 'half-caste institution' at Groote Eylandt, where the Reverend Warren renamed Harry as Jimmy. He thinks the price of his education was high:

> A lot of us didn't know our father and mother, didn't know where we were, it took us four or five years to come back to our own family. Lost our languages, lost our mother and father, we didn't know, maybe five or six [years] we were at Groote Eylandt. Some of them cried and cried and wanted to go back to mainland, so they took them [us] back to Roper. [At age twelve or thirteen Tex was returned to Roper together with Bill Huddlestone.] My mother knew I was there, well she showed up and I was frightened of her because I didn't know anybody, because all that years at Groote Eylandt made me forget all my mother, forget my father.

Tex wanted to become a stockman, but at the missionary's request, he learned carpentry and worked around the mission at fencing and carpentry. After a big flood the old mission at Roper River was shifted to an elevated site at Ngukurr. Tex was recruited into army service and married Ruth, an Aboriginal woman with whom he had four children. But he was gravitating towards the woman of his life. He had first met Nellie when she was only a girl, and he was about fifteen.

> I found Nellie when she was only about this high, she was blond, and I looked at her, and I said 'this will be my wife', and somehow I fell in love with her. Anyhow, I never seen her again till about till she was somewhere about twenty-six. But it kept on my mind—Nellie, Nellie, all the time.

He was working 'all over the place' and earned the name 'Tex' as a rodeo rider. He worked as a stockman at Ted Collins' Beswick Station, as camp overseer on Knuckle Downs, on the railways in Katherine, as head stockman and overseer at Urapanga, and in the Pine Creek mines. Once during a flight to Katherine he took sick, and the plane had to stop at Mainoru. Nellie was there:

> She was married to a fellow—well not married, promised wife, Aboriginal wife—and I looked at her and she looked at me—and—oh, she knew me from way back when she was a little girl. Well, this old fellow, he had two wives, Nellie's sister Dolly, and anyhow, after a while—he was my brother in Aboriginal way, this old Larry—anyhow me and Nellie got together again, we started off you know fall in love and things like that and old Larry said [to her] 'Oh, well, I can't do nothing, he's my brother, you might as well go.'

But releasing Nellie from her promised husband was the smaller obstacle. The Welfare Department (formerly Department of Native Affairs) objected to his re-marriage. The dispute lasted for several years, with threats of prosecution for bigamy. Eventually it was found that his marriage to Ruth had not been registered because it had been celebrated by an unregistered parson. (Many marriages celebrated on missions were not legally binding.) He was informed that the department could not prevent his re-marriage, but it nonetheless meted out some on-the-spot intimidation:

> It went on like that, anyhow they came up and told me 'You're not married'. They had a look in that big book of European marriage with Aboriginal woman. And they found out my name wasn't in there. They said 'We could arrest you now here'—there was a copper alongside, too—but they didn't want to do it. So I ended up marrying in the Presbyterian Church in Katherine, officially now. But I always wonder how I waited and waited and waited till we got married. It took us that long.

To this day, Tex is uncertain of the grounds on which the department really objected to his re-marriage. Bigamy was raised as an issue, but he thinks it was because he was classed as a European, and Europeans were not to marry Aborigines.

> When Native Affairs—he came out getting all the census [Register of Wards], he said 'Your name not here, you're not an Aboriginal, you're a European because your father's a European'. Chinese they haven't got all that, all the laws that Native Affairs had. He said, 'but we keep it a secret'. And nobody knew, even I. Now I know.

To class Chinese with Europeans is more typical of Aboriginal people than of European administrators, but whatever terms the protector may have used, it was brought home to Tex that legally he was 'not Aboriginal'.

What was at issue? If an objection were made to the marriage on the basis of race, it should have equally

The Camfoo family. Nellie and Tex Camfoo at Bulman, with their daughter Christine Camfoo and some of Christine's grand-children, May 1995.

been made to Tex's first marriage with an Aboriginal woman. The department, however, tried to insist on the legality of the first marriage. The department was able to turn a blind eye on polygynous arrangements in what was considered traditional Aboriginal society, such as the sororal polygyny of Nellie, Dolly and Larry. But it certainly sought to stamp out polygamy among those who had been mission-educated.

The admission that a formal objection could not be made to the marriage came cloaked as a collusion: 'let's keep it a secret'. Tex was made to feel that he 'got away with it', an Asian–Aboriginal marrying an Aboriginal woman—not once, but twice.[113]

Tex and Nellie live close to Bulman settlement, at the southern edge of Arnhem Land. Nellie is a highly respected traditional owner, and their house was erected in 1991 on the site of a mine abandoned in 1971. It sits on dangerous terrain where many exposed mineshafts are potential traps for cattle, dogs or children, but it is Nellie's country, and they are content to be there after a working life that took them from Finniss River to Alice Springs.

CONCLUSIONS

In more ways than one, Asians in Australia are implicated in the Stolen Generation. Their presence in large numbers, economic competition with white entrepreneurs, and interactions with Aborigines, gave a strong impulse to Aboriginal protection legislation. Queensland's 1897 Act was transmogrified through successive amendments and adaptations in the two other northern states from a general protective intent towards an increasing obsession with the control of mixed populations. The story of Atima Ahwang is instructive in this context, because in her case file this preoccupation is stated quite candidly.

The experience of the north continued to exert a strong influence on Aboriginal protection legislation. It was the experience of a coloured population, bridging the definable populations of Asians and Aborigines, located in the grey area of the department's reach, and resisting its paternalistic embrace.

Aboriginal protection became the flipside of Asian exclusion. If Asians could not be excluded from pearling, then Aborigines had to be excluded from the creeks, prevented from working on boats, and barred from employment by Asians. If Asians dominated the pearling ports, then Aborigines were evicted from the townships. The increasing concern with a mixed population was based on the idea that it referred 'especially to the case of Asiatics and Kanakas', to 'white men and, *of course*, Asiatics'. The mixed population was larger in the southern parts of Western Australia and Queensland, but in the north it was mixed with Asians, and it was the north that attracted the missions and government stations to deal with the 'problem'.

The mixed population was a problem because it made nonsense of the expectation that, bowing to the force of evolution, Aborigines would die out. For the longest time the bureaucracies sought to distinguish between Aborigines who were 'of the full descent' and those who were not. In the schema of the survival of the fittest the latter should have been seen as the adaptors, the survivors—the fittest. But paradoxically, it was often concluded from comprehensive inquiry that they needed the most protection, while the former might best be left alone. In practice, much of the bureaucracy's energy was spent on eugenic management—authorising marriages, persecuting cohabitation, delineating Aboriginal-free and Aboriginal-only zones, and removing and administering mixed-descent children.

Associating and 'cohabiting' with Asians was by definition an immoral practice for Aborigines, and Aboriginal children of Asian descent were targeted for removal. Some of the stories presented here suggest that Asian–Aboriginal children were more likely to be removed if their parents attempted to live together as a family unit. Cohabitation was an offence under the *Protection Acts* and attracted departmental attention. Those who were abandoned by their Asian fathers had a better chance of being left with their mothers.

We might say that coloured people represented the convergence of two 'problem populations'. Ros Kidd characterised the policy stance towards Aborigines in Queensland as a medical–moral policing rationale, intent on addressing medical and moral issues, but forever knitting them together into a tight complex in the eugenicist language of the nineteenth and early twentieth centuries, which constructed the very idea of 'moral feebleness' in genetic terms.[114] Judith Allen earlier analysed the governmental management of women in such terms. Indeed, it encapsulates well the attitude towards Asians. Anxiety about the Chinese was expressed as illicit sexual relations, unsanitary and crowded housing conditions, and concerns over smallpox, leprosy, opium addiction and gambling, couched in the moral lexicon of filth, laziness and lasciviousness. Like Aborigines, Asians were a problem population subject to a medical–moral policing rationale. Worried about Asians, and worried about Aborigines, and having its white hegemony challenged by the coloured population in the north, the anxious nation was struck at the heart by Asian–Aboriginal families.

In April 1937 the state and federal administrators met for the first time to compare notes on Aboriginal affairs. There was a wide agreement that the 'half-caste' population was a prominent problem. The overall vision was that 'full-blood' Aborigines needed to be contained and segregated, and the mixed population, by now strongly politicised and organised, somehow absorbed. This became the policy of assimilation.

Gradually, and almost imperceptibly, the term 'half-caste' drifted out of legislation in all states, following the Western Australian example of 1936. Queensland's *Aboriginals Preservation and Protection Act 1939* adopted the term 'half-blood'. The last of many amendments to the Northern Territory *Aboriginal Ordinance 1953* extended the meaning of 'Aboriginal' and omitted the term 'half-caste' but allowed the director of Native Affairs to declare 'part-Aboriginals'. Later in the same year the *Welfare Ordinance 1953* which repealed the *Aborigines Ordinance* referred only to 'wards'. Queensland's *Aborigines and Torres Strait Islanders Affairs Act 1965* followed suit with the term 'part Aborigine', until the *Aborigines Act 1971* declared an Aborigine to be 'a descendant of an indigenous inhabitant of the Commonwealth of Australia other than the Torres Strait Islands'. The disappearance of the 'half-caste' was greatly welcomed in Aboriginal politics. Still, it retains some resilience among old-timers as a general reference to mixed descendants.

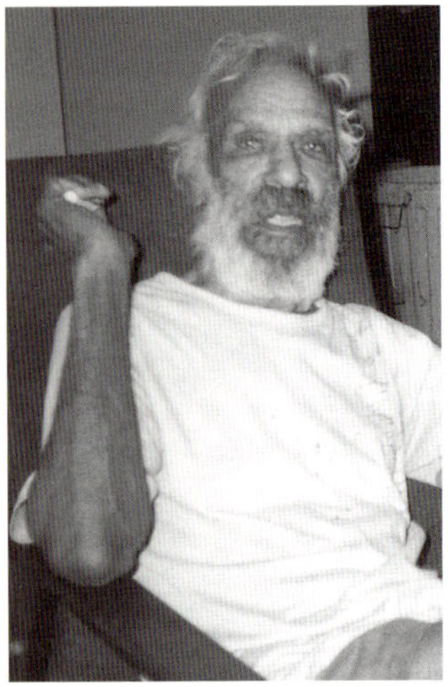

Larry Ahlin.

Larry Ahlin on being 'half-caste'

Larry Ahlin has found it difficult to construct a viable Asian–Aboriginal identity. He continues to describe himself as a 'half-caste', an identity that expresses the sum of his life experiences. He was born in 1927 as the son of Laurrie Wynwylkba (Jinjakba), a Jawoyn Aboriginal woman, and Wong Ah Lin, a Hakka Chinese recruited in Singapore for the construction of the Darwin–Katherine railway. Wong Ah Lin settled in Katherine as a saddler, and then moved to Pine Creek with his Aboriginal wife. Shortly afterwards their two children were taken away.

It is possible that this removal was a result of the agitation of Pine Creek community in 1933 protests against 'a number of part-coloured children' attending the local school which catered for three white and eleven Chinese children. Tim Jones writes: 'The parents of the former refused to let their children attend and this resulted in the police taking action. . . The problem was solved by moving the part-coloured children to Alice Springs.'[115]

Larry and his younger sister were first taken to Kahlin Compound in Darwin, and when this became a girls home, Larry was sent to the Bungalow in Alice Springs. Larry's life became a stripping away of layers of identity. As a ward of the state, Larry was separated from his family, physically, emotionally and legally. Like others in similar circumstances, he had no chance of an inheritance. He says he has very little recollection of his parents. He remembers fossicking for gold with his father, who spoke little English and was very 'growly': 'he simply loved the colour of gold'. Larry found out from the Northern Territory Archives that Wong Ah Lin is buried at Brock's Creek. Brock's Creek Chinatown was the largest Chinese community in the Northern Territory, numbering about 400 in 1886.

Larry reflects positively on the education provided to him as a mixed descendant: 'I had a good scholarship, that's one thing I can say about the government at the time, we had some of the best teachers that were ever brought up from South Australia.'

Encouraged by his academic success, Larry strained for a mainstream identity. He enrolled at the Sydney Technical Institute and became an understudy in journalism. But his private life was in disarray. When he married an Inverell girl of part-Indian descent, he found her family so narrow-minded and colour-conscious that it impacted on his relationship. He enlisted for the Korean War and served with the 3rd Battalion Royal Australian Regiment, a unit which receved a United States Presidential Citation for its actions during the Battle of Kapyong in 1952. During his twelve months in South Korea, where Chinese armies fought on the North Korean side, he must have been confronted with the wartime rhetoric of the American and Australian troops demonising the Chinese enemy. As the son of a Chinese miner, he may have found a large part of his identity under challenge.

After his active military service he returned to Pine Creek where he felt in all respects an outsider. His mother's six sisters filled him in on some family details, and that his mother worried about him while he was away, and died of a broken heart:

> They couldn't hold anything from me, they had to tell me, but they didn't accept me then because I was a half-caste,

and they still don't. They tolerate you but not accept you. And that's the way it is all the way throughout the Northern Territory now.

This was the conclusion he drew from his experience in Aboriginal politics in Katherine. During his six years as chairman of the Jawoyn Association, BHP embarked on the Coronation Hill project to mine gold, platinum and palladium on Jawoyn land. Seeing himself as coming from a mining background, he supported the venture, but the Northern Land Council (NLC) opposed it. Larry's legitimacy as an Aboriginal political representative became contested:

> I felt that I didn't have the right to be there being a half-caste. I was going to hand over to a full-blood Aboriginal and let them handle it themselves, because it was theirs, it wasn't mine. It may have been from my mother's side but then again, at the time they were saying that the half-caste was a non-entity, and you either have to be an Aboriginal—and I couldn't see the enormity of any of it.

Larry's construction of himself is a disappearing trick—the categories he uses to order the world leave no space for himself. 'I don't want to use the word "Aboriginal", because I don't classify myself as one. I'll always be a half-caste, that's the way I see it.'

His primary social affiliation is with his maternal relatives at Binjari, a group that contests the ambit leadership claim of the NLC and settled at an excision south of Katherine. At Binjari the political contest with the NLC is constructed not as an issue of local sovereignty against the large NLC bureaucracy, nor as an issue of appropriate development and lifestyle, but primarily as an issue of 'full-bloods' versus 'half-castes'. Land councils are seen as a phenomenon of the latter. At the time of my visit in 1994 Binjari was advised and financially supported by the Country Party.

Based on the experience of Binjari, Larry sees the Aboriginal future in a retreat to racial purity:

> If the full-blood Aboriginals break away, the half-castes won't have any identification . . . Leave them alone, and they'll do their own thing . . . They want to be left alone, they don't want to be interfered with by Land councils. [At Binjari] They've got big notices stuck all around their community . . . The mixed-bloods are confusing the whole issue because the full-bloods have retreated to be by themselves, because they want no part of them . . . The full-blood Aboriginal now is more or less retreating to themselves. They don't want no part of mixed breed. That's the way it was from the early days.

Accepting this hierarchy of blood, Larry is in an identity vacuum. He constructs himself as non-Aboriginal, mixed descendants as an enemy of the Aboriginal cause, and labels himself as a half-caste, a category which has long been erased from legal existence.

> 'But where does that leave people like yourself?'
> 'Me? It doesn't hurt me one little bit.'
> 'But there are lots of people like yourself, aren't there? You're not in a minority.'
> 'No, I'm not in a minority, and I don't want them. I want to do my own thing. I know what I'm doing and that's the way I want it, because I don't think I'm going to last long, anyway.'

He lives alongside white old-timers who see him, as they always have, as an Aborigine.

CHAPTER 5

Ethnic policy and practice in Darwin

by Julia Martinez

MIXED relations between the Aboriginal and Asian communities in Darwin formed and endured in the face of a largely antagonistic white administration. Asian immigrants were originally brought to Darwin by the South Australian colonial administration, but with the advent of the White Australia policy, there began a regime of restrictions intended to segregate the community into ethnic enclaves and limit the increasing mixed population. The impact of segregation policies was considerable, but despite this, Darwin gained a reputation as a town where everyone mixed together. The segregationists may have held power, but those in favour of a mixed society were in the majority. By the late 1920s Darwin's anti-segregation lobby began to be felt as a political force, but only some aspects of mixed relations were sanctioned. Those of mixed Aboriginal–Asian descent were able to gain significant freedoms, but for many Aboriginal people inter-ethnic relations remained restricted, being officially constructed as inappropriate and even illegal.

COLONISATION AND ASIAN IMMIGRATION

The land that would later become known as Darwin, the capital of the Northern Territory, is Larrakia country. The Larrakia lived in the area now known as central Darwin in various camp sites on the beaches and cliffs. The neighbouring areas were home to the Djerimanga ('Woolner' or 'Woolna') and Kingarakan ('Warnunger').[1] In establishing the town of Darwin (then Palmerston) in 1869 the South Australian colonial government imposed British rule on the local Aboriginal peoples. Having mapped out the region, George Woodroffe Goyder, the surveyor-general, pointed out in his government report that from the indigenous perspective the intended settlement would appear as an 'unauthorised and unwarranted occupation' of Aboriginal land. The acknowledgment of Aboriginal opinion did nothing, however, to deter the colonisation process.

White colonists brought Asian workers to Darwin, so it was in the process of colonisation that the local indigenous peoples met Asians from the Philippines, Singapore, Hong Kong, China, Japan and the Dutch East Indies. One of the first experiences of Aboriginal–Asian relations was between the immigrant Malay and Chinese and indigenous peoples, working together as servants of the colonial elite. In British colonial culture, 'eastern' servants were considered necessary to preserve the prestige and comfort of the colonists. Aboriginal servants were incorporated into this social structure, generally taking on the more arduous or menial tasks. By 1872, with the connection of the London–Australia telegraph line, the staff of the British–Australian Telegraph Company saw to it that this colonial culture was enforced. According to Douglas Lockwood:

> They were Englishmen to the bootstraps who brought their servants from the East. The officers and their ladies rode around in private buggies . . . At night they had Aborigines walking ahead to light their way.[2]

In 1879, the population of the Territory, not including the large Aboriginal population, was put at 460 Europeans, thirty Malays and 3,406 Chinese.[3] Ten 'Malays' had been brought from Singapore in 1874 by Captain Douglas along with the 186 Chinese. Some of the Malays were employed by private individuals and some engaged as the crew of the government cutter *Flying Cloud*.[4] Sowden, writing in 1882, described the Malay crews of the government luggers as 'excellent boatmen' and 'merry fellows'.[5] Most of the Chinese in the Northern Territory were on the gold fields to the south of Darwin, but it was their industry which supported the development of a Chinese commercial centre in Darwin.

It was not until after 1884, with the discovery of pearl shell in Port Darwin, that divers and crew were brought from Japan, the Philippines and nearby Kupang in Timor.[6] The discovery of pearl shell prompted a rush of pearling boats from the Torres Straits, but the industry was abandoned within three years.[7] By 1898, pearling was re-established and the population had become even more ethnically diverse.[8] There were approximately 300 Japanese, most of whom worked in the pearling trade, three owning luggers, while others included 'miners, carpenters, boarding-house keepers, cooks, servants, a doctor and twenty or more prostitutes'.[9] Little is known of the relationship between the early pearlers and the local Aboriginal people. At least some of the Filipino and Malay pearlers remained in Darwin and married Aboriginal women. For example, Antonio Cubillo's ten children with Lily McKeddie established the Cubillo clan, a well-known family in Darwin.[10] In the early years there was relative freedom of movement between the Aboriginal and Asian communities. With the advent of Federation and the White Australia policy, however, there began a period of restrictive administration which dramatically altered the future of ethnic relations in Darwin.

ASIANS AND ABORIGINAL POLICY IN DARWIN

When the federal Labor government took over the Northern Territory in 1911 it immediately implemented policies aimed at racial segregation. The freedom of both Asian and Aboriginal people was regarded as an inherent problem, threatening the future of White Australia. The notion that a mixed society ought to be racially divided was also accepted British colonial policy. Writing in 1914, Elsie Masson, a visitor to Government House, stated that the 'little worlds' of Darwin separated the society along racial lines, with the four main worlds belonging to the white officialdom, Chinatown, the pearling fleets and the 'native' camps.[11]

In 1911 the total population of Darwin was 1,387, with the largest ethnic group being the Chinese numbering 442, including seventy-eight females. The next largest group was the 374 Europeans. The total Aboriginal population was 305 but, using the racial categories of the period, these were divided into 'full-blooded Aboriginals', numbering 145 males and 102 females, and 'half-caste Aboriginals', numbering thirty males and twenty-eight females. The pearling fleets, with crews made up of Asian men, were indicated to be seventy-seven Japanese, fifty-two Filipinos, forty-nine Timorese, twenty-one Malays, seven Javanese, four Siamese, five Singhalese, and five South Sea Islanders.[12] The federal government initiated separate policies relating to each of the three so-called 'coloured' groups, all aimed at limiting, segregating and controlling their populations.

The Kahlin Compound

The federal administration first targeted the Aboriginal population, bringing 'a rigid regulation' to their lives.[13] The *Aboriginals Ordinance 1911* outlined a system in which the CPA would have control over every facet of the lives of Aboriginal people.[14] The central aim was to establish an essentially white population in Darwin and the Aboriginal population was to be kept available to act as servants of the white elite. In 1911 there were 125 Aboriginal workers employed in Darwin, according to the report of J. T. Beckett, inspector of Aboriginals.[15]

The federal government appointed anthropologist, Baldwin Spencer, as CPA in 1912.[16] As a so-called 'expert', his reports were not questioned. He argued that the Aboriginal population of Darwin had 'long since become degenerate' and had 'lost all their old customs and beliefs'.[17] This assessment was given in an attempt to justify his plan to remove the Aboriginal camps from around Darwin and to establish one centralised living area, the Kahlin Compound. The compound was 2.5 kilometres out of town, at the site of the present Cullen Bay Marina. According to Tony Austin, its purpose was to control the movements of the Aboriginal population and to do away with camps closer to town that offended authorities' 'sense of aesthetics and hygiene'. Austin explains that the location was far enough from town to isolate the Aborigines and yet close enough for them to walk to work.[18] Spencer reported:

> Genuine wild natives would be miserable away from their own country, but in the case of a heterogeneous crowd, such as is now gathered together in Darwin, there was no need to pay any heed to this matter. They have all long since got beyond any traditional feeling.[19]

There and gone within a year, Spencer did not stay to see the results of his decisions. The next Chief Protector, W. G. Stretton, wrote in 1913: 'It has been a difficult matter to induce the different tribes to amalgamate and fraternise.'[20]

The effect of shifting the Aboriginal population to the Kahlin Compound had a significant impact on the local Aboriginal people. The main camp site for Larrakia people had been at Lameroo Beach, in central Darwin. In 1936, years later, representatives, who described themselves as 'salt-water' people, explained that they had been told the compound land was given to them. They objected to 'members of other tribes camping and living at the compound', arguing that as a result of this forced mixing, their children were not learning their language, but a mixture of various languages and English.[21] Thus when speaking of the Aboriginal community in Darwin after 1912 it should be recognised that this was already a heterogeneous group, including indigenous peoples from all around the Northern Territory.

Chinatown

The second part of government policy was to reduce the Asian population by encouraging the Chinese to leave Australia. Darwin Chinese were mostly from southern China or Hong Kong and were loosely referred to as 'Cantonese'.[22] Studies by Diana Giese, Suzi Hutchings and others have shown that the dialect groups included Sze Yap and Heung-san and some Hakka.[23] There were clear class distinctions within the Chinese community, with better-off merchants and storekeepers who had sufficient money to travel to China and many poorer Chinese who struggled to survive, working in a variety of labouring jobs. Government policies were focused on the labouring class.

Administrative reports claimed that Chinatown was an unsightly slum, where cramped and unhygienic living conditions endangered public health. These reports were used to order the demolition of several dwellings in Chinatown in 1913. The second strategy used to reduce the Chinese population was to block access to employment. In 1911 Chinese and other Asians were banned from employment in government works, waterside work and fishing. With no source of income, many were forced to leave. Those who were too poor to leave were given free passage to Hong Kong. A group of Chinese, Malay and Filipino residents of Chinatown refused to leave and were offered land at a site two miles from the centre, in the police paddocks, later known simply as Police Paddock.[24] Many of these were ex-pearlers, like Antonio Cubillo, who had married Aboriginal women and made Darwin their permanent home. The administrator, Dr John Gilruth, acknowledged that he had no legal authority to deport those who were unwilling to leave, given that they had arrived in Australia before the 1901 law. Despite many departures, the Chinese population remained steady over the next decade due to the large number of children being born. By 1933 their numbers had decreased slightly, but with an increased white population they made up only 20 per cent of the population.[25] This figure fell to just 10 per cent by 1941.[26]

Pearling camps

The presence of Asian pearling crews in Darwin was also the target of federal intervention. In 1911 there were 138 men employed on pearling luggers. The *Immigration Restriction Act 1901* had granted an exemption to the pearling industry so that it might continue to import Asian divers and crews.[27] In 1912, however, the Fisher Labor government decreed that no licences would be issued to pearlers unless both the divers and tenders were Europeans. A royal commission was appointed, headed by F. W. Bamford, to investigate the industry. With the election of the Liberal government in 1913, new commissioners were appointed and it was finally decided in 1916 that the industry would be allowed to continue employing Asian labour.[28] Nevertheless, the decision was based on the assumption that there would be very little contact between the indentured Asians and the rest of the community as the crews would spend little time on shore.[29] Such restrictions overlooked the association of pearling crews with the Aboriginal population.

Darwin Chinatown.

Photo: National Archives of Australia.

Chinese employers

Legislation aimed at preventing the association between the Chinese and Aboriginal communities was enacted in the *Aboriginals Ordinance 1911*. Federal policy relating to the employment of Aboriginal servants was ostensibly concerned to 'protect' the workers from 'inappropriate' employers. Employment by 'Asiatics' was described as being detrimental for Aboriginal people, the association having supposedly 'debased and rendered them vicious, cunning and untrustworthy'. It was argued that women were 'ruined physically and morally' in Chinese employment.[30] The outgoing South Australian administrator, S. J. Mitchell, claimed that 'Asiatic' employers were supplying their Aboriginal workers with opium and alcohol by way of payment.[31]

These arguments, with all their exaggerated racial stereotyping, found their way into the legislation. Baldwin Spencer, a fierce opponent of the Chinese, declared: 'There are a few decent ones but 98 per cent are low depraved beasts who want deporting.'[32] He proclaimed Chinatown to be a prohibited area for Aboriginal people. He planned to issue 'special permits in the form of brass discs' that would enable Aboriginal servants to enter a prohibited area only when sent on business by their white employer.[33]

The decision to prevent 'Asiatics' from employing Aboriginal servants was queried by Mitchell who believed that some treated their employees as well as Europeans.[34] In 1911 seven Chinese storekeepers and trades people protested to Mitchell: 'Many of us have had the blackboys in our employ for years and have always treated them well and the boys do not want to leave us. This will work a great hardship on us.' These Chinese had been resident in Darwin for an average of thirty years, that is, since 1880.[35] Again in 1912, the Chinese petitioned Baldwin Spencer. Their solicitor argued that they were 'as fit as the average European to employ natives'.[36] A petition was sent by twenty-seven prominent white business people to Josiah Thomas, the Minister for External Affairs, asking for Section 24 of the *Aboriginals Ordinance* to be revised. But the federal Labor government declined to reconsider the prohibition.[37]

Night curfew

In 1918, with the introduction of the revised *Aboriginals Ordinance*, the character of the Kahlin Compound became more restrictive. H. E. Carey, CPA, argued that greater control could be exercised over the association between the Asian and Aboriginal communities if Aboriginal domestic servants were forced to return each night to sleep in the Kahlin Compound. He wrote that, with the present system of allowing Aboriginal servants to sleep on the premises of their employers,

> the difficulty of keeping the aboriginal from loneliness, especially when working hours are over, and yet of preventing him or her from the contamination of evil companions, still exists. While there is a place like the Kahlin, where the natives have much liberty, but can be kept from turning this into license; where the Protector can see they have satisfactory quarters and no unsatisfactory companions (at least of other races than their own); where they can indulge in many tribal customs

and social habits, the difficulty for both employer and employee is considerably lessened.[38]

There were 235 residents in the Kahlin Compound and they were supervised by Compound Superintendent MacDonald 'with strict and impartial discipline'.[39] From an Aboriginal perspective any form of discipline would have been unacceptable and unauthorised, but the adminstration had no sense of Aboriginal people as free agents.

In 1920 the Ordinance was revised in order to prevent Aboriginal employees from visiting Chinatown after work. A night curfew was imposed, requiring them to return to the compound within one hour after sunset.[40] The curfew went from 8 p.m. to 5 a.m.[41] During the 1930s, Chief Protector Dr Cecil Cook gave permission, published each week in the *Government Gazette*, for Aboriginal residents to attend the cinema within the prohibited area of Darwin. This exemption allowed them to stay out until 'thirty minutes after eleven o'clock'.[42] Apart from this, the curfew was strictly enforced. The 1933 Ordinance stated that any Aboriginal person found 'at large' in town one hour after sunset without written permission from their employer was guilty of an offence with a penalty of one month's imprisonment.[43] With these regulations in place, there would appear to have been little opportunity for contact between Aboriginal and Asian people, but for the fact that Aboriginal servants were generally used to run errands in the town centre.

The on-going excuse for this progressively restrictive legislation was that reiterated in the 1928 Bleakley Report, where he argued that the Kahlin Compound was too close to town 'where the presence of a large number of aliens … presented so many of the dangers'. His recommendation that a new site be found was not acted upon until 1938. By this time the population housed in the compound had increased. In 1928 there were 200 Aboriginal workers employed in Darwin, whereas by 1936 there were 348.[44] More Aboriginal people had migrated to Darwin from Melville Island, Daly River and other regions and they were encouraged to take up domestic service. At the 1937 conference held in Canberra to discuss the employment conditions of Aboriginal workers, C. L. A. Abbott, the new administrator for the Northern Territory, gave his approval to such migration, provided that those who stayed found 'work as houseboys' and were 'good workers'. Abbott reported that the demand for domestic labour could not be met by 'half-caste' institutions, despite the fact that there were a total of 279 'inmates in Government institutions'.[45] In 1938 Abbott ordered the Kahlin Compound to be demolished and the Aboriginal population were moved four miles out of Darwin to Bagot Compound. Abbott argued that the new site would 'facilitate effective control of the present aboriginal population who, in the absence of proper facilities for their segregation and housing in a selected locality, are at present residing in insanitary camps situated on beaches and in the bush in and around Darwin'.

In a further attempt to segregate the Aboriginal population from the rest of Darwin society, Abbott cancelled all permits which allowed 'aboriginals to sleep on premises' and those who worked in Darwin were put into trucks at the end of the day and 'compelled to return to the compound to sleep'.[46] The fact that the compound was no longer within easy walking distance from the centre of town made it harder to evade the regulations.

Sexual relations

Andrew Markus, writing in *Governing Savages*, emphasised the administrative concern with 'miscegenation', or 'racial' interbreeding.[47] In keeping with the White Australia policy, the government regarded the increasing 'half-caste' population as a problem. In 1912 anthropologist Baldwin Spencer advised against allowing intercourse between Aboriginal women and men of other 'races'. He stated that he would permit marriage only in cases where the two had children and had been living together for some time.[48] According to J. T. Beckett, Baldwin Spencer intended to repress the so-called 'half-caste' harems in Darwin.[49] This emphasis on the sexual relations between Aboriginal women and Asian men was a relatively new phenomenon in Darwin. In pre-Federation days, there had been five Japanese brothels in Darwin and the presence of Japanese prostitutes took some of the attention away from Aboriginal women.[50]

In order to limit the opportunity for 'miscegenation', revisions were made in the *Aboriginal Ordinance 1918*. Section 53 declared that any person who:

> (a) habitually consorts with a female aboriginal or half-caste; or
> (b) keeps a female aboriginal or half-caste as his mistress; or
> (c) unlawfully has carnal knowledge of a female aboriginal or half-caste, shall be guilty of an offence.[51]

In order to prevent such 'offences', single men who wished to employ Aboriginal servants were obliged to employ both 'husband' and 'wife' in order to qualify for a licence.[52] This did not apply to Asian employers who, though finally permitted to employ Aboriginal servants, were still banned from employing Aboriginal women (but viz. Lily Ah Toy).[53] These rules applied to all but a few Aboriginal women. Women who married men who were 'substantially European' and were living with their husbands were exempted from being defined as 'Aboriginal' under the Ordinance.[54]

The administration continued to be concerned that the numbers of 'half-castes' in the compound was growing as a result of liaisons with Asian and white men. In 1922 attempts were made to restrict the attendance of Aboriginal women at picture shows in an attempt to prevent men from escorting women home. Despite the claim that 'half-caste' numbers were increasing, the 1926 official 'Return of Halfcastes and Quadroons' in the Northern Territory listed only fifteen women for the Darwin district. They ranged in age from thirteen to forty-three and most were of Filipino or Malay descent. They were all employed as domestic servants.[55]

Journalist Jessie Litchfield paints an unsympathetic portrait of such young women. Describing the Saturday night picture show, Litchfield wrote that 'there were young half-caste girls, seductive of eye, clad in silks and satins, and reeking with scent, all giving the "Glad eye" and the "come hither" glance to white men and Malay and Philipino [sic] and Chinese alike…'[56] Her language suggests that their failure to discriminate between ethnic groups was in itself promiscuous.

The degree of administrative intervention increased again in the early 1930s. In 1932 Cook wrote a report entitled 'Half-caste problem', in which he discussed the ramifications for the White Australia policy. Cook cited the 'white' population of the Northern Territory as 2,950 and the 'half-caste' population as 852. He predicted that in twenty years the 'half-caste' population would 'have reproduced sufficiently to become a predominant part of the local population'. His recommendation was to encourage the girls to marry white men and to send the boys away from Darwin. This, he argued, would be a 'method by which the future of this country can be safeguarded in the absence of such radical methods as sterilization of the unfit and legalized abortion'.[57] In 1931 there were twenty-seven males and fifty females living in the Half-Caste Home.[58] The following year the administration announced that the girls were to remain in Kahlin Compound where they could be 'trained' as domestic servants, and the boys were to be moved inland to Pine Creek.[59]

Compounds for Asian men?

For the most part, legislation was aimed at restricting the movements of Aboriginal women. The question of restricting the movements of Asian men employed in the pearling industry was the subject of debate but only limited action. For several years there were too few Asians employed in the pearling industry to warrant special government attention. In 1923, when the Darwin industry was at its lowest ebb, there were two boats employing four Japanese and eight Aboriginal crew. But in 1925, following the revival of the pearling industry, the federal government sent to the sub-collector of customs in Darwin instructions for dealing with the employment of indentured labour.[60] There was some debate in 1928 as to the appropriateness of allowing the pearling crews to live in Chinatown. When Japanese divers asked to rent a house in Cavenagh Street, in Darwin's business centre, sub-collector Pierce wrote:

> The question has been raised as to whether or not indentured labourers are permitted to live in the town, or whether they are restricted to the foreshore when in port. It is claimed by one master pearler that in Broome and Thursday Island, Japanese indents are permitted to live in the town whilst Koepangers and Malays are restricted to the foreshore.[61]

The decision was made to follow the Broome and Thursday Island model, which privileged Japanese above other Asian groups. In any case, the distance from the foreshore camps at Frances Bay to Chinatown was not great and this decision did not greatly affect the interaction between Asian and Aboriginal peoples.

The decision to allow the Japanese to live in the town centre remained in place until the war. In 1936, for example, diver Saka stated that he lived behind the shop of Murakami, the photographer, in the town centre.[62] It was argued that Japanese freedom within Darwin was necessary because divers preferred to live and socialise in Darwin and were thus less likely to work off-shore with Dutch or Japanese competitors. Captain Gregory, writing for the Darwin Pearler's Committee, explained that with eighty Japanese-owned boats operating near Darwin, the drain on skilled divers was keenly felt. He argued that

> the only reason we have been able to keep the divers we have, is that the conditions of working out of Darwin are much easier than those on the Japanese fleet, because they come into port oftener, are able to get

> fresh meat and provisions and also to be ashore for a few days each month, whereas the Japanese boats stay afloat for months, being tendered by schooners and they scarcely ever get on shore.[63]

During the late 1930s, administrative concern over the presence of Asian crews in Darwin increased. In 1936 there were 130 Japanese and 103 Malays employed in Darwin. There were a number of different ethnic groups loosely termed 'Malays' or 'Koepangers', including people from Singapore, Java, Maluku (Aru Islands), Timor and nearby Sabu, and Roti and Sulawesi.[64]

Sergeant Koop, writing in 1936, demonstrates both the relative freedom of movement of divers and crews and the desire of some administrative staff to have that freedom curtailed. Koop complained of the lack of control over indentured aliens:

> The Malay and Koepang divers and crews freely patronise the hotels and become very arrogant and uppish towards other members of the civilian community . . . I am strongly of the opinion that Compounds, for the housing of these indentured labourers, should be established and that they be only allowed in the streets by permits.[65]

But the Chief Pearling Inspector, Nylander, was reluctant to act on his suggestion, arguing that the men on temporary leave from their boats 'naturally desire to make the best of a short-lived change of mode of life'.[66]

McDonald, secretary of the North Australian Workers' Union, took the view that the freedom of Asian crews represented a moral danger to the 'half-caste' women. In 1937 he argued that the pearling crews were responsible for the prevalence of venereal disease. He protested in the *Northern Standard* that they were 'at liberty to visit the homes of the halfcastes without hindrance by the police or any other authority' and gave details of locations in the town centre where Aboriginal women were allegedly meeting with Asian men.[67] His comment regarding the lack of police involvement was untrue. The Darwin Police Court proceedings, which were published in the *Northern Standard*, indicate several cases during the 1930s where police arrested men and women in night raids on houses in the 'prohibited area'. The increasing portrayal of sexual relations as both immoral and criminal in the 1930s did not allow for the development of long-term relationships. In this sense, policy had become more restrictive since 1912 when Baldwin Spencer had at least acknowledged the legitimacy of long-term relationships.

The question of Aboriginal prostitution to pearling crews outside of Darwin, which was an on-going concern of the missionaries at Melville and Goulburn islands, became the subject of lengthy official reports. One report found that ten luggers moored at Buchanan Island and that Aboriginal canoes had been seen going there from Melville and Bathurst islands. At 11 p.m. the boats were boarded by police and three Aboriginal women were found on deck. The women quite readily informed Captain Haultain that they had been given flour, sugar and tobacco by the Japanese men. On another boat three more women were found. They were reported as being 'very frightened' and when 'interrogated' admitted that they, too, had been paid.

In 1936 two Japanese divers employed by R. M. Edwards in Darwin were fined £50 for unlawfully permitting Aboriginal women on board their pearling lugger. Haultain's report suggested that any repeat of the offence and the men would be deported. The severity of the punishment indicated a change of attitude since 1931, when a similar charge incurred a fine of £2. The report also referred to precedents in Broome, where several divers who had been convicted of 'offences against native women' were deported from Australia. The heavy fine was intended to act as a deterrent.[68]

Another report made in 1936 by constable G. L. Don centred on the Aboriginal camp at Garden Point on Melville Island, which was home to about 200 Aboriginal people. At the time there were twenty-nine luggers moored there with over 200 crew members aboard. Don was told that the luggers stopped there every month for about eight to ten days to obtain fresh water. He noticed one Aboriginal–Japanese child and was told that there were others but that their mothers had gone to hide in the mangroves, frightened that the police would take the children to Darwin. He reported that there was flour in the camp that had been obtained from the Japanese. He was told that there were approximately thirty 'half-caste' Japanese children on Melville Island. Don described the place as 'a hot-bed of iniquity' and reported that there were three different Aboriginal groups camped at this site, but that only two were in the habit of mixing with the Japanese men. The third group had apparently threatened to spear any Japanese who touched their women. Don suggested that women were forced to go with the Japanese and noted that three young women from the mission asked to be returned. He wrote: 'I consider the only means of combating this menace is by establishing a Police camp at Garden Point.'[69]

Reports from Goulburn Island in November 1936 provided statements from Aboriginal witnesses. The interviews were conducted by the missionary in charge of Goulburn Island. One Aboriginal woman told of an encounter in South West Bay. Four Aboriginal men and four women went down to the beach after dark and the men called out to the Japanese to send a boat. The woman described the night spent on the lugger with the Japanese men and explained that the men and women of her community had 'pushed us to go because they wanted tobacco'. The second woman confirmed that she gave all her tobacco to an Aboriginal man waiting on shore.

In each account, the process was the same. They shared a meal, washed, had intercourse and slept the evening on board. The women communicated with the Japanese in English. From their descriptions there does not appear to have been long-term relationships or even friendship between the women and the Asian men. One witness said she stayed on deck with another woman because 'she little bit afraid'. The Japanese men were not referred to by name, but only as engineer, diver, second diver and tender. From the women's description, it appears that the encounters were controlled by the Japanese men. The women did not choose their partners, but rather were chosen. Several referred to those women not chosen, stating 'no one would have the other women' and 'no one took me'.[70]

Stories of these encounters were evidently common knowledge in Darwin. In 1938, during the Anniversary Day football procession, a parade float depicted a recent controversial arrest, with the '*H.M.A.S. Larrakin* [*Larrakia*] capturing a Japanese lugger. On the float, a white man impersonated an Aboriginal woman being help captive on board the lugger and plied with tobacco and liquor.'[71] Nakashiba, secretary of the Japanese Society, said that 'public ridicule of a matter of such delicacy was resented'. Other Japanese chose to boycott the Don and Victoria hotels, which had been responsible for the float. The float was based on the real-life drama that was taking place with the capture of Japanese luggers. In defending the float, the organisers claimed that it referred to the 'foreign' Japanese, meaning those pearlers based in Palau in the Caroline Islands rather than the local Japanese. Other newspaper reports, however, did refer to the locally based pearling crews buying goods in the Darwin shops to give to Aboriginal women.[72]

SITES OF CONTACT

Thus far, I have emphasised the official push for segregation in Darwin. But segregation was the preoccupation of a small portion of the white population. Despite its very real impact on the lives of both Aboriginal and Asian residents, it should not be allowed to dominate our image of Darwin society. The heart of Darwin, the quality that gave the town its particular social characteristics, was the polyethnic community. The mixed Aboriginal–Asian population was by no means the largest ethnic group, but they represented the connecting hub between the supposedly separate ethnic groups of Darwin.

Sarah Yu has noted that many of the well-known families of Broome were of mixed background. They were proud of their heritage and described their 'multicultural' culture as unique. Yu's description of Broome has much in common with the stories of pre-war Darwin. The early marriages between Aboriginal women and Filipino, Malay and Chinese men had created a mixed community whose stories celebrate rather than lament the polyglot that was Darwin. These families retained the cultural traditions of their various backgrounds and blended them into a vibrant fusion culture.

Police Paddock

Unlike the strict ethnic segregation of the Kahlin Compound, those living in mixed marriages usually lived in and around Police Paddock, now Stuart Park. This area had been set aside in 1911 for the Chinese, Malay and Filipinos who had decided to remain in Darwin as permanent residents. Many of the families living in Police Paddock belonged to the group whose marriages had been sanctioned by Baldwin Spencer in 1912 because they were in long-term relationships with Aboriginal women and already had children. The members of these families were given more freedom than most Aboriginal people. Unmarried women and young men under twenty-one were the exception, as they were still categorised as Aboriginal and therefore remained under the restrictions of the *Aboriginal Ordinance*.

The polyethnic community of Police Paddock in many ways resembled a typical Southeast Asian village. But residence here was not restricted to the 'coloured' community. Europeans who chose to live and marry into the community were welcomed.[73] Administrative influence over Police Paddock was mitigated by the fact that its residents were largely self-sufficient through fish traps, vegetable gardens and hunting.

Mixed schooling

In 1912, when a wave of White Australian sentiment swept through Darwin after the Territory came under Commonwealth administration, a group of white residents requested a separate white school. Their request was only partially met with the creation of a separate school for Aboriginal children, which had the effect of separating the Chinese from Aboriginal children.[74] The establishment of an Aboriginal school at Kahlin Compound meant that the so-called 'full-blood' Aboriginal children were segregated from the rest of the community. The convent and public school system remained 'mixed', catering for Aboriginal children who were officially categorised as 'half-caste' and 'quadroon', and white and Asian children.

Again in 1925 and 1926, a group of twenty-six white parents petitioned the federal government to have Darwin State School re-organised so as to separate the white children from the 'coloured'.[75] But the government was not prepared to approve the segregation of the school.[76] The government report noted that there were forty-four white, sixty-six Chinese and eleven 'quadroon' and 'half-caste' children at the Darwin school. The Catholic convent school had a similar mix of children.[77] The schools represented an important site of mixed relations and one which crucially shaped the future attitudes of local Darwin residents.

Religion

The Church was another site of mixed relations in Darwin. Christianity in general and Catholicism in particular was favoured by the majority of Filipinos, Chinese and Japanese and their mixed Aboriginal families in Darwin. Many sent their children to the convent school for their education. While most Chinese gave their religion as Confucianism in the 1911 census, by 1933 only 4 per cent followed Chinese traditions, though it was quite common for people to attend both church and temple.[78] During the 1920s the marriage announcements in the *Northern Standard* indicate that a number of Aboriginal couples and Australian-born Chinese married in the Catholic Church.[79]

The labour movement

The Aboriginal–Asian community was also connected by its common labour market position which traditionally saw its members in maritime and waterfront industries. Antonio Cubillo, a Filipino ex-pearler who was married to an Aboriginal–Scottish woman, was one of the first to become involved in the labour movement. When the decision was made in 1912 to enforce a white-only employment practice on the wharf, Cubillo decided to seek the help of the Industrial Workers of the World (IWW), a left-wing union group well known for their stance against racial discrimination. All work on the waterfront was controlled by the newly established Darwin branch of the Australian Workers' Union (AWU). The AWU had a 'colour bar' clause in its membership rules that prevented Asians from joining.[80] In 1915 Cubillo attempted to form a Darwin branch of the IWW. He collected the names and subscriptions of nineteen Chinese, Malay, Filipino, Japanese and Singhalese members.[81] His efforts to re-establish their right to work on the wharf were in vain as the AWU was the stronger union.

Cesar: life at Police Paddock

In 1897 the Philippines rose in revolution against the Spanish. With American aid the Spanish were evicted, America claimed the Philippines, and there followed a civil war against the Americans. The Cesar boys on the island of Kalyvof in Mindanao had sided with the Americans, and one of the brothers was beheaded. Their mother helped to smuggle young Cesar onto a British cargo ship to Singapore. Cesar voyaged to Europe and back as a sailor before he signed up with Captain Edwards who was heading for the pearl shell grounds off Broome. He arrived in Darwin around 1901. His daughter Maria (viz. also Maria Pederson) told me as much as she knew.

> When he came to the Territory there was no Cavenagh Street, it was all mangrove around there. Darwin was just beginning. So he decided to get married. So, those days, you can't—no women around, so his mate, he married a Portuguese–Chinese woman, so he said, 'I'll get you a wife'. So he got my mother from Canton, a Portuguese–Chinese. Up to the day they got married Mum never saw my father. She come off the boat and the arrangement was made, and something like ten or twelve hours after, she was married. Her name was Helena Gonzales.

Cesar had his own twenty-two-foot whale boat for fishing, and the family tended a vegetable garden, chickens and ducks. They lived at Darwin's Police Paddock, where the ten children pondered the gallows from which native prisoners used to be hanged, and which still remained in public view. Poverty dominates Maria's childhood memories.

> We used to think it's Christmas when Mum had sixpence or ninepence to spare and we could go to the butcher. And we used to say to him—that was old Holmes, he was a whiteman, big white chap, he married a little Japanee woman—and when we say 'Mama wants sixpence of meat' he'd give us a lot of meat, he was one of those types, kind towards us. We used to think it's Christmas if we had meat because most of the time we'd have fish and chooks.

Maria said the family spoke *Lengua de Castilan* (an older term for Spanish) and Helena never learned to speak English. As a Catholic from Macao, Helena remained apart from the Darwin Chinese families. Maria only remembers that when she asked the Chinese ladies about their bound feet, it was considered an importune question with dire consequences.

Aboriginal children attended the same school, but Maria had little contact with them:

> My mother wouldn't let us associate with them. We used to speak to them, they used to go to school and we used to sit near them at school. We really only had one or two friends, I guess our own nationality, their mother a half-caste and their father a Filipino. Because only two or three Filipino married the same nationality as my mother, that's all, and the rest of them married a half-caste and [moved] to town. All around Thursday Island you see, all around Broome crowd, there is only like one or two married an Englishwoman. But where we were staying—they call it Stuart Park now, we used to call it Police Paddock, the government gave it to the Filipino chap [Cubillo]—but there was white, Chinee, all nationalities came in and live there. It was only supposed to be just for the, you know, but we all got on well together, it's more or less like community.

Pearling permeated this life at Police Paddock.

My father used to work for Captain Edwards on the lugger. And at lay-up time they'd bring all the sail, rolls of canvas, and Mama used to cut it, we used to be out and away, because the whole verandah used to be taken up to cut the sail and the jib and all that, and Mama used to mark it with a white chalk and Papa used to cut it. Then when that's finish we'd have to get all the twine and them ready, so for day and night, like up to eight o'clock at night, he used to sew with a hurricane lamp. And Mama used to sew the sail; our turn was when the soft part of the sail—you can machine it—Mama had a Wertheim machine and we used to stand there and turn it [crank the handle] and Mama had a stick [to threaten us] and we used to have to behave ourselves. We were glad when school time came so we didn't have to turn that machine.

They'd go out [on the luggers] for three or four months and then they come in again. But my father never go out much. He was more or less shore-based. When the pearl shell came in he used to have to grade them, and then he has to open it, string them up, wash them and have them all ready. There used to be six of them to do that.

Old Captain Edward was good to all the Filipino chaps. He treated us fair, he was really good to us. Most of them were only divers and boat turn-out [Filipinos didn't go into other occupations], and if they said they were a bit short of money, he'd advance them and does things for them. Some of them [other employers] wouldn't help them at all, but he always does, he help them.

Those Filipinos who arrived after 1901 were liable for repatriation, and mixed families tended to be torn apart by this policy.

There was a lot of them went home. A lot of them, went home like that and left them [left their wives and children]. As I said those who came after the Commonwealth [after 1901], they all were sent back, some of the wives don't want to go, they stay back [in Australia] and their husbands went back [to the Philippines] ... Well, I can understand the half-caste woman, why go over there, they don't know anybody, and it's a strange country, a different life. You never know whether your mother-in-law will accept you, because the Filipino very proud nationality, so a lot of them stayed back.

The labour movement in Darwin began as a segregationist lobby under the Darwin AWU but it gradually became more inclusive. In 1922 the AWU was replaced by two rival unions, the North Australian Industrial Union and the Northern Territory Workers' Union (NTWU). There was disagreement between these two over the question of so-called 'coloured' labour, with the NTWU favouring a more inclusive policy. In 1927 North Australian Workers Union (NAWU) was established, amalgamating the two unions and covering the whole of the Northern Territory. The NAWU retained discriminatory membership rules, but allowed 'Australian-born children of Mixed Parentage (European on one side)' into the union, and in practice these rules were loosely administered.[82] Part-Aboriginal workers went on to become a significant part of the NAWU but not without a struggle.

In 1928 efforts were made to extend membership so that 'any coloured person born in Australia who has passed a 3rd class school examination of State school standard' could be admitted.[83] This was supported by Northern Territory Member for Parliament, Harold Nelson, and was aimed at Australian-born Chinese.[84] The motion was rejected with fifty-one in favour and 109 against.[85] In 1930 it was moved that all Aboriginal and Chinese workers be admitted to the union, but again the proposal was rejected.[86]

Mahoney, a communist-inspired unionist, was popular with the 'coloured' community and appealed to all those who believed in equal rights regardless of ethnicity. He lobbied for Aboriginal rights throughout the depression years. In 1931, writing on behalf of the Unemployed Workers' Movement, he declared:

> ... slavery of the worst type is being perpetrated in the Northern Territory towards the aboriginal and half caste race, and we shall do all in our power to force the Government to do away with their present slave conditions ... we demand that they be granted full rights to enter any Trade Union.[87]

This followed the announcement in September 1931 of the Communist Party's fourteen-point program which demanded: equal rights for all Aborigines; full wages; the abolition of the Protection Boards; and the creation of independent Aboriginal republics in central, northern and northwest Australia.[88]

Mahoney was equally concerned to protect the rights of the Chinese and Asian pearling communities.[89] In 1931 he protested against the deportation of Koepanger pearling crews who were on strike and on behalf of the Chinese community over immigration restriction.[90] According to Val McGinness, the 1929 communist-led demonstration on unemployment issues was supported by most of the 'coloured' community. He recalled that 'half-castes, Filipinos, Chinese, Japanese, whites, Italians, Greeks and everything was all mixed up in it'.[91] The Aboriginal–Asian workers who supported Mahoney remained staunch members of the NAWU, but they rejected the hard-line communism of the late 1930s. Catholicism led them to reject the atheistic beliefs of the communists and to support the overtly Catholic Labor leaders of the NAWU. When communist Charlie Priest published an attack on Bob Murray, president of the NAWU in 1936, it was Lawrence Cubillo who gave evidence in court against Priest.[92]

In 1937, the waterside section, with some eighty

members, remained the most powerful group in the NAWU and included men of Aboriginal–Asian background.[93] A list of the waterside workers in 1937 included people of Italian, Greek, Spanish, Chinese and Malay background, and a comment that the 'types and origins' of the workers were 'very mixed indeed'.[94] An examination of the ethnic backgrounds of the waterside workers reveals Spanish–Filipino, Chinese–Australian, Malay–Aboriginal, Irish–Aboriginal, Chinese–Aboriginal and other mixed backgrounds. Arthur Tye, a Chinese–Australian qualified for union membership under the 'mixed parentage' clause.[95] Waterside worker, Johnny Ah Mat, a Thursday Islander of Malay descent, was chosen as union delegate for the sorting shed section in 1931.[96] The Cubillo brothers also worked on the wharf.[97]

In 1940 when the communists took over the NAWU, the out-going secretary, J. A. McDonald, organised a petition to be signed by all those members who supported the original executive. The lengthy list included most of the local Darwin workers and included Greek, Aboriginal, Russian, Italian, Filipino and Chinese names.[98] The Australian-born Chinese—C. Yuen, W. Jan, S. Jan, Peter Ng—were the newest additions to the union, the discriminatory rules having been amended sometime in the late 1930s, the precise date being as yet unknown. With the acceptance of Chinese members, the union could now claim to represent both the Chinese and the Aboriginal–Asian communities.[99] The continued involvement of Aboriginal members in union matters after World War II was demonstrated by the fact that Jack McGinness, president of the Halfcaste Progress Association (re-formed in 1951), went on to become the first Aboriginal president of the NAWU.[100]

Inter-ethnic sport

Perhaps the most public site of mixed relations in Darwin was the sports oval. The importance of sport in the writing of Aboriginal histories has been demonstrated by Colin Tatz and Richard Broome. According to Broome, sporting successes represent 'enduring moments of Aboriginal dominance' and allow historians to emphasise 'Aborigines as active subjects'.[101] In Darwin, the most important sport was Australian Rules football. The game was introduced to Darwin by the captain of the Vesteys football team, Reuben Cooper, the well-known son of Joe Cooper and his Iwaidja wife Alice Rose. Reuben was well connected with Darwin's Asian community, especially given his marriage, firstly to Bertha McKeddie, of Filipina descent, and later to Salamah (Sally) Ah Mat, a Thursday Islander of Malay descent.[102]

Reuben had learnt football during his years at Prince Alfred College in Adelaide.[103] Australian Rules football in Darwin was dominated by Aboriginal players and many of the best known players were of Aboriginal–Asian descent. The most successful team of the late 1930s was the Buffaloes, whose captain was one of the Ah Mat brothers.[104] The majority of Buffaloes players were of Aboriginal descent, including the Snape brothers and Walter Lew Fatt of Aboriginal–Chinese descent and the Cubillo brothers. One of the Ah Mat players, Johnny, was grandfather to Robert Ah Mat, who continues the family tradition today, playing for the Swans AFL team.[105]

As with every social activity in Darwin, Australian Rules football had to struggle against the segregationist lobby in order to maintain mixed sport. In 1926 a group of white players forced the introduction of white-only football, forming the North Australian Football League (NAFL). After that, both Aboriginal and Chinese players were banned from the oval.[106] Writing in the *Northern Standard*, one commentator, 'Fairplay', stated that the

> cloven hoof of prejudice and sectarianism still lives and promises to rise from its ashes in as virulent form as in the past. That the coloured boys in their native land should be debarred by the imported article from playing football...I quite agree there should be a vote taken of Darwin residents interested in fair play, as football will certainly become mediocre without them ...There should be no colour line bringing back the dead past to Darwin...[107]

In protest, the local community boycotted the white-only games, and attendance fell from several hundred to a mere handful.[108] In response to the segregationist policy, those in favour of mixed sport decided to form a soccer league, the Darwin Soccer Association, with two Chinese, one white and one so-called 'half-caste' team.[109]

A Rondalla.
Members of the Cubillo family continue to maintain their links to Filipino cultural traditions.

The Chinese community had been playing soccer in Darwin since the early 1920s when the Chinese Nationalist Party had launched its physical fitness program.[110] A 1923 photograph shows the Darwin Chinese Soccer Team organised by a body called the Darwin Chinese Recreation Club.[111] Given the Chinese experience in the sport, Tommy (Gee) Ming Ket was named secretary of the Darwin Soccer Association. His initial efforts to obtain use of the oval in 1926 were blocked by the Darwin Council. Ming Ket was told that the NAFL had the oval and he would have to apply to them for permission. A letter to the editor from 'Fairplay' argued that the council should have given the soccer players 'a fair go'. The NAFL finally agreed to allow the soccer players the use of the oval.[112] The first teams to play were the Waratahs, an Aboriginal team, who went up against the Chinese Darwin Recreation Club.[113] The formation of the Soccer Association was one of the first examples of formal Asian–Aboriginal co-operation. As is sometimes the case, the joint experience of discrimination prompted an increase in inter-ethnic solidarity.

The 'colour bar' in Australian Rules football lasted for nearly two years before public protest prompted a change. The *Northern Standard* reported that a 'fairly large crowd assembled' to discuss the re-entry of the 'coloured boys' into the Football League. As Member for Parliament, Harold Nelson spoke against the 'colour line' and argued that they did not want to base their society on 'colour and caste', as was done in Singapore. He explicitly rejected this British colonial model of a divided multi-racial society. Bob Murray echoed this rejection of segregation, suggesting that it would be best if they did not simply form one team of 'coloured' players, but divided the 'coloured' players evenly among three mixed teams.[114] With this in mind, the teams were reorganised. In 1933 both the Wanderers and the Buffaloes were comprised of white, Chinese and Aboriginal players. Only the Waratahs remained an all-white team. The younger generation of Chinese and Aboriginal players were similarly organised into mixed teams. The town junior football team was captained by H. Chin and included several Chinese and Aboriginal boys.[115]

Despite the fact that the Australian Rules players had returned to their former sport, the experience of inter-ethnic soccer made a lasting impression and soccer continued to be played by both Chinese and Aboriginal players. In 1937 this was extended to include the pearling crews. A mixed team of local Darwin men including a number of Aboriginal players played against a team of Koepangers. Put Ah Mat, whose family was connected both with the Malay pearling crews and the local community, was chosen as the referee. The Darwin team won the match and the newspaper commentator wrote: 'The little Koepangers played pretty football, and did very well to hold the heavy Australian team to one goal.'[116] This game was significant in that it extended the scope of Aboriginal sporting connections. Having first played against the Chinese team, they had now played against men who belonged in the supposedly secluded world of the foreshore pearling camps. The Japanese pearling crews, however, remained separate.

CONCLUSIONS

Before 1911 it was possible to speak of free mixed relations between the local Aboriginal people of Darwin and Asian immigrants. This was largely a result of the *laissez-faire* attitude of the South Australian government. After that time, the opportunities for Aboriginal people to mix with Asians were severely curtailed by their segregation—first in the Kahlin Compound and later at Bagot Compound. Where relationships continued they were necessarily covert, seeking to avoid the watchful eyes of the white administration. Those who were classified as 'half-caste' Aboriginal, including those of Aboriginal–Asian descent, were, in contrast, allowed substantial freedoms to interact socially with Asians. In particular, those Aboriginal men who joined the union, worked on the wharf and played football were able to develop close connections with Asians. This applied particularly to their relationships with the Australian-born Chinese community. Aboriginal women continued to have close personal relationships with Asian men, but given the strict legislation prohibiting miscegenation, these relationships were necessarily of a covert nature.

Cubillo family lines by Gary Lee

I am a Larrakia man who was born and raised in my people's traditional country in Darwin. The Larrakia are the traditional owners and original inhabitants of the Darwin and Cox Peninsula regions, of the Top End of the Northern Territory, including all the adjacent islands. Our country extends approximately from the mouth of the Adelaide River in the north down around to the mouth of the Finniss River on the south west coast. Prior to European settlement and the establishment of Darwin (then Palmerston) in 1896, my people had experienced long-term relationships with outsiders for who knows how many centuries. Neighbouring Aboriginal groups whose countries bordered that of the Larrakia had ceremonial links with us and among the more prominent of these are the Iwaidja, Gagadju, Wulna, Kungarikan and Tiwi peoples. The Tiwi people and the Larrakia have long interacted, sometimes raiding each other for women, or through ceremony such as when Larrakia people allowed the Tiwi to erect burial poles on our country. The three major Larrakia *dirula* (dreaming) tracks travel from Gagadju country over to Larrakia lands, touching down at the important sites and places of significance, before travelling southwards. This links the Larrakia ceremonially to not just their immediate neighbours but also to those further afield.

The Larrakia had centuries-long associations with Macassan trepangers and traded trepang and pearl shell with them for things like metal axe-heads and cloth. Sometimes women were also 'given' to Macassans, but their visits were eventually stopped by Europeans.

About 150 years ago a southern group, the Wagaidj, began to move onto Larrakia lands on the Cox Peninsula, possibly attracted by the new settlement and its prospects of work and easy access to tobacco and flour. Whatever their reasons, the Wagaidj stayed and eventually all had left their own country to live on the Cox Peninsula. Over time some Wagaidj intermarried with Larrakia, and their ceremonies became mixed. Today the Wagaidj assist the Larrakia to care for Larrakia country, the sites of significance and the *dirula* tracks for which we jointly share responsibility.

The Larrakia people were the first Aboriginal group in the Northern Territory to have their culture and traditions seriously eroded and their population decimated. Our 'reward' for allowing *beragud* (white men) to set up camp was the erosion of our traditional society through introduced diseases such as influenza, smallpox, measles, leprosy and venereal disease. Alcohol and tobacco contributed to further erosion as did following

Life at Police Paddock. Pictured are Edward Cubillo and his Aboriginal mother Lily, in the background, at Police Paddock (now Stuart Park) in Darwin, 1930s. Photo: courtesy of Ana Collins, Katherine.

decades of genocide, dispersal and other impositions designed to limit movement and access to natural and ceremonial resources. The Larrakia have nevertheless endured and survived and we have retained our knowledge of and connections to our country despite the disruptions to our traditional way of life.

I became aware of my Larrakia identity around the age of ten or so, when I was old enough to start taking it in from my Larrakia mother, Mary Cubillo Lee. Her father, grandmother and great-grandmother had passed this on to her and her siblings as she did with myself and my eleven siblings. We were taught our Larrakia heritage including the names of the important *dirula* tracks and sites and from this early age were well aware of our Larrakia identification. Yet my maternal grandfather had a Spanish–Filipino father and my maternal grandmother was a Wardaman woman whose father was Chinese. My paternal grandfather had a Japanese mother and a Chinese father, and to add to the mix, my paternal grandmother was a Yawuru woman whose father was German. Then there is the matter of my maternal great-great-grandfather who was Scottish, who had children with my Larrakia great-great-grandmother.

There never seemed to be a time when I didn't know about my Asian ancestors, or their stories about how they came to be in Darwin and Broome, and the families they had with Aboriginal women. Their stories were so familiar that by the time I started primary school it was all second nature to me. There were plenty of Larrakia and other Aboriginal families with similar backgrounds to ours. All around me were people who looked like I did so as a young boy there was never any doubt or question in my mind. Just as there were never any doubts about my Larrakia identity. I always knew that Darwin was 'my place' and that the surrounding environment was Larrakia country, even as a small boy, although it wasn't until my early teens that I came to appreciate fully just what that meant to me. I never had a problem resolving my other ancestries as a product of two Aboriginal parents with forebears from Asia. My Aboriginality has been formed by my Larrakia and my Asian heritage and I owe it all to my ancestors who helped that happen. This is their story.

My mother's family story is based upon what I've always known and through years of research and countless conversations with my parents, and my mother's immediate and large extended family. I regard this as a rich legacy passed on to me that I believe has informed who I am as an Aboriginal man and Larrakia person today.

My maternal great-great-grandmother was a Larrakia woman named Annie who was born on the Cox Peninsula near the present day Belyuen area, sometime around 1855. There are no official written records about her, no birth or death certificate. What we know about her life before she had children is very scant. My great-great-grandmother must have been in her teens by the time the new township of Darwin was being surveyed and the first streets were being laid out. As the new township of Palmerston grew, Larrakia people were attracted to this new settlement that was growing up around them in the middle of their own country. It wouldn't have been hard for Larrakia people to have contact with these first arrivals in their country. Larrakia people were generally a friendly people who always welcomed outsiders into their country.

There's no doubt that Larrakia people would have lived around the fringes of the new town of Palmerston. Some found work, others were exploited, some women were introduced to prostitution and, because there were no white women in Darwin in those early days, Larrakia women came in very handy to both European and Asian men. Before very long mixed-race children started being born.

Around 1878 Annie Duwun met a white man in Darwin who had arrived from Melbourne. The circumstances under which they met are lost to time but we do have some information about George McKeddie, my great-great-grandfather. He was the third of five children of Scottish free settlers Mr and Mrs McKeddie, from Avoch near Inverness, who had emigrated from Scotland to Melbourne in 1855. He was twenty-three when he arrived in Darwin in 1874 just five years after its establishment. His older sister Bella was already married and settled there. Darwin's population numbered less than 800 European and Asian men but development was proceeding apace and McKeddie prospered. He found immediate work upon arrival with PR Allen & Co. Stores. By 1876 he became general manager of their new Southport branch, a two-day buggy ride or full-day schooner trip away. It was in this position that he and Annie met. In 1879 their first child, my great-grandmother, was born, whom they called Magdalena, or Lily.

By this time McKeddie was a member of the Palmerston town council and had other business interests and prominent involvement in the European social life of the growing town. Other white men of his social standing also had Larrakia de facto wives, including the government resident Charles Dashwood. He had an Aboriginal daughter whom he would not publicly acknowledge even though the whole town knew. The very men who framed policies of protection and laws to prevent the mixing of races had Aboriginal women on the side. Whether because of miscegenation laws or to uphold an image of respectability, most white men chose not to recognise the children they had with Aboriginal women.

McKeddie, however, looked after Annie and acknowledged his daughter, giving her his surname. By all accounts McKeddie was one of those rarities, a settler who looked after his Aboriginal workers well and was widely respected in the area by them. By 1892 Annie gave birth to their second child, Jack. This was around the same time that McKeddie had bought a large pastoral property, encompassing present-day Belyuen Aboriginal community on the Cox Peninsula. He had a large, comfortable homestead built there, where Annie, Lily and McKeddie's long-time trusted Chinese cook and servant, Ah Yang (pronounced Ah Young), lived. Apparently McKeddie bought the property so that Annie and the children could be nearer to her Larrakia family and possibly also to keep them away from the thriving den of iniquity that Darwin already was by the late 1890s.

Within twenty years of its founding, Darwin had grown into a wild frontier town to which all manner of shady characters were attracted. There was a strong gender imbalance and Japanese women were brought to town to work in the brothels in Chinatown and Malaytown, where opium, gambling dens and illegal liquor were also to be found.

Annie Duwun died in 1899 and was buried on the Cox Peninsula at present-day Wangiggi (Mandorah) but we have few other details about her passing. McKeddie owned a house in town and continued to live there with Lily and Jack, assisted by Ah Yang.

At the time of her mother's death, Lily was nineteen years old and pregnant with the first of her eight children. She had met a Spanish–Filipino pearl diver by the name of Antonio Cubillo who was employed on one of McKeddie's two pearling luggers.

Antonio Cubillo was born in Bohol, in the Philippines, in 1875. At age fifteen he became cabin boy on a Spanish ship and spent some years in Europe. Antonio must have heard there was good money to be made from pearl diving in Port Darwin, and on his return voyage, during a stopover in Singapore, signed on for pearling at Palmerston, where he arrived in 1895. It appears that he signed on as a Malay.

Antonio was indentured to McKeddie working the waters of Broome and Darwin. He worked hard and he became a trusted employee and McKeddie's number one diver. He must have had occasions to visit his employer's house in Mitchell Street, where seventeen-year-old Lily lived. She had been well raised, and had graceful manners and was not a boisterous person. They liked each other and Antonio began courting her. McKeddie at first objected to Antonio's interest in his daughter but could do little about it. Much as he liked Antonio, McKeddie's main concern lay in the fact that Antonio was an 'unregistered alien' who could be deported at any time along with his children, regardless of whether they were born in Australia or not. But love won out and in 1898 Lily and Antonio moved into a small hut in Malaytown, then situated at the end of the more notorious Chinatown in Cavenagh Street, down near the Sun Cheong Loong store. Malaytown housed 'Malays', Filipinos and Indonesians as well as Aboriginal and Japanese people. In 1899 the first of their ten children, Christina was born. Antonio was still diving and he and Lily were to have nine more children whose names, in sequential order, were: Alberta (Bertha), Ponciano (Poncie), my grandfather Juan (John), Lorenzo (Laurence), Martina, Eduardo (Edward), Delfin (Dolphin), Ana and Philip. Only Ana survives, living at the time of writing in a nursing home in Katherine.

In 1910 Antonio and Lily were married at the St Mary's Star of the Sea Catholic Church in Darwin. McKeddie set Antonio and Lily up with a steak-and-egg cafe called The Boarding House, near the present-day Tree Of Knowledge at the end of Cavenagh Street. This was to provide for Lily's and his grandchildren's security. It helped Antonio and Lily take good care of their large growing family. There was little in the way of eating places at this time in Darwin. Long and short soup could be bought occasionally in Chinatown, and a Chinese man sold fresh roast pork every day. An Indonesian man sold satee, which was very popular as well. But apart from these few, the Cubillo's cafe was the only proper eating establishment and consequently did very well at the beginning. But Antonio—like just about every other male in Darwin—liked to gamble and he left the running of the cafe to Lily and the eldest sons and daughters. After a while Lily decided to give up the cafe as Antonio was never there to lend a hand and it was getting too much for her to cope with.

Antonio was prominent in the Catholic Church at this time and he had established the first band of any note in Darwin: the Cubillo Brothers' Stringed Orchestra. He had brought with him the Rondalla Spanish–Filipino music tradition which used guitars, mandolins, banjos and octavinas. Xavier Herbert's novel *Capricornia* refers to my great-grandfather's orchestra as

A postcard from Ponciano Cubillo during his visit to the Philippines, dated 'November 13, 1923', at '1874 Oroquieta Street, Sta Cruz, Manila, P. Isles': 'To Sister Tina, Accept this picture as a remembrance of your Brother, Ponciano Cubillo.'

Courtesy of Ana Cubillo, Katherine.

'the Ponto Brothers band of Port Darwin'. Antonio taught all his sons to play various stringed instruments and my grandfather John was the band leader. They played at official functions at Government House and for other civic occasions and were very popular.

In 1912 George McKeddie moved with his son Jack to Emungalen near Katherine where he had bought the store at a place called Nixon's Crossing. In the same year the new government resident, Dr J. A. Gilruth, announced the demolition of Chinatown and Malaytown. The 'unsanitary' and 'unsavory' conditions in this area were not to be tolerated any longer under the new federal administration. The residents of these areas, being mainly Chinese, Filipino, Japanese and 'Malay', had little say in the matter. Antonio and Lily Cubillo left the little tin house in which seven of their children had been born, and moved to a bigger house in Police Paddock.

Antonio undertook several trips to the Philippines, sometimes taking some of his children along, but Lily never went with him. We don't know whether she wanted to go there, or whether she was unable to get a passport, or whether she preferred to stay at home with the other children. We don't know what she thought about Antonio's long absences, but suppose there was little she could do about them. They corresponded with each other and Antonio would send money to her occasionally.

On his last trip in 1935, from which he never returned, he was accompanied by his son Poncie and daughter Alberta. Alberta was grieving from a broken marriage to Reuben Cooper, a very handsome and athletic man who is credited with introducing Australian Rules football to Darwin in 1916. Poncie returned to Darwin after a year, while Alberta stayed with her father. While they were away, Lily suffered a stroke at age fifty-five, which meant she dragged one leg slightly when she walked. The year after, she died in Darwin and was buried by her children. Antonio and Alberta were eventually contacted in the Philippines but could not afford to come home for the funeral. Finally Alberta returned, leaving her father in Manila where he himself died ten years later, in 1945.

I will now turn to my grandfather's life and, even though he was killed long before I was born, I have come to know him through my mother and her mother and this has, in many ways, made him very familiar to me. He was born Juan Roque Cubillo, the fourth child of Antonio and Lily. He had by all accounts a happy-go-lucky nature and was consequently very popular with everyone. He was educated at St Joseph's Primary School in Darwin (now St Mary's). After school he got a job at the Vestey's meatworks on Bullocky Point, the site of present-day Darwin High School. When Vestey's closed down he went droving for a while with his brother Philip, then came back to Darwin and got a job as a wharfie. It was around this time that he first saw my grandmother, Louisa Agatha Lee.

Louisa and Jean Lee were eight-year-old identical twins when they were taken away from their mother, Widji Nelson, a Wardaman woman. Widji Nelson had the twins in 1906 to a Chinese man of whom we only know that he was working at Brock's Creek near Pine Creek at the time, we think as a trader and sometime gold prospector. Their mother had done a good job of hiding them from the authorities, but being Aboriginal–Chinese, the girls were removed. Louisa and her sister were striking to look at—identical girl twins hadn't been seen before in Darwin, let alone Aboriginal–Chinese ones. They had beautiful waist-length black hair plaited down the back. It is said that John first set eyes on Louisa when she and her sister were being boarded onto the mission boat, the *Saint Francis* at Darwin wharf, bound for the Catholic mission on Bathurst Island, where the Native Affairs Department deemed they should be incarcerated.

John and his best friend Tim Angeles wanted to marry Catholic girls and eventually they went to Bathurst Island to speak to Father Gsell. The nuns arranged a meeting between John and Louisa and it is said that the attraction between the two was mutual, whereas Tim and Jean did not strike a spark.

All girls were trained in domestic duties and encouraged to leave the mission once they turned sixteen, having been educated to sixth grade. The twins were sent in to Darwin to work at St Joseph's convent in Darwin. Louisa stayed in the convent until 1926, when she married John Cubillo at St Joseph's church. Her unmarried sister was put into Kahlin Compound and could no longer be with Louisa. She later married a white man by the name of Flynn and had two children to him.

John and Louisa's wedding reception was a big affair held at Antonio and Lily's place, known as 'the Big House', in Police Paddock. They moved into their own place and the first of their nine children, Don, was born in 1928. Their other children in order were: Noeline, Mary (my mother), Francis, Laurence, Steven, Michael, Charles and Catherine. John was working extra shifts at the wharf and providing well for his wife and large family and life seemed to be going well for them. On the morning of 19 February 1942, John was working as usual on the Darwin wharf. He was sitting on the wharf rolling a cigarette at smoko with his good friend George Tye when he looked up and saw a line of Japanese planes overhead. The bombing of Darwin was about to begin. As the bombs rained down, my grandfather started running down the wharf, with ships exploding all around. A direct hit on the *Neptuna* blew him away and his body was never found. His tragic death at thirty-eight years of age was a devastating blow for my Nanna.

Louisa Cubillo and all her children, the youngest being Cathie at three months, had been compulsorily evacuated to Katherine a few weeks before the bombing. They were only allowed one suitcase per family that could hardly hold any spare clothes for nine children. After Darwin was bombed, the authorities put all these women and children on to the backs of cattle trucks to be evacuated further south to Balaclava in South Australia. Just before they left she found out about grandfather's death.

It was to be four years of hardship before they were able to find their way back to Darwin. The evacuee families were told that they had to find their own way back to Darwin if they wanted to leave Balaclava. The women protested to the protector of natives, Mr Neville, who organised trucks to take them, but only as far as Alice Springs, after which they were to be left to their own devices. The women combined forces and organised transport on the backs of trucks, eventually getting themselves and their children back to Darwin.

CHAPTER 6
The polyethnic north

HISTORIES of the far northern townships are but variations on the theme of polyethnic Darwin. Everywhere we find reference to whites being 'outnumbered', because a numerical dominance of whites was not achieved even decades after the implementation of the White Australia policy. The polyethnic society and economy were ethnically stratified. At the apex was the sparse layer of a white ruling elite supported by the latent violence of the state apparatus. These have been the stuff of northern histories. At the bottom were camp Aborigines serving as casual, seasonal and always unskilled labour. These have been explored in race relations histories. But between these two poles was an electrified field peopled by Asians, Aborigines, a few whites, and many mixed descendants making up the bulk of the polyethnic society and ordered by further gradations of ascribed or acquired social worth and wealth.

A systematic investigation of Asians in north Australia tends to demand a differentiated treatment of Chinese, Japanese, Afghans, Filipinos, Malays and so on. However, these ethnic labels are just as problematic as the collective Asian one. They, too, are discursive constructions. They, too, obscure class and religion. They sometimes coincide with nations and sometimes not, and they conjure a conceptual certainty that is not warranted when we think, for example, of the prior migrations of Sama Bajo or Chinese. More poignantly, such differentiations fail to capture the life-worlds of the far north. Dwarfing the few legislative distinctions between Japanese, Chinese and other Asians in Australia, was the plethora of laws, policies and practices that constructed them as a unitary phenomenon, especially so in terms of contact with Aborigines.

This chapter makes some overtures to Aboriginal contact with Japanese, with Chinese and with Afghans as separate issues, but it becomes quickly apparent that whereas the histories of these ethnic groups in Australia differ in terms of the industries in which they were engaged, the periods of their greatest presence, and the regions where they were most prevalent, such ethnic differences are barely manifest in their relations with indigenous people. The stories presented here draw us into the vortex of ethnic mixing until an ethnic disaggregation becomes all but meaningless next to the more dominant image of mixed relations.

CHINESE AND ABORIGINES

Many Aboriginal families today carry Chinese names, despite the weight of legislation aimed against their mixing. It is not necessary to account for individual predilections, but when a pattern of mixed family formation appears, the question begged is what might have made such associations attractive. The most obvious explanation is demographic. The predominantly male Chinese population evidently needed to look outside of their own ethnic group for partners. Chinese women were rare in the far north, and so were European women, who were, moreover, socially out of bounds. As for the Aboriginal population, their gender balance may have been equally disturbed (viz. Pan Quee).

Some informants also commented on the cultural affinities between Chinese and Aborigines. Lily Ah Toy (viz.) remarked on the very similar funerary ritual involving smoke, while Warren Lee Long, of Chinese descent in Cairns, felt there was a much more fundamental affinity expressed as a caring for land instead of its domination, a strong sense of antiquity and roots, a sense of social being rather than individuated being. This is reminiscent of Marcia Langton's idea of the 'metaphysics of abidingness' in Aboriginal culture.[1] Peasant societies typically have a strong sense of family and complex social relations within a simple material culture.

Most importantly for marriage politics, traditional Aboriginal and traditional Chinese culture had a common commitment to polygamy, including arranged marriages and promised marriages, requiring the sanction of the family, not of the state.

AUSTRALIAN CHINESE COMMUNITIES

The Chinese communities who have survived in some northern pockets from the polyethnic era have until recently remained astoundingly homogenous. They are, by and large, the descendants of business Chinese who withstood the decline of mining and, typically being naturalised and having their families in Australia, were not repatriated at the end of any contract. Besides class, the community of Chinese in Australia was also differentiated along ethnic lines, as at home, with strong distinctions between the Hakka and the dominant Han Chinese. No doubt those Chinese who formed family links with Aborigines were mostly labourers from impoverished rural areas. It is also highly likely that they were mostly Hakka Chinese, not well remembered by the surviving Han-dominated Chinese communities in the north.[2]

Families from the polyethnic era know each other and of each other across vast distances, and many family links tie them into a close-knit network. Herbert Sue Yek mockingly warned me: 'We are all related, so don't run any of us down.' I thought I may have discovered a family outside this network when I chanced into a Gordonvale shop run by a Chinese-looking couple with thick Aussie accents, but their ninety-year-old father Eddie Lee Long turned out to be a grandson of Quong Se Duk (or Kwong Sue Duk), about whose vast family, spanning various continents, a video was produced in 1995 with financial assistance from the Queensland Cultural Heritage branch.

Quong Se Duk: a transnational dynasty

Highly mobile, polygynous and wealthy, Quong Se Duk germinated a modern-day family dynasty spanning the globe. He was a herbalist from Guangdong province. Born in 1853, he was the twenty-sixth generation of a family to whom the title of Quong was bestowed in the year 960, and which claims a documented genealogy since the period of the Magna Carta and Ghengis Khan. Quong Se Duk followed the California gold rush, then returned to China to take his first wife Gee Shee in 1874. In the following year he went to the Palmer River. He returned again to China before establishing himself in the Northern Territory where he became a well-connected businessman who was once nominated as government resident. He owned the Sun Mao Lung Company at Southport and later established himself in Palmerston with his second wife Chan Mo Gwei and third wife Yun Yuk Lao. His stone-walled house in Cavenagh Street is the only surviving dwelling from Darwin's Chinatown. In 1889 he brought his first wife with him from China, and in 1898 he took a fourth wife in China and left his first wife there.

In 1902, at age fifty, he moved his family to Cairns. He set up as a herbalist in Sachs Street, Chinatown, and became the Chinese consul. Ida Lee, a daughter of the fourth wife, explained the structure of the household, ruled by the second wife who was a midwife and a very good cook. The fourth wife also cooked, and did the tidying up and the laundry. These two were Christians, while the third wife followed Buddhism. In 1917, now aged sixty-three, the patriarch moved to Melbourne and established a shop in Russell Street where he practised as a herbalist and gold dealer.

He had twenty-three children by the time he died in 1929 at age seventy-six. Of his sons, Thomas and Edward ran stores in Innisfail, Ingham and Townsville. Lesley operated in Babinda and Cairns, and later moved to Sydney and Melbourne. Fred went to Hong Kong and later moved to the USA. Lim went from school in Shanghai to Harvard and Columbia universities, and became a diplomat in the Philippines, and the president of the Bank of Canton in San Francisco. Harry attended Scotch College in Melbourne and opened restaurants in Melbourne. Victor attended Harvard University, joined the Chinese Embassy in Washington, worked at the United Nations, and became an academic in England, Malaysia, Hong Kong and Fiji. In the fifth generation, some 780 people trace their descent to Quong Se Duk.[3]

From Taam Sz Pui to See Poy Corner

Innisfail is reminded of its polyethnic past by See Poy Corner in the central business district. Now the site of a Coles supermarket, it was until 1981 the business of the See Poy family, a modern supermarket-type store even in the 1950s. Innisfail Chinatown had everything from long soup restaurants to gambling parlours, Herbert See Poy (Jnr) recalls. The whole block from Edith and Ernest Street to the Crown Hotel was Chinatown, still lively in the 1930s, 'and then the war, and then that dispersed everything, of course'. 'World War II seemed to be a milestone between the old and the new.'

Taam Sz Pui arrived in Australia for the Palmer gold rush in February 1877 and recorded in a diary those first frightful months in search of gold. Dated in the 'middle of spring of the 14th year of the Chinese Republic' (1925), his diary is written for the benefit of his eldest son, who was to take over the business. It gives his descendants valuable background on his origins, including the Chinese orthography of his name. It takes great care to detail the nature of his obligations to his family in China, how they were fulfilled, and how tortuous his rise to prosperity was. It gives a beautiful insight into the struggles of the Chinese gold seekers, and the building-up of a business based on kin and kindred.[4]

Sz Pui, born in 1854, was from the rural community of Ny Chuen, Nam Hoi district, Guangdong. His mother died when he was only seven, leaving three children. He was raised by an aunt and attended school from age eight to eleven. Later he helped his father to raise fish and plant mulberries, but a flood devastated the family holdings.

Following the rumour of 'inexhaustible gold at Cooktown', he set off at age twenty-three, together with his father and brother in January 1877 via Hong Kong, on a four-week journey to Cooktown. They were taken aback by the 'impoverished condition and starved looks of our fellow countrymen who were either penniless or ill'. Their hopes of good fortune took a heavy blow.

As they set off towards the mountains, only six days after arrival, they had already imbibed stories of cannibal attacks that could not have failed to impress any greenhorns. Consequently 'nobody dared tarry behind to rest or regain his breath'. Five days into the journey they had only covered twenty-six miles and were feeling exhausted. Forty miles out of town they were held up by a flood-swelled river during the Wet and their provisions were running out. Sz Pui returned to Cooktown to replenish supplies. After three months they had progressed 100 miles from Cooktown, still merely going over ground that had been exhausted by others before them. Sz Pui was taught how to pan for gold by Kwok Leung, and was able to obtain '1 or 2 candareens per day, enough to cover expenses'. Finally in July, 130 miles from Cooktown, the group staked a claim on a new rush. Here they could obtain six or seven candareens per day.

Meanwhile news had reached China that large numbers of impoverished Chinese were stranded in Cooktown, unable to make a living, and unable to return home. Sz Pui's second uncle mortgaged the family home and sent £32 through the Man Chuen On store in Cooktown, to cover their return passage. However, Sz Pui's father took ill 'and the money was spent'. Presumably it would not have covered the fare. They were now even more indebted to their family at home.

By December 1877 Sz Pui was on a field 160 miles from Cooktown, where he was 'stranded for a number of years'. He concluded that 'to search for gold was like trying to catch the moon at the bottom of the sea'. After five years he gave up gold digging and worked for £2 per month wages in a restaurant instead. Finally he was able to save some money, which he offered to his father. In 1882 he went to work at the new sugar plantation at the Johnson River, and saved up enough money, £54, to be able to send home his ailing father, who died there the following year. His brother was working in Cairns, and Sz Pui moved to Mourilyan where he joined a combine to open the Kam Woh store. After one of the partners, Lei Kam, was 'expelled' in 1884, the store changed its name to Tun Woh, with partners Luk Fui, Luk Tom and Luk Leung. Rumours of 'impending native attack' led the owners to shift the store to the Johnson River Valley (Innisfail) in 1885, where they were spectacularly successful. By 1888 the three other partners were able to return home with £800 each.

Presumably these payouts left the capital reserve of the store depleted, but by the same token the immense potential of the store had been demonstrated. By now both Sz Pui's grandparents had died, and his sister had been widowed. Sz Pui requested his sister to 'assume the duty as the head of the household', which he would continue to support financially. In other words, he arranged affairs at home so that he could continue to devote himself to the business that promised to support the family and establish him as its most important member. He financed the overseas passage of his nephew Ah Chi (Howard Long Hong), who later inherited an equal one-sixth share of the business alongside Sz Pui's own five children. Sz Pui was now 'an outside partner of Fook Wo Cheung in Hong Kong', who was his buying agent. However, the store was devastated by an 1890 flood, and in the following year Sz Pui was weakened by beri-beri from lack of fresh food. He invited his brother to join the store, but, unimpressed with his business acumen, sent him home in 1892 with £120.

At age forty Sz Pui was ready for marriage. His sister made arrangements with the Chin family, and his

The See Poy shop in Innisfail, 1920s. Photo: courtesy of Arthur See Hoe.

wife arrived in 1897 to join him in the Tun Woh store (still known by this name in 1925), where Sz Pui taught her English. Five children came in quick succession, named patriotically after English royalty or local rivers: Mei Tim (Victoria) in 1898, Mei Kin (Ida) in 1901, Wui Hing (Johnson) in 1902, Wui Wing (Gilbert) in 1905, and Wui Wah (Herbert) in 1907. In 1908 his wife and four elder children went to visit China 'to pay respects to the ancestors' and hold an 'Entering School Ceremony'. While there they acquired property, to be managed by Sz Pui's brother, which 'yielded $1,000 per annum'.

During the years that his family grew, the business suffered a flood in 1904, a storm in 1906, a flood causing heavy losses in 1913, and a storm in 1914 that devastated the township. (His son's memoirs refer to a 1918 cyclone, and a fire in the shop soon after.) Still, Sz Pui prospered. After his first visit home, 'our relatives, cousins and brothers came over one after the other. Each was employed according to his ability and paid according to his capacity' and 'they all became rich in the end'. The diary ends with the words: 'And if you want to perpetuate my work without laxity, observe the ten rules of business. Oh Hing! Oh Hing! Carefully attend to all your affairs. Hereafter I retire with your mother. Taam Sz Pui.'

Sz Pui's wife died the same year, and he followed twelve months later. According to Herbert (Snr), who also left a memoir, the full family name is Tong Chan Tan See Poy. The children were raised with the help of an *ama*, who offered warmth and protection when the parents were strict.

A portrait of the See Poy children in the Queensland Art Gallery. Source: *Courier Mail*, 29.1.2000:W12.

Hing (Johnson) did not take over the business alone. For many years, while the boys were being schooled in China, Sz Pui's eldest daughter Victoria practically ran the business—the only child who did not receive an education past grade five. Victoria, always practical, sensible and strong, became an autodidact. She learned to greet her Greek, Italian, Spanish and Chinese customers in their respective languages, eagerly picking up new phrases from *Victor Hugo Learn to Speak* books.

But there was also a lot of distributing to do, either on horseback or by cart, and sometimes it was an overnight journey pushing a trolley on the railway line to Mena Creek near Mourilyan, where they had a branch, or to the branches at Mourilyan and Silkwood.

Taam Sz Pui, portrait held in the James Cook Museum, Cooktown. Photo: Ganter, from a portrait held by the See Poy family.

Ready for Sunday School.
Edna and Alec See Hoe,
East Innisfail, 1930s.
Photo: courtesy of Arthur See Hoe.

All the children eventually joined in the business, to which a motor car dealership was added in the 1930s, selling the Dodge. The See Poy store became a pillar of commerce in Innisfail. It had the telephone number 3 (after police and fire), and the business sign announced that it sold 'anything and everything'.

That was true, because you could buy a needle, or building material, or lingerie, or hardware, ladies' wear, groceries, stock feed, dynamite, gold-digging equipment, motor cars, trucks—later on, it became the Ford dealer.[5]

Anything except gambling accessories, according to Herbert (Snr), who remembers his father's wrath when one of the girls brought back a mahjong set for sale in the shop, all the rage in Hong Kong in the 1930s. The business employed many Chinese, both members of family and other Australian-born Chinese, including Johnny Sing from Thursday Island, often as a matter of honouring promises of support for the younger members of other Chinese families. The family story weaves in and out of multiple references to Chinese families elsewhere. The See Poys became the focal point of a lively Chinese community.

Most of the children themselves took ABC (Australian-born Chinese) spouses. Ida married Quong Chong from the Quong Se Duk (viz.) family. Johnson married Theodora See Hoe, one of eight children of Ahiti and Wong See Hoe, another Palmer River veteran from the 1880s and a 'leading Chinese merchant' of Cooktown, according to the press report of his wedding in August 1902. (His brother was known as Ah Sam.) Theodora was born in Port Douglas and later lived in Atherton and Tolga on the tablelands. Like the Darwin ABCs, she said 'in those days you didn't go out with anybody, you played in your own backyard'. Ida won a scholarship for her secondary education, but the family could not afford to send her. Theodora came to work in the See Poy shop and helped to finance her younger brother's education at All Souls in Charters Towers ('Tiger' See Hoe). Theodora says the traditional Chinese practice was to send at least one boy of the village for education, usually the eldest son, and that everyone 'put in together' to finance him. Theodora and Johnson married in 1927 and built a beautiful house in Innisfail in 1931 that is likely to become heritage-listed. Theodora and her siblings felt thoroughly Australian. They spoke a little Lung Du dialect at home, but 'we couldn't communicate with our parents very well; they couldn't speak English, and we couldn't speak Chinese'. They were only faced with their Chineseness when they tried to enter professions. During World War II Theodora's youngest brother Alex was refused by the Australian Army and went instead into service with the United States Army in the Philippines.

Herbert attended Canton Christian College at Hainan Island (later renamed Ling Nam University) for six years from 1922. He was accompanied by his cousin Howard, who was returning home, and Gilbert was already at Hong Kong attending university studying for a Bachelor of Science. Life at home was so strict; Herbert refers to his school years in China as the happiest of his life. The college was financially supported from the USA, and had an American curriculum. The school offered all levels of tuition from primary to college, and a senior girls school, and its graduates were entitled to enter Columbia University. With classmates from the USA, Canada and other parts of the world, they played soccer, basketball and baseball. Herbert also played tuba and saxophone in the college orchestra. 'We were often invited to play for the officials in Canton. . . I had the good fortune of having personally met Sun Yat Sen. . . [both he and] Chiang Kai Chek made several visits to the college.'

Times became turbulent.

> I remember the time when Sun Yat Sen was turned on by his subordinate Chan Yu Ming, and Dr Sun Yat Sen escaped on the destroyer *Wing Fung*. I remember when there was a skirmish in the city and a shell hit the guest-house at Ling Nam.

Some members of the See Poy family in Innisfail with the original See Poy shop sign 'Go to See Poy's for Anything and Everything. Estb. 1882. Phone 3.' Presumably the shop had the town's first phone connection after police and fire. Tiger See Hoe, Adrian Lim Joon, Susie How Kee, Gwynne Lim Joon (née How Kee), Theodora See Poy (née See Hoe), Herbert See Poy Jnr.

To his father's great disappointment, Herbert was taught only Mandarin, not Cantonese, and still did not learn 'the correct mannerisms when greeting elders'. In fact, he became a thoroughly modern man. Herbert was recalled from China in 1926 when his father took ill, and then joined the emporium.

Herbert married Muriel Wong Yip from Charleville and built their new house in 1930. Their wedding was elaborately described in the *Cairns Post* (Monday, 13 February 1930) as: 'one of the most notable weddings in the history of Innisfail', the son of Tom See Poy 'whose name is inseparably associated with the history of this centre'. These two went on a four-month honeymoon in China and Hong Kong, but fear of banditry stopped them from visiting the ancestral village. World War II split up the family—Muriel went to Sydney, their son Herbert (Jnr) was taken to Charters Towers, and they could never grow together again, just as the Chinese community was unable to regroup after the war.

CHINESE EMPLOYERS

The remnant Chinese community from the polyethnic period equivocates on its relationships with Aborigines. Typical of the Darwin Chinese, Nellie Fong professes to know very little about Aborigines because of her protected upbringing. Other Australian-born Chinese of the second and third generation in Australia in Darwin, Innisfail and Cairns also had little to say about Aborigines. A few referred to the cannibal myth, and there were a number of references to Chinese–Aboriginal marriages and descendants in the sugar-growing area south and west of Cairns. Cases of Aboriginal–Chinese families like that of Pan Quee (viz.) are well known, and the mixed descendants gain silent acknowledgement if they frequent a Chinese-owned establishment, but a curtain of silence has long descended on them as far as portraying the Chinese community in Australia is concerned.[6] Diana Giese's first publication on the Darwin Chinese made no reference to such families, though her second book on Chinese in Australia includes the case of Gloria Lee, who had an Aboriginal mother from Tempe Downs and a father from Shekki (Shiqi) in Zhongshan, Guangdong. Gloria was sent to China for education, along with her two siblings, in 1919.[7] A community history of the Chinese in Broome, consisting of mainly Cantonese and a few Hakka speakers, makes some overtures towards Chinese–Aboriginal families. It refers to Yau Hong Tai (or Johnny Yu) and Tang Wei, both related to the two authors, but stops short of elaborating on the family of Jimmy Chi, reflecting perhaps current local sensitivities.[8]

Despite the anti-Chinese tone of much Aboriginal protection legislation, especially in Queensland, a number of these Australian-born Chinese families made reference to their Aboriginal employees. In Darwin Lily Ah Toy spoke at length about several of them, and has become a keeper of many stories. George Wah Day's family near Gordonvale, too, has been employing Aborigines for two generations. Though Wah Day had never been naturalised, Aborigines at his cane and vegetable farm were legally employed by permit since at least 1928, and the wages needed to be paid to the police. Mounted police occasionally came for rounds of inspection.[9]

There had always been exemptions to the rule of Chinese exclusion from employing Aborigines, and occasionally such employers, like Lily Ah Toy, became advocates for the people in their employ. Robert See Kee of See Yick and Company at Thursday Island, with offices in Hong Kong and Shanghai, supported an application for exemption from the *Protection Act* by Tommy Chin Fat of Normanton.[10] The mayor of Thursday Island referred to See Kee as 'one of the most influential Chinamen of this town and most European in manner and habits and very wealthy'.[11] His in-laws were a Filipino–Welsh couple.

Many Aboriginal workers held their Chinese employers in high esteem. This is reflected in comments from CPA Roth (Chapter 4—Queensland) as well as in various reminiscences. Ellen Cramond recorded the story of her father-in-law Jimmy Ah Yu at Mt Diamond in the Pine Creek mining fields who was saved from drowning in a wet season river crossing by his Aboriginal employee Deakin.[12]

Deakin worked for Ah Yu for years. Others who worked for him were Young Jack, Nim Fat Jack, and Long Paddy from Mary River, and Tommy Kelsey from Daly River. When Mrs Ah Yu died in 1938 she was mourned with a 'big corroboree down at the camp'.[13]

Ah Kim in Wyndham.
'A gin married to a chinaman—Mrs Ah Kim. Three boys and three girls of the union were taken to China by Ah Kim to be educated.' The *Adelaide Observer*, reporting on the Wyndham races on 30.5.1925.
Photo: courtesy of Darell Lewis.

Wah Day: the dynamics of group migration

George Wah Day's father Wong Wah Day came from Zhongshan in Guangdong in 1894 following his brother Wong Wah Hop who had settled in Mossman, Sydney. The third brother went to Mexico and the four girls stayed behind in Zhongshan. At age fifty-two Wong Wah Day married May Lee Yan, from a village some forty minutes from his own. May was the seventeen-year-old daughter of a former co-worker in the cornfields at Atherton Tablelands, Charlie Lee Yan. A condition of the marriage was that May's younger brother and sister be brought to Australia as well, because their mother had died in childbirth. The youngest girl, Annie Yeo, was raised by a Japanese couple. Wah Day became the first commercial grower of lychees in Australia, in 1930. His Australian-born son George and George's Chinese wife are still farming at Gordonvale.

The Wah Days at Gordonvale.

Nellie Fong and Lily Ah Toy: two views on Aborigines

Nellie Fong and Lily Ah Toy are both born in Darwin from all-Chinese families, and both married into Pine Creek business families. But while Nellie remembers little about Aborigines, Lily has become a storehouse of oral history.

Nellie Fong, the elder sister of the former Darwin mayor Harry Chan, felt that girls growing up in all-Chinese families had very little occasion to socialise with non-Chinese:

> To tell you the truth, I don't go out at all. There's only Jimmie Ah Toy's family, his mum and dad . . . We don't go out at all. One girls doesn't go out. We got our cousins and all that, all them were in the same area, so we got them together . . . We're not allowed to mix with anyone. How can you get married to any Australian boys? But there is one or two of them, later on, not in our generation, but younger, they do. Yes, later, and everyone's the same.

All her children married white Australians. The fourth generation of her family in Australia, her great-grand-children, have hardly a trace of Chinese features.

If they needed some day-labour they could request it from the Kahlin Compound:

> 'We did have Aborigines occasionally to cart water from the well, carry it to the kitchen, for bath, washing, all that . . . We had the natives to carry the water and chop the firewood. By lunchtime, they go back to the compound. That's about all we know about the Aborigine.'
>
> 'They didn't come in the house?'
>
> 'Oh, no, they were very good. We had one old man, we call him Dili, he was a gentle old man.'
>
> 'Where was he from?'
>
> 'I don't know.'
>
> 'Larrakia?'
>
> 'I'm not sure, in those days, anyways. [She was too young to think about it.] He's been there for years till I got engaged [at age fifteen].'

Nellie's father and uncles had a tailoring and drapery business in Darwin. Her mother had been brought from China and did not speak English. Nellie's wedding at age seventeen took place in China, where her Australian-born husband had been raised from about age four to fourteen. He was the son of one of the gardeners who had been engaged in the establishment of the Darwin Botanical Gardens, who then established a business in Brocks Creek. After the wedding, they moved to Pine Creek.

> So we don't have any natives to work for us, we don't use them, we can do all our own work ourselves. Only for, sometime, for them to go to the bush and collect firewood for us and leave it in a heap and then we go and collect it in our little utility, that's all. We don't use them in the garden 'cause they wouldn't know what to do, anyway.

The people who gathered the firewood may have been people like the Pan Quees (viz.), but Nellie had no idea who they might be. Despite the fact that they spoke English, she thought they must 'come from the bush'.

Lily Ah Toy, born in Darwin in 1917, had much the same upbringing, but had far more to say about Aborigines.

I had all my cousins living close together. The Moos lived not far away, and we'd go to football together. No motor cars, it was all a matter of walking. We lived a very restricted life. Nice Chinese girl don't go out running wild or anything like that. We just stayed around our area and played with the cousins and some of our friends come down. In the wet season we used to go out and pick all sorts of wild plums, the milky plums, the billy goat plum that's full of Vitamin C, eating all the wild berries and fruit. Some of the Aboriginals taught us that. And in Pine Creek the Aboriginal people taught us to eat wild grapes and other cucumbers and stuff, they're quite good.

Lily's father Wong Yung came to Australia as an indentured labourer. He became a wood merchant, and built their house from second-hand iron and bush timber, with an ant-bed floor and a well. All seven children helped to bark the timber. They were not a family that could afford domestic help. Still, they were able to get help from the Kahlin Compound and Lily could remember Aboriginal workers since childhood in the 1920s. They might get 'a couple of boys to come and clean the grass for the wet season'. A man called Charlie from the Kahlin Compound worked for them for some seven years.

They'd come in the day and then they had to go back to the compound up here, Kahlin Compound. Daily. Every day they come and every night they go back. We feed them and clothe them, and give them a suit of clothes and the wage in those days only five shillings a week. An ordinary person, a good cook, a Chinese cook, or even a white person, they only earn £1 a week . . . With the Chinese you always eat together. You never think of eating outside.

Lily Ah Toy with Judy Kulwin at Pine Creek.

But we just give Charlie his plate of food, he'd eat what we eat, rice and meat and stuff, he liked that. He'd sit outside by himself with his billycan of tea.

Lily worked as housemaid for a white couple after school, earning 7/6 a week for a half-time job. 'That supplied my whole family with bread' or it might buy a dress. When her father died her mother felt that the house had unlucky spirits, and they moved into Cavenagh Street, where they opened a vegetable shop alongside all the other Chinese shops. The Timorese and Japanese especially enjoyed the salted mustard cabbage, hum choy, and bought large quantities for the luggers. The produce came from Pine Creek and from a market garden at Two-and-a-Half Mile. One of the brothers from that market garden married Lily's cousin and the other became Lily's husband in 1936. They bought a shop in Pine Creek in 1935, where Aborigines were employed in the gardens.

Sunday School at Pine Creek. The Ah Toy children made up a sizeable portion of the Pine Creek Sunday School. Next to Captain Pedersen from the Salvation Army is Joyce Ah Toy (later Cheong Chin), and next to her is May Knight (later Katona). The little one at front in the blue dress is Elaine Ah Toy. The black girl with the white hair bow is Margaret Hart (later Graham). Next to her in a blue dress is Grace Ah Toy. The tall boy in front of Mr Bentley is Edward Ah Toy, and the head peeping up behind is Lawrence Ah Toy. The woman in the black dress is Mrs Bentley, and next to her in a white dress is her daughter Myrtle.

Source: *Australian Women's Weekly*, 19.12.1951.

My father-in-law would tell them what to do, they'd weed, hoe the vegies and they till the ground and water it. But they are very, very conscientious, because they are so proud when they get the bed all tidy and clean, they'd say, 'Come and have a look, missus', and of course you praise them, and when the vegetable or the tomatoes full of fruit—they're really proud of it. And they got the routine job of keeping the water filled and the wood box full and that sort of thing . . . They work for a few months and then go away and come back, or maybe they ask someone else to come. Jawoyn people [locals], some from the Daly River.

Lily and Jimmie Ah Toy ran a bakery, and took over the shop after the death of his parents. There were a number of 'old and indigent' Chinese men in Pine Creek in the 1930s who received food vouchers from the police station. Jimmie used to drive them home with their purchases. Local Aborigines came to the store to trade fresh fish for sugar, tea and tobacco.[14]

Because they had a liquor licence, the Ah Toys were not permitted to have Aborigines on their premises, but they engaged Aboriginal help to unload the stores from the train, for gardening and weeding, and washing, which was done in the next paddock. Deakin and Mabel did housework: cleaning, ironing, lighting the fires in the morning. Mabel had been to Sydney working for Mrs John Lyons, wife of a solicitor, and spoke perfect English, 'she knew exactly what to do' and was very good help. She later moved with the Ah Toys to Darwin. And Deakin reputedly dusted more thoroughly than Lily herself would have done. The interior walls of the bedrooms were made from corrugated iron, and 'he used to wipe each corrugation to clean the dust, and if there's any corner that he can't get at he used to blow the dust out!'

When Deakin died, Lily attended his traditional funeral, and found it to be very similar to a Chinese funeral because they had to step through the smoke, in this case even the dog and the hurricane lamp were smoked. In a Chinese funeral, a little fire would be lit at the gate of the house of the deceased, and all the mourners would step over the smoke. Before the house is entered, everyone washes their hands in a dish of water with pomolo leaves to purify. 'You see, all the badness is gone, we start new again.' For her the smoking ritual meant that the spirit wouldn't come back. Without having to ask any questions about the significance of the Aboriginal ritual, Lily understood it well, drawing on her Chinese tradition.

Unlike many employers of Aboriginal labour, Lily is able to state the country of her former employees. She referred to 'Old Spider, a six-foot-tall Brinkin man from Daly River', to Lily Huddlestones 'from the other side of Daly River, Bennings, they split off from Kybrook Farm, their country is Douglas River', and mentioned that Violet Smith and Judy Kulwin from the Myilly group were both traditional owners of Kakadu. Clearly her relationships with Aboriginal employees ran much deeper than an employment contract. She felt some sense of obligation for those who worked for her, and believes this ran both ways.

Judy Kulwin and her first husband Willie lived in a hut out the back of the Pine Creek shop, with Willie's second wife Kitty, and Willie's brother took his place after his death.

> They always like to bring somebody to take their place, to look after us. So they said to our children, 'We bin grow you up.' They have that loyalty and you can trust them. They come into our house, you know, everything open, clean . . . come into the living room, they don't touch a thing.

When Judy fell pregnant after the war, she was so afraid that the child would be taken away that she hid the girl with an Aboriginal couple in the bush for six years.

> You know how they used to take the part-coloured children away from their parents and put them in the compound and put them in all the missions? Well, the people who looked after Judy, they hid her [baby] by blackening her with charcoal, poor thing.

Finally Judy's older sister Kitty, as the girl's mother in Aboriginal law, brought May Knight to Lily Ah Toy to take her in so she could go to school with Lily's children.

> I knew that this child existed but I never ever set eyes on her until we were approached could she go to school . . . That same girl, given a chance, she worked herself right up at the Darwin University. She still has the respect to me. And her children are also very, very clever.

Little May Knight is captured in a *Women's Weekly* photograph at the Pine Creek Sunday School with the Ah Toy children in 1951. Lily follows the family's progress with interest and satisfaction.

May's daughter had told me that Lily spoke Jawoyn. Lily modestly said she only spoke 'enough to tell them off if they were arguing'. If there was an argument at night she'd go outside and yell at them in lingo, shining the torch on herself so they could see her.

By chance I met Lily Ah Toy again at Pine Creek, where she introduced me to some of her former employees, who called her 'Mum' and were really pleased to see her.

CHINESE–ABORIGINAL COMMUNITIES

The Australian landscape is dotted with faint reminders of former Chinese occupation: Chinaman creeks, China walls, Chinese wells, Chinatowns, Chinaman gardens. There were also many small communities dotted around the north with a core of Chinese–Aboriginal families. In this book I have gathered only a few of their stories, from the Daly in the Northern Territory, at Louie Creek in the Gulf country, at Woods Lake near Burketown, and at China Camp in the Daintree. In such places we may find the mixed indigenous descendants of Chinese pottering about their market gardens as if time had stood still.

China Camp on the Bloomfield

China Camp, on the Creb track to Wujal-Wujal in the Daintree, is a garden oasis in the bush. It was established by Chinese tin miners, and is now occupied by a few old Aboriginal men who continue to maintain links to country, affording younger members of their families an occasional spell. Peter Fischer and George Kulka maintain a fairly self-sufficient lifestyle, with poultry and a rich harvest of fruit and vegetables: mangos, bananas, papaya.

The first archival reference to China Camp is in 1888 as a tin field. It was part of the Cunnamurra run and mining claim selected by William Baird, who discovered the Annan River tin deposits in 1885 and gold on the Wenlock in 1896. In 1888 the tin field-housed 110 Chinese and 132 Javanese and Malay tin miners. Robert Baird opened a store 'for the Chinese and tin scratchers at China Camp'.

Peter Fischer, age seventy-eight, at China Camp, in the Daintree with visitor Ioannis Manousakis, 1997. China Camp is a garden oasis on the Creb track.

Chong at the Woods Lake market gardens

Woods Lake gained its name during the search for lost explorers Burke and Wills in 1861, when Aboriginal guides led William Landsborough and his party to this waterhole after crossing the Plains of Promise. It was an 'unbroken sheet of water' teeming with whistling ducks and grey crane and other 'aquatic fowl'. Landsborough gave it the name of his lieutenant in charge of the *Victoria*. It was a two-mile-long lagoon that became until 1963 the main water supply for Burketown, the colonisation of which started shortly afterwards.

By the 1880s Woods Lake was a flourishing Chinese market garden, supplying the town with fresh food as well, and even selling to Thursday Island. There were two large market gardens at Woods Lake, and another one at Louie Creek that delivered vegetables as far as Camooweal, a four-day journey by spring cart. Jimmy Ah Fin and Lee Gee were the local bakers in Burketown. Indeed there were so many Chinese in the Burketown area, which supplied the mining fields of the Gulf, that the cemetery had a Chinese section, but it has since been eroded by floods.

From Doomadgee to Mornington Island, Aboriginal people remember 'the Lakes' as a place where one used to call in for vegetables and fruit. The Burketown police letter books make frequent reference to Aborigines camped there, and to Chinese–Aboriginal children, but from 1891 to 1911 the only actionable incident at Woods Lake was the conviction of Jemmy Ah Sue for supplying liquor to an Aboriginal named Minnie in 1906. Indeed, in response to opinions expressed on opium smoking, the local sergeant wrote in June 1907: 'I have not seen one instance of use of opium either at the blacks camps or Chinese stores or gardens in this district.'[15] Woods Lake was the site of a number of legal marriages between Chinese and indigenous people. But in the 1930s the official mood changed and the local protector targeted a number of mixed families for surveillance, including one at Louie Creek. In January 1935 the Aboriginal camp at Woods Lake was unoccupied.[16] In that year, the Removals Register records that a group of twenty-three were removed in a single swoop from Turn-Off Lagoon to Mornington Island for 'immoral associations'—often a euphemism for associating with Chinese.

Nellie Chong at Woods Lake, near Burketown, 1997. This used to be the Chinese gardens outside Burketown. The former Woods Lake is rapidly drying up. Nellie's father Chong Que Ang arrived at age fourteen in Australia, and married Sarah Ah Sam of mixed descent. One of Nellie's uncles was taken back to China and settled there.

Woods Lake, 1939.
Sadie Watson (née Ah Quey) carrying Maudie's daughter Gertie, Maudie Kum Sing carrying her daughter Violet. Herbie Watson, Jessie Watson, Archie Kum Sing (wearing a hat), and at front, Nancy Watson, William Sewter, Rachel Kum Sing, Kate Watson (later Yamaguchi), Alfie Kum Sing.
Photo: courtesy of Kate Yamaguchi, Mt Isa.

By the time I visited Woods Lake, Nellie Chong and her sister Louie, ill at the time and in her eighties, were the sole remaining residents of 'The Lakes'. Nellie was tending her Chinese cabbages and other vegetables, but everything looked dry. For the past ten years or so the water has gradually been drying up and the lake is receding. Nellie says the lagoon is simply silting up from the run-off carried into it by many creeks. The last season had been so dry that a patch of twenty-two mango trees was being eaten up by white ants.

Nellie's father was Chong Que Ang, known as Tommy Chong. He had arrived at age thirteen, possibly as a stow-away, from Guangdong. Judging by his approximate age at his death in 1957, he must have been born in the 1880s, and he arrived around 1893. In 1908 he married Sarah Ah Sam (also referred to as Sarah Ah Quom or Acum), who was the daughter of Minnie and the Chinese cook at Lawn Hill. Ah Sam had previously resided at Woods Lake in 1895.[17] Sarah lived at Lawn Hill Station and was sixteen at the time of her marriage. The local protector noted that the 'Turn-Off Lagoon police speaks well of these people'.[18]

Sarah's only surviving brother was living in China with his grandfather, and her sister Lora married Rinzo Yamaguchi (viz.).

Tommy and Sarah Chong used to cook on stations in the Gulf area, including Lawn Hill, then they became gardeners, and eventually Tommy went sandalwooding and boundary riding. Nellie was the youngest of six children born in 1934. She remembers him as 'a good father, one of the best'. Nellie grew up to love gardening, and carried on looking after her gardens next to a full-time job in town, when they had no water pump, and gathering cow manure to make liquid fertiliser.

The department records described Minnie as a 'Leichhardt aboriginal' (the Leichhardt River flows roughly from Mt Isa to Burketown), and one of the local elders told Nellie where she was from. Still, Nellie insists she does not know where her Aboriginal grandmother Minnie came from, and finds it difficult to identify as Aboriginal: 'I have to, I suppose so. But I just live the way we lived as a child growing up—not like these here now, claiming land, fighting over this, fighting over that.' She is on a Special Lease, on common land, a remnant of history. Since she does not want to be included in land claims, there will be nothing for her daughter to inherit either from her Chinese patrilineage or her Aboriginal matrilineage. In terms of rights to land, 'we all grew up on it, all together, Europeans and coloured and all that. We're all together now. We're all one.'

THE CANNIBAL MYTH

No doubt the most well-known anecdote of interactions between Chinese and Aborigines is the alleged cannibalistic preference of Aborigines for Chinese. Part of local historical knowledge particularly in the Palmer River area, it is amply described in *River of Gold* by Hector Holthouse and was resurrected into public debate by Pauline Hanson in the 1990s.

The Palmer gold rush followed from William Hann's explorations in 1872–73, and it is possible that Chinese were landed at the Bloomfield to avoid government taxes as early as this.[19] By 1877 the Daintree was opened for selection and Cairns and Port Douglas were established as provisioning stations. In 1880 Harry Fraser and the formidable Christie Palmerston were gold prospecting in the Daintree.[20] Palmerston, his name engraved on the goldfields landscape with a river, is a well-known, if not celebrated, historical figure of the area. He was intent on dominating the mining in this area and on keeping Chinese away. He was known as a great antagonist of Chinese, and forged strategic alliances with local Aborigines. Holthouse, in characteristically offensive language, describes the dynamics as follows:

> Christie Palmerston was one of the most remarkable men the north ever knew. To the diggers he became a friend in need, to the Chinese a death-dealing terror, and to the cannibal blacks a legendary figure who moved among them unmolested . . . He had an uncanny knack of handling the wild blacks. At a time when white and Chinese diggers alike were being killed and eaten by them, he was always able to make friends among any tribe he chose and recruit young bucks who would follow him anywhere. For years he roamed the unexplored ranges with a private army of myalls, picking up gold wherever he could find it, defying the law whenever it suited him. But for the Chinese he had a fanatical hatred. He raided them ruthlessly, robbed them of their gold and stores, killed them by the dozen, and, it was alleged, bartered those he took prisoner with the cannibal blacks knowing they would be used as food . . . No one ever saw him digging for gold, but he always seemed to have a good supply of it. Old diggers muttered darkly that it came from miners who had been murdered by the blacks . . . In the early days of the rush Palmerston had organized his myalls into gangs to carry rations up from the coast. When coolies began to compete, he retaliated by raiding their pack trains with his blacks, stealing their stores to sell to the diggers himself, and, according to some of the Chinese storekeepers at any rate, paying his cannibal recruits by letting them have the Chinese prisoners as food. The blacks by then were doing so much raiding on their own account that no one could tell whether Palmerston had any part in it or not . . . There was nothing Palmerston seemed to enjoy better than finding a big gang of Chinese scouring the gravel in some isolated gully. With his myall mob at his heels, he would charge down on them, firing wildly, screeching the same hideous cockatoo battle cry as the blacks themselves, and, as often as not, scarcely distinguishable from them.[21]

Holthouse's account of attacks on Chinese, veiled as Aboriginal attacks, is supported by other sources.

Sometimes Aborigines were deliberately implicated in a killing by leaving Aboriginal spears or other artefacts at the scene. But the reference to cannibalism as a culinary practice is ludicrous. Holthouse's first chapter, entitled 'Cannibal Country', contains a number of professed first-hand accounts of cannibal activity on the Palmer, none of them referenced to a source, and his invocations of a 'preference for Chinese' are too macabre to warrant repetition. Generally the evidence for cannibalism in such sources is of the type where 'They also found the whole body of a dead blackfellow, freshly cooked, and ready for eating.'[22] Michael Pickering, in an exhaustive review of evidence for cannibalism in Australia, found that the greatest number of references to it were repetitions of a much smaller number of reported incidents, often falsely parading as first-hand accounts, and that of the reported incidents most were unreliable. They either inferred cannibalism from evidence which simply could not yield it (such as finding only 'the charred hand of a white woman') or clearly reflected a misreading of mortuary practices which involved burying the bones after they had been cleaned of flesh by firing. After careful examination of a vast amount of textual references, Pickering was left with only a handful of reliable first-hand accounts that involved the ritual consumption of certain body parts, such as kidney fat.[23]

The elders associated with China Camp near Mossman will not deny the practice of cannibalism in the past, though they usually ascribe it to some other group, not their own.[24] But when I cited some passages from Holthouse to Peter Costello at Hopevale, originally from Musgrave, he said: 'That book should be destroyed. Tell him to burn the book.' His son David added: 'These are the things that destroy Reconciliation.'[25]

The alleged cannibalistic preference of Aborigines for Chinese was part of the lore into which new arrivals were quickly immersed when they arrived in the ports delivering them to the goldfields, with barely an idea what to expect.

This is how it occurs in the memoirs of Taam Sz Pui, who set off into the mountains behind Cooktown with a group of Chinese six days after their arrival. Because they had already heard about cannibals in the area 'no-one dared tarry behind to rest or regain his breath'. Sz Pui's descriptions of the arduousness of the journey reports no incident with Aborigines, but ten months into their journey, in December, they set up camp at Mitchell River where they 'heard natives at night'. They were so worried that they kept watch all night and left the next morning.[26]

Sz Pui's memoir hints that the fear of cannibalism exerted a powerful discipline on a motley crew of exhausted workers. It was simply too useful a myth to disappear quickly, in the face of personal experiences with Aborigines. Decades later, Japanese recruiters spread an equally useful myth among their Aboriginal recruits, that sharks were attracted to white skin. It meant that it was dangerous to go swimming diving with white people, and much better to sign on with the Japanese.

Sam Ah Bow and Sam Lee On, who later settled at Louie Creek (viz.), also carried this lore. They were part of an epic migration from the Northern Territory into Queensland and said that along the way they had been treated to stories of Aboriginal cannibals, who reputedly preferred Chinese to any other victims.[27]

Tim Jones refers to a number of Aboriginal attacks on Chinese miners in the Northern Territory, and there were attacks on Chinese shepherds. Noel Loos argues that the Chinese may have been more liable to attack because they were less protected by police, less well armed, and ventured into unpoliceable territory. If Chinese appeared to Aborigines as colonisers, they were attacked in areas where there was armed resistance. But they were not a favoured target, and definitely not subject to cannibalistic motives. Against the vast number of Aboriginal attacks on Chinese must be read the evidence of harmonious relations between them.

The 1895 migration of Chinese miners from the Northern Territory to Queensland occured as a result of sharpen-ing legislation in the Northern Territory, when in 1895 a Goldmining Bill was tabled to bar 'any Chinese or Asiatic alien' from taking out mining leases, and the *Chinese Exclusion Act* was amended to facilitate the eviction of Chinese from golfields. This, together with the exhaustion of alluvial fields, set in train a wave of migration into Queensland.

Some slipped through without paying the Queensland poll-tax, but many were apprehended. In 1895 the Burketown paper reported that thirty-five Chinese had been arrested and placed in the lock-up, harness room and other places. The following year about a hundred were arrested at Camooweal and escorted back to the nearest water-hole in the Territory and left there. In 1898 another twenty arrived at Cloncurry escorted by two constables and a tracker . . . They had been three months on the road through lonely and unsettled country, and many had died from thirst and hunger. It was a relief to be arrested in Queensland and given food and clothing.[28]

JAPANESE AND ABORIGINES

With the Japanese community in Australia that has survived from the pre-war period, matters stand a little differently. This community was severely disrupted as a result of internment and repatriation. It is well known that many of the Japanese had wives and children here and in Japan. But during interviews in Japan among those who were repatriated, it was unthinkable to mention the chance of any Aboriginal relatives. This was partly due to the social setting of the interviews in Japan, often in the presence of other family members and always translated by my female travel companion, and occasionally in the presence of journalists. It also had to do with the high social standing accorded to 'Arafura divers', in whose memory a number of monuments have been erected, and who, as pioneers and conveyors of wealth, enjoy a status comparable to Anzac veterans in Australia.

Those Japanese who did manage to return to the north after the war were generally the very people who already had indigenous families there, so their mixed marriages have become part of the family heritage and are openly acknowledged.

Louie Creek: Chinese–Aborigines of the Gulf

Louie Creek was another site of intensive interaction between Chinese and Aborigines. Louie Creek straddles Lawn Hill Station and Lawn Hill National Park, described in the travel literature as being 'like an emerald in the desert'. Its Aboriginal art sites reveal longstanding indigenous occupation.

There were a number of Chinese at Louie Creek, prominent among them Sam Ah Bow who married Opal, a Wanyi (Lawn Hill) woman originally from Brunette Downs in the Northern Territory, in 1898. Of their five children, three were taken back to China, and two married Chinese men in Australia. Loma was twelve when her three siblings—seventeen-year-old Gomthen, thirteen-year-old Emma and seven-year-old Amy—left for China in 1903. The youngest child was Queegin (or Quinsen), known as Dolly. Ethel Clark, a great-granddaughter of Ah Bow and keeper of the family history, says: 'A lot of these Chinese–Aboriginal people in the Gulf country here are all related in some way. It's so funny. The Ah Kits, and the Ah Wangs, and the Lee Ons and the Timms, Ah Fat, and somehow or other they all intermarried in this younger generation.'

Sam Ah Bow was from the Chu Kum Bow family in Tyfokong, Guangdong. He was part of an epic Chinese march from Darwin to 'China Wall' at Nicholson River in the Gulf. From there they travelled by ship to Burketown, and many went on to Croydon and Georgetown and as far as the Atherton Tablelands in search of gold.

Ah Bow became the gardener at Lawn Hill Station. He was naturalised and in 1907 he took over the Louie Creek leases from the estate of miner John Charles Ingram, who had held them for only a year. Tim See Too had already started up gardens on the lease but he moved on to Farley Creek nearby. Louie Creek had a beautiful spring, which has since dried up. The Ah Bows had goats and their own cattle brand as well as extensive gardens. They held three leases amounting to 130 acres. Two of these leases were taken up by Ah Bow's daughter Dolly in 1935, but all were lost to the family in 1985, through non-payment of rates, because none of the descendants was aware of them. At a family reunion at Louie Creek in 1988, they found an irrigation sluice, tools and Chinese artefacts, but by 1991 it had all been destroyed by a fire. Only the dam remains, referred to as 'Chinaman Dam'.

The Ah Bows became a focus of community at Louie Creek. Opal was a midwife who delivered many children in the Burketown district, including all her own grandchildren. Aboriginal women from Burketown and Doomadgee would come to Louie Creek when it was time to give birth to their babies. Sam Ah Bow was an intrepid keeper of records, leaving a wealth of information for his descendants who believe that he had much traditional healing knowledge. He indicated that his father was Detfung, a doctor. Louie Creek was also a focal point for Chinese, who would come visiting or just stop over on their way through, or work for Ah Bow. Chinese hawkers came to obtain supplies of bananas, oranges, plums, mangos and all kinds of produce. There were three separate camp sites: the Chinese in the gardens on one side of the creek,

Aborigines on the other side, and Europeans who worked at the mines or fencing.

Dolly, the youngest daughter of Opal and Sam Ah Bow, was very young when she married Johnny Ah Kup in 1918. Johnny, also from China, was reputedly a great cook. They lived at Louie Creek until 1936. Their eldest daughter of eleven children, born in 1920, was removed under the *Aborigines Protection Act* in May 1935 at age fourteen and was signed on as a domestic at Gregory Downs, Planet Downs, Kunkulla and Almora Station. Several people, including Dolly's brother-in-law Johnny Leon, tried to act on her behalf until July 1938, when she was finally permitted to 'manage her own affairs', but without being granted an exemption. In the process, the whole family came 'under surveillance'. Not unlike the local protector in the case of Atima Ahwang (viz.), local protector Thornton at Gregory Downs had formed an opinion about undesirable associations between Aborigines and Chinese at Louie Creek, and waged a battle against Ah Kup's reputation.

By the time I met Dolly Ah Kup in Cloncurry, she had twenty-two grandchildren, forty-two great-grandchildren, and twenty-four great-great-grandchildren. One of them is Alexis Wright, the author of the powerful novel *Plains of Promises*.

Loma Ah Bow, the only other child of Opal and Sam Ah Bow not repatriated to China, also married a Chinese. She was fifteen when she married Sam Lee On, aged fifty-five. He was also known as Ah Saw, born in China in 1857 as the son of Lee Gow, storekeeper, and Wang Gue. He arrived in 1875 from Hong Kong with two brothers, who later returned to China, apparently having done well at the Palmer. Like his father-in-law, Sam Lee On had been part of the Chinese migration from Darwin and had worked on the goldfields and gradually worked his way to Lawn Hill. He worked as cook and gardener at a number of stations. In 1914 his employer was Charlie Ah Chong at Camooweal, who had a market garden employing five Chinese. Ah Chong, too, had married an Aboriginal woman, Maggie, from Lawn Hill Station in 1912.[29]

Sam Ah Bow of Guangdong walked from Darwin to the Gulf of Carpentaria in search of gold. He settled with his Aboriginal wife Opal at Louie Creek (Lawn Hill—pictured) until his death in 1932. A sizeable Chinese– Aboriginal community emerged around the station.

Photo: courtesy of Ethel Clark, Mt Isa.

The children of Loma and Sam Lee On were: William (or Ah Kong), born in 1908 and Johnny (or Dang Kong), both born at Gregory Downs; Moody (or Sing Kong), born at Lawn Hill; Jessie and Albert (Ben Kong), born at Louie Creek; and Daisy, Arthur, Dulcie, Maysie, Benjamin and Fred (or Ah Tai), born in Camooweal. Loma bore eleven children, of whom four died early. She herself died at Fred's birth in 1928, at age thirty-seven. Whether by chance or through some other cosmic connection, her three elder sons, all drovers, had gathered at home just before her death. Moody had just returned from his very first 2,000-kilometre droving trek. William, the eldest, and Johnny, the second son, met up by chance at the People's Palace in Brisbane and decided to come back together, reaching Cloncurry just a week before Loma died in Camooweal.

Lee On took over Ah Chong's bakery in 1924 under the business name 'Leon and Sons'. The spelling of this family name has gradually changed to Leon. All the boys became excellent cooks and took over the cooking in their families. William took over the bakery in 1932 so that his father could return to China, where he died in 1940 at age ninety.

Moody ended up working as cook at Brunette Downs, the birthplace of his grandmother Opal. During his four-year stint there, he cooked for the deputy prime minister and his thirty-six-strong party visiting the Northern Territory for a week. He remembers Mrs McEwen personally congratulating him on his cooking.[30]

Eventually the boys were drawn to Mt Isa mines where William worked from 1947 to 1973, Moody from 1948 to 1963, and Johnny until his retirement. At Mt Isa they and their children maintained the tradition of keeping an open house. Moody's daughter Ethel Clark said,

> This place here, from the time it was built to just the last few years, it was a place for all the Aboriginal people from the stations. They came in, they waited here to have their babies, or they came here to do their Christmas shopping, it didn't matter because most of them were Aboriginal people, they came in and they stayed here, and they lived here . . . There weren't places in town like hostels for the women from around the stations to come, so this is where they all lived, and that's from Cairns and anywhere. We always had the link with the Aboriginal side and the Chinese side . . . Mt Isa itself has been a really multiracial place from the beginning . . . Dad can go anywhere around town and people look after him, black, white or any colour. If they know who he is they bring him home. The black people respect him and the white people respect him . . . But now, in the last five years there's more racial tension than ever before. There's been a whole new group of people coming into Mt Isa. Over the years there's been a lot coming, the Germans, the Italians, there was a huge Finnish and Irish population here, Greeks, and they were the sort of people that came here to work and they stayed here. But now these people are leaving and a new group have come in, it's a whole new scene now.

Albert Leon has joined an overseas Chinese (*huaqiao*) association in Sydney and is attuned to the Chinese identity politics, which distinguish between being Chinese, and being of Chinese origin. He is aware that mainland China has sometimes used the presence of people 'of Chinese origin' as a basis for territorial claims—but reminds us that 'it's not only the Chinese that does it'. He argues that Chinese were highly prominent in Australian economic development: 'Everywhere in Australia, if there's a town that could prosper, there's always one Chinese family there. If there's no Chinese in that town, that town is no good, because the Chinese won't settle unless they can make money. And they left descendants.'

Steven Alberts in Broome spoke about his mother's relationship with Okumura Masetora. He was a 'top diver' in Broome before the war, and was one of those who returned after the war. Being already married with children in Japan, the couple waited for some twenty years until they married, by which time they had several grandchildren together. Though Alberts was not one of Okumura's children, he says,

> I grew up with all the Japanee mob, they all became our relatives. And they used to send their money home to Japan. And because I was the only kid there, every time we get Christmas or Easter or whatever, I'd get heaps of presents from all the Japanese, so I had all these toys from all these heaps of Japanese.

Alberts says the Japanese helped to support the Aborigines from the hill camps, and indeed these two communities supported each other. When the luggers came in they would bring seafood and tinned food

> and they used to bring all these turtles, all lined up on the beach, so all the people from the hill used to come over, 'pick any one you want', and they were free for all the people, and that used to be the thing... We used to stand on the hill when all the luggers came in, me and my auntie and my mother. We could see all the luggers come in, fantastic sight, one by one . . . And all the different camps they had. From there right up to where 'Seaview' is now [the hillside on the foreshore of town], there used to be all different Aboriginal camps. Heaps of women were waiting for their men, not only Japanese—Chinamen and all.[31]

This open acknowledgement of relationships is also reflected in the way the history of the Japanese community in Australia has been represented. Yuriko Nagata's study of Japanese internees refers to Arthur Yamaguchi at Mt Isa, who has a Japanese father, Rinzo Yamaguchi, and a Chinese–Aboriginal mother, Lora. At Thursday Island a number of men with local families were among the Japanese rounded up in 1941. Listed in an inventory of aliens compiled prior to the round-up were: Tomitaro Fuji, married with one child to Josie Chin Soon of Chinese–Torres Strait–Samoan descent; Iwazo Takai, married with three children to Sophia Baba of Malay–Torres Strait descent; Kyuhichi Shibasaki, married with three children to Jean Ah Boo of Malay–Aboriginal descent; and Seikitchi Takimoto, who was known to live with a mixed descendant.[32] On Thursday Island stories abound of other relation-ships that were torn apart as a result of deportations.[33] Yuriko Nagata established that only thirty-eight Japanese repatriated to Thursday Island after the war, including six males and six females with mixed Japanese parentage. Nakata Tamiya, or Tom Nakata, was the first to return to Thursday Island in 1947, and found shelter with the Dewis family of Malay–Islander origin.[34] He married Cessa Mills, one of Thursday Island's own Mills Sisters, a popular singing group.

Yamaguchi: 'I bin miss him'

Rinzo was the son of Manzo and Orie Yamaguchi, farmers in Rokue village, Kumamoto prefecture (Japan). He was born in 1875 and came to Australia from Kobe in 1896 to work in the Palms sugar mill near Mackay, then worked in Townsville and Cairns before he came to Burketown. In 1919 he married seventeen-year-old Lora Ah Sam from Woods Lake in Burketown. Lora's mother was Minnie from Burketown, and her father was Ah Sam. Rinzo (known as Harry) and Lora worked at Riversleigh Station (now famous for its fossils), Lawn Hill Station and Burketown, and on Avon Downs, Alexandria and Wologoran stations in the Northern Territory. By the late 1920s Rinzo had a lorry and supplied outlying stations with fruit and vegetables from Burketown (presumably Woods Lake)—a job in which he was sometimes entrusted with messages and errands, such as from the police stations. Their only child Arthur was born in 1921, and they moved back to Burketown to open a bakery in 1930. The Chinese bakeries had long disappeared.

At age sixty-nine, Rinzo was arrested in December 1941. He had failed to register as an alien, and protested that he had been naturalised at Cooktown in 1909 or thereabouts, though he no longer had the documents, which were all destroyed by a fire in Burketown in 1912 while he worked as a cook in the Commonwealth Hotel. He remembered the name of the sergeant who had taken his oath, and the charge of £13. The authorities did not believe a word of it, recalling that it had been policy since 1903 not to naturalise Asians. (A fire destroyed all Burketown Council records in 1927.) Against the advice of the Burketown sergeant, whose custody involved letting Rinzo sleep on the verandah, he was interned at Hay. His wife said, 'I bin miss him. Cryin', cryin' all night. Dogs bin miss him too because he had to feed them and play with them. Them dogs was howlin' and I was howlin' too, meanin' I started the dogs. Everybody said: "You start your dogs howlin' like that, it's no good. Everybody don't like it." I said, OK.' Despite intensive lobbying by his son, a member of the North Australia Observer Unit, he was not released from Loveday until February 1945.[35]

The legacy of these historical circumstances is that the Japanese descendants in Australia today belong largely to families that are well integrated with indigenous communities, whereas the descendants of the prewar Chinese population in Australia stem mostly from business families who had brought their wives from China and were able to establish quite homogenous communities whose members view themselves as Australian-born Chinese or simply as Australians. The differences between these communities today do not reflect differences in interaction with Aborigines.

Needless to say, not all liaisons that issued in offspring resulted in the formation of families. I encountered a number of anecdotal references to the Aboriginal children of Japanese fathers who are not acknowledged either here or in Japan, and some such descendants are unsure of who their fathers were. William Brown of Mackay believes that Kono was his father.[36] Others refer to him as 'Toksan' and say that he looks the 'spitting image' of Kono.[37] A renowned lugger captain, Kono Tesaburo from Ehime, born around 1893, was well known by a number of my interviewees in Japan, some of whom had been interned together with him. He is also remembered by name by a number of Aborigines from the eastern side of Cape York, who had worked with him. Like many in the marine industry, he did not always play by the rules, sometimes taking Aboriginal crew outside of Australian waters to poach around New Caledonia or Papua New Guinea. Kono was among the Japanese trepangers who operated on a system based on large schooners, staying at sea for three months at a time, and carrying some twelve or thirteen indigenous divers to fish between the Barrier Reef and the islands of southern New Guinea.[38] It must be cautioned, however, that a number of Kono family members were engaged in the Australian fishery. Peter Costello at Hopevale said that among the Japanese who came to visit Hopevale and entertained good relations with Father Schwartz was an 'old fellow' whose son sailed with him, by the name of Konu.[39] Kono Chiyoju, born around 1912, and 'very popular' among the Japanese, was also employed by Morey Company and interned. And in 1926 reference was made to a Kono Kohachiro who jumped ship to stop over in Mackay for two months but was otherwise also employed, like captain Kono, on the Morey Company's *Mildred*.[40]

William Brown, Mackay. Photo: courtesy of Narelle Brown, Mackay.

Abandoned: Ah Kui on the Daly

Topsy Ah Kui Kunnarajie, a Malak-Malak woman at Daly River, only knows her Chinese father's name as Ah Kui (pronounced as a:'kwi). He lived at Tipperary Station and came only occasionally bringing money. She remembers the first time she saw him: 'When I seen him and looked like him [saw what he looked like], I jumped back, cause I never seen him, you know. I was frightened a little bit, too, from my Papa.' It's not that he was a rough man, he just looked so different, with 'long plenty currem currem' (*karem-karem*, long hair). She believes he may have retired in Darwin. Her mother died at a young age and she was raised by another woman. Sometimes she was teased for looking different, 'they callem me Chinaman'.
To compensate for this difference, she points out that Mrs Ah Toy, the well-known Chinese businesswoman from Darwin and Pine Creek, 'they callem me sister'. Topsy is a full member of the Daly River Aboriginal community and is active in the women's resource centre that produces acrylic art and renowned silk-screen prints.

Many Aboriginal descendants know even less about their Chinese fathers, often not even a name.

Topsy Ah Kui Kunnarajie, a Malak-Malak woman at Daly River, June 1994.

Pan Quee and the 'combo state': a Daly River story

No sooner had the first South Australian settlement in the north precariously attached itself at Escape Cliffs in 1864, than land sales in Adelaide got underway. Exploration parties were quickly organised, and the first of these, headed by T. B. Finniss, a former colonial secretary, South Australia's first premier and now—briefly—the first government resident in the Northern Territory, so named the Daly River in 1865. Glowing reports on its potential aroused speculative commercial interest, and by the late 1870s the Daly River land had been taken up on paper. Conveniently close to cheap overseas labour pools, and with promising black soil, the Daly held rich prospects for tropical plantation farming.

Colonisation was off to a bumpy start. The first cattle station lasted only from 1882 until 1889. In 1885 plantation farming got underway on a 20,000-acre lease, but ended in fiasco with a jealousy shooting the following year. A Jesuit mission set up at Uniya in 1886, shifted in 1891 and closed in 1899. Chinese gardeners arrived in the area in 1890 and settled at the old Uniya site, which they abandoned in 1897. The discovery of copper in 1882 led to a massacre in 1884, and the mine was closed in 1895. In 1892 the white population in the Daly River area, apart from missionaries, numbered just two.[41]

In 1899 a new start was made. The Daly River Cattle Station, later Tipperary, was taken up again, and the copper mine resumed. The government smelter was shifted from Darwin to the Daly in 1904 and the white presence was reinforced by a police camp in 1906. The federal government, too, was seduced by the agricultural potential of the Daly, and attempted to settle a yeomanry of farmers on free blocks of up to 320 acres—big enough for plantations, though the importation of cheap Asian labour was no longer favoured.

There was no shortage of vision. The leaders of a Russian colony in the Atherton Tablelands were federally financed to assess the feasibility of Russian farmers on the Daly in 1911. One of them was the highly educated agricultural specialist Konstantin Vladimirov who, as Elena Govor observes, came armed with an ubiquitous umbrella and revolutionary songs. He had been inspector of fisheries in Turkestan and submitted a sixty-four-page report to the Department of External Affairs on the prospects of the Territory, with a systematic description of its geography, agriculture and pastoral industry.

Harry Morgan at Daly River, June 1994. He only knows that his father was 'a Chinaman'.

The other, Leandro Illin, submitted a ninety-two-page typed travel diary including a depressing picture of the treatment of Aborigines at the hands of frontier station owners, the removal of mixed-descent children to Bathurst Island, and their trials by law which were incomprehensible to the Aboriginal accused. It deeply offended his Russian intellectual conviction of the equality of men. He later married an Aboriginal woman in the Atherton Tablelands and experienced at first hand how, in having an Aboriginal family, one was stripped of one's citizenship rights. He concluded that the Territory would be suitable for Russians if it were alcohol-free.[42]

Not only Russians were being courted to settle the Territory. The inspection party consisted of a number of members of the federal parliament, senators, and high-ranking officials including Sir Hubert Murray, governor of New Guinea, and Sir Josiah Thomas, Minister for External Affairs, who was willing to throw his support behind targeted immigration schemes. The new colonisers were to be scientifically supported by a demonstration farm that, at the time of this august visit, consisted merely of a handsome sign, and had by 1916 become an Aboriginal reserve.

The 1911 party had a chance to speak to a number of already established settlers, many of whom were keen to sell up to the government. By 1921 the last few remaining settlers were offered free fares to return south. It is likely that those who remained had formed Aboriginal families.

A new wave of hopeful settlers was attracted in the 1920s by the success of peanut farming. Some of the names associated with the Daly—L'Erber, Zacharow, Bausman, Leinonen, Althous, Khari and Harmanis—suggest that a mixed Continental presence emerged. By 1947 an inspector of lands observed that most Daly settlers were living 'in the combo state'.[43]

Among those living in circumstances described by the lands inspector was Jimmy Pan Quee (pronounced as pen'kwi). He had taken up a peanut farm on the Daly in 1929, and formed an Aboriginal family. He was born around 1889 and died in 1959, and three types of sources each give us a different impression of him: the memories of his Aboriginal family, the notes in official records, and some local songs.

Jimmy Pan Quee was a local legend. Johnnie Wiltshire, an old-timer at Bamboo Creek, gave me an impromptu performance of a variation of *Poor Bugger Me*, which consisted of a litany of complaints ending with 'bugger big Charlie, bugger Pang Quee'. Sexism and racism are blended into another portrayal of frontier society in Jim Burgoyne's ballad *Down on the Daly* (ca. 1935). It lists Pan Quee among the 'characters' of the Daly, 'noted for their hospitality', and intimates that access to Aboriginal women was part and parcel of social relations, such 'that you'll never want to go away from the Daly River Oh!'[44] The Pan Quee of these songs is a reckless exploiter of Aboriginal sexuality.

Pan Quee had been the manager of a Hop Kee & Company shop in Darwin's Cavenagh Street since 1906, selling 'all kinds of Chinese and English goods and Chinese Medicine'. He must have been around seventeen years old when he became manager of the shop. By 1914 he advertised as a wood carter and contractor, still from the shop at the corner of Cavenagh and Barry streets.[45] By 1925 he appears on the electoral roll as living at Fletcher's Gully, and in 1929, at age forty, he took out a lease on the Daly.

The police journals reveal that Ah Hoin and Charlie Mo On were living in Pan Quee's camp with Aboriginal women. In December 1924 the birth of a 'half-caste female Selina Que' was registered on the Aboriginal reserve (the former demonstration farm).

A group consisting of 'half-castes Kitty, Bubbles, Nellie, Johnny, Silina Que, Pan Kee, and Aborigines Ruby & Lucana' were taken to Darwin in June 1925. The terse language of the police journal does not reveal how many families were in this group, but presumably this was the removal of at least two families, belonging to Pan Quee and Ah Hoin. However, Kitty, her two 'quadroon' children and Lukana were found again at the Aboriginal camp on the Daly in August 1926. In October the constable, evidently trying to remove them, reported that they had 'gone bush at present' and inquired about them at Pan Quee's camp. By November he had them 'detained', and sent 'Kitty, Johnny and Silenque' to Darwin. They do not reappear in the records of the Daly River police.[46] In the official records Pan Quee was the irresponsible progenitor of waifs for the care of the state.

According to local memory, however, Kitty and her Aboriginal husband Lukana stayed with Pan Quee until his peanut farm collapsed.[47] The children of Kitty and Pan Quee were taken to the compound in Darwin, but Kitty's daughter from her Aboriginal husband remained with her in the Pan Quee household.

Pan Quee moved to Humpty Doo and had another daughter with a Larrakia woman called Hilda: 'He used to buy me everything, buy clothes, get tucker, shoes, dress. He had an old army Blitz.'[48] This girl was not removed, perhaps because Pan Quee did not live with her mother.

Kitty's son John was transferred from Kahlin Compound to Bathurst Island, and when he was old enough to be released from Aboriginal institutions, he played a central role in reuniting his family. He re-established contact with his mother. Kitty was now living at Pan Quee's station in Humpty Doo with her Aboriginal husband Lukana and her father Yuliera. During the war they had all gone bush so as to avoid compulsory evacuation. John also reintroduced his sister Marjorie (presumably the girl referred to as Silenque and Silina in the police journal) to Humpty Doo. After the war, when the Darwin Chinese were being resettled outside the town centre, John bought a block of land at Knuckey's Lagoon together with Charlie On. It was a saw-milling station that supplied firewood to Darwin, and it became home to them all. The local and family recollections suggest Pan Quee as the stoic head of a household accepting the Aboriginal family that sprawled around him. Marjorie recounts:

> He looked after my sister Joan [daughter of Kitty and Lukana] and my mother and old Lukana was here too with them . . . He used to live here by himself, while my brother [John] and them used to live over there, there's an old house there, you can see it there, that's where my brother and my mother [Kitty], and Arthur [Joan's son] and his family are staying there now. He died here, on the block, too, old Jimmy. My mother used to do his clothes, but he used to cook for himself. He used to mix with the Chinese people in Darwin, he'd take their firewood, he'd go around to Sun Choong Lung in Darwin, he'd mix with them there, sit down and have a yarn, until late at night he'd come back, cook his own tucker. My mother used to never wait on him with food and things, he used to come back and cook it himself . . . He didn't like white people.[49]

Arthur also remembers Pan Quee: 'He used to give

Kitty Pan Quee (Madjaga), wife of Lukana and Jimmy Pan Quee. Photo: courtesy of Arthur Pan Quee, Knuckey's Lagoon.

us herbal medicine, won't go to a doctor. [He'd say] "I'd rather cut my throat."'[50]

Among the Chinese community in Darwin, Pan Quee is also remembered, though perhaps not so fondly. It is said that he spoke the local Brinkin language, and fathered a number of Aboriginal children.[51]

The Pan Quee household does not lend itself to a romantic image of Christian monogamy and conjugal dedication. It is the kind of arrangement that spawned the disdainful image of the 'combo state'. Both Aborigines and Chinese had strong traditions of polygamy, and the Pan Quee household appears to have devised its own conjugal arrangements based loosely on such traditions. Kitty uprooted herself and Lukana from the Daly to go to Humpty Doo, and later to Knuckey's Lagoon with Pan Quee, and John left his job at the wharves to create an economic basis for them all at Knuckey's Lagoon. It seems that this household was an economic unit held together by a deep-running sense of commitment.

The Aboriginal women in this family showed a strong preference for entering into relationships with Chinese. Kitty's mother had another daughter by a Chinese at Bridge Creek, and presumably Kitty was also part-Chinese. Kitty had two children with Pan Quee, and her third daughter, from her Aboriginal husband, had a son with another Chinese. Pan Quee himself had children with at least three Aboriginal women.

The predominance of mixed conjugal relations at the Daly River observed by the lands inspector may have arisen from a strong gender imbalance. Immigrant communities were usually unbalanced and this may have been mirrored on the Daly by an imbalance in the Aboriginal population. It is known that the 'Coppermine killings' of September 1884 resulted in the deaths of 'at least 150 Aborigines including many women and children'.[52] This suggests that the targets of recrimination and attack were mostly Aboriginal males. Marjorie observed that her family was far from unique:

> A lot of them, most of them Daly River people are half Chinese from all those miners there. And from the islands, there, some of them are Japanese, Malaysian, you know like Broome people and all them and Bathurst Island and all. They're from the boats used to come with those people and they used to come inland to all the native people, get friendly with the native people. While the Chinese down there in the Daly River area, Brocks Creek area, all those you see half-Chinese people everywhere, kids. You see the features, they are half Chinese.[53]

Whereas Kitty's Chinese–Aboriginal children were removed from the mixed household that could have supported them, children like Topsy Ah Kui, who had been abandoned by their Chinese fathers, were less likely to attract official attention.

Fleeting and irresponsible encounters typify images of Chinese–Aboriginal relations in the official documentation, and in the memory of many Aboriginal descendants. A legislative and policy framework that rendered such liaisons punishable must certainly have discouraged men from taking responsibility for their Aboriginal children. Still, many did try, though few managed to prevent the removal of their children. The stories of Ahlin, Sahanna and Camfoo explore the impact of such removals on the identity of the children.

ABANDONED CHILDREN

Whether the mixed Aboriginal children descended from Chinese or Japanese, or from other Asians, many, perhaps most, grew up without their fathers. A number of factors colluded to create this phenomenon: the incidence of casual liaisons, the traditional Aboriginal ascription of paternity which devalued biological paternity, the family commitments of such men in their home country, the likelihood of their deportation at the end of their contracts, the laws prohibiting cohabitation, the policies discouraging mixed marriages. Finally, such children—whether their fathers cared for them or not—were defined as 'neglected children' and were likely to be removed. This usually meant that they lost their mothers as well.

In areas of intensive interaction, the mixed descendants tended to be targeted for removal. Sunlight Bassini referred at length to the massive numbers of removals of Lama Lama people from Port Stewart in Princess Charlotte Bay:

> My dad was working with the Japanese. He was working round Australia's water, pearl-diving with the rest of the people from community, from Aurukun, Edward River, everywhere, Lockhart River, Cape York, working with everybody. Japanee gathering the boys from different tribes ... I'm sixty-two. I was born here in Coen and my dad was working with the Japanese, like pearl shell, from Port Stewart, my family was living there, too. That's where the old Japanee used to come around and pick the people, no white fellow there, only Aborigines, they were living out in the bush. Till the police mucked them all up, like you had the half-caste, and sending the half-caste people away . . . they took them down to the mission. Really. They took them to Woorabinda, that's where most of the half-castes went.[54]

He explained how helpless everyone felt, not knowing why they were sent away, or what they could do about it, who to appeal to, how to reconnect. In the 1990s they were still finding family members who had been removed all over Australia, and had travelled to Melbourne to consult anthropologist Donald Thomson's photographic collection to assist in the family reconnection process.

Similar stories are told about Laura and the Goldsborough area in North Queensland, and Mornington Island was full of mixed descendants from the Gulf. Lily Ah Toy makes the same point with reference to Pine Creek. In the Northern Territory many were sent to 'half-caste' institutions including the Tiwi Islands. The policy of targeting Asian–Aboriginal children was sharply perceived in Aboriginal communities, who resorted to hiding mixed-descent children and blackening their skin with charcoal. But it is difficult to read from the records. Frequently the explanation given in the removals register, that the removal was justified because of 'immoral associations', is the only hint we get that it was provoked by contact with Asians.

Interviews with former Arafura divers in Japan revealed that they had little idea of the pressures exerted by the *Protection Acts* on the Aborigines with whom they worked.[55] By the same token, Aboriginal children of Asian men might grow up unaware of the complex set of regulations governing their fathers. As a result the tendency is to infer that Asian men who abandoned their

Aboriginal children did so by choice. Len Royee at Gordonvale believes that one of his great-grandfathers was Chinese.

> They went back to their own country and whatever and died and didn't make contact whatever. That's what happened. Some stayed here and some went south and that sort of thing and had another family and that was it—they just forgot about what happened here.[56]

A number of descendants who have tried to trace their Asian ancestors found to their surprise a quite different story. Sarah Yu recorded such a story in Broome:

> Ollie Smith grew up in the local St John of God Orphanage in Broome. For most of her life she had thought that her Asian father had abandoned her and her Aboriginal mother and returned to Indonesia. It was only when she read the welfare files held on herself and her mother that she uncovered a different story. As she says, they 'held more secrets than I could have imagined'.

Repatriation of Timorese pearling workers from Broome, ca. 1937. This photo shows families being torn apart. Standing at the shore waving at the men are their Aboriginal wives, children and friends.

Photo: courtesy of Margaret Robinson, Broome.

Ollie discovered that her father was Wella Kalle, a 'Koepanger', who had been arrested and fined £20 for long-term cohabiting with Rita Smith, Ollie's 'half-caste' mother. The Native Affairs Department chose to make an example of Kalle to the Broome community, particularly to the 'half-caste' women there. Kalle was deported back to Kupang, despite the support of his employer McDaniels, the Pearlers' Association, senators, the Minister for the North West and other respectable members of the Broome community—all of whom argued that there was a shortage of experienced divers in Broome and that Kalle had their confidence. Although the department professed a duty of care to the Broome native population, little concern was shown for the fate of Rita and her child, whom Kalle had accommodated and fully supported. When he was deported to Kupang in December 1951, Ollie, at age three, was placed in the Broome orphanage. At age six, she became a ward of the state under the *Child Welfare Act 1947–59*, because she was not a 'native-in-law'.

As in many of the Stolen Generation stories, history repeated itself in Ollie's family. Rita's mother Dora had been removed to Beagle Bay Mission, after her Asian husband had been deported, and Rita, too, had grown up in the mission dormitory.

In 1995, after many inquiries, Ollie received a letter from her father and met him in Kupang. He told Ollie of how he used to meet Rita in the back lane of her granny's house, next to the gambling house. He had loved her mother, and would have had more children if he had been able to stay. His was a story of what might have been.[57]

I have already made the point that the anecdotal evidence suggests such children were more likely to be removed if their fathers attempted to raise them, because of objections to the formation of coloured communities, and because cohabitation laws provided an added leverage for intervention. Removal meant not only the separation from family and community, but also that the children, as wards of the state, became unable to inherit from their Asian fathers.

Mixed-descent children had no right of inheritance. Under the Western Australian *Aborigines Act 1905* the chief protector was the legal guardian of every Aboriginal and half-caste child under sixteen years of age (Section 3), and he was entitled to manage the property of Aborigines even without their consent 'to provide for the due preservation of such property' (Section 6). When Aboriginal children inherited property from their non-Aboriginal fathers, the inheritance was usually remitted to some trust fund 'for the benefit of Aborigines'. The upshot of this policy was that many children who were born into settled and well-off family settings were removed to missions and deprived of the material inheritance that would have given them a head-start. Such is the story of Moonlight Valley in a remote part of the Kimberley, unconnected with pearling or mining. Here it was the presence of 'Afghans' that caused official concern.

Sianna Sindhi: Moonlight Valley and its heirs

Sianna Sindhi, or Sahanna, was among a number of Afghan cameleers who arrived in Wyndham around 1908. He was born around 1871 and participated in the British war against the Baluchis before he arrived from Karachi as a camel teamster in 1899. When camel haulage became threatened by motor cars in the 1920s, Sahanna started a cattle run on the Salmond River, between the present site of El Questro and Karunji, where the steep banks of the river run in an east–west direction, admitting the moonlight. The first archival reference to the Moonlight Valley run is in 1937, but Sahanna had already obtained his own brand certificate (SE2) in 1929.

Pastoral activity in this area commenced only in 1920, when returned servicemen were granted properties in the area. James (Scotty) Salmond obtained a 100,000-acre pastoral lease called Karunji. The Kitja people from Salmond River moved to Karunji to work for Salmond. When Sahanna arrived, 'Tommy' and 'Daisy' showed him where he could 'sit down' on Tommy's country on the Salmond River. Daisy's country was further upstream. This family moved to Sahanna's station with their daughters Mary and Winnie.

The records of the Moonlight Valley lease are no longer complete, and it is uncertain whether the lease was in Sahanna's name, perhaps on the strength of his being an ex-serviceman and British subject, or whether it was held through a dummy owner—the latter being more likely.

The relationship between Salmond and Sahanna was uneasy. Cattle rustling was rife in the Kimberley. There had been depredations on Sahanna's cattle on the southern and western boundaries of the run and one constable alleged that Sahanna's run was on part of Karunji Station. In September 1931 stolen horses were found on Salmond's plant, as their owners, Sultan Mahomed and Jaffa Khan of Four-Mile in Wyndham, had suspected. When his rent-free period of five years ran out, Salmond ran into financial difficulties that he blamed—as pastoralists in the northwest were wont to—on the 'depredations from Aborigines'. He requested rent reduction and relief and became indebted to D. W. Rust, an ex-serviceman on a nearby property. By 1932 Salmond, who had once had 3,000 head of stock, had run out of cattle. He transferred his lease to Rust and became cook at Bedford Downs Station.

All stations in the Kimberley had to rely on Aboriginal labour, but Sahanna could not obtain a permit to employ Aborigines. Being Asian he was not considered a respectable employer. In 1935 and 1939, when he was sixty-four and sixty-eight respectively, he fathered a child each with Mary and Winnie. The elder child, Jack, remembers sometimes going on camel rides with his father, to pick up stock from the Wyndham wharves for the various stations. 'He went to just about every station in the Kimberley. He had a fair amount [of camels] anyway. I just came for the ride. He had big plans for me, he told me. He was going to send me somewhere, he didn't mention where he was going to send me, apparently to a school. But that didn't eventuate. He died before that happened.'

It was after the birth of the children that pressure on Sahanna was increased to play by the rules. In 1937 local constable Fawcett suggested to Sahanna that the way out of his trouble would be to employ a white manager. The assumption was that a white man would safeguard the kind of morality that could be officially sanctioned with a permit to employ Aboriginal labour.

In 1938 Sahanna complained of cattle killing and was visited by P. J. Plant, a Wyndham constable. During his investigations in the area in June and July 1938, Plant helped himself to two killers (beasts) from Sahanna's stock, and there were no further complaints from Sahanna. Still, Plant returned in October and November. Plant was applying for a lease for himself in 1940, and in April 1941 he formally acquired the leasehold of Moonlight Valley. It is not clear why he acquired the leasehold, but the transfer took place while Sahanna was evidently under pressure about the need for a permit to employ Aboriginal labour. In July 1941 Sahanna made a will in favour of his brother Sultan with a small consideration to the wife of Wyndham shop-owner Lee Tong (viz.) and the daughter of Plant. This may have been an acknowledgement of debts or of assistance rendered in holding the lease.

Eventually a white man, Peter Reynolds, was employed at Moonlight Valley, and a 'permit to employ' consequently granted. Some twelve Aboriginal adults and three children lived at Moonlight Valley. In 1943 Reynolds—the white guarantor of order and morality—killed Mary's husband Lefthand Nabu in a jealousy shooting. This murder shattered the small Moonlight Valley community.

The Department of Native Affairs at once withdrew the permit to employ Aborigines. The spectre of prosecution against Sahanna was raised, and Sahanna sought the help of the Wyndham native hospital to see what he could do. He wanted to bank a couple of hundred pounds for his children, and make a will in their favour. He was told to see the chief protector.

The adults of Moonlight Valley were taken to Perth as witnesses in the murder trial. Only Mary's mother Daisy stayed behind with little Jack Sahanna. During the trial it transpired that Reynolds was an army deserter by the name of Burfoot, who had been fabricating stories about himself.

While in Perth as a witness to the murder trial, Sahanna himself came under pressure from the chief protector. He was threatened with prosecution for cohabiting. Bray forced Sahanna to admit to his paternity of the children and agree to pay maintenance of twelve shillings and sixpence per week for each child to the department. Clearly this meant institutionalisation for the children, and as moves were already underway to remove three-year-old Mary Ann to Moola Bulla, Sahanna pleaded for them to be placed in the Holy Child Orphanage in Broome, not in the remote Beagle Bay Aboriginal Mission. He wanted Jack to be allowed to stay at least another year, and to wait until Mary Ann turned five. As a sign of goodwill and generosity, he made an immediate downpayment of £30.

Sahanna made out a new will in favour of his two children, Kemel (Jack) Sahanna and Meriam (Mary Ann) Sahanna. The department insisted that the commissioner for native affairs would be the executor of the will, that the children could not take possession of their inheritance until they were at least thirty years of age, and that the commissioner 'should have the right to dispose of the property at any time'.

Sahanna's bargaining position was weak—after all, he faced the possibility of prosecution—but he carried himself with dignity. He not only negotiated confidently with the protector, he went and gave a press interview: not about the murder, not about his problems with the department, but about his position as an Afghan–Australian. He had not been to Perth for forty years, and the obvious changes in the big city gave the seventy-two-year-old a measure of his age. The strangeness of the city brought into relief the familiarity of the place he had created for himself in the world, and of the family he had formed with the Moonlight Valley people. He reflected about a life that had taken him from the Baluchi wars—where he had fought for the British—to the isolation of Moonlight Valley where the nearest neighbour was forty miles away.

Perhaps the interest of the press and the reading public could restore to the old man some of the dignity that the protector denied him.

The commissioner consented that Mary Ann should be allowed to stay with her family until she was five, but despite Sahanna's pleading for time, the department prepared to transfer little Jack at once. The commissioner wrote to the mother superior of the Broome orphanage, offering ten shillings per week for each child 'and you could also collect Child Endowment'. Two shillings and sixpence per week was to be placed in a trust account. The usual rate of maintenance for children allocated to missions was five shillings per week. 'Would you like to have the children?'[58] The mother superior replied that they were still evacuated in Beagle Bay and had no space for boys, but would be happy to receive the girl at once, adding that it was much better for her to be removed at a young age. The bishop was willing to accept the boy into the Beagle Bay Mission.

Sahanna was instructed to arrange for the transfer of the children as soon as possible after the wet season in 1944. But the Aboriginal witnesses in the murder trial had not reached home yet. They had been taken to Moore River Native Settlement to wait out the Wet. On the same day as Bray wrote to Sahanna to prepare for the removal of the children, he also wrote to Broome to arrange for Mary Ann to be intercepted there before she reached home.

By January 1944 Sahanna had returned to Moonlight Valley, and his brother Sultan from Wyndham's Four-Mile was there also. Not letting up, the Turkey Creek constable now raised the matter of illegal employment of Aborigines and prosecution against Sultan for cohabiting. But the Aboriginal members of the station were still *en route*, and the two old men were without their workforce. In February news of Sahanna's death reached the department. Mrs Russ of Gibb River Station told Sister Margaret on a visit to Derby that Sahanna had been found drowned in a pool of water near his homestead: 'He must have fallen off a mule or may have been thrown.'[59] Sahanna drowned in Koolamun Creek, and foul play was rumoured in Wyndham. No inquest was conducted into the circumstances of Sahanna's death. He was buried in an unknown location.

In April 1944 the ten adults and two children from Moonlight Valley were discharged from Moore River. But nobody informed them that Sahanna had died, or that the children were to be taken away, or that a will had been made in favour of the children. Mary Ann was taken into custody in Broome. 'Her mother was most upset on leaving the baby and wanted to remain here and live at Beagle Bay with her and was only persuaded to go on my promising to ask Mr Bray if he would allow her to return to the Beagle Bay Mission to live.'[60] There is no record of any efforts to allow Winnie to join her daughter at Beagle Bay. Sister Cecilia confirmed the arrival of Mary Ann at Beagle Bay on 1 May 1944, observing that she did not have a blanket and 'only a few rags of dress'. She asked the children's legal guardian, the chief protector, whether some blankets might be sent for the children.

In September 1945 the Broome orphanage inquired after the whereabouts of Jack Sahanna, who had still not reached them as promised. As it happens, his removal was witnessed by a correspondent for *Walkabout* magazine, who even published a photograph of 'little Sarhanna' beside the mail plane that carried him off. For *Walkabout* readers, this story was framed not as a removal, but as the inexorable march of progress.

> A tiny brown child sitting all alone beside an aeroplane agleam on a vast plain, mountain-ringed—the picture remains as a symbol of the New Australia that is forming, slowly but surely . . . of ever-growing fleets of civil aircraft that glisten in our skies . . . The reason why that small dark child created a symbol for me is because I saw him first just so: dramatically backed by a silver Lockheed when he was travelling alone on the newly inaugurated Kimberley Stations Medical and Mail Service . . . We had come into Argyle Station to board the 'Doctor's Plane' in order to reach Hall's Creek . . . Mrs Durack had been ill for some days . . . The plane crew and a couple of passengers came across to the brush-shelter. The R.M.A. *Kimberley* remained solitary, out on the strip.
>
> Or so I thought until I walked across and saw the child. There he sat, Yogi-fashion with crossed legs, a tiny brown human, incredibly small and lonely, set against the huge silver Lockheed . . .
>
> The child had picked up two sticks and was beating them together, singing a little refrain under his breath, to pass the time and, I do not doubt, to allay the terror of being thus utterly alone, already 150-odd miles by air (a fortnight's journey by horse) from Karungie, where he had that morning boarded the plane. Beside him lay the tiniest swag in the world, his entire possessions rolled in a minute ground-sheet, which with native caution he had fetched out from the plane, keeping it handy, just in case.
>
> He sat on the earth and beat his sticks as his aboriginal mother and her ancestors had done for centuries. But the lustrous eyes he lifted to me held a reserved mystical query that puzzled me; and his tiny nostrils had a fine-cut angle of pride. His name explained. This was Sarhanna, aged eight, son of an Afghan and a lubra. His mother had died when he was a baby. His father had reared and provided for him. But now his father also was dead, and Sarhanna *en route* to be cared for and educated at the Beagle Bay Mission, close to Broome.[61]

The description of forlorn Jack is priceless. Only the detail of his mother's death got mangled in the story. That way it certainly made a more palatable story about the modern trappings of progress.

I met Jack's mother in 1995. The women never returned to Moonlight Valley where the deaths of Lefthand and

Sahanna had occurred. In the space of a few months Mary had lost her Aboriginal husband in the shooting, Mary and Winnie had lost their children, and they had all lost the patron who enabled them to live together in their own country. Mary shrouds herself in silence over that part of her life. Winnie remembers it. Peter Reynolds served five years for the murder of Lefthand. The people of Moonlight Valley served a lifetime for what followed.

A forced removal cannot be said to have taken place where there is evidence of parental consent, according to the federal court findings in the *Stolen Generations Case* in 2000.[62] This means that Jack's and Mary Ann's was not a forced removal: their father consented to their institutionalisation. That he wanted to postpone their removal, that he objected to their placement in a native mission, that he was threatened with prosecution if he did not consent, or that the mothers were not consulted—does this not matter before the law?

It was now left to the department to execute Sahanna's will and act as legal guardian of the children. In this task it failed miserably. It showed no interest in defending the property from fraudulent claims. Plant claimed to own the land as well as all the improvements on it, and half the cattle. Wyndham locals knew—and still say so—that Plant was only a nominal owner, and that Sahanna had been running the station for over fifteen years before Plant arrived. But his claim was settled in full and without disputation. Out of the remainder of the estate were paid all outstanding debts and expenses. The remaining 400 head of cattle were rounded up and taken to the butcher shop now owned by Plant. As Gus Bottrill, who first documented this case, points out, if Plant had been the owner, then the cost of winding up the estate should have been his responsibility. All that was left of Sahanna's estate of 75,000 acres and 2,000 bullocks was the sum of £27, and the children never saw any of it.

Charlie McAdam remembers another part of the story:

> 'A couple of years after I left Beagle Bay I did a couple of trips to Broome and I run into his mother. I don't know that mob, Wyndham way, but we were just having a yarn and an old lady said to me, "You haven't seen Jackie?"
> "Jackie who?"
> "Jackie Carlton."
> "Yeah, he's in Beagle Bay."
> "Oh, that one my own son, that one bin taken away."

Retracing Moonlight Valley. Don Campbell and Winnie Gallagher after successfully locating Moonlight Valley from the air, May 1995.

It was a sad thing. I remember talking to the old lady. "That one was my son." Yeah.'[63]

I locked myself in the first time I went to Jack Sahanna's place on the outskirts of Broome. Greeted by a sign 'Keep Out. Ghaddafi country', I imagined bloodhounds and self-shooting guns, and then figured that the only way to find out whether I was welcome was to ask. The house was well set back from the cattle gate, which did not offer the urban convenience of a door chime or an intercom system. I asked my son to open the gate, instructed him to close it behind us, and drove in. We found nobody at home, no bloodhounds, and no guns pointed at us, but my conscientious seven-year-old had not only closed the gate, he had snapped the padlock shut as well. So when I first met Jack the next day, I had to deliver an apology and a new padlock. Within half an hour of speaking to him, I was pacing up and down his kitchen trying to tell him how wrong he was. His story got to me. He ended up saying he'd been looking for someone to write his story, and I retorted 'Well, you've found her'. We stared at each other in surprise and made friends.

Jack had tried to use the avenues of common law to obtain justice. He had viewed the issue as one of property and inheritance, and 'nothing to do with race'. He had engaged a solicitor and had been informed of the statute of limitations: it was too late to make a retrospective claim on the property of which he had been swindled. But Jack had never been informed that there was a will in his favour, that he was supposed to inherit property with his sister. He was at a loss to understand how the statute of limitations could be applied to his case.

Jack Sahanna at the point of his removal from Moonlight Valley.
Photo: *Walkabout*, 1.10.1946 (vol. 12, no. 12), p. 11.

Jack calls himself a self-made man. He is happy with the education he received to Grade 6. He was trained as a blacksmith, and when he finally left the mission, it took him only a couple of hours to get a job. He says, 'I worked for a decent person. He could see that I was working alright and he gave me all the opportunities in the world. Anything I wanted to do, he let me do. He gave me any help that I needed. After nine years I finished up with a tradesman's certificate.' That's how he built his own substantial house: 'I'm proud of this place, I built it myself. I didn't do the brickwork, of course. This is something to be proud of. I designed and built it myself. Verandah all around. Beautiful.'

On the mission he became estranged from his family and background. He grew up 'in a blooming dormitory and [was] brought up by Hitler's men. All

Jack Sahanna at home, Broome 1995.

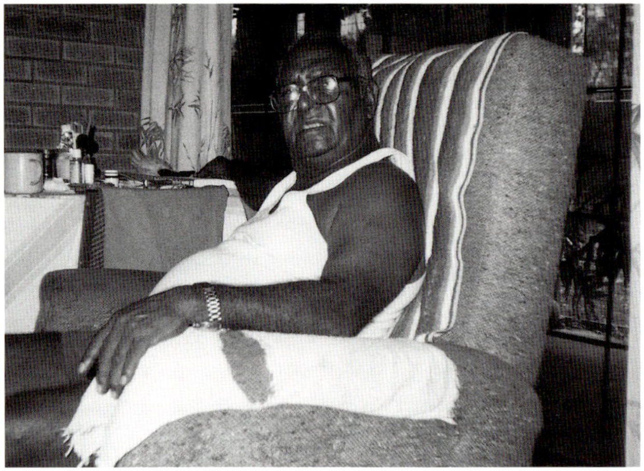

these German missionaries. Bishop Raible. And they were strict. But I appreciate everything they've done for me. It made a man out of me.' And having become that man, Jack wanted 'nothing to do with Aboriginal Legal Service or anything. I like to do everything by my own self.'

By his own self, as an Australian individual and equal citizen, he sought redress from the law. But the disadvantage of race has everything to do with his position. The state had appointed itself as his legal guardian because he was Aboriginal. Because he was Aboriginal, it was not deemed necessary to inform him of his inheritance. Because he was Aboriginal, it was possible to spend his money on his behalf. The chief protector acted entirely within his powers. Jack Plant must be long dead. The period of redress has expired under the statute of limitations. Common law holds no recourse for Jack.

As an adult, he found that his mother and aunt were still alive in Wyndham, and met his brothers and sisters from a second marriage. It was difficult for him. It challenged his identity. While I was there he agreed that we should all go to Moonlight Valley, but nobody felt confident that we would find the way. Winnie used to walk from there to Wyndham when she was young. She was keen to go, but would she be able to guide us in the car after so many years? Would we be able to navigate the camel tracks? Would there be any tracks?

On my next visit to Broome I was armed to the teeth with four-wheel-driving equipment including GPS and two-way radio, and arranged with the State Emergency Service to delay the seasonal burn-off. Don Campbell and Winnie Gallagher accompanied me on a reconnaissance flight from Wyndham and we located the homestead and storehouse and determined its GPS position, and mapped out a possible vehicle access route. Jack's wife made sure that his truck got serviced so that we could drive in convoy.

But events had overtaken our plans. An access road was proposed through the Kimberley, and the land council sought to contact all traditional owners along the route to consult over consent. His Aboriginal family had nominated Jack as a traditional owner of Moonlight Valley. Jack was in a dilemma. He had thought of Moonlight Valley as his father's property. He had tried to win it back and failed. But it was also the traditional country of his mother. It was offered to him symbolically. His family was waiting for him. He had been thinking about this for months, examining his motives. If he went there, he committed himself to being a traditional owner, to being Aboriginal. He developed a heart condition. He became unable to travel. What should he do now?

AFGHAN CAMELEERS

Sianna Sindhi, or Sahanna, at Moonlight Valley and his brother Sultan Punjab, or Sultan Mahomed Booch, belonged to a community of Afghans that had settled in Wyndham. During the gold rushes in northwestern Australia, camel teams quickly became an invaluable supply line. The people usually referred to as 'Afghans' were able to undercut cartage rates of white teamsters and a keen racial competition developed. All manner of difficulty was placed in the way of these cameleers, including sometimes the refusal of rights of commonage to graze camels. Such difficulties led to a cameleer strike at Port Hedland in 1908, as a result of which a number of cameleers moved to Wyndham. Most of them were in fact Indians, from east of the Durant line that separated British India from Afghanistan. Despite this, their designation as 'Afghans' denied their British citizenship and their battle for secure tenure in Wyndham lasted sixteen years—actually, until motor cars were introduced, displacing the camel runs. Sianna Sindhi and Sultan Punjab had been trading on the Eastern Goldfields (Esperance, the Murchison and Onslow to Port Hedland) before coming to the Kimberley. The names of the other Wyndham cameleers have been rendered as: Jaffa Khan, storekeeper Zaman Shah, workers Palli, Alloo and Hiada, Omrah or Omera or Imbra, Paul or Pal Singh, and Lal Mahomet Belooch.

Cameleers came to Australia from Beluchistan, the Punjab, Kashmir and the Sindh province—areas that now straddle north India, Pakistan and Afghanistan. As well, a few came from the Middle East and Egypt. They were initially imported to Australia under indenture agreements as camel handlers. The first three arrived to accompany the celebrated Burke and Wills exploration in 1860, and in 1865 Thomas Elder imported thirty-one handlers with 124 camels to establish a cartage business. Large-scale importation took off in the 1880s.

Afghan camel teams became invaluable until the 1920s for crucial inland transport routes through semi-arid and arid territory, supplying stations, mining camps and public works sites. The supplies they carried supported the construction of the Adelaide–Darwin telegraph line, the Transcontinental railway line from Kalgoorlie to Port Augusta, the Queenland border fence, and in Western Australia the rabbit-proof fence and the Canning Stock Route. They carried supplies along the 500-kilometre Birdsville Track from Marree (formerly Hergott Springs) to Birdsville in Queensland, along the Strzelecki Track to Innamincka, and from the Oodnadatta rail head to Alice Springs, Tennant Creek and Newcastle Waters. They also serviced various supply routes from the Western Australian ports into the inland. Cemeteries in Broken Hill, Marree, Alice Springs and Coolgardie hint at the former concentration of 'Afghan' populations.[64] Their memory is celebrated in the national icon of the 'Ghan' rail connection to Alice Springs, a route that was previously only serviceable by camel teams.

In 1886 the first camels arrived in Derby to service the goldfields supply lines, and by 1887 Meer Dost Khan and a syndicate of Afghans had imported 600 camels to Fremantle. In 1888 Elders, a large pastoral company, assisted the establishment of Afghan-owned cartage enterprise. The brothers Faiz and Tagh Mahomet from Kandahar established their own business and went on to sponsor many more Afghans, many of whom eventually became independent hawkers. 'By the 1890s the ownership of camels in Australia was well and truly in the hands of Afghan merchants.'[65] As in the pearling industry, the interests of large companies such as Elders, which favoured the importation of camels, diverged from those of smaller owners who resisted their competition. And as in pearling, white Australians were able to mobilise the powers of the state to delimit the economic opportunities of such competitors seeking to fix them into particular positions in the workforce.

As soon as camel haulage became an Afghan-owned enterprise, it started to meet with public and official resistance and became a 'problem'. During 1892 the Western Australian Parliament turned its attention to the problem of hawkers from 'India or other Asiatic countries' who made themselves 'a nuisance and terror to law-abiding settlers'. It was alleged that they usually visited out-of-the-way farms and stations when the 'husbands were away and only the women and children were at home', and being 'strong hulking-looking fellows', 'often put the womenfolk in great fear being aliens and coloured men'. The appearance of some of them, it was claimed, 'was enough to intimidate any lonely female, and make her purchase against her will'. An interesting image was being conjured up here, but the real issue was that complaints against the competition from hawkers had been raised by white shop-owners. The latter were referred to in this debate as 'legitimate traders', by implication rendering 'illegitimate' the non-white hawkers, who had obtained and paid for their licences. Attorney-General Burt expressed hopes of being able to deal with this problem administratively, but was frustrated, because it was found that most of these hawkers were British subjects. The Western Australian Parliament's happy solution to this dilemma was to abolish altogether the *Hawkers' Act 1882*, and with it, hawking licences. Hawking by Asians had been turned from a discursive illegitimacy into a substantive one within a few months.[66]

Meanwhile the Afghans themselves were subject to occasional harassment. Christine Stevens records various incidents of harassment by bullock teamsters in New South Wales and Queensland, leading up to debates on immigration of 'coloured aliens' which resulted in *Imported Labour Registry Acts* prohibiting resident 'coloured aliens' from importing others.[67]

In 1901, in the wake of a change in government in Western Australia, Premier Throssel and Commissioner of Crown Lands Moran, seeking to curb the importation of Asians, dealt shamefully with businessman Faiz Mahomet. He had already worked as a Jemadar under the British in the construction of the telegraph line from Karachi to Beluchistan. An order in council which exempted him from the newly imposed prohibitions was cancelled a month after being proclaimed, while Mahomet was already in Karachi to organise the transportation of 500 camels and several camel drivers. He had chartered a ship and sustained huge financial losses during this business trip.[68] Stevens refers to a similar incident in 1907, when quarantine concerns were raised. After exhaustive investigation, ten months quarantine at a remote station and the killing of some of the camels, no disease was found. The owners incurred a substantial debt. Stevens records this as the last importation of camels to Australia.[69]

The lexicon of concerns is familiar. As with other Asians, it was not simply the Afghans' economic competition but also their easy access to Aboriginal workers that caused government concern. During his last year in office in 1908, CPA Prinsep introduced a new regulation, whereby Afghan camel drivers were not permitted to employ natives under the age of twenty.

It was well known that there was much interaction, including family formation, between Afghans and Aborigines. Michael Cigler described the social dynamics of Marree, one of the sites of intensive Afghan presence. In the 1950s Marree was, like many towns, divided by the railway line, with the European quarters on one side and Aborigines and Afghans sharing the other side. Social interaction between the latter two was strong, and the two parts of town each had their own shops. There was only one school with two classrooms, and no ethnic distinction was made here, but in the picture theatre, the centre aisle served as a colour line. Cigler believes that 'To a large extent, the separation of Afghans in the town from Europeans was a result of their feeling of affinity for and intermarriage with the Aborigines.'[70]

On the eastern gold field the number of camels had risen from forty-two in 1891 to 4,000 in 1896. An Anti-Afghan League was formed and submitted petitions, and a Royal Commission into Mining in 1898 examined the competition offered by Afghans.[71] It was as a result of this political mood that Afghans came from Port Hedland into the Kimberley, where they engaged in long battle to secure tenure.

A group of them obtained permission to camp at Four-Mile in Wyndham in 1908, where they built camel yards, twenty-four houses, a mosque and a well within two years. Lal Mahomet applied for a lease at Three-Mile in 1914 but was refused because of an objection from a publican. The refusal was based on the *Land Act* regulations prohibiting 'alien Asiatics' from obtaining leases. In 1915 Pal Singh was declined the lease of a small block vacated by Durack. In 1917 the Afghans engaged a lawyer to have their camp declared a reserve under Section 39 of the *Land Act*. The Wyndham magistrate responded by convicting two of them for 'harbouring' and urged the 'removal' of the camp. A reserve was declared much further away from town, at eight or nine miles distance. The Afghans responded that it had no water. The reserve was amended in April 1918 and Lal Mahomet again protested that it was unsuitable. In November the police started to clear the camp at Four-Mile and the Afghans obtained ministerial approval for staying on their old camp, having pointed out that the

The Afghan camp at Wyndham. Mona Williams at the remains of the Afghan camp at Four-Mile.

distance from town of the new reserve would impact greatly on cartage rates throughout the district. In April 1919 they gained the support of the local protector who argued that at least the old camp at Four-Mile was easier to supervise in cases of cohabitation or contact.[72]

The number of Afghan cameleers in Australia is difficult to gauge. For immigration purposes, papers for camel handlers only became necessary with the *Imported Labour Registry Act 1897*, and from 1904 a passport was required to enter Australia. Until then the camel handlers were recorded as 'Indians', 'Afghans', 'Turks', 'Syrians', 'Asians' and 'other'. Researchers have resorted to using the number of camels imported to gauge the number of handlers required for them. Whereas the immigration of Afghans peaked in the 1880s, the camel haulage industry was at its peak between 1900 and 1905.[73] This means that by the turn of the century the industry must have been conducted largely by cameleers of between ten and twenty years residence, and the public agitation was directed against men with an already substantial attachment to Australia. Eventually it was not public resistance, but the motor car that brought an end to the camel teams and camels were left to roam. By the 1920s the camels, having adapted well to Australian environmental conditions, came to be considered as a pest. The *Camel Destruction Act 1925* permitted the shooting of feral camels. Today Australia is the world's only exporter of feral camels, with lucrative exports to Saudi Arabia.

Polyethnic Wyndham

Halal meat is still available in Wyndham, which once had a sizeable Afghan population. The Aboriginal descendants of the Wyndham Afghans are now difficult to trace. At the time of my visit the only living 'Afghan' was a Peshorie, Shaikh Abdul Kadir bin Hadji Ali. He was born 1912 in Peshawar, near the Khyber Pass separating Afghanistan from the former British India, now Pakistan. He came to Broome for the pearling industry, is a naturalised Australian, and a devout Muslim. His Aboriginal wife Phyllis, on the other hand, was raised on a Catholic mission: 'We couldn't get married in the church, we had to get married in the presbytery, because he had different religion.' Abdul had suffered two strokes recently, and before I went to see him, Phyllis pleaded: 'Don't religion him, please.' He had become infuriated when in hospital a Christian Father tried to pray for him. His failing health brought him closer to his faith, whereas while they were raising their five children together, it had never been an issue.

The family moved from Broome to Wyndham in 1965, after the pearling industry collapsed. Phyllis found it 'more better than Broome. Friendly people, I just felt free.'

Next to the Afghan community that settled there,

Wyndham has always had its share of Chinese businesses and market gardens. Today it is seen as one of the more ethnically tolerant townships, and many of its indigenous residents prefer it to Derby.

Billy Lee Tong is one of the living reminders of Wyndham's polyethnic past. His family maintained links with his ancestral village in China, where Billy's father had a second family. He runs the only remaining Chinese shop in Wyndham, a saddlery, making swags and child-seats.

Billy's father Charlie Lee Tong Fu was born in Guangdong in 1866. Reputedly, because of his good looks with a flat nose, 'an attempt was made to buy him from the family and raise him as an actor for the aristocracy'.[74] He arrived in Darwin in 1882 at age about sixteen or seventeen, and with a group of Chinese started to head south to go peanut picking. After the group disbanded he worked at Rosewood Station on the Ord River. Later he became cook and drover in Halls Creek, working for Tom Bradshaw. From droving cattle into Wyndham he became friends with an old Chinese who owned a shop there and invited him to become a partner, but Lee Tong preferred to continue droving. When the old man died, Lee Tong discovered that he had inherited the Wyndham shop.

Charlie married Cecilia Chin Hee, an orphan who had been brought up by the widow Selina Hassan, of mixed Malay descent. In 1921 they settled down to life as businesspeople in Wyndham. Other Wyndham Chinese at the time included the Fong Sams who owned the Victoria Hotel, and Fred Gee Hong Yet, the cook at the Three Mile Hotel and later owner of a cafe in the Port. They started to sell groceries, and Cecilia became a tailoress and produced Assam and Safari suits. Reputedly she could make eight pairs of trousers a day. After a few years they had saved up some £60 or £100 and sent this back to the old man's family in China 'to repay the inheritance'. Billy says that when his father gained an attractive contract to supply Forrest River Mission with provisions, the bishop in Perth received protest letters objecting to the Church's dealing with a Chinese business in preference to Europeans.

Lee Tong used to visit China regularly by steamer from Darwin. He had a wife and two daughters there, and after his first wife's early death the girls were raised by other family members. After Lee Tong's death Cecilia continued to send back money for the support of these girls from her husband's first marriage. Eventually, possibly because their overseas contacts were incriminating them in the eyes of the communist government, the family wrote not to send any more money: the girls had grown up and could look after themselves. Billy says he'd still send them about £200 at Christmas time. Billy speaks some Cantonese and has been back to China three or four times. He maintains a correspondence with his niece in Baulou.

POLYETHNIC FAMILIES

Though it may be desirable for analytical purposes to distinguish between Aboriginal relationships with Afghans, with Japanese and with Chinese, these neat distinctions become meaningless in the hubs of polyethnicity powered by the pearling industry where Filipinos, Indonesians and Timorese as well as many other nationalities were also resident. Members from all these ethnic groups married into Aboriginal families, and horizons of cultural experience were vastly expanded as a result. In addition, there were marriages between Chinese and Japanese, between Pacific Islanders and Malays, and so on, and between the descendants of such mixed marriages. A host of languages, religions, culinary habits and cultural practices existed side by side in these polyethnic communities. In the third generation a child in such a mixed family may have four grandparents speaking four different languages, and as a result end up learning only English or a local creole. The cultural traditions of such families were a matter of negotiation.

In a number of families four ethnic lines of descent converged in the second generation of immigration—for example, Filipino, Malay, mainland Aboriginal and Torres Strait Islander descent. Such families are the core of the coloured community that gave the far north its character. These families form such vast networks that if we traced those who are referred to in this book across three generations, including the vertical links of each sibling in each generation instead of tracing them horizontally through a single line of descent as I have done, hardly a family would remain unconnected to the network.

Consider this example: the Jamaican trepanger Douglas Pitt (born 1844) formed families with both Chopa Wacando (or Sopa Calemo) from Noumea and Sue Wazan from Murray Island. Taking only the patrilineage of the first two generations emanating from these unions, we find among their children's generation Magno Loren and Ceriaco Losbanes from the Philippines, and among their grandchildren's generation the following names: Pitt, Sailor, Savage, Guivarra, Sweeney, Raymond, Jacobs, Saveka, Mills, Marsden, Ware, Nain, Mye, Mosby, Akee, Reading, Walters and Panzo Cedar. In the matrilineage we find: Ses, Modee, Williams, Morrison, Kewait, Kemble, Crozier, Noble, Hedricks and Seiko. In the fourth generation patrilineage we need to add: Dan, Christian, Jose, Mazza, Flower, Lohr, Plummer, Pelham, Preece, Bulli and Pau. This family tree, though incomplete, traces to the sixth generation, now growing up.[75] Few descendants from Torres Strait could claim to be completely unconnected to this web of relations.

Badu Island Malaytown

Many of the first-generation immigrants who embarked on mixed families had already travelled extensively before they entered Australian pearling. Lui Samoa, a whaler, had been to Liverpool, Africa and New Guinea before he came from American Samoa. A Samoan Bible was part of his sparse luggage. At Mapoon he obtained a wife from Saibai Island in Torres Strait and they moved to Badu Island. One of their daughters, Kathleen, describes how her own marriage was arranged: 'You know in those days, parents had to choose the man for you to get married. Like in the Bible, they used to choose wife for their boys or choose the boy for their girls. That's what they used to do on the island and this one was chosen... My father came home and told me,

'Malay pearling workers at Thursday Island', ca. 1920. Eight of these fourteen 'Malay pearling workers on Thursday Island' have been identified. Wearing the suit is Subdin bin Hussen (later Subdeen Hoosen, referred to in one document as Sudin bin Oobane, arrived 1914), and on the far right is Wahab bin Tahal. Both of these men are from Ambon. In the centre row on the left is Doolah bin Hondo, wearing a dark shirt is Ollie (or Willie) Dewis from Timor (referred to in one document as Olie Daybees, arrived in Australia in 1914), next to him with his legs crossed is Tommy Loban, and next to him in a white shirt is Hendrik Lewin. Second from left in the front row is Omar (or Hassan) bin Awel from Kampung Tengah-Tengah in Ambon, who arrived in 1914, and on the far right is Sayyed Barba. It is also believed that Tooriki bin Hassan (or Turki) and Manungi are in this photo. Others who arrived in 1914 were 'Tamsie Cassine' and 'Baquu bin Amat' (Bargo bin Ahmat). Photo: courtesy of Balfour Ross photographer, Thursday Island.

"There's a boy here, I'd like you marry him."'

Kathleen had already set her sights elsewhere, and an argument followed with her mother as the spouse's advocate. Her Samoan father, more used perhaps to the sexual independence of girls, supported Kathleen and asked the spouse to take his ring back. After some further talks Kathleen agreed to marry Marsat Ketchell, who promised to provide for her invalid father. At first their relationship was rocky. Kathleen accused him of not providing properly for her father and found Ketchell to be very jealous. She returned to her parents. Afterwards they settled down and produced thirteen children. Kathleen became a loyal partisan for her husband in the internal politics of Badu and looks back on her marriage with satisfaction.

Marsat struggled with English at the Badu Island school, and even into old age always got his wife to interpret for him when he had to converse with an English-speaker. But his mental agility was noted by his teacher and family. He completed an apprenticeship with the Papuan Industries Limited (later Island Industries Board) and became a skilled boat builder, able to draw plans and adapt designs.

Marsat's father was Chee Krimon, a Muslim recruited in Singapore for Darwin, who worked his way to Torres Strait. He married a Badu Island girl named Igari (née Bamaui) and became the first baker on Badu. On Badu the superintendent changed his name to Ketchell. 'They said that's more soundable, like.' Chee and Igari gave an equal share of Qur'anic and Biblical names to their eight children: Marsat, Samat, Aaron, Leah, Alia, Ruth, Jane and Nauma. Kathleen remembers her father-in-law as a 'real Malayan. He was like fair skin, grey hair, like. Very fair. He never speak language from Torres Strait, he just spoke English, not real good English. He had a garden and when the vegetables were ready, he just gathered up all the family and they dig and they take the food home. That's all they do . . . They don't sell anything there, they just give it away, like.'

Chee never attempted to initiate his sons into the faith, only asking that they abstain from pork. His family probably did not follow these instructions, because Kathleen noticed that he always had his own plate, cutlery and cup that were never shared. 'He was a good man, very good man. Very hard working.' His bread, made with coconut leavening, enjoyed great popularity, and he also made *tuba*, a kind of kava drink, but never drank it himself. They all lived at a place called 'Malaya town' on Badu, also inhabited by the numerous family of Albert Bowie with a similar background to Chee.[76] The ethno-spatial organisation of Badu Island was to play an important role in the wrangle between Atima Ahwang (viz.) and the Queensland protection bureaucracy.

THE RULES OF POLYETHNICITY

When I speak of a 'polyethnic north' I do not mean the harmonious blend of many cultures. Polyethnicity refers to the close proximity of peoples from different ethnic backgrounds, and the frequent family formation across ethnic boundaries. Polyethnicity means both the blurring of boundaries through family formation and their codified maintenance as markers of social status.

The northern polyethnicity was underwritten by finely graded rules of etiquette that dictated where one lived, which school one attended, with whom one socialised, and even where one sat in the picture theatre. A famous example is the Sun Pictures in Broome, where it was always 'blacks at the back' on wooden benches, while the white elite had fine squatting chairs in the middle.

These etiquettes could become so ingrained and unchallenged that they could be understood as habits of preference or economy. This is how Lily Ah Toy describes the seating arrangements at the Don Pictures in Darwin:

> All the good seats were deckchairs down in the front, and further up it was all planks and we'd sit on those. And the Aborigines they would always sit in one corner. As children we always sat on these hard wooden seats, we'd never sit down there where the posh people are. You can still see the same film for sixpence.[77]

But those who breached the etiquette found that it could be enforced. Like all indigenous people who mentioned them to me, Pedro Guivarra found these rules obnoxious: 'You go to the pictures, they put a torch in your face, as soon as they see that, they show you to the back seat, a wooden seat like that, you got to go and sit there. You're not allowed in any dances.'

On close inspection, the polyethnic north consisted of a multitude of definable ethnic spaces in close proximity, even down to the smallest spaces, such as a pearling boat. Pedro Guivarra explained:

> When you sign on a boat, part of that boat, you're not allowed to go there. It's only a small boat, you'd think you can walk anywhere or sleep anywhere. But the protectors tell the Japanese, now this fellow is a half-caste, he stays at quarter, you know at the back, the other two New Guinea, they stay at the middle cabin, you know, they not allowed at the back, and the mainlanders, they're Aboriginal, they stay right on the forehead.[78]

Allowed to sit anywhere at last: Theresa Chi in the Sun Pictures cinema, Broome, April 1995.

Maria Pederson: maintaining distance

Maria Cesar, the daughter of a Filipino pearling worker and a Portuguese–Chinese from Canton, married a Dutch railway fettler by the name of Pederson in 1929. For the next twenty-four years, Maria shifted home to move with the railways from Pine Creek to Twenty-two-Mile, to Rum Jungle, to Mataranka. Because schools were not available in these railway camps, they had to send their children away, but with her last baby, Maria baulked. She refused to let the child go, and settled in Katherine. She took over the tearooms in the main street and managed the cafe for fifteen years, from 1952 to 1968. She is still with her youngest daughter who transformed the cafe into a gift shop, surveyed from the back rooms by Maria's watchful gaze.

I asked Maria about her relationships with Aborigines in Katherine. She replied:

> They come in and those days they weren't allowed to drink, they were always sober, they come in, they buy food. We give them their food and off they go, they'd be sitting on the bench there eating it up. I got no trouble with them. It all depends how you treat them, I suppose. I never had any trouble with them. They say to me 'Hallo, *kadjeri*', that's their lingo for old woman, 'Hallo, *kadjeri*, where are you going?', 'I'm going to church', 'Alright' they say and they go off and I go my way. When they're broke, they'd come and say '*Kadjeri*, ohh, I'm hungry'. They wouldn't have a dollar in their purse, I'd just give it to them and off they'd go . . .

Growing up at Police Paddock, many of Maria's childhood friends and their children must identify as Aborigines. Still, her view of Aborigines is across a deep racial divide. She is well disposed towards Aborigines as long as they don't drink, but stops short of taking them on as individuals. Even those who worked for her for over a decade remained only superficial acquaintances about whose backgrounds little is known.

> Put it this way, they all say this, and their skin may be dark but if they take a liking to you and you be a friend for them, you be a friend for a lifetime. They protect you. When the kids were small and we were at Mataranka, I had Don and Ida working for me, I had them for ten or fifteen years. They used to say, 'I got no money, you give me tucker, bit of clothing and bit of tobacco and we come and help you.' 'All right.' So I always made sure that they had their few bob but I always made sure that they've got their tobacco and food. They used to take the kids out. 'Don't you go far out, you look after them now.' 'We'll look after them.' Oh, they'd come home sunburnt, they [the children] were happy, they [the Aborigines] went swimming and taught them how to dig a hole for the turtle and all them, oh, they used to be happy when they came back. They'd go away round about Christmas time or early before the winter starts, they want to go walkabout. Those days, if you give them money, I don't know what they do with it but they still come back and say, 'I'm hungry.' So it's better for you to give them a couple of bag of flour and a bag of sugar and a couple of pound of tea and some bully beef and soap and hair oil. Oh, they used to be grand with the hair oil and powder. You'd give them that, oh, they as happy as Larry, and the tobacco what they can chew and off they go and when they come back they

work twice as hard, they had their break. I always found them alright. Even now, when I walk down the street they always call out and talk to me and I talk to them.

I questioned Maria further:

'If they went walkabout at Christmas time, where would they go?'
'I don't know. I just give them their tucker they just go to their tribe or wherever they all go.'
'Do you know what tribe they were?'
'I think they were Matara—I think Borarua crowd.'
'Borroloola? Oh? Which one?'
'Bororula crowd they were.'
'How come they came all the way up from Borroloola?'
'No, they were, we were up in Mataranka, they used to walk—well hitch-hike—from Bororula to Mataranka.'
'[Established that it must be Borroloola.] That's a long way. Do you know how they got here, to Mataranka?'
'They'd been in Mataranka for a long time, they must have been brought to Mataranka when they were kids.'
'What work did they do for you?'
'Ida used to do the washing for me and Don used to keep the yard clean, and we used to have wooden stoves, they used to chop the wood for us.'
'But the washing isn't done every day, is it?'
'Yeah, I used to wash every day, having the kids. One thing, I don't like dirty clothes around the house. And my husband, digging and packing and pick and shovel, he used to get dirty when he come home. She ironed, too, but not so nice as Clare, the other native woman I had, she was a young girl, gosh, she ironed beautiful. She used to come and give me a hand and do the washing. They used to do that for some tobacco and matches and something to eat, or hair oil, oh, they're grand with the hair oil and powder.'
'Did they learn that on the missions, to wash and iron?'
'Yeah, a lot of station women, like Elsie Station, and all them they used to get these girls when they were young and they used to train them as a housewife, as a cook, as a laundress, and they are really good. You go to Elsie Station when Mrs Charles was there, the place was spotless, lovely bread cooked, lovely garden and everything.'

Living at close range with Aborigines did not necessarily raise an awareness of the policies governing them, of child removals and mission training, and departmental control of earnings (viz. also Nellie Fong). But essentially Maria faced the same problem as indigenous people emerging out of the coloured community—with the decline of the polyethnic spaces after the war there was no ideological space for being in-between. Like her husband and children, Maria became part of the white community. I asked her how she identified herself ethnically. 'Well, my father is a Filipino, my mother is a Portuguese–Chinese, we come under the Filipino, I suppose.' Had she been back to the Philippines?

We couldn't afford it, and when they all got married we never bothered. As I always tell the kids, they want to go and see the place where Mama was born, Canton. I don't know any family there now. I went to all the islands, Tahiti and all them, then we went to America with my other daughter, but I didn't make it to the Philippines. One day I will [chuckles].

POLYETHNIC TOWNSHIPS

Even in a small business centre like Broome, the icon of polyethnicity, there was an area referred to as Chinatown. It was located along Carnarvon Street with the Chinese Club, Chinese boarding houses, and some fifteen Chinese businesses, and running into Sheba Lane with the Guomindang store and several more Chinese businesses. Europeans tended to run businesses that required special licences, such as liquor outlets, chemists, pearling companies and cinemas. These were slightly concentrated along Short Street and Dampier Terrace close to Streeter's Jetty. The Japanese and other Asian premises were scattered throughout the central business district framed by Short Street, Dampier Terrace, Napier Terrace and Carnarvon Street. Further along the foreshore, on the hillside, were the 'native camps'.

In the Torres Strait a number of islands had ethnic enclaves, such as the South Sea settlement and the 'Malaya town' referred to by Kathleen Ketchell at Badu, the Catholic community of Filipinos on Hammond Island, the South Pacific Islander settlement at St Paul's on Moa, and 'Port Lihou' formed by Solomon Islanders and their indigenous wives at Prince of Wales Island.

Thursday Island, too, had a Malaytown, and a 'native area' towards the back of the island. The Japanese business centre was referred to as 'Yokohama'. It had a public bath, stores, a brothel, and boarding houses in Millman, John and Douglas streets, where during the lay-up season the Japanese recruits were accommodated according to their areas of origin, in 'Ehime House', 'Kushimoto House', and 'Shionomisaki House'. Just before World War II, Douglas Street housed the Matsushita store, the Sumioka store, Yumamoto's laundry, Tanaka's laundry, Mizukami's laundry, Nishimura's long soup shop, and the residence of the Shiojima Company's business manager and his family. Victoria Parade contained the business premises of the Ebisu Company with the residence of the shopkeeper. Hargreave Street housed Yamashita's sauce factory and home, two Japanese dressmakers, and a Japanese watchmaker. Hamada's long soup shop was in Millman Street, and another Japanese dressmaker was in John Street.

Thursday Island was intended as a white administrative settlement, with restrictions on native residents. Even so, the Europeans were always in a minority. In 1894 over 700 Japanese residents alone numbered more than the European population, and within three years there were twice as many Japanese as Europeans on the island. In addition there was a considerable number of other Asian residents, and a coloured population boosted by in-migration from the islands when these became reserves. By the 1890s most shops on the island were owned by Asians.

Chapter 5 has already demonstrated that ethnic spaces were to a degree managed and contained. 'Native camps' were everywhere designated, and in Darwin a concerted effort to disestablish Chinatown in 1911 was accompanied by the establishment of Police Paddock as a 'coloured quarters'. A number of state agencies could be involved in the management of ethnic spaces. These included government residents and the mayors or administrators who succeeded them, the Aboriginal protection bureaucracy, public health officials who could raise and enforce concerns over overcrowding and sanitation, lands departments who issued leases, police who were usually consulted for 'local information' and who enforced restrictions, and customs who maintained an interest in the accommodation of indentured workers. From Martinez' account in Chapter 5 we see that others freely offered opinions. Among them were pearlers, pearling inspectors, union officials, newspaper editors, and visitors. Her reading of the management of ethnic spaces in Darwin is closer than any available from Broome or Thursday Island and is equalled only by a study of Malaytown in Cairns by Jeremy Hodes.

Studies of such townships, in Broome by Sarah Yu and in Darwin by Julia Martinez, suggest that a shared *kriol* language ought to be added to the list of bonds uniting communities. The Malaytown Tropical Troubadours of Cairns had their Police Paddock counterpart in Darwin in the Cubillo Brothers' String Orchestra, noted in Xavier Herbert's *Capricornia*. Cairns Malaytown, in turn, became the model for 'Luggertown' in the 'Port Cowrie' of Vance Palmer's 1937 novel *Legend for Sanderson*.[79]

Coloured communities were strongly imprinted on the romantic imagination of the north in the 1930s. It was a time when the racial future of Australia was again widely reflected on. This time it was clear that Aborigines were not about to 'die out'. Their numbers were recovering under the admixture of mixed descendants and 'coloureds', and a range of futures was mooted involving either the segregation of 'full-bloods' and the assimilation of all others, or the drawing in of 'coloureds' under the mantle of Aboriginal protection. Many saw 'coloureds' and 'half-castes' as the spearhead towards a better acceptance of Aboriginal people in the mainstream. Xavier Herbert's novels included a range of such characters sympathetically described to underline the injustice of racial prejudice. Vance Palmer, referring to the Torres Strait descendants on the mainland such as might be found in Malaytown in Cairns, described them as 'almost a separate race of people—intelligent, finely built, educated well in the State schools, different both from the Aborigines and their island fathers'.[80] Racialised vocabulary also featured strongly in the novels of Ion Idriess. He refers to Derby girls of mixed Malay, Chinese and Aboriginal descent as 'little tigresses' with 'the flash of white teeth', clothed in 'natty uniforms' or 'close-fitting evening dress', with a sensuality quite absent from the white and Aboriginal women in his text.[81]

Malaytown in Cairns

The extended Pitt family became the core of Malaytown in Cairns, one of the lesser-known polyethnic townships of the north. Embraced by Kenny, Draper and Bunda streets, on Alligator Creek, it was on the swampy side of town. The better-drained elevated areas, drier and less affected by mosquitoes, were on the eastern side of a railway line which divided the 'battlers' from the 'wealthy'.[82] Malaytown must have started to form around the turn of the century, because in 1904, the Department of Public Health, after responding to an outbreak of bubonic plague by burning down sixteen dwellings after a 'systematic house-to-house inspection', referred in a report to a 'motley township [that] has recently opened up, inhabited by Chinese, Japanese, Javanese, Malays and Cinghalese'.[83] When a police station was established there in 1909, the police inspector in charge requested that it be officially referred to as 'South Cairns', because it may offend the Europeans of the precinct to be designated as residents of 'Malaytown'.[84]

In the 1920s Torres Strait Islanders became the dominant population of Malaytown, and it became a more substantial settlement. Jeremy Hodes observes:

> A comparison of two photographs of Malay Town in 1922 and circa 1932 shows a more settled community, with increased vegetation and additional dwellings which appeared to be more substantial and better maintained than previously. The boats on Alligator Creek also appear to be newer and larger. This change is especially pronounced when it is considered that the latter photograph was taken at the height of the Great Depression.[85]

Malaytown in Cairns attracted mixed descendants from the islands and elsewhere because it meant an escape from the embrace of the Department of Native Affairs. It also afforded better educational opportunities, because the children went to Cairns Central State School. Lee-Bryce, the Thursday Island protector, viewed favourably the exodus of coloured families from reserve islands, because 'they are what may be termed a "flash lot" and not desirable residents'. He referred particularly to the Pitt family as 'a great trouble'.[86] His struggle with the defiance of coloured community is demonstrated in the story of Atima Ahwang (viz.). Hodes observes that little attempt was made to extend the reach of the department over residents of Malaytown in Cairns, and only two of its residents ever had their wages controlled by the department. Hodes judges the men of Malaytown as being 'uniformly strong willed, independent and successful men'.[87]

From interviews with Cairns residents who grew up close to Malaytown, Hodes forms the impression that the residents there, referred to collectively as 'coloured people', were well respected by the locals. A 'Fisherman's Appeal' was published by Douglas Pitt in the *Cairns Post* on 4 February 1920 requesting public donations after a cyclone had brought him financial ruin. As Hodes observes, this 'demonstrates the respect held for Douglas Pitt and his family by residents of Cairns and district and is probably unparalleled elsewhere in Queensland during this era.'[88] Keith Johns from Bunda Street 'has fond memories of Malay Town and its residents', recollecting that 'many white children used to swim in the Alligator Creek with the Malay Town children, and would go fishing crabbing and prawning with them as well as play cards'. Johns recalls also that Malaytown residents welcomed these visitors.[89] However, this impression is tempered by the observation that 'it was mainly the '"lower class" of whites who went there' while 'middle class families, who lived further away from Malay Town, rarely went near there'. Hodes finds different attitudes refracted from those who went to a private Catholic school and those who shared the local state primary school with Malaytown children. He concludes that class, not race, was the determinant of attitude to 'coloureds' which could range 'from outright racism and hatred to friendship and intermarriage'.[90]

The polyethnicity of Malaytown meant more than co-residence. Hodes observes that 'most of the families were related by marriage and kinship ties' and there were a number of mixed families. What emerged was a close-knit community able to offer mutual support. For example, when Fred Walters moved there with his family from Yarrabah in 1935 they stayed initially with a Singhalese fisherman, Thomas Da Silva and his Aboriginal wife Ida. Among the residents of Malaytown before World War II, Hodes lists seventy-five Torres Strait Islanders, twelve Malays, eight Africans (mostly Bullio family), seven Aborigines (mostly married into Torres Strait families), seven Sri Lankans and Sikhs (mostly from the African–Sikh Singh family), seven Chinese (all members of the Sang family), five Europeans, three Japanese, three Australian South Sea Islanders, and one Jamaican. This means that the 'Chinese, Japanese, Javanese, Malay and Cinghalese' community of the turn of the century had been significantly transformed as a result of migration from Torres Strait.[91]

Typical of the polyethnic township, the children of Malaytown grew up with a secure sense of community and identity bonded by family links, co-residence, shared schooling, economic collaboration and co-dependence and class position. 'Even though eking out a living was difficult and the conditions of the settlement resembled a squalid fringe camp, some of the younger residents looked back fondly on their childhood experiences. They remember growing up in Malay Town surrounded by a warm and caring community.'[92]

They also emerged with a cultural repertoire that permitted the expression of various ethnic traditions. Much singing and dancing often attracted white visitors to Malaytown. 'Most Saturday nights the dancing was accompanied by lively music supplied by the Jacobs and Pitt families. Benny Jacobs was on the turtle back mandolin, Doug Jacobs and Tom Guivarra on the steel guitar, Francis Guivarra on the banjo mandolin, and Arthur Pitt on the Spanish guitar.'[93]

The 'Tropical Troubadours' of Malaytown included members from the Pitt, Jacobs, Guivarra, Paterson, Anno, Delacruz, Noble, Meredith and Walters families dressed in a range of Pacific Island attire.

POLYETHNIC ACCOMMODATIONS

The close proximity of ethnic groups in the polyethnic north afforded easy access to a range of culinary and dress experiences. It was as easy to buy long soup or sate, and soy sauce, rice and chilli have become standard ingredients in much indigenous cuisine in the north. Starchy Ahwang said that at Thursday Island 'you don't wear trousers, you wear *sarong* all the time. And *tabi*, Japanese boot.'[94] *Tabi* is the traditional sandal that inspired the all-Australian thong. *Sarong* is still the preferred at-home wear of many Strait residents and Strait descendants further south, but photographs capturing formal or ceremonial occasions and people at lugger work suggest that singlet and shorts, or shirt and trousers, were just as easily donned, and those who could afford or borrow a suit would wear it for formal occasions.

Yet beneath the cultural admixture, lines of differentiation continued to be drawn and reinforced. In the pearling ports, ethnic groups were often explicitly played out against each other. If one ethnic group started to agitate over wages or conditions, master pearlers would look towards the importation of a different group. But even without such definable occasions, ethnic difference constantly simmered in an industry where racial distinctions were used to draw class distinctions, in the sense that the hierarchies of labour were ethnically stratified. Master pearlers distinguished between pools of labour in ethnic terms, and often crewed vessels with only one group, or in an explicit ethnic hierarchy. Those who worked in the industry perceived this acutely. Pedro Guivarra reflects,

> And they make us split, they want that split there, so you got no trouble, and they create that thing, 'I'm better than you.'
>
> And they call them names, Daudai, that's the lowest name you can call any blackfellow New Guinean. Agai is another low name you could put for anybody, that's an Aboriginal, that's an old word in the north, it's really bad. If you mentioned it today, they'd kill you. They made it that way, keep everybody apart. Keep the Agai away from the half-caste, the half-caste away from the Japanese, you know, 'I'm better than you' all the way down. No good.

Guivarra sees the separate administrative arrangements for Torres Strait Islanders as part of that ethnic management.

> They were protecting them in them days, that's how they make the split with the people, very bad. Even the Act covering the Aboriginals and the Act covering the Islanders, two different Acts. And that's where they fight all the time. That mob fighting this mob, this mob fighting that mob, you know.

He sees these distinctions, which translated into different management regimes, as the source of much ethnic friction.

> 'Did you ever fight with the Japanese?'
> 'Many a times.'
> 'With knives?'
> 'Anything. When we were kids [at Thursday Island], we used to wait for them, say after the pictures, when they come out from the pictures and sing out for the little dorey, them little boats, they used to sing out, just call the name of the boat, and the bloke used to jump in the dorey and come and pick them up, take them out to port after the picture. We used to be waiting on the beach for them. And then we all did in.'[95]

Ethnic friction, nurtured by the finely graded rules of

polyethnicity, usually simmered below the surface. If it occasionally erupted in violence it was usually widely reported, such as the 'Koepang race riot' in Broome in 1920. Tension between Timorese and Japanese in Broome was well known. The 'Koepangers' were occasionally used to replace the Japanese. They came mostly from Sabu, Alor and Roti and were recognisably different 'with long flowing hair and very little clothing'. They were socially distinct from the Malays and lived in humpies on the foreshore. Japanese and other Malays in Broome considered them natives.[96] There were disturbances in 1907 and 1914 involving several hundred people in Broome.

Despite such occasional clashes, the relative absence of conflict between ethnic groups in the pearling ports has often been remarked on. Bain observes that even the outbreak of the Sino–Japanese War did not imprint itself on relations between the Chinese and Japanese residents of Broome.[97]

Contrasting with this image of polyethnic accommodation was a white rampage in Normanton in 1888 resulting in the burning of coloured quarters and the eviction of all coloureds—a large proportion of the total population of Normanton. Normanton was the service town for a mining hinterland, and 1888 was the year when anti-Chinese sentiment became galvanised in the second—and last—spate of legislation targeted specifically against Chinese. It was after 1888 that the north became 'seriously polyethnic' and exclusionist legislation in all states became framed in terms of anti-Asian, and pro-white, sentiment. The Normanton miners were at the spearhead of this shift.

The concern with which the white community noted race riots bespeaks a considerable level of fear. It was a fear generated by the stepping out of assigned roles—talking back, fighting back—that ruptured the rules.

Michael Schaper, studying the records of the Broome race riot of Christmas 1920, reaches the same conclusions as Guivarra. In this conflict, over 1,000 Japanese were set against some 400 Timorese, with a force of almost 300 specially sworn-in white constables trying to maintain order for three days. Schaper examines the stratified society maintained by Europeans, with its differences in wealth, status and living conditions: 'Tensions generated by the relative differences provided fertile grounds in which conflict was likely to arise.' The toll of this conflict amounted to between three and six fatalities, of which the only white victim was an officer who died of heat stroke, and sixty injured. It was hardly a major debacle in an industry with a 10 per cent death rate. But the 'Koepanger race riots' stayed long in the memory of Broome. They were deeply disturbing and well noted by the press because it had been so difficult to maintain white hegemony during those three days: 'The Japanese walked over the whites when they were after the Koepangers … It makes them think they are as good as whitemen, and they then take law and order into their own hands.'[98] Such attitudes were clearly alarming, capable of eroding the basis of Broome's polyethnic society. White residents united as the ethnic group whose job it was to maintain order, while offers from the Malay community to assist as special constables were declined. Constables were under strict instructions not to shoot, because any fatality caused by whites would implicate them in a struggle that was first and foremost defined by ethnicity. Broome's request for a display of white power through the presence of a navy warship was endorsed by the premier and the Prime Minister.

How Normanton became white

When Normanton whites went on a rampage on the morning of 13 June 1888, the bodies of three white men were subsequently found with dagger wounds, for whose murder the Malay Sedim was charged. On 16 June a 'monster meeting' was held where lynching was suggested, and all coloured and Chinese men were 'seized and dragged out and thrown into the street'. A resolution was passed to urge the immediate removal of all aliens from the colony. At midnight a 200-strong mob gathered at the riverbanks with ropes and tarred firesticks, and 'razed to the ground and fired' eighteen houses owned by coloured residents. The residents of Malaytown fled, with only forty returning the next morning to a safe house on the outskirts of the town. The newspaper noted that they were armed 'and trouble is feared'. Immediately forty special constables were sworn in. All coloured domestic employees in town were discharged, and 'all coloured people excepting the Chinese were placed for safety on board the hulk *Rapido*' on 17 June after four more houses had been burned in Malaytown. 'Nearly all of the coloured people in Normanton are now quite destitute.' On 18 June a 150-strong mob again assembled at the wharves until 3 a.m. The town was patrolled by citizens, and some 'forty coloured people were brought in from the countryside and placed on the *Rapido*'.

Anyone who was not white was deemed guilty by association in a town intent on turning itself white. One coloured man carrying a swag, and evidently just arriving, was hounded by a party of horsemen for three miles to the landing. Another, Allio Donelly, 'a Spanish subject' and longtime resident as carter, married to a white woman, was also seized and confined on the hulk, as was a black American passenger on the coach from Croydon. Those captured were confined on the hulk until they arrived at Thursday Island by steamer *Birksgate* on 2 July. Disembarking were '84 coloured men, chiefly Malays but including Spanish, French and American coloured subjects who were expelled from Normanton ... The newly arrived contingent numbers more than the whole of the white population here', the Thursday Island correspondent observed.[99]

Pearl Hamaguchi on the politics of polyethnic marriage

Pearl's story has all the charm of Cinderella, but there is no fairy godmother, only a handsome prince. She was born with the stigma of being the illegitimate child of a Broome identity. In solid partnership with her husband Hiroshi and her sons, she is today a successful businesswoman, true to her name, in pearls. The family have built themselves what few can achieve: the house of their dreams. It retains a hint of the pearling days with its ample use of timber, wide verandahs and spacious rooms. Like Pearl herself, it is comfortable, graceful and unpretentious. Pearl's account provides vivid glimpses into the codes of conduct of a polyethnic community.

Pearl's mother, Mary Barbara Lynott, was from Ruby Plains near Halls Creek and her father was Scottish. At age four, Barbara was removed to Beagle Bay, and later sent to the convent run by the Irish nuns in Broome. With the nuns, the Sunday treat was walking to Chinatown, 'because that's where the hub of shopping and everything was. "But you must cover your faces when you see the Asians, don't let them see you." So these poor half-caste girls, part-Aborigine, they were told not to cohabitate with Asians or white men. But anyway, we still cropped up.'

Torn from her family, and with no father for her children, Barbara led a difficult life. In 1942 she and her children evacuated to Beagle Bay together with other families, including several pregnant women. The bumpy car ride would have taken several days, so a boat was hurriedly obtained from an old Filipino to reach the mission that was already hopelessly overcrowded. They returned to Broome in 1946.

So they came back after the war and all these women now had instructions from the mission to register for your coupons, for tea, milk, sugar, whatever, the basic things, at the Native Welfare office. The likes of my mother and a few of her friends, they had Asian children like me, and the man looked at us: 'Who's the father?', you know, growling. 'Asiatic?' 'Yes, sir.' No rations for me. I didn't qualify. Quadroons or quarter-caste, or whatever. I had to share my mother's rations.

Barbara found a job in the hospital laundry, hand-washing the linen and uniforms with a scrubbing board, suffering from chronically sore arms.

It was not only the washing, hang the clothes up, starch the clothes, all the nurses' uniforms, starching all these things. And in the fifties it was real white master mentality. If it wasn't right, they'd throw it back in your face ... And my sister and I, we'd go home from school for lunch. We had only a little Primus stove, and we'd have to heat up what we had the night before, we'd make our own lunch. And running around with no shoes, I'll never forget, we were so poor.

The year we turned fourteen we knew that was our final year at school. We said, 'Sister, please Sister', pleading with the Sister to be allowed to stay on in school. But 'No, Pearl' or Rose or Mary. 'There's only two of us and too many of you, we just can't cope, we can't keep you on at all.' That was the convent school. Coloured children, mostly, and black, you know, full-bloods. Upper-class coloureds didn't mix with the blacks. They had a govern-

Pearlie Hamaguchi and her son Neill, a member of the Broome band Kuckles, June 1995.

Hiroshi Hamaguchi of Broome (right) and a friend on their arrival as recruits in the pearling industry. Photo: courtesy of Pearl Hamaguchi, Broome.

ment school there, but coloured families had to go before the Parents and Citizens Association, and they probably would have said 'no they're not good enough to mix with our children', you know, it was that mentality. The likes of my mother didn't even try. She was brought up by the nuns and it was good enough for her.

They did accept some coloured children. There were families here that were established, they had property, and their husbands were pearling divers or merchants. These people in those days called themselves 'Eurasian'. Mother never really felt at ease with that, she always thought of herself as inferior.

My mother told me, 'Because you are half-Asian, you have to either marry Japanese or Chinese' because my father was of that descent. 'Don't marry a white man!' Broome in those days, you had to stick, keep to your own grouping. Of course older people have better experience, hard life I suppose, and most daughters take their mother's advice ... Especially in those days, people of white Anglo-Saxon always thought they were superior, that sort of attitude. A lot of my mother's friends married white men, and she felt most of the time it wasn't happy marriages because they weren't as free. They weren't allowed to mix with their own people any more, coloured people weren't encouraged to their house, and they had to give up a lot of their culture and thinking.

After the war, Broome master pearlers again recruited in Japan and a hundred Taiji men arrived in 1955. They were signed up by Streeter and Male and accommodated just across the street from the company's shop that employed Pearl. Among them was Hiroshi Hamaguchi.

They were just over the road, and we were young girls, and we used to say to each other, 'I bags that one, I bags that one.' And I suppose they were saying they bags us, the usual thing. You could take your pick in those days, it was twenty boys for one girl, you know, with lots of luggers in those days. And Saturday they had picture, movie theatre. And I'd be standing there and getting [offered] tickets here and tickets there, 'Please, sit with me', 'Please, sit with me', and so on, being shouted, you know, they'd buy the tickets. Well in the fifties and sixties it was like that. And the luggers came in, you know, very exciting. All these handsome young boys.

Hiroshi claims tongue-in-cheek that he had all the movie tickets booked, anyway, but according to Pearl a ruse was not necessary. When I asked him why he over-signed his contract after the first three years, he looked at Pearl, and she answered:

I suppose I was the reason he never went home. Don't blame me, Dad. It was love at first sight, hey Dad? We got married in 1960, five years after. We didn't go to Japan till after twenty-two years. He just likes this, he likes the Broome lifestyle.

Hiroshi had to quit diving after six years when he contracted diver's bends. He worked in mining for a few years until Pearls Pty Ltd (PPL) commenced pearl cultivation at Kuri Bay. He already held a master's certificate, but then learned written English to obtain the Australian master's certificate, and took charge of the transport of live shell. In 1984 Hiroshi was made redundant.

> In 1983 PPL closed down. If you know the history of Broome, Male and Company had big problems, because there was a terrible shell plague, it killed the shell . . . So he said, 'What do I do with my life? I think I'll ask for my own pearling licence.' He knew this game inside out, that's all he'd been doing, pearling industry. So we bought a boat, fisheries issued us with a licence. A very little fishing boat, second-hand. One of the older boys was the skipper. Now we've got four boats. Our company is Hamaguchi Pearls, the farm is thirty-five miles south, at Gordon Bay. The oldest one is our farm manager, the second one is skipper of the big shelling boat, the third one is a public servant, the fourth one is the engineer on the boat, the fifth one has just completed his gold-smithing certificate, and the baby is eighteen, he's just started as our diver.

This made Hamaguchi the first Asian in Broome to hold a pearler's licence in his own right.[100]

Hiroshi and Pearl never considered settling back in Japan. They think it would have been too difficult for Pearl: 'In those rural villages you're always Mr Hamaguchi's foreign wife.' Hiroshi obtained Australian citizenship in 1962 and feels very much at home here. He is only reminded of his otherness by newcomers to Broome. 'People ask me, "Where you come from, Japan?" I tell them, "I came here before you're born."'

Apart from the spatial organisation of ethnicity, the assignment of roles in a hierarchy of labour, and the dictates of social interaction, marriage politics also played their part in the maintenance of polyethnicity. We have already noted that missionaries and protectors had firm ideas about 'suitable matches' and were often able to enforce these. But obviously parents could also weigh into the argument with racialised views about suitable matches.

There is one other element of polyethnicity that is easily overlooked. Living at close quarters with people who engage in very different cultural practices from one's own may develop in people a facility for *teenmurti*. This is the ability to see no evil, hear no evil, speak no evil—the trained turning of a blind eye and deaf ear to practices which may be offensive, and for this a woman's veil can be turned to use as a subtle shield of honour. Isobel d'Antoine, for example, remembers the reaction of the Catholic nuns to Captain Owen, an eccentric pearler in Broome, who would water his mango trees stark naked in the front yard. The nuns marched the children past his house with the command 'Eyes left!' and covered the side of their faces with their veils. I have observed this *teenmurti* in Papua New Guinea, when on a modern air-conditioned passenger ferry to Lae, an American G-rated movie was projected onto a vast screen at the front, eagerly followed by all. The movie ended in the close-up on a passionate kiss, and glancing around to see if anyone was offended, I found that all the women around me had been suddenly overcome by slumber. It meant that there was a possibility they may not have seen the scene, and did not have to deal with it. They neither had to accept it nor attempt to distance themselves from it. They had simply not taken notice of it and could therefore overlook it altogether.

The spatial and behavioural rules of polyethnic co-existence are of course racist rules, because they are racialised rules propping up difference. But the maintenance and defence of such rules can be observed at every level in the hierarchy that they underpin. We see this in stories from Lily Ah Toy, who, having spent many hours on wooden seats, argues that wherever you sat in the cinema, you still saw the same movie for less money, or in the protestations of Pearl Hamaguchi's mother that she 'never felt comfortable' with the class of coloured people who saw themselves as 'Eurasian', and that the convent school was 'good enough for her' children. We see it in the distinctions drawn by Larry Ahlin between 'full-bloods' and 'half-castes', in Cesar's description of Police Paddock, and in Aboriginal descriptions of the spatial organisation of the Pan Quee household. A significant degree of acquiescence to the rules of difference, and the ability to overlook what was repugnant, was what rendered polyethnic communities strikingly functional. That acquiescence was disrupted in World War II and was never to be repaired.

Pedro Guivarra Jnr: mixed lineages

Newcomers to the polyethnic north often did not understand it, and this could cause tension. The young men of the luggers were thoroughly cosmopolitan, like Darnley Island-born Pedro Guivarra whose family had moved to Thursday Island to get away from government supervision. Like so many local boys he gravitated straight from school into pearling. He started off as pearl cleaner with Farquahr Company, with a crew from New Guinea and Mapoon, and rose to become a respected diver. During World War II he was a navy gunner with overseas service, and his brother became a 'rat of Tobruk'. The first time he was himself in charge of a lugger after the war, he took it to Darwin with a seventeen-strong Torres Strait crew:

> And I went out to a pub, at the back of the pub to buy sate, and on my way out, a girl was sitting down on a log, and she said, 'What have you got there?' and I said, 'Sate. Do you want some?' And I went over to give her some, and she took a long time picking it, and suddenly I felt this—this new Australian bloke come out, and he can't speak much English, but he just grab me by the neck and pulled me away, and I said, 'Hey, you, I'm doing nothing here', and the girl tried to explain to him that I was giving her sate, and he wouldn't take any [explanation], he just picked up a log and threw it at me, and I ducked away, and I went right in front of the pub at him and starting to fight. And he pulled out a cut-throat razor to cut me, and one of my mates from the boat grabbed his hand, and he cut my mate across there, so him and I end up nearly killed him. I kept on hitting him, hitting him, because he had that razor in his hand, cut-throat razor . . . He nearly died, he was bleeding through the mouth and nose and ears, but I was a big man then, I was sixteen stone.[101]

Pedro was arrested 'and they reckon I was never going to get out'. Horides, a Greek pearling master, put up bail for him, but Pedro jumped bail and took off to Cairns. This is when he married Gloria Boota, who had no idea that he was a fugitive from the law. Horides caught up with him and brought him back to Darwin to work off his debt, confident that things could be smoothed over. When he arrived in Darwin, Pedro sent a telegraph to his new wife to let her know he arrived safely. As he was leaving the post office, he was arrested again. Gloria received two telegrams that day: 'Arrived safely in Darwin', and 'In gaol'. Pedro was charged with assault and grievous bodily harm, fined and reprimanded. 'You must be good boy now, you're a good worker, you got a good boss now.' Difficult as it was for him to come to terms with it, paternalism and the influence of the pearling elite worked in Pedro's favour. 'They reckon the world is not crook.'

Pedro Guivarra (Snr) and Annie Wazan. Photo: courtesy of Guivarra family.

Abetha (left) was adopted by Pedro Guivarra and Annie Wazan and grew up as a sister to Peter, Frances and Thomas Guivarra. She was under threat of removal from her adopted family. She later married Songhi Mills. Carmen Seiko (centre, born 1898), grand-daughter of William Walton, married Peter Guivarra in 1919, and they had five children: Walter, Joey, David, Pedro Jnr and Mary. On the right is Kitty Savage.

Photo: courtesy of Guivarra family.

According to the philosophy of historical dialectics, every oppression carries the seeds of its own demise. The mixed population of the north was the product of a particular system: it was a class system based on racial stratification that brought Asians to the north, that imposed boundaries on Aborigines, that made the marriages of 'half-castes with half-castes' appear attractive, and that sought to bind this mixed population to laws and rules governing Aborigines.

Coming down south from the polyethnic north, they were often taken aback at the unabashed discrimination meted out to them.

> In Cairns at that time, if you go into a milk bar to buy a glass of milk, you can stand there till every white person is served in that bar. We used to stand there and just look at them and they used to go and serve everybody until they come to you and said, 'Look, I'm sorry, the management said you're not to be served in here, see.'

It was difficult to bear, especially after serving in the war. The bare face of oppression was a radicalising experience.

> I used to march in the street, me and my wife, five of us used to march with placards in the main street in Cairns. We used to get the placards pulled out of our hands, smashed up by the police, locked up, but we come out and do it again . . . We fought like hell. We never stop, we don't care. Been locked up, bashed up in there . . . We do that all the time until we started an Advancement League up in Cairns . . . And everybody attended the meeting, there used to be ten or fifteen there every night, every night, every night, so the trade union joined up with us, they affiliated with the Advancement League. And they sent us to Canberra for a conference. We came back and off we went, and it was one of the strongest black organisations in Cairns after that conference. Charlie Perkins was only a college boy, he was at that conference . . . Education, better homes, legal service. We screamed and screamed and screamed. But the trade union behind us was the force at that time. If it wasn't, altogether we'd never make it, because we didn't know where to go, how to go about it. There was too much law against black people at that time. I knew nothing when I left Thursday Island. Nothing there.

The marine industries and their easy mixing of peoples have been Pedro's world for generations.

> We're the offspring of Douglas Pitt, they come over to Murray Island, he had, what, three wives in Murray Island, then he decided to go to Darnley Island, and we're [the result of that,] coming down the generations. My grandmother [Annie Wazan] was Douglas Pitt daughter. He was a big bêche-de-mer fisher, he's a Jamaican. One of my grandfathers is Filipino, and another [great-grandfather] is from England, [William] Walton.

Both Annie Wazan and her sister Felicia married Filipinos. Annie and Pedro Guivarra (born around 1869 in the Philippines) had three sons—Peter, Frances and Thomas—and adopted Abetha, from the first marriage of Annie's sister Louisa, as their fourth child. Abetha later married Songhi Mills, another outspoken island leader from Naghir Island and famous diver, skipper of the *Milton*. Of this generation, only Abetha

Mills was still alive at the time of interviewing.

She remembered how the family came to move to the mainland. Francis and Thomas had found work on the Mossman sugar mill and cane farms, while Peter and his wife and children, and Annie herself, were still at Darnley. The two brothers advised Peter to move to Thursday Island, where they owned a house, because he had sugar diabetes, and it might have been difficult to find medical help when he needed it at Darnley. But as they were preparing to move, the protector intervened, saying that Abetha was under the Act and not permitted to leave. This must have been around 1928 as the department tried to extend its legislative reach.

In 1919 Peter Guivarra, posing as a Filipino in his marriage application, married Carmen Seiko of mixed Iama (Yam Island, Torres Strait) descent, and they had five children: Walter, Joey, David, Pedro (Jnr) and finally Mary, who was born at Thursday Island in 1929. Pedro Jnr was raised into the pearling industry: 'My father [Peter Guivarra, born 1895] used to be a sail maker for them boats, he used to work for Sinclair Company. When I was a little boy I used to give him a hand, wax all the twine while he's sitting down, and if he want another one I put it in the needle and wax it for him, sitting down all day. He used to skipper them luggers, and then lay-up time he'd sit down sewing all the sails. [He used to work bêche-de-mer too.]'

It was for the sake of Mary's first husband that the family home on Thursday Island was sold by Peter's eldest son Walter, in order to bail him out of prison. These people had all died by the time I met their aunt, Abetha Mills, who still expressed misgivings about that sale. Somewhere on its ground must be the silver butter dish from her grandmother that was buried for safe-keeping before everyone was evacuated from Thursday Island. She managed to rescue some furniture to Naghir Island only to watch it being eaten by white ants, and everything else was looted. She still knows the name of the family on another island where years later she was invited to sleep on one of the mattresses looted from her family's estate.

So these were some of the grandchildren of Annie Wazan and Pedro Guivarra (Snr). The grandchildren of Annie's sister Felicia became Filipinos. After Felicia's death her Filipino husband Magano took his children back to Manila. Only one of these, Bella, returned in the 1980s, leaving her children and grandchildren behind. The story goes that during World War II Bella's son Lawrence was employed in a Manila factory producing aircraft parts for the Japanese airforce, and he was busily sabotaging the planes, dressed in women's clothes so as not to be detected.

CHAPTER 7

The decline of the polyethnic north

THE war experience of northern Australia was vastly different from that in the south. During World War II the pearling ports, along with the whole of the Northern Territory north of Alice Springs, came under military control. The pearling ports became important infrastructures and therefore military targets. The pearling vessels were confiscated for war-related service and the industry ground to a halt. There were over ninety air-raids on northern targets, but even before these started, the north was in disarray because of the evacuations of civilians on a vast scale. Aboriginal populations, too, were moved around, and because of their good pre-war relations with Japanese, their loyalty to Australia was questioned. For many, contact with the military in one form or another was an eye-opener and set the scene for a 'new deal'. The Northern Territory's infrastructure received a massive boost as 32,000 Australian and 5,000 American troops were stationed in 'Fortress Darwin' and the military presence in the Territory peaked in late 1942 at 100,000 troops.[1] For the first time ever whites became numerically dominant in the north. World War II became the occasion for a fundamental reconstruction of the ethnic identity of the north.

THE NORTH UNDER ATTACK

On 7 and 8 December 1941 Japan entered the war with attacks on British and American military installations in Malaya (Kota Baru), Thailand, Singapore, Guam and Hawaii (Pearl Harbor). Australia immediately declared itself at war with Japan, Finland, Hungary and Romania, and later, in March, with Thailand. The Japanese entry into the war had been anticipated. Two battalions of the Royal Australian Army 8th Division had been garrisoned in Darwin in readiness for action in the Pacific since April, joined by further units by November. The Japanese in Australia had already been enumerated and described in secret police lists. The Thursday Island list of one stateless (Germanic) and 488 Japanese residents had been compiled on 29 May 1941. Warrants of arrest had already been drawn up and only needed to be signed on 8 December.[2] A barbed wire fence went up around Thursday Island's 'Yokohama' district with 8.75 miles of wire that had arrived a week earlier.[3] The numbers of Japanese residents in Australia had been on the decline. On 8 December the Japanese who were not out at sea were rounded up everywhere. Eventually 359 were taken from Thursday Island, sixty-seven from Darwin, and 212 from Broome, to internment camps in the south.[4]

Northern Australia became a forward defence post for the Pacific war theatre. Alan Powell gives an account of the role of Darwin in the Pacific War. All but two of the units from Darwin were immediately dispatched to Timor, Ambon and Singapore where they suffered great casualties. On 21 January 1942 Japanese forces attacked mainland New Guinea, by early February the Japanese had overpowered the Australians in Ambon, on 15 February Singapore fell. Malaya was taken soon after, and at the end of the month the Australians were defeated in Timor. Darwin and Port Moresby had long been used as American refuelling stations *en route* from Hawaii to the Philippines. The first American servicemen arrived in Australia on 22 January, and in February a large force evacuated from the Philippines to a new base at the Batchelor airstrip on the Northern Territory coast. Cloncurry and Daly Waters served as stations for the transport of fighter planes between Brisbane or Townsville and Darwin or Batchelor.

To support 'Fortress Darwin' road works commenced on the Barkly Highway to link Mt Isa to the Stuart Highway, and to link Alice Springs to the Darwin railhead at Birdum (Larrimah) by sealed road. Japanese submarines and reconnaissance planes were frequently sighted on the northern coasts in January and early February 1942. As early as June 1940 a volunteer Air Raid Precautions group had been formed in Darwin, but because they were given no powers of control they had resigned in protest on 26 January 1942. They had achieved, however, with federal permission granted on 12 December, the evacuation of 2,200 women and children from Darwin within four weeks. The first shipment was by *Zealandia*, and the last on 18 January by air. Most of the white population had now left, with only sixty-three white women remaining. Most Aborigines were also removed from Darwin.[5] From the remainder of the Territory, mixed-descent mission children had been sent to New South Wales and South Australia in late 1941 and early 1942.

On the morning of 19 February 1942 Darwin became the target of the first of many air attacks on north Australia. The missionary at Bathurst Island was able to give warning to Darwin Coast Radio twenty minutes before a 188-strong fleet of Zeroes, bombers and dive-bombers arrived. But no air-raid signal was sounded, and five American Kittyhawks (P40s) landed in Darwin just minutes before the attack. The post office and port, and two merchant ships near Bathurst Island, were the targets of this raid. Eighty minutes after the all-clear signal, 54 Betty bombers (Mitsubishi II) renewed the attack. The death toll reported to the Australian public was seventeen, but the air-raid resulted in over 240 casualties (viz. Cubillo). A disorganised exodus from Darwin followed.[6] Lily Ah Toy (viz.) remembers that the raid on Darwin resulted in a flood of evacuees to Pine Creek, but it was not until Katherine was bombed, on 22 March, that panic broke out and there was a scramble to the south.

Broome, too, had become a refuelling port for the RAAF, and Mary Albertus Bain describes its wartime chapter.[7] At the outbreak of war the town consisted of about 400 white and 1,000 'coloured' residents. In January 1942 all luggers were confiscated—forty-four were purchased for war service and sixteen, destroyed. After the bombing of Darwin, (white) women and children were evacuated from Wyndham, Derby and Broome, with sixty-three of them being shipped south on the *Koolinda*. The coloured population was evacuated to Beagle Bay and there were hardly any women and children left in Broome. Coastal shipping became liable to attack as the Japanese forces were advancing on Java in the lead-up to the Battle of Coral Sea in May 1942.

The town now became a way station for the Dutch in the East Indies and Americans from the Philippines evacuating to Perth and Sydney. In the last two weeks of February 1942 up to 8,000 evacuees were shipped through Broome, mostly women and children but also US service personnel. The resources of Broome were overstretched and often evacuees had to stay overnight until refuelling was completed.

On 3 March there was an air attack on Broome airport and harbour. The evacuees in port suffered some seventy casualties during an hour of sustained bombing until every machine was hit—six American bombers

(B24 Liberators and B17 Flying Fortresses) and sixteen Dutch flying-boats. A formation of Zeroes (Mitsubishi O) attacked the Wyndham airport and radio station on the same day, also flying out of Kupang, and the next day it was Darwin's turn again.

Requests were made for air evacuation from Broome. American personnel and RAAF officers were airlifted next day to Queensland, and some wounded Dutch evacuees were taken south, but the local civilians remained unaided. Many Aborigines and 'Koepangers' went bush, and a civilian road convoy was organised to evacuate. According to Bain only sixteen men remained—shop-keepers and officials with infrastructural responsibilities. Most from the convoy returned after six days because floods had rendered the roads impassable. Hugh Edwards indicates that of the Europeans only some forty remained in Broome, shrinking to ten by 1944. All agree that the port of pearls became a ghost town.[8] Port Hedland, too, was practically empty except for evacuees flooding in from the north and islands.[9]

On 14 March 1942 the Horn Island RAAF base in Torres Strait was bombed for the first time. Thursday Island had requested defence protection in 1939 for its 1,500 residents. A 600-strong garrison was stationed there to safeguard shipping routes and in 1941 the RAAF airstrip was built at Horn Island. By the time of the air attack, Thursday Island, too, had been evacuated. On 28 January 1942, 495 residents had departed by *Zealandia* and *Ormiston* to southern townships. Among them 280 coloured and twenty Chinese were taken to the Cherbourg Aboriginal reserve (formerly Barambah). During February and March more coloured women and children were sent to Cherbourg.

The Japanese advance seemed unstoppable. The war had shifted towards Australia and from February to May 1942 a Japanese invasion of the Australian mainland seemed imminent. General Douglas MacArthur arrived from the Philippines on 17 March to set up headquarters in Melbourne, and on 29 March he placed the north of the Northern Territory under military control. All white women north of Katherine were ordered to leave; other civilians could leave if they wished unless required for essential services.[10]

A number of military installations became targets of air-raids, including Katherine airstrip on 22 March, Townsville where the first of three attacks occurred on 25 July, Port Hedland on 30 July, the navy installation at Exmouth Gulf on 20 and 21 May 1943, and Drysdale River Mission (later Kalumburu), with a nearby airstrip, on 27 September 1943. Heavy battles were fought over Darwin again on 15 March and 2 May 1943. Bain refers to sixty-four air-raids in Darwin, seventy in the Northern Territory as a whole, fourteen in Western Australia, and ten on Horn Island.[11]

SPYING

The precision and careful targeting of the bombing raids caused much speculation. Local folklore has it that at the end of the Broome raid, a V-formation of bombers was observed flying low over the 'Japanese section of the cemetery'.[12] Such spatial accuracy is difficult to credit, but the story reflects the mood. In Broome there was great suspicion of Fifth Column activity, and rumours about certain prominent figures 'who had good business relations with Japan' are still nurtured. Torres Strait

Islanders would claim that it was thanks to their good relations with Japanese skippers that their villages were spared.[13] Others claimed that Thursday Island was spared because it contained the Japanese cemetery, or because a Japanese princess was buried there, or because it was thought that some Japanese were still residing there. None of these explanations is as convincing as the presence of military targets in the harbours, airports and communications centres. The targeting at any rate demonstrated a close familiarity with the coast and its ports.

Suspicions about Japanese lugger captains had become widespread in the 1930s when Japanese fleets started to encroach in the coastal waters of Australia. It was alleged that they charted the reefs for the Japanese Navy.[14] The Military Commandant in Darwin observed in 1940 that 'many of the lugger crew boys who have visited Darwin this season have come ashore wearing Japanese Army F. S. Caps'.[15] Japan was at war with China since 1939 and Yuriko Nagata observes that the Thursday Island *nihonjin-kai* (Japanese Club) made various financial contributions to Japanese national defence.

Cartellisation of the Japanese economy accelerated in the 1930s, unifying the state and the economy and merging interests of trade and defence under the economic dominance of *zaibatsu* like Mitsubishi and Mitsui, which practically controlled Arafura pearling in the 1930s. In 1938 all Japanese South Sea fishing activities were placed under the Nippon Shinju Kabushiki Kaisha.[16] A local historian in Wakayama, Ogawa Taira, said in 1987 that ships from Kushimoto 'were requisitioned by the Japanese Navy as spy ships to Palau, the Philippines, New Guinea, Borneo, Java, etc. They carried cargo and personnel, and made charts of the foreign ports, noting where water, bananas, potatoes and so on could be obtained. They were instructed to do so three years before the outbreak of war. I spoke to one of the captains myself.'[17]

Fears of Japanese espionage under cover of pearling were longstanding. As early as 1909 the Bishop of North Queensland had approached External Affairs with the suspicion that Japanese trepangers were 'systematically taking soundings of the reefs and channels in our waters'.[18] It was the year of publication of a much-discussed book, *The Australian Crisis*, by C. H. Kirmess, which suggested that in the case of a defence crisis, northern Australian Aborigines would rally to the Japanese. War hysteria rekindled all these suspicions.

ABORIGINAL LOYALTY

Because of their close links with Japanese, several Aboriginal communities were evacuated during the war. The whole of Cape Bedford (now Hopevale), with a German missionary and lugger connections, was removed on 17 May 1942 to Woorabinda where they suffered a disastrous death toll.[19] Within nine months sixty of the 235 relocated to Woorabinda had died.[20] The evacuation appears to have been initiated by a former superintendent of Yarrabah who wrote to the Townsville military commandant in January 1942 pointing out the 'possible menace to the people resident in North Queensland' emanating from the Aboriginal reserves on the eastern seaboard. Unless they were under military control 'it is possible for these aboriginals to convey information by signalling in native fashion . . . to the invader. The Yarrabah boys, I know, were always frequenting that portion of Cairns known as Malay Town, the headquarters of late Japanese Fishing crews.'

He ended with a few of his own poignant observations about the general character of the 'blacks'—cunning, unreliable, given to bribery and natural instinct.[21] Northern Command made inquiries with Padre Campbell, also a former superintendent of Yarrabah, who discounted the likelihood of effective smoke signalling. He also observed that Lockhart Aborigines 'have not been well treated by the Japanese crews', whereas Cape Bedford, with a German superintendent, 'may be a source of dissemination of information to the enemy'.[22] Nobody seemed to recall that a group of twenty Cape Bedford residents had been the first Aborigines in Queensland to volunteer for military service in October 1939, a month after fifty Darwin Aborigines had been accepted for militia service. While the loyalties of Aborigines as a group were questioned, some 400 Aborigines from Western Australia, close to 1,000 from the Northern Territory, and a total of 3,850 from Queensland including Torres Strait Islanders went into military and quasi-military service for Australia. More would have volunteered had they been accepted.[23]

In the whole pearling belt, from the Kimberley to the Cape, there were strong fears that Aborigines might become an 'active Fifth Column' in the case of invasion.[24] Still, the response was quite inconsistent. While Cape Bedford Aborigines under the German missionary Schwartz had been removed, nearby Bloomfield (later Wujal-Wujal), also with lugger connections, also Lutheran, was not. The German missionaries at Beagle Bay had been interned in 1940 and the mission placed under Army Intelligence control. Nearby Lombadina was left alone after the arrest of the German missionaries.[25] The army considered closing down Hermannsburg Mission under Strehlow in central Australia but did not proceed.

In the Northern Territory, too, Aborigines were under suspicion of likely fraternisation with the Japanese enemy. An army patrol in the Northern Territory reported around May 1942 that coastal Aborigines were commenting favourably on their relations with Japanese and pointing out that 'white men have not given them anything and on a number of occasions have molested them and their lubras'.[26] Robert Hall argues on the contrary that they had 'a long history of attacks on Japanese seamen' and that the Balamumu 'were almost hereditary enemies' of the Japanese.[27] (See Chapter 4, Northern Territory.) My impression is that they simply thought less in the ethnic categories distinguishing Japanese and Europeans and more in terms of defending their culture against any transgressors. Hall cites a number of incidents where Aborigines reportedly claimed allegiance to German missionaries or Japanese pearlers to point out the injustices meted out to them by Australians in treatment and dispossession. The Bishop of Carpentaria thought along the same lines. It was their neutrality that rendered Aborigines suspicious.[28]

COLOUR-CODED EVACUATIONS

The evacuation of the north followed neat hierarchies of colour. White women and children were offered opportunities to evacuate before the northern townships were attacked, and Asian and coloured civilians were fitted in where possible. But there was much procrastination on safeguarding Aborigines in the north. Indeed, the evacuation plans for Aborigines were inspired not by concern for their protection, but to forestall collaboration with the enemy and to clear areas of potential contact with personnel.

In Western Australia the wholesale evacuation of coastal Aborigines between Derby and Carnarvon was recommended by the military in June 1942 because of fears over their loyalties.[29] Unable to gain the support of Director of Native Affairs H. I. Bray for evacuation, eventually the army settled on draconian controls for Aborigines. They were barred from towns and from September required a military permit to travel, work and remain in an area. In the far north unemployed Aborigines were assigned to supervised camps, while further south anyone unemployed was sent to Moore River. The latter was also the destination of those suspected of pro-Japanese sentiments, and so acquired the form of a detention camp with a corporal attached. Port Hedland, where ninety-five soldiers were garrisoned, became a prohibited area.[30]

Aboriginal people in the Northern Territory were often moved to make way for the military. They were moved from the coasts to 'supervised camps' at Snake Bay on Melville Island, Delissaville on Cox Peninsula, Adelaide River, Katherine, Maranboy, Larrimah and Mataranka. Delissaville was in turn evacuated to Katherine in April 1943. Powell observes that this kept the women away from the military personnel, made supervision and rationing easier, cleared the coast for battle, and prevented any collaboration in case of a Japanese invasion.[31] It also facilitated the formation of special unpaid military units and army access to Aboriginal labour.

In Queensland the evacuations of missions was uncoordinated. Military headquarters had no clear picture who was ordering what, and nobody wanted to take financial responsibility for the evacuations. At Mornington Island, for example, a Captain Hall gave 'very strong advice to evacuate the women and children and the half-caste native women from Mornington Island'. He probably meant 'white women and children', because these were picked up soon after. Northern Command knew nothing about Hall's advice. The Bishop of Carpentaria, too, understood from a visit by Lieutenant Beaman from Military Intelligence that 'Beaman was fairly definite in his conviction that Cowal Creek, Lockhart River and the Presbyterian mission natives would have to be moved'. But Queensland Headquarters insisted that 'no Military pressure produced the evacuation from these three (3) stations'.[32] The bishop complained to the deputy director of Native Affairs: 'I found the Lieut. Beaman was forming opinions on insufficient and in some cases inaccurate information; that his idea of co-operation and mine did not correspond. His idea seemed to be that the army would give orders and the Mission authorities would pay costs.'

The bishop indicated that 'we have roughly 1,000 people to deal with' and suggested the acquisition of cattle properties to house such evacuees.[33] The bishop took exception to Beaman who had visited all Cape York missions and recommended wholesale evacuation claiming that of the resident Aborigines 'not one percent could be relied upon to be loyal'.[34]

Meanwhile the Aurukun missionary, without clear instructions, had already formed his own back-up plan. Seven weeks before the air attack on Darwin he had 'made the following plans if we are forced to evacuate'. All the biggest girls were to be married off; small children were to be returned to the care of their parents, the others left in charge of the missionaries. Everyone was to split into small parties and hide in the swamps and scrubs of the Archer and other rivers. Canoes and dinghies had already been hidden on the Watson River to ferry them across, and provisions had been taken to prepared positions up the Archer River. His wife was to be taken southeast to the nearest whites for evacuation further south. Missionaries McCarthy and MacKenzie himself were to remain in hiding with small parties to try to get messages through to Military Headquarters.[35] Similar plans were put into action by others in charge of remote missions and reserves in the Northern Territory.

The patriotic intentions of MacKenzie notwithstanding, in January 1943 the mission authorities were requested to now evacuate Mapoon because National Security doubted their loyalty and felt also that venereal disease 'constitute(d) a menace to any troops who may be stationed in that area'. The mission authorities took strong exception on both grounds and wished to know who was spreading such rumours.[36] Lockhart River, Mapoon and Cowal Creek were close to black US troops. Higgins Field aerodrome (Jacky Jacky) near Cowal Creek was consequently moved to Vrilya Point sixty miles further south.[37]

The Queensland Department of Native Affairs did not acquire cattle properties to evacuate Aborigines. It announced its plans for the evacuation of the Cape York Peninsula Aborigines in September 1942, when the Allies had already gained the upper hand, and civilians had started to return to Cairns. Cowal Creek, Lockhart River (404 residents) and Port Stewart (near Coen) would be 'mustered' to Mitchell River. The 212 Aboriginal residents of Cooktown were to join the Cape Bedford people at Woorabinda. Those from Normanton, numbering less than 100, were to be taken to Doomadgee. This would clear the east coast of the peninsula north of Mossman of all Aborigines.[38] None of this eventuated. The department had been preoccupied with coloured evacuees.

COLOURED EVACUEES

In the scramble for northern evacuation, coloured evacuees, not normally under the umbrella of protection bureaucracies, fell under the control of the Queensland Department of Native Affairs. The Catholic mission on Hammond Island and the Catholic convent at Thursday Island became subject to compulsory evacuation. Though 'none of them were wards of the state', the department arranged for their accommodation in the south.[39] The first party of ninety-four arrived in Townsville on 2 March 1942, and the second party of ninety-one on 11 March after delays when the *Goodwill* ran aground on Cape Melville. They were quartered in the quarantine station and medically examined by Sir Raphael Cilento and Dr Todd Stephens and declared free of disease. They included eleven Malay indents, one Singhalese, and 'the balance were Malayan–South Sea Islander, Malayan–Chinese and Malayan–Torres Strait Islander strain'. They 'readily accepted the proposal to proceed to Cherbourg settlement as a clearing station for their future employment'.[40] The Prime Minister cabled the Queensland premier to underline that they were to be sent to localities where work could be obtained so they could 'become self-supporting as early as possible'. The Commonwealth would pay sustenance for compulsory coloured evacuees for one and up to three months, thereafter the state was responsible for their financial welfare. The much more generous sustenance for white evacuees did not carry the same time limit.[41]

From Thursday Island people continued to arrive in Cairns on launches and luggers. Native Affairs was having difficulty accommodating them, and was not happy with the way they 'crowded together', sometimes thirteen in one cottage. They were mostly women and children staying with friends and relatives or renting workers cottages vacated by the civil evacuation of Cairns. Several of them received military allotments because their husbands served in the Thursday Island militia. In April 1942 the acting superintendent of Palm Island, Foote, was sent to Cairns to assess the evacuated coloured population there. He was to ensure that they were receiving any child endowments and other federal payments they were eligible for, but most of all to see what they were doing about finding employment. Protector O'Leary, now deputy director of the department, explained that 'these people are by breed, living conditions etc. practically similar to the party that we controlled at the Quarantine Station, Townsville'.[42]

In May 1942 Foote ascertained that there were over 200 coloured evacuees in Cairns (155), Mossman (33), Babinda and Deeral (20), and Brisbane (20). Those in Cairns were concentrated in Malaytown and its surrounding suburbs, now called Portsmith and Parramatta Park.[43] O'Leary asked whether the Yarrabah Station could accept 123 mixed-descent people 'whose removal from Cairns for health and other reasons is desirable'. The arrival of American personnel, including black soldiers, was expected and Foote predicted that 'one can imagine what would happen and the trouble they would cause the Police so soon as these negroes got amongst the evacuee women'. He recommended that those who were unwilling to move on should have their allowances suspended.[44]

ARMY TAIM

By mid-1942 the Allies were gaining some leverage on the Japanese advance. The Darwin radar started to function by late March, and in June the radar system was expanded to cover the whole northwest and Arnhem Land coast. Air defence capacity was boosted when Spitfires replaced Australian Kittyhawks in January 1943.[45] The evacuations had been so extensive that by July 1944 only 1,563 white civilians remained in the whole of the Territory. Consequently the military drew extensively on Aboriginal labour.

Administrator Abbott had planned to scatter the part-Aboriginal and Asian residents along the Stuart Highway, but Chinese community leaders objected to this, and Asians along with 1,300 part-Aborigines were evacuated from the Northern Territory. This left only Aboriginal labour for deployment by the armed forces.

The military's vast need for 'fatigue labour' drew Aborigines from the Tiwi and other nearby islands into Darwin. The administration on the other hand sought to clear Darwin of Aborigines. Bagot Reserve was closed in December 1941 and Aboriginal camps at Knuckey's Lagoon (viz. Pan Quee) and Shoal Bay were raided in March 1942 to engage residents in work at the Mataranka aerodrome.[46]

Aboriginal labour was used for an army piggery at Alice Springs, and an extensive garden at Adelaide River. Eighty Tiwi men were quartered at Darwin's Larrakeyah Barracks for service with the port craft from March 1944 to April 1945. Aboriginal camps also formed around the army installations all along the route from Darwin to Alice Springs. Many Aborigines performed day labour work—some remember cleaning ammunition shells—and by April 1945, 662 Aboriginal men and seventy-two Aboriginal women were on the army payroll. Powell confirms that 'The men did everything from chopping firewood and working the army farms to handling ammunition, driving army vehicles and stripping engines for reconditioning'. Seventy-two manned small port craft, and the women worked mostly in the military hospitals and hostels.[47]

In Arnhem Land the lighthouse keeper at Cape Don (Dundas Strait, on Cobourg Peninsula) employed local Aborigines and they saw Cape Croker bombed during the war. (After the war they continued to sign on with Japanese skippers and the small community that emerged there harboured no grudges against Japanese when I visited.) Airstrips at Groote Eylandt, Milingimbi and Gove were used for military purposes. So were Bathurst Island, Drysdale River, Mainbulloo and a host of other airstrips in the Darwin–Katherine area. While the air force was building remote airstrips, the army worried how they could be defended.[48]

Powell observes that the birth rate increased among the Aborigines in the ambit of the army. They felt more secure, and more valued than under Native Administration. Brigadier Dollery, the commander of the Northern Territory Line of Communications Area, proposed a doubling of the Aboriginal pay (five shillings a week) and the formation of an Aboriginal Employment Company with pay scales equal to whites. Nothing came of this proposal.[49]

The army was more insistent than the navy and air force on the 'substantial European background' of its recruits, but after the first air attack on Darwin there was an acute manpower shortage and Aboriginal volunteers were enlisted in greater numbers. Several anthropologists including A. P. Elkin supported the idea of Aboriginal military service, and there was a strong Aboriginal rights movement that pinned its hopes on military service as a way to citizen rights. Similarly the Chinese Legation lobbied for acceptance of Chinese citizens into the armed forces. Four hundred Chinese had enlisted by June 1942.[50]

Apart from formal enlistment and civilian support work for the military, between 200 and 250 Northern Territory Aborigines participated in the war effort in a number of *de facto* military units under local service commanders. The first of these was formed in 1941 among the very people who had suffered persecution for killing Japanese at Caledon Bay. The Northern Territory Reconnaissance Unit, under anthropologist Donald Thomson as squadron leader, consisted of 'native bush warriors' trained for coast watch and guerrilla patrol. The expense of this force was three sticks of tobacco per week each and costs for Thomson. The Yolngu were not enlisted, not paid, not outfitted or accommodated, not rationed, not issued with fire-arms, and not eligible for repatriation benefits. Thomson pointed out how important it was to establish a white presence among the people who had been in contact with up to 700 Japanese pearlers annually.[51]

Major W. E. H. Stanner, also an anthropologist, formed the 2/1 North Australia Observer Unit with over 700 men after the attack on Darwin. They patrolled the bush and coast from Yampi Sound near Derby to Normanton in the Gulf. Many of them went on to active service in New Guinea in 1944.[52] Missionary Jack Gribble at Snake Bay in the Tiwi Islands led a twenty-six-strong coastwatch unit, and the 'Black Watch', a forty-strong rescue unit, worked under Jack Murray as an army volunteer defence corps at Delissaville on Cox Peninsula near Darwin. The members of the Snake Bay unit were armed and wearing navy uniforms and might be appointed to the rank of 'petty officer', but like those at Delissaville and Arnhem Land they were neither enlisted nor paid. These units formed an early warning and rescue belt around Darwin.[53]

In Queensland there was much less effort than in the Northern Territory to actively involve mainland Aborigines in home defence. Still, Palm Island residents were organised into work gangs to stand by for manpower requests and in August 1942, in the lead-up to the battle of Milne Bay, the army hastily recruited at Lockhart River for the Torres Strait Defence Force.[54]

The Torres Strait Defence Force incorporated the Torres Strait Light Infantry Battalion, coastal artillery, a small craft unit and a number of other units.[55] On recommendation of the Queensland protector, they received £3 per week instead of the army scale of £8, though there were no legal grounds on which such a distinction could be sustained. Still the roll-up was so enthusiastic that it practically depleted the islands of able-bodied men capable of tending gardens and maintaining houses. A total of 775 served in this force, and a number of other Islanders served in regular units of the Royal Australian Army, Navy and Air Force, and in the US Army which was less wedded to colonial images of blacks and aliens.[56] Beckett observes that

> almost all those who were physically fit between the ages of sixteen and thirty-five, at some stage served in this force . . . which was staffed below the rank of sergeant by Islanders together with a few Malays and Aborigines . . . A number had received training as drivers, clerks and radio operators, and several had been promoted to non-commissioned ranks.[57]

The 'Malays' were in fact mixed Asian–Aboriginal descendants who were not under the Act, and received the full scale of pay. This rankled with the others, and, together with other factors, led to a sit-down strike in December 1943. As a result their pay, which had slipped to some 39 per cent, was raised to 66.6 per cent of the full scale.[58]

In Western Australia Beau Davis, pearler and naval officer in charge of Broome, patrolled the coast from Broome to Darwin with seven Chinese, Timorese and Malays, including Lockie bin Sali and Lenny Leonard. Contrary to the practice in the other two states, Davis used trade goods to encourage coastal Aborigines to stay put and supply local information.[59] Pastoral station workers were trained for defence, and although the plan had been to restrict training and access to weapons to whites, Cyril Longmore, journalist, friend of Prime Minister Curtin, and AIF Captain in World War I, trained a 13-strong Aboriginal volunteer unit at Liveringa Station in July 1942. He wanted to form a 250-strong Native Auxiliary Corps but the Director of Native Affairs Bray felt that Aborigines could not be trusted with rifles and knew 'nothing about patriotism or loyalty'. He suggested that Aboriginal platoons could be attached to the stations. Hall points out that Bray seemed more concerned about the stations' access to cheap labour than about the safety or ability of the people in his care. Neither Longmore nor Bray had any knowledge of the Aboriginal units in the Northern Territory or Queensland, and the army command was not forthcoming with such information. The unit was not formed.

Besides these Aboriginal units, there were many Aborigines who rendered service as guides and interpreters.[60] Longmore pointed out that no army unit moved in the bush without an Aboriginal guide. Heavily armed guerrilla groups were formed on a number of pastoral properties, including Mainbuloo and Victoria River Downs, and these also had Aboriginal guides.[61]

The newspapers were silent about the Aboriginal participation in the war effort and a general awareness of their war effort did not filter through to the public until well into the 1960s.[62] Western Australia passed the *Natives (Citizenship Rights) Act 1944* offering citizenship to current or former serving personnel with an honourable discharge, and it was touted by Bray's annual report on Native Affairs as an 'enlightened policy'.[63] But it required applicants to 'dissolve tribal and native associations' and H. D. Moseley, who had been royal commissioner into Native Affairs in 1939, and responsible for security in Western Australia during the war, observed in 1946 that of over 400 Aborigines who had enlisted in the state, only two had been granted citizenship by this Act. In 1949 the Commonwealth *Electoral Act* granted voting rights to Aboriginal ex-servicemen.[64] Benefits did not extend over the former members of quasi-military units, and a long struggle for recognition of service followed. In 1961 a House of Representatives Select Committee on voting rights for Aborigines heard evidence of Aboriginal war service with considerable surprise. One of its members, Kim Beazley, wrote to Senator Gorton as Minister of the Royal Australian Navy in support of recognising the contribution of the Gribble patrol.[65] The history of Chinese participation in the Australian war effort, on the other hand, is still being written. Ian Welch has assembled a preliminary list of over 1,000 Chinese-Australian servicemen in World War II.[66]

In the Torres Strait, where active indigenous participation in the war was most intensive, the wartime experience had deep effects. Because all usable vessels had been requisitioned and the men drawn into year-round war service—unlike the seasonal lugger work—the traditional economy had been severely disrupted and a dependence on store foods had emerged with attendant health consequences. But more importantly it dislodged the Department of Native Affairs as an authoritative body over Islander affairs. The flight of the protector in the face of approaching war was for Islanders an apt expression of the support they could expect from the Queensland government.[67] 'Army taim' showed up the colonial nature of the protection bureaucracies, with a lexicon of practices and ideas ('cunning, indolent, unreliable, requiring protection') that was not quite shared by the military. Hall observed that across the board Aborigines and Torres Strait Islanders found ready acceptance among their white comrades.

Asians at Port Keats

Wadeye was the only place I visited in the north where the memory of Asians was predominantly negative. The mention of Asians conjured memories of Japanese warplanes flying over.

The activity generated by a massive deployment of troops to 'Fortress Darwin' attracted many Aborigines. Among them was Johnny Juler, with chest cicatrices and a pierced nose to carry an ironwood splint 'to keep that law':

> When the war come people went to airforce, working the road, highway, we working. But we coming out here [Port Keats coast]. That airforce, people had to hide in the bushes somewhere around here. Lots of airforce and gun. After that, me and my brother working with the airforce, working through every area. Captain said plane might come along put a war with us and we shootem back.
>
> Then we bin work boat now, that nother plane which it come along from Wyndham, come along plane, somewhere around there, maybe four mile out from here to where they burn that plane. One man, he burned, died, Englis, one bloke died. We run from there me and my brothers, one slow coming behind us [chuckles about the slow one], we seenim that bloke, looking at that one fire [we kept running towards the fire].

There was nothing they could do to help the English pilot from the crashed plane, his leg was severed, he was badly burnt and he died.

Once they found some stranded Malay trepangers, too:

> We had people up here finding them *jindi*, they callem *jindi*, could be Malayan people [indicates strong build]. There was a number of people we thought was a woman—clothes look like a woman [indicates sarong]. 'Where you come from?' 'We come out to Broome but our land long way out' . . . 'Well, we short of tucker.' 'We take you back to our home, we gib you tucker, put you on a plane, go back to Darwin.' 'Alright then.'

The pre-war contact with Asians is now overwritten with more recent impressions.

> I want to makem young men [initiate young men]. But me really old man. I was born in wildlife. No *kukleg* [cooked food, rice]. My mother, my father, my grandfather, no *kukleg*, that food him from Japanee. And they brought in that calico, wear calico then.

Johnny Dumoo, translated by his daughter Annunciata Longmirr, and in the company of Celesta Dumoo and several grandchildren, told the story of how the men went to fight the Japanese who had been abusing local women as an exchange relationship went awry. Nimarluk, after whom Nitmiluk National Park is named, was among the elders who killed the Japanese. But this was not a proper women's story, and the teller, translator and interviewer felt awkward, more so because we each brought a different approach to the issue. It seems a long time ago now that women were used as the currency in an exchange relationship, and mission time has transformed the moral universe. Women still have the rough end of the stick here, and the moral universe at Wadeye needs to change yet more.

SURVEILLANCE

Next to making lists, quantifying, specifying and enumerating people, another wartime administrative occupation was qualifying: judging, pre-judging loyalties and attitudes. This was done, like other management activities, in convenient ethnic categories. Category misfits attracted suspicion.

Among the Japanese rounded up at Thursday Island were several with local families: Tomitaro Fuji married to Josie Chin Soon with one child, Iwazo Takai married to Sophia Barba with three children, Kyukichi Shibasaki from Miwasaki married to Jean Ah Boo with three children, Seikitchi Takimoto who was living with a Thursday Island woman at Blackall Street, and Sao Tanaka, owner of a laundry in Douglas Street, Thursday Island, who was the mother of eight Australian-born children, one of whom had married a Malay–Torres Strait descendant, another a Chinese, and a third married Tsunehiki Mana at the internment camp. Most of these internees had been residents of some forty years, and for all of them the police description ran 'no doubt his/her sentiments would be with his/her native land Japan'.[68]

Those who were not interned with their Japanese family members came under close surveillance. The families of Fuji, Takai and Shibasaki were taken to Cherbourg in February 1942 on the Katoora along with 'coloured residents'. Monitoring the letters sent by the Japanese internees, it was noted that several were on friendly terms with 'a number of Australian citizens mostly women'.[69] Nine women came under suspicion of 'pro-Japanese sentiments', and six were singled out for investigation by Queensland state police in February 1943 and interned at Gaythorne in Brisbane.[70]

Anima Ahmat was interviewed about her feelings about Japanese. She admitted to corresponding with one of the internees at Hay, with whom she had been living for seven years.

> She would not say that the Japanese had treated her better than the white people, but she has had more to do with the Japanese and always found them to be very good people.
>
> Inquiries from the staff at Cherbourg show that this woman associates mainly with other evacuees from Thursday Island, and has little to do with the aboriginal inmates at Cherbourg, but appears to be very sympathetic towards the Japanese.
>
> As the result of my inquiries I am of the opinion that Anima Ahmat is in sympathy with the Japanese and that she would prefer the Japanese to the white people, also that she considers herself superior to the aboriginals at Cherbourg.[71]

Her removal from Cherbourg was recommended 'in view of the possibility of the 1,000 aboriginals being affected by her propaganda'.[72]

Jean Shibasaki (née Jena Ah Boo) was also taken to Gaythorne. Perhaps she spoke a little too candidly when she stated during the attitudinal assessment at Murgon (Cherbourg) 'that the white people treated the coloured people well but did not mix with them the same as the Japanese who treated them very well'.

'Further inquiries' at Cherbourg 'reveal that she spreads Japanese propaganda amongst the natives. It is stated that she praises the Japanese and never misses an opportunity to tell the aboriginals how good the Japanese are to the coloured people, and that there is no need to be afraid of them.' It does sound rather like the sort of information that might have been conveyed by the white superintendent, though he could not have heard her make such statements since 'she is very careful of what she says in the hearing of the white officials'. The police pompously concluded: 'Shibasaki's attitude and activities are likely to influence the natives against the British Empire and in favour of the Japanese, and that her continued residence and association with the inmates would tend to make them a menace to national security in the event of an invasion.'

A précis of her case intriguingly argues, 'Shibasaki is a person of doubtful origin . . . but her ancestry is such as to show sentiments that could be classed as anti-British.'[73]

One must wonder about the claim of such in-grained sentiments. As to her doubtful origins, Jena Ah Boo was born on Thursday Island in 1912 as the daughter of Assan Ah Boo (or Abu Hassan) who was from Malacca on the Malaysian west coast and therefore a British subject, and Lass Seden, also born in Australia. Lass's mother was from Badu Island and her father, Amber Seden, was from Surabaya in (Dutch) Indonesia. It was a perfectly typical lineage for someone from Thursday Island, but for Murgon police in southern Queensland apparently so unfathomably complicated as to be doubtful.

Jean Shibasaki had never been in the grip of Aboriginal protection before. She had already caused enough paperwork to fall foul of the Aboriginal administration bureaucracy. After her evacuation from Thursday Island to Cherbourg in March 1942, she had been released into the care of her parents at Bundaberg at the end of the year. There she applied for rations for herself and her six children and was granted relief from January to May 1943, but in fact she only received rations for three weeks before the local officer argued that if she needed rations she should apply to the Department of Native Affairs to be returned to Cherbourg. It was during this dispute over rations that she was arrested. Her six children—Jamel, Hismile, Nonyna, Miyoko, Hisako and Isao (Billy)—were to be left with the grandparents in Bundaberg. But Jean refused to part with them, and all were interned at Gaythorne. She was now informed that she had lost her British nationality on her marriage to Shibasaki in 1929, and was required to register as an alien. In July 1943 she was released from Gaythorne under restriction order to her parents at Bundaberg, but only after both her parents and two brothers had been extensively interrogated and committed themselves to her and her children's support. Billy, incidentally, grew up to become deputy mayor of Thursday Island.

May Woodhead, an adoptive sister of Jean Shibasaki, was also taken to Gaythorne. According to her family, May, in her usual notorious way, had got up and sung Japanese songs at a party at Cherbourg.[74] Another woman to be interned was Lear Barba, who had been living with Seijiro Machida, and had three Japanese-fathered children. She told Yuriko Nagata that apart from the three married couples a number of women of Malay–Islander origin were living with Japanese, but only 'the outspoken ones' were interned.[75] Outspoken people were never welcome by those in charge of Aboriginal reserves. Knowing how easy it was to challenge the authority of protectors and superintendents, and how 'examples' were set, it seems rather that the menace which these women presented to the 'British Empire' rested not in their attitude towards the enemy but in their attitude towards Aboriginal protection.

JAPANESE INTERNMENTS

Altogether some 16,700 persons from over twenty ethnic and national backgrounds were interned in Australia as either 'enemy aliens' or 'naturalised British subjects of enemy origin'. For purposes of internment, ethnic labels were as widely conceived as they were in the popular imagination. Third-generation Australians of Japanese or of mixed-Japanese descent were as much candidates for internment as Japanese citizens temporarily in Australia. Almost a quarter of all internees were Japanese, either from Australia (1,141) or from the East Indies, the Pacific, New Zealand and Formosa (Taiwan) (3,160).[76] Almost 70 per cent of the Australian Japanese internees were from the far north.[77] Bain comments that the number of Japanese internees was small compared to the total number of resident aliens, but her source, which is not an official or published one, underestimates the number of Japanese internees in Australia by about half.[78] Indeed, the net of Japanese captives was very thorough and systematic.

At first the Victorians were taken to Tatura, Sydneysiders to Liverpool, and 223 mainland Queensland Japanese residents were temporarily held at Gaythorne in Brisbane. Later, families were quartered at Tatura and the single men from Thursday Island were taken to Hay in New South Wales, and those from Darwin to Loveday in South Australia. Only a small number of Japanese internees from Australia were at Cowra.

At Thursday Island about half the Japanese were at sea the day Pearl Harbor was attacked. Tatsuno Ryuhichi learned of the outbreak of war from a sympathetic fellow-worker:

> I was on Yorke Island, and an Islander came from the mainland, he used to work with us, and said, 'I have sad news, war started. So when you get back to Thursday Island a launch will pick you up.'[79]

Their children continued to go to school every day until the first consignment was shipped on the *Zealandia*. The *Zealandia* also carried sixteen Darwin internees, who were all members of families headed by Japanese, and evacuees from Darwin—whites were in roomy cabins, non-whites in cramped conditions 'almost as bad as enemy prisoners'.[80]

Inoue Ushimatsu, at Thursday Island since 1934, must have been on this first consignment:

> We felt the air of the approaching war but we didn't exactly know that the war was coming. Six of us were drinking at Yorke Island, and we ran out of alcohol, so we went back to Thursday Island. We were met there by a police launch and they told us that war had been declared. They put us in a barbed wire enclosure. We had no belongings. After a few days we were allowed to get our belongings from our *haus*. The whole Japanese settlement was fenced, but actually it wasn't too bad, because that's where we would have stayed, anyway. After two weeks, towards Christmas, a cargo boat shipped us to

Sydney. The conditions were terrible. We were in cow pens, there were no toilets and everything was so dirty, we got diarrhoea from the water. It took one week to get to Brisbane, on New Year's Eve we got to Sydney.[81]

It was a bad journey on rough seas. They ran out of fresh water and had to drink 'semi-desalinated' water. The *Marela* shipped the remaining Japanese from Thursday Island.[82] Horimoto Shinichi was among the lucky stragglers:

> I was near the coast of Papua New Guinea when war was declared, and a launch came to look for us. When we came back all the boats were in the harbour. There were mines in the Torres Strait Waters. Most [Japanese] had been taken to Sydney, only forty-seven of us were left at Thursday Island. We waited for a week and then a passenger ship took us. It was very comfortable, they brought us the menu to choose from and an interpreter translated for us.[83]

The Darwin Japanese were rounded up by Ancel Gregory—pearler and naval officer, a friend and business associate of pearler Yasukichi Murakami, and widely suspected of being a spy for the Japanese.[84] The Broome Japanese reportedly gathered in Carnarvon Street to await internment. Some one hundred internees including five women were crammed into the prison, and the others were placed under restriction orders. Not everyone was in a hurry to bring the luggers in. Masatora Okamura's boat was located by an Aboriginal patrol, but 'took it easy' until they ran out of food. They returned on 18 December and were taken to goal. Eventually 185 crowded in the goal built to hold forty to fifty prisoners, and Broome residents kept sending food to the gaol. On 17 January the families of internees were brought in for detention. On 28 January the *Koolinda* carried 212 internees from Broome and thirty-four from Port Hedland and further south, to Fremantle. They arrived at Tatura on 19 February, the day of the first air-raid on Darwin.[85] There were no complaints about their treatment.

Mrs Yamashita (Tei Shiosaki) of Thursday Island, most likely after her release from internment. Tei Shiosaki was born in Australia but raised in Kushimoto. When she came to Thursday Island at age twenty, she was unable to speak English. Nagata found that there were many such Kigoo Sansei—second-generation Japanese (*sansei*) returning to Australia after a period in Japan (*kigoo*). They were Australian-born Japanese who as children were sent to Japan for education. Photo: courtesy of Joe Yamashita, Thursday Island.

Among those at Tatura were Thursday Island residents Haruyoshi Yamashita and his wife Tei (née Shiosaki) with seven children. Hearing that some children had been released to attend schools, they sought the same exemption for their children, but no school could be found to accept them.[86] As a consequence, the children learned Japanese during their period in internment, and one of the sons later studied in Tokyo.[87] Yamashita was a community leader at Thursday Island. He was president of the *nihonjin-kai* and acted as interpreter and *oyakata*. Former divers remembered him fondly:

> 'Yamashita was like a father to us. He took care of everybody, also concerning the wages.' (Seike Ukio) 'Yamashita made sure we kept good appearances if we went to town, no shorts were allowed.' (Takao Koonosuke)

Haruyoshi Yamashita, prominent businessman at Thursday Island. When he returned from internment to Thursday Island at age sixty, he found all his businesses destroyed. He then worked in the store of a Chinese friend and purchased that business after five years. He died two years later, but the shop is still in the family. Photo: courtesy of Joe Yamashita, Thursday Island.

RETURN TO THE NORTH

Yamashita owned a shop and residence, and a soy sauce factory, and ran a guesthouse at Thursday Island. His investment in Thursday Island was evidently substantial, and he sought to return there as quickly as possible. Yamashita sought early release from detention to return to Thursday Island and rebuild his business but was informed that his business and residence was destroyed and there was nothing for him to return to, and that he was better off in the camp. He did not achieve an early release. When he was finally released, pressure was placed on the passenger line to make it difficult to secure a passage for him and his family.[88] Still, eventually they returned in 1947. They now had nine children and Yamashita was sixty years old and 'a very tired man, both physically and mentally'.[89]

The policy was not to release any Japanese 'for their own protection'. Nagata found that of the 4,301 Japanese interned in Australia, only sixty-nine were released before February 1946 (sixteen women, fourteen children, twenty men over age sixty-five, and nineteen men with white wives). This explains the difficulty experienced by Yamashita and Arthur Yamaguchi (viz.) who sought an early release.

Many of the interned Japanese pleaded with the authorities to be allowed to remain in Australia, but at war's end the government was determined to force the end of an era through wholesale deportation. The few Japanese who were able to avoid deportation were advised not to return to the north. The authorities insisted that there were no jobs and no accommodation for them. Neither were coloured evacuees rendered any assistance in returning north. Many coloured evacuees and a number of Japanese who had lived on Thursday Island re-settled in Cairns instead.

Yuriko Nagata has established that of the 359 Japanese arrested at Thursday Island, only thirty-eight returned to the town after the war. Among these were only seven first-generation Japanese. The remainder were Australian-born, either with Japanese parents (sixteen) or of mixed Japanese descent (twelve), and three were third-generation Japanese. Of those with mixed families at Thursday Island, Takai had died, while Fuji and Shibasaki were reunited. After six years of absence they had become strangers to their younger children.[90] Mrs Tanaka and her eight children and new son-in-law were among the few who were allowed to return to Thursday Island after the war. Jirokichi Nakata with his wife Shigeno and five children also returned.[91]

Only nine Japanese found their way back to Broome of a pre-war population of 300. Among them were Chi, Matsumoto and Hatsu Kanagae, who had been one of five single women arrested. Several who had substantial business interests there had been deported, like Yasutaroo Hama, Broome resident of forty-five years, who owned two houses including a boarding house and property valued at £800. Others were discouraged from returning. The Shiosaki family learned in Perth on their way back from Tatura that 'everything they owned in Broome had been destroyed'. They decided to stay put in Perth.[92]

In Darwin the atmosphere was reportedly very hostile to Japanese. Those at Tatura were told that only one attempted to return, but could not get off the plane. As a result of this story, Yoshio Murakami settled in Cossack with his Australian-born wife Masuko, and her mother and brothers stayed in Perth before returning to Darwin in 1956 and 1957.[93] Prominent pre-war community leaders and pearlers Jiru Muramatsu and Yasukichi Murakami had died and it was years before a small Japanese community dared to re-establish itself.[94]

RAZED TO THE GROUND

The experience of the Japanese and Chinese returning north after the war is strikingly similar across all polyethnic spaces. 'I was amazed at the desolation' said Jirokichi Nakata of his return to Thursday Island in June 1947. Thursday Island was depleted. Amira Mendis recalls that in 1947 the Thursday Island community consisted of some fifty people.[95] The Japanese houses and shops in Douglas and Hargreave streets were destroyed, with only the shell-stores of white master pearlers remaining. 'There was nothing left. As far as we know, the army dismantled it during the war. Other houses too.'[96] Billy Shibasaki remembers his return as a child: 'When we came back, all the places [the Japanese had] lived in were all demolished. Some of the places were shot up.'[97]

The assault was not confined to Japanese residences and businesses. Cairns Chinatown in Sachs Street (now Grafton Street in the CBD), Malaytown in Cairns, and Police Paddock in Darwin all disappeared during the war.

Several pre-war Chinese residents gradually made their way back to Darwin and found 'there was no Chinatown'.[98] Agnes Hannan, who has extensively documented this period in the history of the Darwin Chinese community, found that Chinatown 'had disappeared except for the concrete slabs on which it had stood': 'Chinatown was gone, swept away by the looting, burning and bulldozing of the locally based Provost troops after the bombing.'[99]

Diana Giese, having conducted extensive interviews among Darwin Chinese, writes: 'It had been razed: burnt, reduced to ground-level rubble and overgrown with grass, as completely as if the country had been invaded and the enemy had wanted to obliterate all evidence of the Territory Chinese.' But the only occupation had been by other Australians.[100]

Bill Wong described to Giese how he tried to go home, but found that his home had disappeared: 'I went back to where I used to live. And there was no home there. I looked down the gully for my cousin's house—all gone. All the market gardens were gone.'[101]

Lily Ah Toy explained: 'The army helped themselves . . . The houses were bombed, were looted; there was nothing.'

It is impossible to determine how much damage was sustained during the fifty-eight air-raids on Darwin, but it was the clean-up, consisting of burning, bulldozing and filling up wells, that caused the most irreparable damage. Eddie Quong told Diana Giese: 'I remember a couple of elderly ladies coming back to their shop from Melbourne. When they saw it bulldozed, they just sat down and cried. They had buried their valuables in the backyard. Their fortunes were gone.'[102]

Jimmie Chi's Chevrolet

The Chi family has become part of the legend of Broome. James Chi (Snr) was the Australian-born son of John Chi and Yae Yamamoto, both businesspeople. James liked to dress well and live well. He had something of a reputation for being a *bon vivant.*

He ran a taxi service with the first motor car ever licensed in Broome, a Chevrolet with the numberplate BM-1. Jimmie Chi's taxi brought the mail to Lombadina, and Elizabeth Puertollano (née Hunter) at Beagle Bay remembers that it was he who arrived with the message to pick up the German Fathers at Lombadina for internment.

James himself was arrested as an enemy alien in December 1941. He was first arrested on 20 December and released the same day—probably because of overcrowding—and taken in again a week later together with 185 detainees in Broome gaol.[103] He ended up at Woolenock Labour Camp at Renmark, South Australia. This was a subsidiary of Loveday, supplying firewood to the camp and to the River Murray irrigation pumps. There were only about seventeen Australian residents at Woolenock, alongside 216 detainees from New Caledonia and thirty-nine from the East Indies.[104]

The file of his internment suggests that Chi was subject to some victimisation, though whether by the Japanese inmates or by the staff is not clear. Chi wanted to see the official visitor to inquire about his possessions, but was always out working when the visitor arrived. The spokesperson for the Japanese internees, Shigeru Yamaguchi, told him that any such matters would have to be channelled through him, but that he himself was not forewarned of these visits. The camp commandant was adamant that Yamaguchi always knew of pending visits.[105] Yamaguchi does not appear in Yuriko Nagata's study of Japanese internees. This suggests that he was from overseas, because the compound leaders were usually well-known leaders of the Japanese communities, most of them employees of the big trading companies in the Dutch East Indies. They held much influence over the internees.

In March 1943 Chi instructed a solicitor to inquire about the notice of appeal against his internment, which he had lodged a year before. The deputy director for security in South Australia replied that there was no record of this application.[106] Several of eleven Australian-born inmates at Woolenock kept applying for a release hearing unsuccessfully. Jimmie Chi told Yuriko Nagata, 'I put my application for hearing many times while I was interned . . . but no hearing. I don't know why, but that Captain Brown [Camp Commandant at Woolenock] was not cooperative about this at all.'[107]

The records of Chi's internment also reveal that the military authorities recklessly destroyed this man's economic base. The story that unravels in the file is that Chi had left his car with W. B. Ellies, son of the Singhalese jeweller, who was also evacuated shortly afterwards. It was parked in a rented garage. When the ground staff of the US Air Force arrived in Broome in mid-February 1942, they inquired at the police station for useable cars, and took possession of Chi's car. It was used by officers of the 22nd bomber squadron until 3 March, when all US personnel were evacuated by air. Afterwards it was used by the

Jimmie Chi's Chevrolet.

Photo: courtesy of Pearl Hamaguchi, Broome.

Australian Army demolition squad, and then by the 19th Battalion until 19 December, then it was taken to Port Hedland and used by Australian Army headquarters, and in March 1943 it was returned to Broome a total wreck. The Broome motor garage had been turned into the army garage, and its owner became sergeant in charge of workshops in the area. The garage had used BM-1 to provide spare parts for BM-100, the 'saloon car' of the American Army. The chassis, motor, gear-box, differentials, front and rear axle assembly, radiator and wheels were dismantled and spare parts from another civilian vehicle were added to BM-1. When Chi returned to Broome, only the body of the car was left. It had been fitted with two army tyres, and one tyre was missing. The army accepted no liability and he was asked to sign a receipt for his car.[108]

His dinghy with outboard motor could not be located. It had been used by the Royal Australian Navy until September 1945. His double-barrel 12-gauge shotgun and Browning Automatic.22 rifle were last seen at the police station. His radio set had been handed to the military authorities. Chi claimed £150 for the car, which had cost £250 in 1937, and £50 for his home and restaurant, which were destroyed. The substantial file that documents this wild goose chase for information conjures a sense of mockery lacing the terse exactitude of its reports. Chi's struggle for compensation was a grapple to recover some dignity: he sheeted it home to the authorities that he was not Japanese, and not Chinese, but an Australian-born Australian citizen who could hold them, after all, accountable.

By the time the residents returned, natural decay had added to the devastation: 'Substantial stores had been burnt to the ground. Roofs had fallen in; white ants had attacked; rubbish was piled high in rooms emptied of furniture. The wells had been filled with rubbish.'[109]

It was much the same in Broome. While Broome was practically deserted, Sheba Lane burned down. It had been the site of a Japanese brothel, the Guomindang store, and the Lee Ah Chun and Wing Lee buildings. Bain writes that Chinatown took on an air of decadence intensified by looting.[110] When Jimmie Chi Snr (viz.) returned to Broome from internment, he found that 'the place was razed to the ground, Chinatown was looted'.[111] His house and restaurant were burnt, the restaurant equipment sold, and his car was wrecked.

From his efforts to retrace his possessions, we gain an idea of the plunder of useful possessions by the military.

POST-WAR ETHNIC RECONSTRUCTION

After the war Darwin attracted many newcomers with its improved infrastructure—its population rose from 1,566 in 1933 to 2,538 in 1947 and 8,071 in 1954.[112] This massive growth facilitated the ethnic reorganisation of the town. Before the war, fifty-three of 500 acres in the town area had been registered in the name of eighty Chinese residents. But in 1945, before they were allowed to return, all land and housing had been taken over by the government under the federal *Darwin Lands Acquisition Act*. Charles See Kee described it as 'Everybody had nothing. Government had taken over everything.'[113] Like the Japanese, many Chinese did not attempt to resettle in the Territory. Those who tried to reclaim their land faced, as Giese put it, 'Kafkaesque situations' as responsibilities were shifted between departments, state and federal agencies, cabinet and post-war reconstruction until well into the 1950s.[114]

Agnes Hannan's study of post-war Darwin demonstrates that the demise of polyethnic townships all across the north was not a coincidence. It was part of a formulated federal policy to prevent the re-formation of polyethnic spaces under the guise of assimilation. Hannan unearthed some particularly candid statements of that policy. At parliamentary level it was felt that Chinatown was too 'filthy and dilapidated' to have a place in the new Darwin which 'has to be made a city of which Australia can be proud'.[115] Administrator C. L. A. Abbott aimed for the 'elimination of undesirable elements which Darwin has suffered from far too much in the past'. What he meant was: 'The acquisition of this area by the Government will give control over all people returning and will entirely prevent the Chinese quarter forming again. If land is acquired from the former Chinese residents there is really no need for them to return as they have no other assets.'[116]

The chief surveyor agreed to a proactive implementation of the assimilation policy. Without fear of contradicting himself, he declared: 'It is undesirable that persons of the one nationality (non-European) should be permitted to congregate in a particular area.'[117]

To this end all Chinese-owned properties were targeted for resumption. A Cavenagh Street property was acquired for the purpose of a fire station in order to 'assist to prevent further expansion of Chinatown'.[118] The first merchant to be invited to return to Darwin, and the only one whose premises were still intact, was Thomas

Brown and Sons, who had only traded in Darwin for three years before the evacuation, while long-established Chinese merchants were put at arm's length in the reconstruction of the town.[119]

The whole episode brought about a radical social reconstruction of the Chinese community. Just before the war Chinese had made up 10 per cent of the non-Aboriginal Darwin community (down from 20 per cent in 1933) and owned 25 per cent of land. After the war Chinese land ownership in the CBD dropped to 3.5 per cent and their numbers, although fairly steady (316 in 1933 and 301 in 1954) became a much smaller proportion of Darwin's growing total population (5.3 per cent in 1947, 3.7 per cent in 1954). The Chinese were becoming a diminishing minority.[120]

The number of Chinese land owners fell by 50 per cent (from eighty to forty), and the acreage they held fell by 67.5 per cent (from 53 to 17.25 acres). This means that fewer Chinese were landowners, and the land held by them was in smaller allotments. The conditions for improvements placed on land ownership in the framework of post-war reconstruction and expansion meant that it was no longer possible to lease unimproved land for market gardens in the town area. In a climate of credit restrictions and building materials shortages, the conditions of leases made land ownership extremely expensive and Hannan believes that this, together with the low valuations placed on resumed properties, meant that only those who had held properties outside the CBD, as well as inside it, found it financially justifiable to return.[121]

Eventually some 75 per cent of the pre-war Chinese residents returned to Darwin, but the community was transformed. The multiple tenancies of the half-acre blocks that had characterised Chinatown became impossible. Before the war, eleven Chinese families owned sixteen blocks housing sixty shops in the southeastern end of Cavenagh Street. Each block housed up to five shops as well as residences above or behind, and most were held conjointly by several members of a family. This intensive use provided extra income for the landowners, affordable rents for the shops, the combining of business and family concerns, and close co-residence. After the war, Chinese business became concentrated 'in the hands of two or three families' who owned ten blocks in the CBD, with only one business to a block, and one (a hotel) taking up three blocks. Returning Chinese families had been offered preference for blocks in the outer suburbs, with the result that residence had to be separated from business and the Chinese community became scattered.[122]

> A grandiose plan had been conceived for an entirely new town. It was intended to present Australia's northern gateway as an entrance worthy of a rising European power. What was left of the old town was ignored.[123]

The Chinese were dispersed around the now expanded town, and Christine Inglis observes that they became downwardly mobile as fewer had access to business ownership and self-employment.[124] This needs to be tempered with the observation that many entered employment in the public service, airlines and banks. Hannan also remarks that ethnic and political factionalism was replaced after the war with a new pan-Chinese solidarity, and that a number of Chinese community members entered public office. Charles See Kee became the first president of the Darwin Civic Committee in

1947, and the Darwin Town Council inaugurated in 1957 also comprised a Chinese member. Harry Chan became mayor and president of the Legislative Council in 1966. Raymond Chin became an executive member of the Darwin Returned Servicemen's League (RSL) from 1957 until 1971, and in an illustrious public service career rose to clerk of the Legislative Assembly in 1982.[125] Darwin has had two Chinese mayors, one of its many distinctions that recommended it in the late 1980s as 'Australia's Gateway to Asia'.

Hannan provides ample evidence that the new Darwin was constructed on a social *tabula rasa* as the northern gateway of a rising European power. But the effort to prevent the regrouping of Asian communities was not confined to Darwin, where the strong arm of federal planning provided a particularly effective mechanism. Everywhere the re-appearance of polyethnic townships was actively hampered by refusing assistance for the return journeys of coloured evacuees. The Ah Toy family (viz.) from Pine Creek continued to lobby to be allowed to return, and were very nearly passed over in favour of a newly formed North Australian Co-Operative Society owned by a European.[126]

THE REINTRODUCTION OF JAPANESE

Elsewhere in the north the question of Asian communities was framed in terms of the reconstruction of the pearling industry, which was completely paralysed. Most Broome pearlers had moved south, and of the impressive pre-war fleet no more than six useable vessels remained.[127] The North Australia Development Commission, in charge of northern post-war reconstruction, strongly supported the resurrection of the pearling industry, underlining its significant defence value, but stopped short of arguing for a reintroduction of Asians to support it. It recommended the better training and integration of Torres Strait Islanders in the industry to replace the Asians who had dominated its workforce before the war.

The industry was at any rate shifting towards the harvesting of trochus shell, accessible by swimming diving with goggles, and the post-war fleet eventually became a motley collection of vessels operated by many adventurous newcomers. Still a number of the pre-war master pearlers resumed their business interests and continued to call for the reintroduction of Japanese divers. This was because of the longstanding racial idea that the Japanese had a 'special faculty' for finding shell, and were irreplaceable. In Queensland the tension between the pearlers' desire to reintroduce the Japanese workforce that had served the industry so well, and the vocal resistance of the RSL to Japanese recruits, was curiously resolved by the introduction of 106 divers from the American mandated territory of Okinawa in 1958. Whether this creative compromise pleased both the RSL and the master pearlers or neither, the Okinawan experiment was widely considered a failure by both the recruits and their employers.[128]

Nagata finds that at Thursday Island the Japanese returning from internment had a much better reception than elsewhere, but it was in Broome that new Japanese recruits were first reintroduced to the pearling industry. A thirty-two-strong group arrived in 1952 via Darwin, where anti-Japanese sentiments ran so high that they were advised to stay indoors.[129] This group was engaged by Streeter & Male and Morgan, and was headed by Oku Syunichi, who had worked in Broome periodically since 1919. His son Oku Saioshi was also part of the group:

> We were all from Taiji, Susami and Wabuka. Our government was reluctant to permit the recruiting of Japanese nationals to Australia. Civilian air traffic had not yet been established, so we travelled by Qantas via the American airbase in Iwakuni. The cost of the voyage was met by the employer. Our three-year contracts provided for regular transferral of part of our wages to our homes. During the stopover in Darwin we were met with protests from Australians and found the airport barricaded. We had a police escort, but we didn't really know what it was all about, we couldn't understand what they were shouting.[130]

Also in this group was Masatora Okamura, who later married an Aboriginal woman and stayed on.[131] In 1955 a larger group arrived, including Hiroshi Hamaguchi (viz.) who also married a local woman.

Still, it was the end of the polyethnic north. The post-war federal Ministry of Immigration took a strong stance against Asian immigration and Arthur Calwell promised the nation that no Japanese war brides or pearlers or workers would come into Australia 'while I remain Minister'.[132] He back-flipped four years later and the first Japanese war bride arrived in 1952 amidst much publicity carefully groomed to present an 'assimilated' image.[133] Under Calwell's Ministry of Immigration, Australia opened up to first a trickle and finally a gush of immigrants as displaced persons and refugees arrived. Among them were a large number of Chinese from Papua New Guinea and Chinese seamen escaping from revolutionary China, swelling the ranks of the resident Chinese population in the south.

CONCLUSIONS

The war washed over north Australia like a massive tsunami, flattening the structures of the old colonial order and germinating new ideas for the recolonisation of the wasteland it created. The assimilation policy formulated in the late 1930s was practically implemented in the north during wartime, with regard to both Aborigines and Asians, but hardly as expected. Evacuations, deportations, relocations and military deployment brought massive upheavals. Nobody willed it, nobody planned it, but it was the end of the old order. Aboriginal management bureaucracies—having ascertained their dominance over all things Aboriginal against the Churches and against 'coloured' people striving to evade their reach—were displaced by other agencies in the management of Aboriginal affairs, with military authorities taking a temporary lead role. After the withdrawal of the military, the Aboriginal management bureaucracy was never to reach its former influence again. It gradually withered before the citizenship aspirations of indigenous peoples who had glimpsed the world outside the narrow horizon of managed lives.

Conducted in confusion, haste and improvisation, the evacuations were nevertheless layered along time-honoured ethnic hierarchies: best not to challenge what order was left. This was no time to respect grey areas, in-between zones, fine gradations. Many coloured people were drawn into the vortex of Aboriginal management.

They would add their voice of protest against its regimentation after the war.

As the tide of evacuations washed away the civilians who had defined the old colonial order, Aborigines were left behind to provide labour for the military that had flooded in. They, too, were uprooted and relocated, but not to the safety of southern states. Military planners had always envisioned that the homeland would be defended by persons of 'substantially European background', an expectation reflected in their recruitment guidelines. But in the north everything was different, as usual. Men of indigenous and Asian descent offered their service even if they were not properly enlisted and fully paid, and became indispensable for homeland defence.

War was a time for confusion, suspicion, rumour and fear. Straining against a descent into disorder, countless officials prepared innumerable lists—provisional, local, partial lists; lists of enemy aliens, internees, evacuees; lists of those yet to be administered, located, relocated; lists on which to base planning, to rescue reason. Enumerating, statistically recording, accounting for people, categorising people so as to predict, understand, pre-judge them, to know their minds before they had made them up, all this became important for war-time administration.

The war was a moment of vast historic significance in north Australia for reasons that are likely to have escaped most of its witnesses: for the first and only time, north Australia was actually 'mostly white'—a state of affairs that had been discursively claimed since 1788. No amount of social engineering through immigration, family formation and Aboriginal policy had managed to bring about what the upheaval of the war occasioned within a few months.

The post-war agenda aimed to keep it that way. The ranks closed across all branches of administration to discourage the repatriation of coloured communities, prevent the reformation of polyethnic townships and ethnic enclaves, and resist the drift into townships of remote Aborigines who were likely to form the nuclei of new, mixed, fringe communities. Just as the north was finally turning white, and one might speak confidently about a 'white Australia', the south of the continent embarked on its long journey towards becoming multicultural as it dawned on policy makers that a monocultural nation was not, after all, tenable.

MALAYTOWNS such as in Cairns, Darwin, Badu Island and Innisfail were, next to Broome and Thursday Island, the hubs of northern polyethnicity where Asian–Aboriginal identity was most publicly played out—in communities of people who were similarly placed, who reinforced, affirmed and validated the identity that had grown from family relations, schooling, socialising and work. In these places, being coloured was a life-world, an all-encompassing horizon of experience.

Chinatowns in the metropolitan centres, and even as far afield as Croydon and Cloncurry, are now reasonably well documented.[1] They are well on the way of turning from cultural curiosities to part and parcel of the Australian heritage awareness, powered by the renewal of a strong presence of ethnic Chinese in Australia. Japanese enclaves are celebrated as local history of former pearling ports with the touch of exoticism that historical distance, and the proportional insignificance of Japanese in Australia today, affords.

The polyethnic character of such Chinatowns and Japanese enclaves is barely noticed, and the demise of Malaytowns has been all but unrecorded. It is tempting to brush these as quaint phenomena, colourful but inconsequential historical footnotes. But Asian–Aboriginal contact has bestowed a significant legacy on Aboriginal identity today: it is no coincidence that 'yella fella' has come to denote all mixed Aboriginal descendants.

THE END OF BEING COLOURED

Being 'coloured' was for many mixed indigenous descendants an identity that was able to both affirm indigeneity and keep at arm's length the colonising mechanisms which oppressed indigenous peoples and the labels which denied them recognition as valuable fellow Australians. With the demise of the polyethnic north and the erosion of the 'half-caste' category from legislation, it became difficult to remain 'coloured'. Larry Ahlin (viz.) said, more recently, that 'you either had to be an Aborigine'—or not. There was no in-between, because increasingly the social and economic rights of Aboriginal citizens became mediated through their Aboriginality. Ahlin speaks of himself as a 'half-caste', holding to an identity that is no longer socially available.

In principle a person of mixed lineage ought to have a range of identity options. A number of mixed-descent people revealed in their narratives how they tried out a non-indigenous identity. Many found out that 'not being Aboriginal' was not an available option—not because the Aboriginal part of their family demanded that they return to the fold, but because non-Aboriginal society rejected them as a fully fledged member.[2] Tex Camfoo (viz.) is still ambivalent about whether or not he was an Aborigine under the Northern Territory Ordinance, but has settled the matter in practice and no longer worries about it. Jack Sahanna (viz.) was proud to be 'a self-made man', just as the missionaries had taught him to be, until it became clear that the Aboriginal part of his ancestry had already determined his life chances and would continue to do so. His children have no such trouble. They know where they belong.

One way or another, Aboriginal people everywhere are faced with the need to come to terms with mixed histories. A former chairman of the Marpuna Aboriginal Corporation to re-establish Old Mapoon reflects a common sentiment: 'We can't help what happened in the past for what we are in the present.' Mixed histories are not to be silenced, but to be accepted into an understanding of what it means to be Aboriginal today.

ABORIGINAL/NON-ABORIGINAL: TICK ONE

Australians are routinely faced with a host of forms—census, hospital admissions, enrolments, welfare—that require them to be either Aboriginal, Torres Strait Islander, or neither. A tripartite definition of Aborigines has replaced the various definitions of the *Welfare Acts* and *Protection Acts*. Being Aboriginal now means being of Aboriginal descent, to identify as Aboriginal, and to be recognised as Aboriginal by an Aboriginal community. This definition no longer encourages the counting of particles of blood to distinguish between 'full' and—by implication—'lesser' Aborigines that were preoccupations of Aboriginal administration. This has facilitated a vast change in Aboriginal politics where mixed descendants have always been at the cutting edge. The bifurcation of racial categories into 'Aboriginal' and 'non-Aboriginal' has been an expedient platform from which to demand better access to economic and political citizenship for all Aborigines.

But this bifurcation also offers the potential for great divisiveness. Among non-Aborigines there is a vast degree of envy of welfare schemes and funding opportunities targeted specifically at Aborigines. Just as the need for and legitimacy of affirmative action for women has always been under siege from the rhetoric of a 'fair go', so the denial of a need for affirmative action for Aborigines is couched in principles of equal opportunity. No amount of hard data on health, life expectancy, access to education, substance abuse, the incidence of domestic violence and incarceration, that amply documents disadvantage, has been able to seriously dislodge the perception that better opportunities for one part of the population must mean a disadvantage for all others. Persons who identify as Aboriginal without conforming to colonial ideas of Aboriginality leaven such discontent.

In Aboriginal communities internal dissent over the question of the authentic Aboriginality of particular persons can be toxic. Whereas the polyethnic communities of the past permitted some liminal status for individuals, some Aboriginal communities themselves are now seeking a closure over who may and who may not be considered Aboriginal. Corrosive new discursive types have appeared: the 'paper Aborigine' authenticated by one community but contested by another; the 'bogus Aborigine' who identifies as Aboriginal but without a paper trail and whose authenticity is contested; and the 'fake Aborigine', such as the Eddie Burap persona of Elizabeth Durack. However, these labels are very loosely applied and capable of inflicting great personal injury.

In the 1990s eligibility for ATSIC elections became a touchstone of dissent. The new landscape of economic and political citizenship premised on Aboriginality appears to require the drawing of reliable and testable boundaries, and for good reasons. The tripartite definition of descent, self-identification and community acceptance resists such a closure, and for equally good reasons. Whereas the law courts have so far upheld the tripartite principle of definition, popular rhetoric, steeped in blood and skin colour, has always privileged descent over the two other tests of Aboriginality, both within Aboriginal communities and outside of them. The discourse of blood has received new poignancy with the availability of 'genetic fingerprinting'.

THE VICTIMS OF BINARY IDENTITY POLITICS

Doubts have long rankled about the authenticity of many Tasmanians claiming Aboriginality. Michael Mansell from the Tasmanian Aboriginal Centre has gone further than most in voicing such concerns, alleging that there are 'frauds' and 'impostors' among those claiming eligibility for ATSIC elections. In the 1998 ATSIC elections eleven Tasmanian candidates were challenged about their Aboriginality, and two were excluded as a result of a Federal Court ruling. In the 2002 elections 1,100 persons who sought inclusion on the electoral rolls were challenged. When twenty of these resolved to determine their Aboriginality through DNA testing, a vigorous public debate erupted. This debate raises difficult scientific, ethical and political questions. It is about the reliability of mitochondrial DNA (the genetic material traced through the maternal line), the legitimate ownership of the tissue sample serving as a base line, the tenuousness of the claims to Aboriginality of some, and who has the powers to determine what does and does not constitute an Aboriginal person.

In a postcolonial world the external imposition of identity is no longer acceptable. At United Nations levels, the Working Group on Indigenous Peoples resolved that such determinations must be the prerogative of indigenous peoples themselves. This position is mirrored by comments from the ATSIC commissioner for Tasmania and indeed by Justice Merkle of the Federal Court, who was asked to make a determination in 1998.[3]

The Tasmanian Aboriginal community has always been under challenge. It was prematurely declared extinct with the death of Truganini in 1876, widely acclaimed as the last 'full-blood' Tasmanian. The struggle of Aboriginal Tasmanians for recognition has been long and hard, and required a dislodging of colonial visions. Doubts are now raised that in its effort to regroup into a political force, the community was too liberal in its acceptance of mixed descendants who may have trouble establishing a paper trail of authenticity.

These debates are not confined to Tasmania. In 1995 contestations over eligibility for ATSIC elections in Roma, Queensland, landed in the Federal Court, and in 2000 a Hervey Bay family made headlines when it was found that Aboriginal descent could not be established. This family had always defined itself squarely within the local Aboriginal community. In defence against a charge of illegal fishing, one of its members claimed traditional fishing rights, and to quash the defence the Queensland Department of Primary Industries established that this family was 'of purely Sri Lankan descent'. The *Courier Mail* reported this story as front-page news. It cited other community members as supporting the view that this family had long fraudulently claimed Aboriginal benefits, and had therefore deprived 'genuine' Aborigines.[4] The same argument was raised by members of the Tasmanian Aboriginal Centre with regard to ATSIC eligibility and access to ATSIC funding.

The paradoxical effect of such contestations is that those most hostile to affirmative action for Aborigines find their most vociferous support in members of

Aboriginal communities who raise concerns about the administration of and eligibility for such schemes. Instead of consolidation of a national Aboriginal community against continued hostility from outside, there is an implosion.

The either/or idea of Aboriginality is unable to take account of history. This bifurcated identity politics creates it own victims. For many, 'being Aboriginal' is the result of intensely personal inner struggle and chafes against the politicised and public nature of identity. Gordon Matthews has published a gripping narrative of his identity journey that twisted him not once, but twice. He was adopted into a white family with some unresolved questions about his biological father. Prompted by the stereotyping meted out during his school years, Matthews gradually immersed himself in an Aboriginal identity. While studying in Tasmania he finally embraced this identity and turned it to advantage as the first Aboriginal career diplomat in the Australian public service. He eventually managed to find his white biological mother and discovered that his father had not been Aboriginal, but Asian. Matthews' autobiography traces in vivid detail the angst, agony, shame and loss of reconstructing his ethnic identity when elements of his personal history peel themselves off the hazy backdrop of half-known, half-assumed, half-ignored coulisses to demand attention at centre stage, requiring the script to be revised and the roles to be reallocated in the midst of the performance of identity in full public view. At the end of the book the reader is left with a sense of utter devastation. Matthews makes a valiant attempt to pick himself off the floor with some faintly optimistic comments about the possibility of patching up personal relationships, but this story defies the craving for a happy ending.[5]

Sally Morgan's account of identity as a personal journey has received far more attention. Indeed, it became a bestseller with over 70,000 copies sold. With only one identity reconstruction—perhaps as much as anyone can bear—*My Place* speaks more confidently about becoming Aboriginal. Published at the height of debate about the position of Aborigines in a national identity in the Bicentennial, and at a time when changes in adoption laws and the assistance of various organisations had facilitated the reconnection of adopted children and their biological parents, it spoke for the experience of a generation who had travelled various distances along the road of reaching out towards the Aboriginal part of themselves. While Matthews' jigsaw puzzle is shattered under the forensic investigation, Morgan's falls into place, she finds 'her place'.[6]

Having established her Aboriginal descent, Morgan was able to assume an Aboriginal identity and seek Aboriginal community recognition of it. She fulfils all three dimensions necessary for being Aboriginal, but her Aboriginal identity did not remain unchallenged. Among her most outspoken critics was well-known author and poet, and former head of Aboriginal Studies at Murdoch University, Mudrooroo, who saw *My Place* as an outsider's view of Aboriginality. He felt that 'just because something is written by a person who identifies as an Aborigine doesn't make it an Aboriginal work'.[7] By 1996 Mudrooroo's claim to Aboriginal descent was widely held to have been reliably disproven by a genealogy produced by one of his sisters who traced their black ancestry to a black American.[8] He was practically sentenced as a 'fake

Aborigine'. It would be difficult to doubt the sincerity of the author of *Wild Cat Falling*, *Us Mob*, and *Writings from the Fringe*. His identity commitment is reflected in his name changes from Colin Johnson to Mudrooroo Nyoongah, Mudrooroo Narogin, and finally to Mudrooroo. The search for identity among people of indigenous descent who were raised as 'whites' is wrought with danger. Fiona Noble calls it a Russian roulette that can end in a public hanging: those with public profiles draw a larger crowd.[9] It is not uncommon for a family to become deeply divided when some of its members embrace their Aboriginal identity and others deny it.

Mudrooroo's story, in full public view, demonstrates the self-destructive power of a binary view of Aboriginality. This binary view also lurks in Morgan's account so that Isabel Tarrago cautiously objects that Morgan glosses over 'the cultural diversity of Aboriginal Culture'.[10] Bain Attwood, with scalpel-like precision, points out that in finding the Aboriginal part of herself, and privileging it, Morgan denies the white part of herself and purchases into the view that either being, or not being, Aboriginal are the only two legitimate options available, just as the census categories suggest.[11] Many who have, like Mudrooroo and Morgan, travelled along a path of identity recovery have found only the absence of boundary.

WAYS OF BEING ABORIGINAL

Binary oppositions have a comforting rhetorical certainty about them: you either are, or are not (Aboriginal, Jewish, Chinese, etc.), you can jump the fence, make the grade, be in or out, with us or against us. Indeed, for large parts of the Aboriginal population, Aboriginal identity is perfectly unproblematic: they live in communities who continually affirm and reinforce this identity—they have no option but to embrace it. It is under conditions of displacement, either temporary or permanent, that identity becomes difficult. Fiona Noble interviewed people who were raised as 'white' and have since either found proof, or harbour strong feelings, that they must be of Aboriginal descent. She encountered not two, but three identity positions: besides those who embrace Aboriginality, and those who opt out, there are the 'half-steps'. They may understand themselves as 'being of Aboriginal descent', but this position raises its own uncertainties. It is a private, intimate solution, not sanctioned by any policies or definitions. Such people want to tick all the boxes on the forms that regularly face them with their uncertainties. Their identity is situational. Even those who have resolved to 'opt out' may sometimes strategically deploy their Aboriginal ancestry, in a family argument or to demolish racist comments. Noble found that every time another half-step embraces Aboriginality, it implicates their parents and siblings. Many such families hold an uneasy truce about identity.[12]

Such reflections are repeated manifold in other ethnic groups who have borne the brunt of historical displacement: being Jewish, being African-American, being Caribbean, being German in the Sudetenland, have all become problematic. Steeped in scholarly traditions, and wrought by political transformations, high Chinese culture has brought forth a rich harvest of reflections on the identity of displacement. A few scholars have developed typologies. Wang Gungwu examines four ways of being Chinese outside of China: *huashang*, *hugagong*, *huaqiao* and *huayi*. The *huashang* is a Chinese merchant, a pioneer abroad who can offer opportunities to other members of their group and who is likely to maintain links to the ancestral home, while the *hugagong* is a Chinese labourer abroad, a coolie whose economic options have displaced him. These two are economic positions that affect the ability to maintain links. The *huaqiao* is born in China and merely sojourning abroad, while the *huayi* is of Chinese ancestry born abroad. The latter is the position of most overseas Chinese today. It still allows for a range of identity options: '*Huayi* are Chinese by descent but only sometimes Chinese by consent.'[13] It is the *huayi* identity that is most interesting here, but least possible to typologise.

Wang Ling-Chi offers a more poetic typology according to *gen*, roots. To the sojourners he refers as *luoye guigen*, fallen leaves that must return to their roots. To those who have tried to assimilate into their dominant host societies, by anglicising their names or stripping themselves of language and cultural practices, he refers as *zhancao chugen*, suggesting weeds that have been thoroughly uprooted, because hostile host societies resist their assimilation on new ground. Those who have struck an accommodation are *luodi shenggen*, seeds planted in foreign soil and striking roots, resettled without striving for home. Those who search for their roots and ancestors are *xungen wenzu*, cultivating ethnic pride and exploring family history, and discovering in the process their otherness in both worlds.[14] Wang omits to mention that it is possible to transit several of these positions in a lifetime.

Henry Chan rejects all of these typologies for reasons that are equally relevant in the context of Aboriginal identity. He argues that they essentialise the diasporic experience and 'reinforce the politics of difference', a difference that is more imagined than real. He argues that 'there is not, and never was, a single community we can call the Chinese community in Australia'. Migrants from Guangdong or Fujian might have identified themselves as Tangren (descended from the Tang dynasty), or according to district (Zhongshan, Siyi, etc.), or according to village. These are situational identities. Local traditions could encourage or prevent the migration of whole family groups, leading to differences in the migration experience, and even small overseas Chinese populations sometimes comprised several temples indicating several communities. This is why 'intra-communal disputes and violence were more common than inter-racial ones' among Chinese in Australia. Chan concludes that a unitary view of Chinese in Australia is nothing less than an acceptance of the Yellow Peril ideology, 'a figment of the fervid imagination of nineteenth-century white racists and of their counterparts in the late twentieth-century Hanson movement'.[15] To throw off the yoke of externally imposed unitary identities that maintain and eternally reconstruct difference and otherness, requires an insistence on a differentiated view able to take account of myriad ways of being situated in identity.

The policy instruments of mainstream Aboriginal politics have abolished situational identity, excised the grey areas, conquered the in-between. Together with the obnoxious, imposed idea of the 'half-caste', the self-ascribed 'coloured' has also been abolished and there is no room for just 'being of Aboriginal descent'. But beyond the rhetoric, many lives are lived in just such liminal spaces. It is not just that identity is always potentially problematic—more so for displaced people. It is situational.

There are good historical reasons why the boundaries of 'Aboriginality' must be hazy. Noble has dealt with only some of those reasons: those who were severed from their Aboriginal backgrounds by removal or adoption may find it difficult to retrace their steps, and there is also a generational layer of mixed descendants who were either not told, or opted out of an Aboriginal identity. But beyond that there are the historical shifts in definitions. Sifting through 700 pieces of legislation John McCorquodale found sixty-seven ways of defining Aborigines: by race, territory, affiliation, blood, lineage, self-identification, and myriad other ways.[16] Different definitions produce different outcomes. The Aboriginal protection bureaucracy has always wrestled with its difficulty of determining who is an Aborigine. The bureaucracy was far from clear how far its powers stretched but inserted itself in the lives of mixed descendants at crucial moments in order to gain leverage on eugenic management. This is reflected in the stories of Tex Camfoo and Atima Ahwang. The curious result in Queensland was that one could be 'deemed to be an Aborigine', or could be retrospectively classified as 'having been an Aborigine' for a period of time, and that instances of 'being Aboriginal', 'being half-caste', and being 'neither Aboriginal nor half-caste' could occur between siblings of identical parentage. In the Northern Territory one might be simultaneously treated as Aboriginal (regarding drinking rights) and as white (not a ward of the state) once the 'half-caste' category was dropped from legislation. All of these discursive gymnastics caused uncertainties.

We have seen in Chapter 4 that the eugenic management of mixed populations became the prime preoccupation of Aboriginal policy from its inception at the turn of the century to the 1930s. Just when it seemed that the eugenic management battle was won and the bureaucracy was at its apex of powers over people of indigenous descent, a massive political backlash, spearheaded by disenfranchised mixed descendants, unfolded to stay the bureaucracy. Chapter 7 showed how the experience of World War II further weakened the hold of the Aboriginal protection bureaucracy as an imposed quasi-government of indigenous peoples.

The struggle against paternalism was long drawn-out. As elsewhere in the world, it consolidated black people into a common purpose. Complex hierarchies of colour inherited from a colonial past were debunked as a phenomenon of the divide-and-rule strategy. In Australia a number of alliances and organisations emerged to militate for citizenship rights of all black people, buoyed by the intellectual impact of postcolonial Africa and the Black Power Movement in the USA (viz. Pedro Guivarra). Mixed Islander descendants played prominent roles in advancement leagues and citizenship organisations, and in the establishment of Aboriginal legal aid, housing, cultural and health services.

Queensland's DAIA (Department of Aboriginal and Islander Advancement/Affairs) was not a complete misnomer—it meant to include under its ambit not only Torres Strait Islanders but also the descendants of South Sea Islanders who had been brought to Queensland for the sugar and pearling industries. It was not until 1975 that South Sea Islanders received official recognition from the Queensland government as a separate ethnic group, still under its ambit. Only after the demise of the DAIA did 'being Aboriginal' in Queensland become confined to being mainland Aboriginal, and Islanders were eased out of Aboriginal organisations. By the 1990s Islander descendants in Queensland had been sequestered from Aboriginal politics.[17]

The receding tide of coloured communities, and increasingly tight boundaries of Aboriginality, left many stranded. Len Royee, in the sugar cane strip of north Queensland, is one of them. He feels excluded from the community renewal galvanising around land claims:

> It is disturbing, for me anyway. I get accused a lot and it's not our fault . . . like, I'm not an Aboriginal, I'm not a Solomon Islander and all that sort of thing—I'm in-between and I am a man with no land sort of thing. I'm just a bit of flotsam on the sea, come in, go out, come in, go out. You know, like that . . .
>
> Chinese, Hindu, we got all of them in the family. See, some of my Aboriginal people they say, 'Look, we want this just for us Aboriginal people up there, we don't want no white man or whatever.' I said, you can't do that any more. I said our people are intermarried: Chinaman, Whiteman, Irish—you name them. You can't exclude them, you have to bring them in. I've got Hindus for cousins and all, yeah, half-Hindus.[18]

The histories told here demonstrate that in the past such mixed families were squarely constructed inside the problem population that caused the department to want to rein them in. Many people were 'turned Aboriginal' against their wishes. Just as vigorously they are now washed out, becoming *zhancao chugen*, weeds pulled out by their roots.

There is much cynicism about those who now wish to reclaim their Aboriginal identity. Material advantages appear as an obvious motivation and sufficient explanation for the increasing number of citizens who now define themselves as Aborigines or Torres Strait Islanders in the census.[19] But the erosion of an in-between status, of being able to be 'coloured', also means a loss of belonging.

There are no data on which to pin quantitative estimates. We have only stories: stories upon stories that layer themselves into a history. These stories tell that the north is full of people who still remember its polyethnic past, for whom being coloured is the fabric of identity. Stories from people who have embraced Aboriginality, or who have opted out, or who are still unsure which way to go. It is little surprising that many are still making up their minds, that the census reflects a growth in Aboriginal population that is not explicable by natural growth. This growth is worrying: it should be worrying—every time another half-step makes a full step it may mean another family divided in argument.

The polyethnic north supplies a powerful historical explanation for the turbulence now apparent in Aboriginal identity politics. We also find in these stories from the north a sense of Aboriginality that is not predicated on binaries. A vast range of cultural productions simply celebrate the shared histories and mixed lineages.

ARNHEM LAND: MIXED HISTORIES, CULTURAL REVIVAL

Arnhem Land Aborigines nurture the memory of their Macassan connections in paintings, stories and dances, school texts and popular songs, through local museum displays and mutual visits. These signs of cultural revival at the Top End celebrate connectedness in a history without Balanda.

Renewed interest in the history of Macassan contact was stimulated by the *Hati Marege* project. The visit was marred by controversy when the Northern Land Council objected to flying the Bicentennial Flag on the vessel, arguing that there was no historical link whatsoever to 1788. The representatives of two national governments were involved in the arrival ceremony and, until a day before its arrival, there was considerable official uncertainty about whether the vessel would be permitted to dock on Aboriginal land. What had become boiled down to an argument over the symbolism of a flag was a deep rift between indigenous and Balanda views of the ownership of the Macassan–Aboriginal history.

The visit resulted in a range of cultural productions and activities. The event itself featured in John Darling's documentary *Below the Wind*, which told the story of the various peoples involved in this historical trade relationship.[20] The *Hati Marege* project germinated in 1985 when Peter Spillett placed an article in the *Northern Territory News* with a picture of Ibu Saribanong looking for her Yolngu relatives. Michael Cooke from Batchelor College was at Galiwin'ku at the time and remembers that 'this newspaper article generated real excitement, and old memories and stories were rekindled in an effort to surmise the Aboriginal family in question'.[21] Working in association with Spillett, Cooke co-ordinated the group of Batchelor College students referred to earlier to record oral history interviews and prepare for a field study in Makassar in June 1986.

A sense of excitement about Macassan connections is discernable right across the Top End. In the early 1990s people at Maningrida became very active in reconnecting with this contact history. Johnny Bulunbulun started in 1992 to produce a series of about twenty-five paintings reflecting Macassan stories from a Yirritja song cycle. These have received national acclaim. One of them can be found in the hall of the Darwin airport. The paintings feature his clan totem Lunggurrma, the north wind 'which brought the Macassan trepangers to the shores of Arnhem Land', and the Barayana, the white wet season clouds that it brings.[22]

A cultural exchange visit to Kupang and South Sulawesi was organised at Maningrida in October 1993: 'The main purpose of this visit was for the traditional custodians of an Arnhem Land–Macassan exchange ceremony to renew ties with their Macassan counterparts.'[23] They performed the Marayarr Murrukundja, a Rom ceremony of diplomacy lasting for three nights and ending 'with the presentation of a large decorated pole which represents the mast of a Makassan *perahu* on rough seas. People mourn the loss of the pole when it is presented to the recipients, just as they feel sadness at the departure of their Makassan friends and family at the end of each trepanging season.'[24] Their visit received nationwide media attention in Indonesia, and trucks with blaring loudspeakers announced the performance of the '*orang aborijin dari Australia utara*', but the Australian media were silent.

The group was told that their Macassan audience understood a number of words used in the ceremony. This was the first time that Johnny Bulunbulun, who had grown up with stories about light-skinned Macassans, saw for himself the people about whom he had heard so much, and he spotted an antique ceramic storage pot of

The Marayarr Murrukundja Ceremony Goes to Makassar

A report of the Bawinanga Aboriginal Corporation/Maningrida Arts and Culture cultural exchange visit to Kupang NTT, and South Sulawesi, Indonesia.
October 1993

Murray Garde
Cultural Research Officer, Bawinanga Aboriginal Corporation

Maningrida artists visit Makassar, October 1993. Pictured are: Johnny Bulunbulun, songman; Terry Gandadila, didjeridu player; and dancers Laurie Marburru, Charlie Djinmalala Brian, Roselyn Gundjiriyardji, Philip Morris, Alfie Cooper, Tommy Steele, Terry Mangapal and Laurie Guraylayla.

the kind he had included in his paintings but had never seen. The pot was purchased for the Djomi Museum in Maningrida. Again the group marvelled about the wealth of common words, and compiled lists of such words. On their return, they started to interrogate their world of names and sites looking for long-forgotten Macassan connections, and even turned up shards of pottery at known Macassan sites.[25]

Also in 1993, the Sunrize Band from Maningrida received nationwide airplay with *Lembana Manimani*, three years after *Takirrina* had been produced at Milingimbi by Wirrnga. 'Lembana Manimani' is the Makasar name for Maningrida, meaning 'bay of beads', after the red abrus seed they introduced there.[26] The Sunrize lyrics reflect the positive way in which the Macassan contact history is remembered. Yothu Yindi from Yirrkala have in their repertoire *Macassan Crew*, with references to the morning star, to Daeng Gatjing, and other significant Macassan referents.

As a result of the connections made by the Maningrida group during their 1993 trip, a group of basket weavers embarked on a cultural exchange visit to Biboki in West Timor in early 1995. They learned *ikat* tying and dyeing using traditional techniques and local resources, and taught the Biboki women their fibre preparations, spinning, dyeing and looping of string bags and coil-woven baskets.[27]

Balanda researchers also returned to the chapter of Macassan contact in the 1990s. Scott Mitchell conducted archaeological work on Cobourg Peninsula and Croker Island, and the supply of swags and camping gear of the North Australia Research Unit were divided in 1995 between my flying visit through the coastal communities and Annie Clarke's archaeological expedition to Groote Eylandt.

FAR RIGHT: Yothu Yindi performing before an audience of many friends and relations, Darwin, 1995.

Yothu Yindi

Macassan Crew

Yendharama birrapirra

Tradewinds blow
The southern cross
Taking their prau
Across the sea
They came in peace
Through the Ashmore Reef
Smoke and steel
And the Tamarind seed

Steer it up right
Steer it up true
Navigate the morning star
Brave Macassan crew

Sailed on through
The hole in the wall
The place we call Rarrakala
To the shores of the far North East
Smoke, steel, and the Tamarind tree

Gapala Mangatjay
Gapala Gurrumulnga

Navigate the morning star
Brave Macassan crew

Miyaman Matjala
Miyaman gurrumulnga
Dayngatjing Garrnhdalu
Daymulung Wila'wila'yun

Miyaman Mangatjay
Miyaman Gurrumulngu
Dayngatjing Garrnhdalu
Daymulung Wila'wila'yun

Steer it up right
Steer it up true
Navigate the morning star
Brave Macassan crew

Sunrize Band

Lembana Mani Mani

I've seen the pot in Entrance Island
And the spirit of Macassar
Lembana Mani Mani
Was once a trading post
People during that time
Had a wonderful time
They entered Territory waters
But no-one didn't mind
They came long long way from home
To get what they really wanted

Some of them got speared
And some ran away
Some sailed back home and didn't give a damn

Lembana Mani Mani Maningrida
Lembana Mani Mani Maningrida
Lembana Mani Mani Maningrida
Guj-ngarli aburr-wena
Bilay wnega aburr-bona gurda
Marnnga jiny-bunggiya jiny-nyorkiya
Ngarduwa gubi-nana arawa gun-mala mala
Birripa gugu arrawa gun-guna aburr-makapchunga nula
Aburr-jekarra aburr-wena burruwa
Gun-mala mala arrawa nyubi-nana Australia
Majang mbi-garrana

Lembana Mani Mani Maningrida
Lembana Mani Mani Maningrida
Lembana Mani Mani Maningrida

We commemorate and celebrate
For those visitors from Macassar
They left back for us to remind only their spirit
Today we see lots of people
Have Indigenous blood
To me it is not only
The event that took place
But a history—what happened 20,000 years ago

They took back home with them
All those rough-skinned sea slugs
Some wanted women
Black fellas wanted wine
Either you're an enemy or a friend of mine

Lembana Mani Mani Maningrida
Lembana Mani Mani Maningrida
Lembana Mani Mani Maningrida

Wirrnga Band
My Sweet Takirrina
by Lapulung Dhamarrandji

For many years these stories were told
among the remote shores of Arnhem Land
Macassan sailors navigated the great seas
seeking their ways towards the Yolngu people's land.
They sailed across from Ujung Pandang and navigated the seas
to our country, Marrege, Australia.

chorus
My sweet Takirrina, My sweet Takirrina, Takirrina, Galiwin'ku
My sweet Takirrina, My sweet Takirrina, Takirrina, Galiwin'ku

They sailed across the great Java seas
and navigated the seas to an island called Takirrina
trading goods and making better friendship
by gathering off the shores a good old trepang
Macassen men - how brave they were
they once came ashore on a coastal Yolngu land

chorus
My sweet Takirrina, My sweet Takirrina, Takirrina, Galiwin'ku
My sweet Takirrina, My sweet Takirrina, Takirrina, Galiwin'ku

Macassan prau sail north-east Arnhem Land shores
wandering so silently through the lonesome roaring seas
Macassan men – how great sailors
they once came ashore at a place called the Gulmanngur.
In the year 1988 Macassan prau revisits Arnhem Land
we celebrate the year 1988
all the Yolngu people throughout Arnhem Land

chorus
My sweet Takirrina, My sweet Takirrina, Takirrina, Galiwin'ku
My sweet Takirrina, My sweet Takirrina, Takirrina, Galiwin'ku

In 1996 theatre director Andrish Saint-Claire started to prepare for an indigenous opera on trepang. He brought a group of Macassans, including Yotjing, a descendant of Husein Daeng Ranka, to Elcho Island for the dance performance of an exchange ritual. In 1997 a return visit was made to Sulawesi by a group led by Mattjuwi Burrawanga. This visit included a funeral ceremony at the grave of Mangellai Daeng Maro, who had died in 1978, and a public performance celebrating Mattjuwi's reunion with his Macassan family, before an audience of nine thousand people. Again the Australian media took no interest in the event. The theme of family reunion was once more celebrated during the Darwin festival in 1999, and brought to Federation Square in Melbourne during 2001 as a Yolngu contribution to the Centenary of Federation celebrations.

BROOME: CULTURAL DYNAMO OF THE KIMBERLEY

Broome Aborigines embrace shared histories, cuisines, and a unifying Broome creole. Here the Shinju Festival (pearl festival) is just as easily organised by Aboriginal associations, and anyone participates in the Hang Seng (Chinese Feast of the Dead). 'Pearling songs, Japanese dancing and karate exhibitions are part of the town culture,' reports the Centre for Aboriginal Studies in Music (CASM) in Adelaide, of the Aboriginal culture in Broome. Broome is recognised as the musical focus of the whole Kimberley.

As well as the usual country and western background and rock developments, many of the musicians have a strong affinity with the atmosphere, subject matter and style of calypso and reggae.[28]

Keith Lapulung, formerly of the Wirrnga Band, a friend, and Regina Ganter at Milingimbi.

Jimmy Chi (Jnr) is a central part of this creative culture. He helped to found the Broome Musicians Aboriginal Corporation to support young musicians. As a member of the Broome band Kuckles, he performed at the third International Cologne Song Festival in 1982, and was asked: 'What's Aboriginal about your music?' It evidently jarred with expectations of traditional sounds. He maintains that the calypso-like music 'is Aboriginal, not reggae at all'.[29] It is Broome-Aboriginal. Jimmy Chi's musicals reflect the vibrancy of that community. It is able to lampoon the mixed-up histories when the Aboriginal boy turns out to be the bishop's son, and the German tourist is revealed as Aboriginal. *Bran Nue Dae* was widely acclaimed as 'the first mainstream Aboriginal musical' when it opened in Perth in 1990. His second play, *Corrugation Road*, is about schizophrenia and identity.

Jimmy Chi's path into being Aboriginal was rocky and affected him deeply. He says that his schizophrenia was produced by his mixed ethnic background and the responses it solicited. He has a Japanese–Chinese father

Bran Nue Dae. The cabaret performed with unflagging enthusiasm at Broome's Cable Beach Resort, 1995.

and an Aboriginal–Scottish mother, and says his experience of racism started at school, from Aboriginal classmates. He argues that any racism—by Aborigines, whites or anyone else—is part of the problem, not part of the solution. It stops people from becoming whole:

> I'd like to research those other ethnic groups that I belong to as well. I think to become a complete human being you've got to look at the history of all your composites. I feel I can make a contribution to Australia, as an Aboriginal. I can't say I'm Asian, I can't say I'm Chinese, I can't say I'm Scottish. I can say I'm Aboriginal; but will the Aboriginal people themselves look on me as Aboriginal?[30]

Chi understands the power of cultural production: 'I think that writing and theatre and music have a lot to do with changing people's attitudes.'

Sarah Yu observes that permanent relations between Asian men and Aboriginal women became more frequent after the war, when the Aboriginal bureaucracy loosened its grip. When the coloured families who had been evacuated to Beagle Bay returned to Broome, many houses became homes to Asians, Aborigines and coloured people, 'often a family to each room'. There was much exchange of food. Aborigines used the Asian-built fish traps, and food was also a medium for courtship:

> Food was at the heart of interactions between the Asians and the Aboriginal people of Broome. This was at a time of poverty, when people survived on rations. There was no refrigeration, often no power, and people had to buy supplies of fresh vegetables from small general stores or Asian vendors. The Asians introduced chilli and spice to the local diet.[31]

Rice and curry are staple Aboriginal diet. Another legacy of this shared history is the Broome Creole: 'What kind bro?', 'He got no birrkup', and the 'gedouchoo' we find in Mark bin Bakar's media personality 'Mary G.', originally from Radio Goolari, and now on national television.[32]

FAR RIGHT: Broome's colourful past. The visitor is greeted in the town centre by bronze statues of the Japanese 'founding fathers' of Broome pearling.

Tensions continue to exist between various groups. But what defines both Broome and Broome Aboriginal culture today is its polyethnic past. An Austrian visitor once observed that Broome was the only town he knew that had signed its own death-certificate: it defined itself through its past.[33] But this memory of the past is also capable of germinating a future.

TI, MY BEAUTIFUL HOME

Music is also important in the culture of Thursday Island, and like Broome, it reflects a history of mixed relations, with a South Sea twist. Local cultural performances are just as likely to include some Malay or South Sea elements as the traditional performances that distinguish the Torres Strait Islands from each other. The Mills Sisters have been an important part of that cultural maintenance with a repertoire of Island songs, like *Oh, TI, My Beautiful Home*. Seaman Dan, a former pearl diver—the original Diver Dan—who is gaining wider reputation by the mainstream includes *Terang Bulan* (Malayan Moon) in his repertoire. This is also one of the favourites of Rocky Ahwang, a younger brother of Atima Ahwang (viz.).

A third-generation member of the Ahwang family has embraced Islam to reconnect with his severed patrilineage. He feels, like Jimmy Chi (Jnr), that he has to reach out to all the parts of his ancestry. Thursday Island has a lively Muslim congregation consisting mostly of the descendants of Malay pearling workers. Funerary and religious practices have been passed down through families. Like Christian practices on Thursday Island, Islam has a local flavour. There are no calls for prayer, and the imam is an Australian-born convert. Dress codes and prohibitions are loosely interpreted, but halal meat has always been available, as in Wyndham, and there is a sincere engagement with Qur'anic wisdom and practical guidance.

In the fourth generation, a young woman from the Ahwang lineage started to track her roots into the Pacific a few years ago. She described how amazing it was to go to this remote island and find a woman who looked just like her, and who carried herself in just the same way,

Saleh Ahwang, Mackay, 1997. Saleh has returned to Islam, the faith of his grandfather.

TOP LEFT: Cessa (née Mills), one of the three Mills Sisters of Thursday Island, with husband Tom Nakata.

BOTTOM LEFT: Malay dance at Thursday Island. Malay descendants at Thursday Island, including Raima (née Fukumura) and Noreen Yorkston (née bin Awel) perform at the primary school cultural festival, early 1970s. Photo: courtesy of Hagiga bin Doraho, Thursday Island.

Rocky Ahwang and wife Joan at Scrub Hill, Hervey Bay, June 1997.

Born in 1909, Rocky (Noranee) was practically blind at this time, but still strumming on his guitar. He translates *Terang Bulan* as:

Clear moon—you're shining
bright for me
Buaya timbul—he's buried but
he's not dead.
See, everything has meaning.
Mulut lelaki—don't talk to me
lying all the time.

Malayan Moon (transcribed and translated by Niken Lim)

Terang bulan	Clear moon
Teranglah dikali	Shining bright on the river
Buaya timbul disangka 'tlah mati	Crocodile (womaniser) turns up, I thought it was dead
Jangan percaya mulut lelaki	Don't trust man's words
Berani sumpah (ta)pi takutlah mati.	They dare to swear but they are scared to die (they're quick with promises, but not ready for consequences)

making the same hand movements as herself—recognisably a member of the same family. There are signs of ethnogenesis everywhere: reclaiming the various dimensions of mixed lineages.

MIXED RELATIONS EVERYWHERE

Younger voices are starting to add to this yearning to discover the 'other parts of themselves', besides being Aboriginal. Hannah McGlade, a Nyungar from the southwest of Western Australia with some Chinese ancestry, writes of a dream, or 'a visitation', from

> a Chinese man, huge in stature but not at all frightening, more as if he had been around for many years. I was very tiny by comparison, little me, I was wearing my kung fu shoes but they were far too big for my feet and I could not move at all. Without speaking the old man looked at me—and acknowledged me. Somehow I knew what to do. I took a few small steps in my too big shoes.[34]

McGlade began to research and write her family's mixed history, and started to contribute her perspective to histories of the Chinese in Australia. She began to think in terms of postgraduate work.

Gary Lee from Darwin also took on his family's history as a project. He produced the play *Keep Him My Heart*. Subtitled *A Larrakia–Filipino Love Story*, it insists on both the Aboriginal and Filipino parts of the Cubillo family (viz.). This work, too, caused much discussion within the extended family, with the result that his contribution to this book remains half-written.

Beyond Thursday Island, Torres Strait island culture, too, reflects a dynamic sense of indigeneity, with aeroplane dance machines, luggers and other icons of modernity integrated into traditional performances. It is also receptive to South Sea Islander influences. Jeremy Beckett observes that like other ethnic identities, Aboriginality is constantly created.[35]

The embracing of mixed relations evident in such cultural productions from the north calls for a tempering of positions, a consideration of complexities, a resistance to closure. Rigidly conceived Aboriginality that draws its salience from externally imposed, colonial ideas of essential 'pastness' silences many about their personal histories, and sustains racism. Kevin Keeffe argues for Aboriginality-as-resistance to colonial views, displacing Aboriginality-as-persistence, as pastness, that is content to perform Aboriginality according to widely held expectations of what it ought to be.[36] A pan-Aboriginal identity can only be credibly sustained by making room for all the local Aboriginalities. Local Aboriginalities, like that of Broome, Arnhem Land, or the Torres Strait are shaped by their particular histories: they are open to the mixed relations these histories have bequeathed on them.

A similar shift in ethnic politics has taken place in the Caribbean. Though with different historical constellations from north Australia, there, too, Indian, Chinese and African lineages have become entangled in a colonial past where hierarchies of colour were strenuously maintained. First formulated in the late 1930s, 'negritude' became an important leverage against colonial culture, capable of galvanising blacks and coloureds into a united political force around a simple black–white binary. Negritude emphasised cosmic connections to distant Africa, but Caribbean intellectuals found themselves defined as outsiders by Africans. More recently the cultural productions from the Caribbean emphasise creoleness. They reflect a heterogenous society that is neither African, nor Chinese, nor Indian nor French, but ultimately Caribbean, and draw on a unifying Creole language that reflects cultural diversity. Prominent in this canon are: *In Praise of Creoleness* (*Eloge de la créolité*, 1989) by Bernabé, Chamoiseau and Confiant,

Mixed Relations.
In 1989 indigenous singer/songwriter Bart Willoughby formed the band Mixed Relations. The band comprised four males and four females, with two members being non-indigenous. This combination of gender and race, in addition to Dreamtime creation stories of the Seven Sisters, inspired the band's name, Mixed Relations.
Photo: courtesy of Bart Willoughby and Fiona Noble.

Poster advertising Gary Lee's play about the Cubillo family.

and Raphael Confiant's childhood memoirs (*Ravines du devant-jour*, 1993). It is a canon that 'shows us the creole milieu of rural Martinique, with its blend of four races, its intersecting religions and beliefs, and its complex and often divisive social structure'. Among the cast of characters one is described as being 'at the interface of fourteen race mixtures and uncharacteristic of them all'. Ever present 'is the Creole language that holds together this multi-faceted society'.[37] Beverley Ormerod observes that

> Negritude was a necessary stage in the long political and psychological struggle of black West Indians to gain mental freedom and personal dignity . . . It created a mental space that would later enable Caribbean writers to take stock of their increasingly multiracial society and to take for granted their right to depict it.[38]

It is just this right that has been claimed by the cultural producers of the north presented here. They embraced their Aboriginality and defined it from within. The challenge is for the Australian public to understand and accept these definitions.

MIXED HISTORY AND AUSTRALIAN IDENTITY

These northern histories implicate not only indigenous identities. They revise the most well-rehearsed truths of Australian history. Along the Arnhem Land coast Macassan contact has become a core of collective identity, but in the national historical imagination it is barely a footnote. It is not defensible to write national histories—which ought to speak for the whole continent—as if they started in the southeast in 1788. The Macassan contact is too well documented to be relegated to pre-history, and it was too important for settlement strategies to be ignored. Nor do such histories accurately portray white history in Australia: in the north the bicentennial is still a long way off. The idea of an isolated continent, linked to the world by the arrival of the British fades into irrelevance next to this Macassan contact history. Yolngu, just like Torres Strait Islanders, were well connected with the outside world before the British arrival and became isolated under colonial impact.

The notion that Australia has a long white history that only came under barrage in the 1970s is more rhetorical than substantial. While white sovereignty was claimed over the whole continent since 1829 (with the creation of Western Australia), white settlement did not make substantial inroads into the north until the 1860s. In numerical terms, it remained tenuous, and was not finally achieved until World War II. Asian, Aboriginal and coloured populations, either together or singly, outstripped a thin white layer. In the far northern townships, the dominant lived experience was not of a white Australia but of a polyethnic one.

Interviewees

Ah Chee, Norma, Derby, August 1994
Ah Kit, Phyllis, Mount Isa, 10.8.1997
Ah Kui, Topsy, Daly River, June 1994
Ah Kup, Dolly (née Ah Bow), Cloncurry, August 1997
Ah Loy, Phyllis, Thursday Island, 19.7.1997
Ah Mat, Frank, Darwin, 13.6.1997
Ah Toy, Lily, Darwin, June 1994
Ahlin, Larry, Pine Creek, May 1995
Ahwang, Rocky, Hervey Bay, 20.6.1997
Ahwang, Saleh, Mackay, 26.6.1997
Ahwang, Starchy, Mackay, 26.6.1997
Alberts, Steven, Broome, 3.9.1994
Ambidjambi (Frank Ambi), Minjilang, Croker Island, 3.6.1995
Bassini, Sunlight, Coen, July 1997
bin Doraho, Hagiga, Thursday Island, 20.7.1997
bin Hadji Ali, Shaikh Abdul Kadir, Wyndham, 27.8.1994
Brown, Narelle, Mackay, 6.8.1997
Bulunbulun, Johnny, Maningrida, June 1995
Bunggaru, Jimmie, Maningrida, 6.6.1995
Burchell, Billy, Wonga Beach, Mossman, 3.7.1997
Camfoo, Tex and Nellie, Bulman, 14.5.1995
Campbell, John, Wyndham, September 1994
Chi, Theresa, Darwin, June 1994
Chong, Nellie, Mornington Island, August 1997
Clark, Ethel, Mount Isa, 9.8.1997
Collins, Ana, Katherine, September 1994
Costello, Peter, Hopevale, 8.7.1997
Danaja, Peter, Maningrida, 6.6.1995
Davies, Irene, One Arm Point, Dampierland Peninsula, June 1995
Dukulurruwuy, Rita, Milingimbi, 14.6.1995
Dumoo, Johnny, Wadeye, July 1994
Fischer, Peter, China Camp, 4.7.1997
Flinders, Bob, at Hopevale, 19.1.1986
Fong, Nellie, Darwin, June 1994
Foster, Marjorie, Knuckey's Lagoon, Darwin, 6.6.1994
Gallagher, Winnie, Wyndham, May 1995
Garrwiritja, Joe Mowandjil, Milingimbi, 13.6.1995
Gray, Fred, Howard Springs, 4.6.1994
Green, Daisy, Georgetown, July 1997
Guivarra, Pedro and Gloria, Gladstone and Thursday Island, 1994 and July 1997
Guivarra, Ricky, Mackay, June 1997
Gunderra, Willie Danjati, Galiwin'ku, 10.6.1995
Haji Ali, Phyllis, Wyndham, 26.8.1994
Hamaguchi, Pearl and Hiroshi, Broome, September 1994
Horimoto Shinichi, Susami, Wakayama (Japan), 20.10.1987
Hunter, Dot, Broome, 5.9.1994
Juler, Johnny, Wadeye, July 1994
Kenyon, Joan, Humpty Doo, June 1994
Ketchell, Kathleen (née Lui), Cairns, 2.7.1997
Kulka, George, China Camp, 5.7.1997
Lapulung, Keith, Milingimbi, 14.6.1995
Lee Tong, Billy, Wyndham, August 1994
Leon, Albert, Mount Isa, 9.8.1997
Leon, Moody, Mount Isa, 9.8.1997
Marika, Rarriwuy, Dhimuru, Yirrkala, 8.6.1995
Mattjuwi (Burruwanga), Galiwin'ku, 12.6.1995
Mendis, Amira, Thursday Island, July 1997
Mills, Abetha, Mackay, June 1997
Morgan, Harry, Daly River, June 1994
Mulurinji, Nelson, Cobourg Peninsula, 2.7.1995
Munyarryun, Bawurr, Dhimuru, Yirrkala, 8.6.1995
Nakata, Cessa (née Mills) and Tom, Thursday Island, July 1997
Ogawa Taira, Tanabe, Wakayama (Japan), 21.10.1987
Oku Saioshi, Taiji, Wakayama (Japan), 15.10.1987
Patlas, Cliff, Cobourg Peninsula, 2.6.1995
Pederson, Maria, Katherine, 15.9.1994
Puertollano, Theresa, Derby, 29.8.1994
Que Noy, Albert, Darwin, June 1994
Que Noy, Arthur, Winnellie, Darwin, June 1994
Robinson, Margaret (née Roe), Broome, September 1994
Royee, Len, Gordonvale, 26.7.1997
Rraying, Joy, Milingimbi, 14.6.1995
Sahanna, Jack, Broome, September 1994, May 1995
See Poy, Herbert Jnr, Innisfail, June 1997
See Poy, Herbert Snr, Innisfail, June 1997
See Poy, Theodora, Innisfail, June 1997
Shibasaki, Billy and Sariba (née bin Garape), Thursday Island, 19.7.1997
Tatsuno Ryuhichi, Honai, Ehime (Japan), 23.10.1987
Unoue Ushimatsu, Miwazaki, Wakayama (Japan), 18.10.1987
Wabuka Kyomi, Susami, Wakayama (Japan), 20.10.1987
Wah Day, George, Pine Creek, Gordonvale, 26.7.1997
Williams, Mona, Wyndham, September 1994
Wulanybuma, George, Galiwin'ku, 10.6.1995
Yamaguchi, Arthur and Kate, Mount Isa, 6.8.1997
Yambikbik, Brian, Cobourg Peninsula, 2.6.1995
Yiela, Sandy, Lockhart River, 3.1.1987
Yumbulul, Terry, Galiwin'ku, 10.6.1995
Yunupingu, Joe Djalalingpa, Yirrkala, 8.6.1995

Notes

CHAPTER 1: TREPANG: AUSTRALIA'S ASIAN CONNECTION

1 Ian Crawford, 'Late prehistoric changes in Aboriginal cultures in Kimberley, Western Australia', 1969:90.Crawford suggests that 'Marege' might initially have been used to refer especially to Melville Island. *PaMarege* became a reference to trepang fishermen.

2 Sometimes, especially in the eastern area, pronounced as Mangajarra, and rendered by Ronald Berndt and Catherine Berndt as 'Mankasaran' (*Arnhem Land—Its History and Its People*, 1954:40). I have adopted the spelling used in Yolngu Matha publications from Milingimbi. It closely approximates the Makasar term 'Mangkasara'.

3 'Macassans' is used here not as an ethnic ascription (which ought to be Makasar) but as a reference to the voyagers in the archipelago who traded to the port of Makassar (called Ujung Pandang from about 1974 to 2001). I prefer this term to 'Indonesians' because it is more specific and has been used in much previous literature.

4 Berndt & Berndt, *Arnhem Land*, 1954:40.

5 Crawford, 'Late prehistoric changes', 1969:87, 88.

6 Charles Campbell Macknight, *A Voyage to Marege—Macassan Trepangers in Northern Australia*, 1976:1, 40; D. John Mulvaney, *The Prehistory of Australia*, 1975 (1969):25–8.

7 Macknight, *A Voyage to Marege*, 1976:16.

8 Ibid., 8; Mulvaney, *The Prehistory of Australia*, 1975:25–8.

9 Macknight, *A Voyage to Marege*, 1976:14.

10 The Dutch made attempts with a 'factory' at Damar (Zuidwester Eilandt) in 1646 and again at Fort du Bus in West Papua in 1828.

11 The first Chinese junk in Makassar was recorded in 1615 and the first Chinese trader in Amboyna in 1623. G. Cokayne to Sir T. Smythe, 16.7.1615, in W. Foster (ed.), *Letters Received by the East India Company from Its Servants in the East*, 1899(3):137; F. Valentijin, *Oud en Nieuw Oost-Indien*, 1726:55; V. Purcell, *The Chinese in Southeast Asia*, 1951:459; in Crawford, 'Late prehistoric changes', 1969:99.

12 Thomas Forrest described the items traded by *taukeh* at New Guinea in 1775, referring to Chinese traders from Ternate and Tidore: 'The Chinese provided iron tools, chopping knives, axes, blue and red cloth, China beads, plates and bowls, receiving in return Misoy bark, slaves, ambergris, trepang, tortoise shell, small pearls, black parrots and large red parrots, birds-of-paradise, and many kinds of dead birds, dried in a particular way.' Makassar General to Bantam, 13.4.1665, India Office Records, in Crawford, 'Late prehistoric changes', 1969:100; Thomas Forrest, *A Voyage to New Guinea and the Moluccas from Balambangan*, 1780:106 in Macknight, *A Voyage to Marege*, 1976:13.

13 Owen Stanley in J. L. Stokes, *Discoveries in Australia*, 1846, vol. 2, 335–7, cited in Macknight, *A Voyage to Marege*, 1976:13.

14 G. W. Earl, foreword in D. H. Kolff, *Voyage of the Dutch Brig of War Dourge*, 1840, in Crawford, 'Late prehistoric changes', 1969:101. The naturalist Alfred Wallace also comments on such journeys in 1856.

15 Willem Robert, *The Dutch Explorations, 1605–1756, of the North and Northwest Coast of Australia*, 1973:147.

16 '*Het Zuidland . . . wordt van Timor en Makassar wel eens bevaren, doch geeft onzes wetens niets als tripangs, zijne gedroogde kwalvisch en was.*' Governor General of DEIC, Batavia, 1754 in Robert, *The Dutch Explorations*, 1973:146. To write '*zijne*' (meaning 'his') instead of '*zijnde*' (being) makes little sense in this sentence and could be a typographical error in Robert.

17 Jean Etienne Gonzal, in command of the *Rijder* and *Buis*, visited the Kimberley in June–July and captured two Aborigines. The VOC directors considered that of these two vessels, one had achieved little and the other nothing. Their reports of Australian potential were as discouraging as those of other Europeans.

18 The account of this journey relates how the natives at Port Essington attempted to tow away the *Nova Hollandia*, which was lying at anchor with three little vessels (*schuities*), and then attempted to tow the anchor buoy, also without success, suggesting that they were so unused to strangers as to be unfamiliar with anchors. Of course traditional sea-going craft in the area did not carry anchors.

19 H. T. Fry, 'Cathay and the way thither: the background to Botany Bay', 1969–71:497–510, 137ff; Alexander Dalrymple, 'An account of what has passed between the India directors and Alexander Dalrymple; intended as an introduction of a plan for extending the commerce of this kingdom, and of the Company, in the East-Indies, by an establishment at Balambangan'; Forrest, *A Voyage from Calcutta*, 1780:78; Crawford, 'Late prehistoric changes', 1969:102.

20 Crawford, 'Late prehistoric changes', 1969:103.

21 Macknight, *A Voyage to Marege*, 1976:97.

22 Anne Clarke, 'The "Moormans Trowsers": Macassan and Aboriginal interactions and the changing fabric of indigenous social life', 2000: 315–35.

23 F. Péron & L. de Freycinet, *Voyage de découvertes aux terres australes*, 1816, vol. 2:248 in Crawford, 'Late prehistoric changes', 1969:98.

24 Macknight, *A Voyage to Marege*, 1976:97.

25 Alfred Searcy, *In Australian Tropics*, 1907:46.

26 Mulvaney, *The Prehistory of Australia*, 1975:47, and Alan Powell, *Far Country—A Short History of the Northern Territory*, 1988 (1982):36, 52.

27 K. G. MacIntyre, *The Secret Discovery of Australia*, 1977; Crawford, 'Late prehistoric changes', 1969:100. See also Charles Boxer, *Francisco Vieira de Figueiredo*, 1967; Marco Ramerini, 'Timor Leste'.

28 Clifford Sather, *The Bajau Laut—Adaptation, History and Fate in a Maritime Fishing Society of South-eastern Sabah*, 1997:9.

29 Ibid. *Turije'ne'* is the Makasar term.

30 Ibid., 17.

31 Ibid.,16.

32 Jim Warren, *The Sulu Zone, 1786–1898*, 1981: 209–11.

33 Sather, *The Bajau Laut*, 1997:40.

34 Ibid., 37ff.

35 Ibid., 6.

36 Ibid., 7.

37 Ibid., 14, referring to James Fox, 'Notes on the southern voyages and settlements of the Sama-Bajau', 1977, 133:459.

38 Lloyd Warner, *A Black Civilization—A Social Study of an Australian Tribe*, 1958; D. F. Thomson, *Economic Structure and the Ceremonial Exchange Cycle in Arnhem Land*, 1949; Berndt & Berndt, *Arnhem Land*, 1954, with regard to northeast Arnhem Land, and Crawford 'Late prehistoric changes', 1969, with regard to the Kimberley.

39 Berndt & Berndt, *Arnhem Land*, 1954:15, 73.

40 Ibid., 15.

41 Ibid., 35.

42 Burrumarra said that the Birindji stories had been kept secret until 1989, when he revealed a range of stories and images for the flag *rranga*, which was to be a symbol of Makarrata—the treaty promised by the Fraser government for 1988.

43 Berndt & Berndt, *Arnhem Land*, 1954:17.

44 Crawford, 'Late prehistoric changes', 1969:291.

45 Ibid., 136–7.

46 Ian McIntosh, 'The bricoleur at work: Warang Dingo mythology in the Yirritja moiety of north-east Arnhem Land', 1992; Thomson, *Economic Structure*, 1949:51.

47 McIntosh, 'The bricoleur at work', 1992:44.

48 Ibid., 30–4, 46. McIntosh here argues with Hiatt, McConnell, Morphy and Malinowski.

49 A photograph of this map appears in Michael Cooke, 'Makassar and northeast Arnhem Land', 1987:v.

50 Patunru, *Sedjarah Goa Jajasan Kebudajan di Makassar*, 1967. Later published as *Sejara Gowa*.

51 Peter Spillett (Daeng Makkulle), 'Gotong Royong: Hubungan Makassar-Marege', 1987:20.

52 Macknight, *A Voyage to Marege*, 1976:81, 98–9.

53 Clarke, 'The "Moormans Trowsers"', 2000: 315–35. Other essays in the same volume also make the observation that the archaeological record suggests that the Australian inland was inhabited earlier than the coasts. Scott Mitchell, pers. comm., Darwin, May 1995.

54 Ibid., 44. King later became a commissioner of the Australian Agricultural Company, which experimented with opium crops in the Hawkesbury region.

55 Matthew Flinders, *A Voyage to Terra Australis*, 1814:213.

56 Pobassoo or Pobasso are English-speaking approaches to what is more likely to have been Pu (for *bungawa*) Bassu. Macknight refers to a place named after Bapa Baso (Father Nail), an expert *perahu* builder whose camp was just south of Woodah Island in the Gulf of Carpentaria. Macknight, *A Voyage to Marege*, 1976:96.

57 Péron & de Freycinet, *Voyage de découvertes*, 1816 (2):247, in Crawford 'Late prehistoric changes', 1969:103.

58 Powell, *Far Country*, 1988 (1982):34.

59 Flinders, *A Voyage to Terra Australis*, 1814:250–1.

60 Brown's journal 1802–03, cited in Macknight, *A Voyage to Marege*, 1976:162.

61 Powell, *Far Country*, 1988:41.

62 Phillip Parker King, in Crawford, 'Late prehistoric changes', 1969.

63 Powell, *Far Country*, 1988:47.

64 Ibid.

65 Ibid., 49; Searcy, *In Australian Tropics*, 1984 (1907):219ff.

66 Major Campbell, 1834, cited in Berndt & Berndt, *Arnhem Land*, 1954:216.

67 Powell, *Far Country*, 1988:50; Searcy, *In Australian Tropics*, 1984:219ff.

68 Searcy, *In Australian Tropics*, 1984:19, 47.

69 *Historical Records of Australia*, Series 1, vol. 14, 350–1 and vol. 15:153–4.

70 G. W. Earl, *Observations on the Commercial and Agricultural Capabilities of the North Coast of New Holland*, 1836; and W. B. Wildey, *Australasia and the Oceanic Region*, 1876:78; cited in Berndt & Berndt, *Arnhem Land*, 1954:74, 216.

71 The years given in brackets indicate the period of operation of a convict settlement. Norfolk Island (1788–1814) had already ceased to operate, while Port Arthur in Tasmania (1830–77) and Swan River in Western Australia (1849–86) were not yet established.

72 Confalonieri was one of 27 Benedictines arriving in 1846 with Rosendo Salvado. George Earl divided the Cobourg people into the Yarlo, Yaako, lyi and Oitby tribes. Norman Tindale records them as Wurengo, Jaako, Iwaidja and Oitbi.

73 Ibid.

74 Searcy, *In Australian Tropics*, 1984:40.

75 Powell, *Far Country*, 1988:54.

76 R. B. Douglas to Commissioner of Crown Lands, 5.8.1872, in Macknight, *A Voyage to Marege*, 1976:100.

77 Searcy, *In Australian Tropics*, 1984:22.

78 Ibid., 67.

79 Ibid., 97.

80 C. C. Macknight, entry in *Northern Territory Dictionary of Biography* (NTDB) vol. 1, David Carment et al. (eds), 1990.

81 Ibid.

82 The party consisted of Robinson, Lorance, Francis, Brown and 'a black boy'. Macknight used the journal of Lorance as a basis for 'Journal of a voyage around Arnhem Land in 1875', 1981:135–45.

83 Historical evidence tendered in *Mary Yarmir & Ors v. Northern Territory of Australia & Ors, Federal Court of Australia*, 6.7.1998, Olney J presiding. According to Searcy (1984:22), the site was known as Adjaka to the Croker people, and as Ujung Tambanunu (Oojoontambanoonoo) to Macassans.

84 Searcy, *In Australian Tropics*, 1984:100.

85 Macknight, NTDB, 1990.

86 Berndt & Berndt, *Arnhem Land*, 1954:69.

87 Macknight, NTDB; Berndt & Berndt, *Arnhem Land*, 1954:69.

88 Macknight, *A Voyage to Marege*, 1976:105.

89 Robinson, manager of Cobourg Cattle Company station at Port Essington, to Little, 12.2.1882, cited in Macknight, *A Voyage to Marege*, 1976:106.

90 John Morris, 'The coming of the Macassans to the islands of the Tiwi', n.d. (1960s):17–18. Macknight, *A Voyage to Marege*, 1976:118ff.

91 Macknight, NTDB, 1990. A. A. Cense, 'Makassaars–Boeginese Prauwvaart op Noord-Australie', *Bijdragen*, Vol. 108, 1952:262. Reuben married Bertha McKeddie, of Filipino descent, in 1920. Reuben's second wife was Salamah Ah Mat from Thursday Island. He established the Australian Rules Football code in the Northern Territory, and died while working for the Australian Army in 1942.

92 Searcy, *In Australian Tropics*, 1984:79.

93 SAA 790/1883/632 in Macknight, *A Voyage to Marege*, 1976:108.

94 In 1883–84 seven vessels came to Marege and three to Kayu Jawa, and in 1884–85 thirteen came to Marege while six went to Kayu Jawa. Macknight, *A Voyage to Marege*, 1976:111–16.

95 Ibid., 117.

96 Ibid., 123.

97 Ibid., 97.

98 Donald Denoon, Philippa Mein Smith and Marivic Wyndham, *A History of Australia, New Zealand and the Pacific*, 2000:38.

99 Ibid., 42.

100 Ibid., 57, citing James Belich, *Making Peoples: A History of the New Zealanders*, 1996.

CHAPTER 2: DEEP HISTORIES: INDONESIANS AND ABORIGINES

1 C. C. Macknight, 'Journal of a voyage around Arnhem Land in 1875', 1981:135–45. This is the journal of Lorance travelling with Robinson, SAA 790/1876/74.

2 Interview with Bawurr Munyarryun and Rarriwuy Marika, Timuru, Yirrkala, 8.6.1995.

3 Interview with Terry Yumbulul, Willie Danjati Gunderra and George Wulanybuma, Galiwin'ku, 10.6.1995.

4 Interview with Bawurr Munyarryun and Rarriwuy Marika, Yirrkala, 8.6.1995. The words of the song in question have been recorded by Rarriwuy Marika interviewing Wandjuk Marika in May 1986. It is rendered in Peter Spillett, 'Dreamtime stories from Makassar and Marege', 1998:16, as '*Wathikatikha, wathikathika, wathabilipatha, wathakuwaka, drri thar-risami, gapulwanungurr, nhugukassa, balipali nana nana, windirrituku, barra' piya*.'

5 Djäwawungu, Dhä-Dhuditjpuy Mangatharra, Milingimbi 1979.

6 Spillett, 'Gotong Royong', 1987:18.

7 Bopaniwung, Dhäwu Dhuwal Gopiyawuywainguwuy. Ga Mangatharrawainguwuy. Milingimbi Literature Centre, 1988.

8 Macknight has used an account from Daeng Sarro recorded by Cense to identify the places referred to by Macassans. Charles Campbell Macknight, *The Farthest Coast*, 1969:180–5.

9 Interview with Joy Rraying, Rita Dukulurruwuy and Keith Lapulung, Milingimbi, 14.6.1995.

10 Ian McIntosh, 'The bricoleur at work: Warang Dingo mythology in the Yirritja moiety of north-east Arnhem Land', 1992:58.

11 Interview with Bawurr Munyarryun and Rarriwuy Marika, Yirrkala, 8.6.1995.

12 Interview with Peter Danaja, Sunrize Band, 6.6.1995.

13 Andrish Saint-Clare, pers. comm. July 2001, referring to his video screening of Yolngu dances in Makassar in 1994.

14 David Paul Zorc, 'Yolngu-Matha dictionary–Macassan loanwords project', 29–30 May 1986 (MS). See also Nicholas Evans, 'Makassan loanwords in Top End languages', 1992:107–91.

15 Zorc, 'Yolngu-Matha dictionary', 1986; Michael Cooke, 'Makassar and northeast Arnhem Land—missing links and living bridges', 1987:56; Alan Walker and R. David Zorc, 'Austronesian loanwords in Yolngu-Matha of northeast Arnhem Land', 1981:107–34.

16 Ronald Berndt & Catherine Berndt, *Arnhem Land: Its History and Its People*, 1954:52; Spillett, 'Gotong Royong', 1987:9; Walker and Zorc, 'Austronesian loanwords in Yolngu-Matha', 1982:127.

17 John Darling, *Below the Wind*, 1994.

18 Interview with Joe Djalalingpa Yunupingu, Yirrkala, 8.6.1995.

19 Charles Campbell Macknight, *A Voyage to Marege—Macassan Trepangers in Northern Australia*, 1976:126.

20 Gunanu and Bätjang were the names of known persons in Arnhem Land of the same generation as Mangellai, and reputedly light skinned. Bätjang died as a young man in the 1920s and left no descendants. Gunanu died at Elcho Island in the 1940s as a middle-aged woman. See Cooke, 'Makassar and northeast Arnhem Land', 1987.

21 Ibid.

22 E. O. Robinson, manager of Cobourg Cattle Company station at Port Essington, to J. A. G. Little, 12.2.1882, in Searcy, *In Australian Tropics*, 1984:47.

23 Ibid., 67.

24 Macknight, *A Voyage to Marege*, 1976:135.

25 Searcy, *In Australian Tropics*, 1984:47.

26 Spillett, 'Gotong Royong', 1987:14.

27 According to Mattjuwi, then, Garrngar was abducted to Makassar and had Gunano (2) there, and the Gunano buried at Elcho Island is grandmother to himself and Gunano (2). Garnggar and Gunano (2) must have remained in Makassar, because they did not return, and Gunano (1) had probably never been to Makassar. But Gunano (1), born around the turn of the century, cannot have been mother of Garnggar who was old enough to be abducted before 1907. Cooke, 'Makassar and northeast Arnhem Land', 1987:32–6, and interview with Mattjuwi, Galiwin'ku, 12.6.1995.

28 Spillett, 'Gotong Royong', 1987:12.

29 The house is featured in Macknight, *A Voyage to Marege*, 1976, photograph 18. According to Spillett, the Batchelor College students identified it as being built from north Australian ironwood and stringybark. Spillett, 'Gotong Royong', 1987:28.

30 Spillett, 'Gotong Royong', 1987.

31 The Berndts thought it was a work-related injury sustained from falling off the mast. Rarriwuy Marika recorded a story told by Wandjuk Marika in May 1986, which explains it as the result of a beating from the captain, for losing the captain's cap, but ascribes this injury to Domi, Djaladjari's brother. There may have been reasons of protocol for this switched identity. David Burrumarra, cousin/brother of the two,

told Ian McIntosh that it was Djalatjirri who received a blow to the back from the first mate. Berndt & Berndt, *Arnhem Land*, 1954:51. Spillett, 'Dreamtime stories', 1989:26, referring to an interview in May 1986. Ian McIntosh, *The Whale and the Cross—Conversations with David Burrumarra MBE*, 1994:86.

32 Berndt & Berndt, *Arnhem Land*, 1954:53.

33 Ibid., 56. The spelling given is 'Kambu'malagu' for Kampung Maluku; 'karei Deintumbo buga' for Daeng Tompo, the *bunggawa* (*karaeng* is also a royal title); and 'Batadjowa' for Patti Jawaya. Djaladjari lists the following Makassans: Jadjung, the *perahu* captain at Kambu'tumbu; Deintumbo at Kambu'basi or Kambu'batji; Bunggasinga at Kambu'kalasu; Chinese at Kambu'djinga; Malays and their headman Dara at Kambu'maleiju; Madi, a *bunggawa* at Kambu'biru; Papadjin, a *perahu* headman at Kambu'guda in the plain country near the lily swamps; Mitjindi, a *bunggawa* at Limbu'timbarun or Limbu'katuwung; several *bunggawa* at Ranguwa near the beach; and Kupangers and Japanese at Kambu'dadi along the creek and lily swamp. He also visited Laelae, Gundingari, Djamaluna, Banda and Manggarei islands, northwest of Makassar. (Spelling by Berndt and Berndt.)

34 Interview with Bawurr Munyarryun and Rarriwuy Marika, Timuru, Yirrkala, 8.6.1995.

35 According to McIntosh, *The Whale and the Cross*, 1994:8, Bukulatjipi became a surname of Warramirri people in the 1960s. It refers to an ancestral hero whose site has been occupied by the Nabalco mine at Gove.

36 John Cawte, *The Universe of the Warramiri* 1993; McIntosh, *The Whale and the Cross*, 1994.

37 Cooke, 'Makassar and northeast Arnhem Land', 1987:56–8.

38 Interview with Terry Yumbulul, Willie Danjati Gunderra and George Wulanybuma, Galiwin'ku, 10.6.1995.

39 Spillett, 'Gotong Royong', 1987:20.

40 Macknight, *A Voyage to Marege*, 1976:84

41 Spillett, 'Gotong Royong', 1987:22. Berndt and Berndt (*Arnhem Land*, 1957:57, 59) reserve the term *wuramu* for 'Crook Men' or 'collection men' (thieves), inhabiting the mountains behind Makassar, who sporadically ransacked the city. Occasionally it may refer to Dutch customs officials who collected duties. Later *wuramu* became a reference to carved wooden figures in northeast Arnhem Land, and Makassan posts placed on graves to symbolise a dead person's spirit. *Wuramu* also refers to a collection ceremony of the Yirritja moiety (Berndt & Berndt, *Arnhem Land*, 1957:63).

42 George's 'father' (grandfather?) Mayunga was the brother of Dayngmangu.

43 McIntosh, *The Whale and the Cross*, 1994:18, 22. It is more than likely that this name also exists in Makasar. Macknight mentions that the Bay of Mangko', Northwest Bay, commemorates one of the leaders of the Macassans.

44 Gulmanngur (Gulman, Gulmannuru) on Elcho Island functions as an important referent in such stories. (It also features in the song, *My Sweet Takirrina*.) But it is absent from Daeng Saro's exhaustive list of Macassan sites. Husein is known to have had a camp in Melville Bay, referred to as Lembana Panrea (literally: Carpenter's or Tradesman's Bay). That a number of Yolngu stories associate him with Elcho Island may reflect the movement of Husein's Aboriginal family from Melville Bay to Elcho Island, or it may reflect the way in which Husein, like other Macassans, moved from camp to camp. Daeng Sarro said they would stay a fortnight at Takkarena (Elcho Island, the old mission site), and five or ten days at Melville Bay. Cense, 'Makassaars–Boeginese Prauwvaart op Noord-Australie', 1952:263.

45 This was one of the stories collected by Batchelor College students. Bobby Wunyimarra Ganambarr said it had been recorded a few years ago by Matjarra, as told by Dhawa Danygulil at Milingimbi. In Cooke, 'Makassar and northeast Arnhem Land', 1987:13–14.

46 Cooke, 'Makassar and northeast Arnhem Land', 1987:6.

47 Spillett, 'Gotong Royong', 1987:31.

48 Ibid., 30. Similar paintings including hand silhouettes blown with red ochre and x-ray figures also occur in Irian Jaya.

49 Interview with Joe Mowandjil Garrwiritja, Milingimbi, 13.6.1995.

50 Berndt & Berndt, *Arnhem Land*, 1954:ii.

51 Spillett, 'Gotong Royong', 1987:22, 23, 27.

52 Berndt & Berndt, *Arnhem Land*, 1954:28.

53 C. W. M. Hart & Arnold Pilling, *The Tiwi of North Australia*, 1960.

54 Ibid., 98. See also G. W. Earl, *The Native Races of the Indian Archipelago: Papuans*, 1853:210; Alan Powell, *Far Country—A Short History of the Northern Territory*, 1988 (1982); John Mulvaney, *The Prehistory of Australia*, 1975 (1969):45.

55 Phyllis Mander Jones, *The Tasman Map of 1644 Sydney*, 1948; J. E. Heeres, *The Part Borne by the Dutch in the Discovery of Australia 1606–1765*, 1899.

56 Searcy, *In Australian Tropics*, 1984:46.

57 A. A. Cense, 'Makassaars–Boeginese Prauwvaart op Nord-Australie', 1952:262.

58 Michael McCarthy & Lesley Silvester, 'Australian Contact Shipwrecks Program', 1998.

59 John Morris, 'The coming of the Macassans to the islands of the Tiwi', n.d. (1960s); Peter Spillett, 'Dreamtime stories', 1989:10.

60 Spillett, 'Dreamtime Stories', 1989:10.

61 Ibid., 10.

62 Ibid., 9.

63 The sites of Macassan activity referred to on Melville Island were Wulawunga, or Air Force Creek, south of Point Piper, which contains a well, and around Karslake Island, with a camp at Ulurankgu southeast from Cape Lavery, where the well is now covered over.

64 Interview with Brian Yambikbik, Nelson Mulurinji and Cliff Patlas, Cobourg Peninsula, 2.6.1995.

65 Ibid.

66 The sites of Macassan activity remembered here were on the reefs southeast of Warruwi, at Sims Island, and at Anuru Bay [Aurari Bay], southeast of which there is a Macassan grave, at Malala. Spillett, 'Dreamtime stories', 1989:10–11.

67 Ibid.

68 Searcy, *In Australian Tropics*, 1984:81.

69 Maningrida is located on Kunibidji land, and the Mabarnard/Djukurridji clan are the landowning group. Others at Maningrida belong to the Kunbarlang, Nakkara, Burarra, Kuninjku, Gorrgoni, Gunardba, Rembarrnga, Djinang and Gupapuyungu people.

70 Interview with Jimmie Bunggaru, Maningrida,

6.6.1995.

71 *Northern Territory News*, 17.6.1995:29.

72 Interview with Joe Mowandjil Garrwiritja, Milingimbi, 13.6.1995.

73 Interview with Mattjuwi, Galiwin'ku, 12.6.1995.

74 P. M. Worsley, 'Early Asian contacts with Australia', 1955:1–11.

75 Ian Crawford, 'Late prehistoric changes in Aboriginal cultures in Kimberley, Western Australia', 1969:287, 290–91, 107.

76 Péron & de Freycinet, *Voyage de découvertes*, 1816(2):245–51; Phillip Parker King, 1827(1):138; J. J. Vosmaer, 'Korte beschrijving van het Z.O. schiereiland van Celebes', 1839, xvii:195–484, R. J. Sholl, Journal, 1865, all cited in Crawford, 'Late prehistoric changes', 1969:103ff.

77 Searcy, *In Australian Tropics*, 1984:189.

78 Crawford, 'Late prehistoric changes', 1969:208.

79 Ibid., 107.

80 Ibid., 277.

81 Ibid., 280ff.

82 Ibid., 115, 119.

83 *West Australian*, 2.6.1911, in Crawford, 'Late prehistoric changes', 1969:118.

84 Battye CSO 638/35 in Crawford, 'Late prehistoric changes', 117.

85 Crawford, 'Late prehistoric changes', 1969:124.

86 Ibid., 126, 128.

87 Ibid., 136ff.

88 Australian Customs Service, 'Coastwatch improvement program strengthens detect and deter capacity', 1999; Senator Andrew Bartlett, 'Parliamentary Speech,' 25.11.1999, www.democrats.org.au/parliament/bartlett/19991125border.htm

89 These populations are still distinguishable by language, boat type and other cultural differences: people from Madura (East Java), Makasars, Bugis, Bajau Laut, and Butonese. James Fox, 'A report on eastern Indonesian fishermen in Darwin', 1992:15.

90 Bruce Campbell & Bu Wilson, 'Indonesian fishing off Australia: crime or tradition', 1992:2–4.

91 Both Jill Elliott and Democrat Senator Andrew Bartlett commented negatively on the press coverage. Jill Elliott, 'Indonesian fishermen: a Western Australian perspective', ca. 1994, distributed to the members of the Kimberley Indonesia Friendship Association. A shortened version was published as Jill Elliott, 'Fishing in Australian waters', 1996.

92 Elliott, 'Indonesian fishermen', 1994.

93 Fox, 'A report on eastern Indonesian fishermen', 1992.

94 Rod Sachse, 'Indonesian fishermen—an overview', ca. 1994, distributed to the members of the Kimberley Indonesia Friendship Association.

95 Anthony Reid, 'Indonesian fishermen detained in Broome: a report on the social and economic background', 1992.

96 Mark Erdmann, 'An ABC guide to coral reef fisheries in Southwest Sulawesi, Indonesia', 1995, distributed to the members of the Kimberley Indonesia Friendship Association. Among the techniques observed by Erdmann are life finning, electroshock fishing using car batteries, cyanide fishing (squirting potassium cyanide to stun the fish), and blasting (using dynamite).

97 Under the Suharto government, five-year plans demanded intensification of fishing, and the licensing of foreign vessels helped to lift the statistics. At Lembeh Strait, in northern Sulawesi, a Taiwanese trap net became known as the 'Curtain of Death'. From 1997 to 1998 it stretched across the strait killing dolphins, whales, turtles, dugong and other large fish. Mark Erdmann, 'Leave Indonesia's fisheries to Indonesians!', 2000.

98 Reid, 'Indonesian fishermen detained in Broome', 1992:6.

99 In 1992 the fleet consisted of (1) traditional Rotinese fishing for trepang and trochus in the MoU zone, which is legal unless a motor or other modern equipment is carried. The Rotinese have close connections with the people of (2) Tukangbesi, who also engage in traditional fishing in the MoU zone, though their rights to that fishery have not been officially recognised. They are generally tolerated, but eleven of their boats were apprehended. (3) Fishermen from Tiori Strait in southeast Sulawesi ventured into the AFZ as far as King Sound fishing for trochus. Seventy of their small, motorised vessels were impounded and 1,000 crew arrested, many of whom were gaoled in Broome. (4) Fleets from southeast Sulawesi have also entered the AFZ in the Northern Territory and Queensland in search of shark fin. Their boats are motorised and somewhat larger, and thirty-one vessels have been apprehended. (5) A commercial fleet out of Dobo (Aru) and Merauke (Irian Jaya) also enters the AFZ in search of shark fin, on large motorised boats owned by companies based in Jakarta. Sixty-five of these vessels, and three industrial drop-liners, have been apprehended. Campbell & Wilson, 'Indonesian fishing off Australia', 1992.

100 Elliott, 'Indonesian fishermen', 1994.

101 Ibid.

102 Campbell & Wilson, 'Indonesian fishing off Australia', 1992.

103 Elliott observed about those detained in Broome that 'at no stage during the period since 1988 has any government official or delegation taken the opportunity to discuss the problem with these men. The same can be said for the various Australian representatives who visit Indonesia to discuss the illegal fishing problem.' Elliott, 'Indonesian fishermen', 1994.

104 Graham Duncan, 'Misadventures in the button trade', *Good Weekend*, 30.3.1991.

105 Interview with Irene Davies, One Arm Point, June 1995.

106 Erdmann, 'Leave Indonesia's fisheries to Indonesians!', 2000.

107 Northeast Arnhem Land includes Milingimbi, Ramingining, Galiwin'ku (Elcho Island), Gapuwiyak (Lake Evella) and Yirrkala. The region includes some forty clan groups, each with their own dialect.

CHAPTER 3: PEARLING: 'ALL KIND OF NATION'

1 This is the title of an article by Athol Chase in *Aboriginal History* 5 (1) 1981:7–19.

2 Mary Albertus Bain, *Full Fathom Five*, 1982:19.

3 Sholl to Colonial Secretary, 24.2.1869 in Bain, *Full Fathom Five*, 1982:25.

4 Chester to Colonial Secretary, 10.10.1871, ColA 2499/71, QSA.

5 Bain, *Full Fathom Five*, 1982:75.

6 Ibid., 23.
7 Ibid., 28; Bill Dalton, *Indonesia Handbook*, 1978:235.
8 Bain, *Full Fathom Five*, 1982:29–31.
9 Ibid., 34. The incident occurred in 1880.
10 Ibid., 35.
11 Report of the Hamilton inquiry into pearling, 1897, cited in Regina Ganter, *The Pearl-Shellers of Torres Strait*, 1994:31.
12 R. McRae to Colonial Secretary, 8.3.1875, in Bain, *Full Fathom Five*, 1982:32.
13 Bain, *Full Fathom Five*, 1982:29.
14 Anne Atkinson, *Asian Immigrants to Western Australia, 1829–1901*, 1988.
15 W. S. Weerasooria, *Links between Sri Lanka and Australia*, 1988.
16 Bain, *Full Fathom Five*, 1982:284–8.
17 Ibid., 41.
18 Ibid., 41.
19 Ganter, *The Pearl-Shellers of Torres Strait*, 1994:35ff.
20 Searcy, *In Australian Tropics*, 1984:78 and Bain, *Full Fathom Five*, 1982:76. Bain describes the vessel as the former property of the Rajah of Pas Sair, noting it as a 112-ton brigantine with eight long boats and twenty-one dinghies.
21 Bain, *Full Fathom Five*, 1982:79.
22 Ibid., 1982:34, 81; Searcy, *In Australian Tropics*, 1984:315.
23 David Sissons, 'The Japanese in the Australian pearling industry', 1979:5; Bain, *Full Fathom Five*, 1982:92.
24 Bain, *Full Fathom Five*, 1982:87; Sissons, 'The Japanese in the Australian pearling industry', 1979.
25 The preamble of the Act referred to Indians, Chinese, Africans, Malays and Pacific Islanders. Bain, *Full Fathom Five*, 1982:95.
26 Ibid., 96; K. Watanabe, 'Sasude-to oyobi Toresu-Kaiko Tanken Hokoku', ca. 1894:39.
27 Douglas, 1898:427 cited in Ganter, *The Pearl-Shellers of Torres Strait*, 1994:105.
28 Evidence by Wells, Flamsteed and Graham, in John Mackay, 'Report of the Royal Commission appointed to enquire into the working of the Pearl-shell and Bêche-de-Mer Industries', 1908 (2):242, 239; F. W. Bamford, 'Royal Commission on the Pearl-Shelling Industry Progress Report', 1913:110.
29 Evidence by Evanson, in Mackay, 'Report of the Royal Commission', 1908:236.
30 W. Dashwood 'Pearl-shelling industry in Port Darwin and Northern Territory', 1902 (2):21–91; Mackay, 'Report of the Royal Commission', 1908; F. W. Bamford, 'Royal Commission on the Pearl-Shelling Industry Report and Recommendations', 1914–17, vol. 5:831–41.
31 Bain, *Full Fathom Five*, 1982:104.
32 Ibid., 98–9.
33 J. P. S. Bach, 'The pearling industry of Australia: an account of its social and economic development', 1956:292.
34 Based on figures by Bach, 1956:277, 278, 280.
35 Ganter, *The Pearl-Shellers of Torres Strait*, 1994:117.
36 Ibid., Chapter 4, for exploration of the question of extra-territorial pearling.
37 Ibid., Chapter 6, for description of Australian pearlers' disunity as a major marketing weakness.
38 Ibid., for development of these arguments, too.

CHAPTER 4: ABORIGINAL PROTECTION, ASIAN EXCLUSION

1 Regina Ganter, 'Letters from Mapoon: colonising Aboriginal gender', 1999: 267–302.
2 Nicholas Hey, report to the Colonial Secretary, 1.7.1897, Mf186, AIATSIS.
3 Evidence by Hey in John Mackay (Chair), 'Report of the Royal Commission appointed to enquire into the working of the Pearl-shell and Bêche-de-Mer Industries', 1908:218.
4 Ibid., 1908:220.
5 Athol Chase, '"All kind of nation": Aborigines and Asians in Cape York Peninsula', vol. 5, no. 1: 1981:13.
6 Interview with Sandy Yiela, Lockhart River, 3.1.1987.
7 Interview with Bob Flinders, at age seventy-two, at Hopevale, 19.1.1986. Flinders is referring to the Queensland Department of Aboriginal and Islander Affairs, and the disastrous wartime evacuation of Hopevale residents to Woorabinda reserve in Central Queensland.
8 Interview with Ambidjambi (Frank Ambi) at Minjilang, Croker Island, 3.6.1995.
9 W. Parry-Okeden, 'Report on the North Queensland Aborigines and the Native Police', vol. 2, 1897.
10 Nicholas Hey, Annual Report for Mapoon 1906, Mf186, AIATSIS.
11 Arthur Richter, Annual Report for Aurukun, 1907, Mf171, AIATSIS.
12 Desmond Manderson, *From Mr Sin to Mr Big*, 1993:36. See also Cathie May, *Topsawyers: the Chinese in Cairns 1870 to 1920*, 1984:226–8.
13 Examination of Roth by the Legislative Council of Queensland, 8.10.1901, QPP vol. LXXXVII 1901:1136. Initially Walter Roth and Archibald Meston were appointed as northern and southern protectors respectively. Meston was eased out of office and Roth became chief protector in 1904. Regina Ganter and Ros Kidd, 'The powers of protectors: conflicts surrounding Queensland's 1897 Aboriginal Legislation', 25 (101):536–54.
14 Roth to Under Secretary, Home Department, 21.1.1901, QSA A/58764.
15 QPP vol. LXXXVII, 1901:596.
16 Statement by Putt, Atherton Farmers' and Progress Association, in Roth 20.9.1898, QSA col. 142.
17 Examination of Walter Roth, 8.10.1901, QPP vol. LXXXVII, 1901:1141.
18 Constable McKenna, Mossman Police Station to CPA, 23.8.1901, QSA A/58764.
19 4.3.1901 and 26.9.1901, QSA A/58764.
20 CPA to (Murray Island woman) 19.2.1913, QSA A/58767; Normanton Protector to CPA, 8.1.1906, QSA A/44680; Cairns Protector to CPA, 23.3.1905, QSA A/44680; Roth Progress Report, October 1902, QSA A/44679.
21 John Dimmock, Landclaim Book, with kind permission of the Carpentaria Land Council. Supplemented with details from QSA A/69441 and QSA A/69434.
22 Edward Byron Reuter, *The Mulatto in the United States*, 1970 (1918).
23 Still the most incisive description of the lugger strike and its effects on Torres Strait is Nonie Sharp's 'Culture clash in the Torres Strait Islands: the maritime strike of 1936', 11 (3):107–26.
24 Until 1872 all Torres Strait Islanders were regarded as Pacific Islanders 'not under the influence of any civilised power', and those north of 10th degree latitude—in the northern half of the Strait—were so classed until 1879.

25 Interview with Starchy Ahwang, Mackay, 26.6.1997.

26 Lee-Bryce, Protector at Thursday Island to CPA, 14.3.1914, QSA A/58761.

27 Ibid.

28 Removals Register, 1914:65–6, QSA Z2688.

29 Clara Riley to CPA, 11.7.1914, QSA A/58761.

30 28.9.1914, 'Order for Removal of Aboriginal under Section 9/1897 and Section 3/1901', QSA A/58761; and 22.7.1914, CPA to Under Secretary, Home Department, QSA A/58761.

31 CPA to Lee-Bryce, 21.7.1914, QSA A/58761; and Clara Riley to Atima Ahwang at Barambah, 4.10.1914, QSA A/58761.

32 Lee-Bryce to CPA, 14.8.1914, QSA A/58761; and CPA to Under Secretary, Home Department, 22.7.1914, QSA A/58761. This letter was annotated 'Bleakley to see me.'

33 Lee-Bryce to CPA, 16.2.1915, QSA A/58761.

34 Lee-Bryce to CPA, 4.10.1915, QSA A/58800; and interviews with Rocky Ahwang, Hervey Bay, and Starchy Ahwang, Mackay, 1997.

35 CPA to Protector at Thursday Island, 23.10.1917, QSA A/58761.

36 Atima Ahwang to CPA Bleakley, 9.11.1917, QSA A/58761.

37 Protector at Thursday Island to CPA, 16.6.1919, QSA A/58761.

38 Walter Filewood to CPA, 14.10.1920, Filewood to Home Secretary, 20.10.1920, QSA A/58761.

39 CPA to Home Secretary, 18.5.1921, QSA A/58761.

40 Protector at Thursday Island to CPA, 24.6.1921, and Crown Solicitor to Under Secretary, Home Secretary's Office, 26.7.1921, QSA A/58761.

41 Protector Holmes at Thursday Island to CPA, 7.4.1921, QSA A/58761.

42 Protector Holmes at Thursday Island to CPA, 10.8.1921.

43 Protector O'Leary at Thursday Island to CPA, 1.6.1923, QSA A/58761.

44 CPA to Protector at Thursday Island, 6.8.1923, QSA A/58761.

45 Crowther in WAPP 1886:192.

46 Hansard for the Legislative Assembly, 14.1.1892, WAPP 1892–93:245ff.

47 Ibid.

48 Forbes, Secretary of the Aborigines Protection Board to Onslow, Administrator of WA, 17.5.1892 in correspondence re APB, WAPP.

49 Aborigines Department Report for 1898–99, WAPP 1899.

50 Chief Protector Prinsep, Aborigines Department Report to June 1900, in WAPP 1900.

51 Sub-inspector Duncan at Derby, re Kimberley, in Aborigines Department Report, WAPP 1903–04.

52 Appendix 5, WAPP 1903–04.

53 G. S. Olivey, WAPP V&P, 1903–04, Aborigines Department Report to June 1903, Appendix 7.

54 Ibid.

55 WAPP 1903–04, Appendix 9.

56 Prinsep, Annual Report of the CPA to June 1904.

57 Prinsep, CPA report to June 1902.

58 Two of the nine boys were married to Beagle Bay girls in 1918, three ran away in January 1919, one had been taken away for being troublesome, and by 1919 there was only one left. Eugene Perez, *Kalumburu*, 1977.

59 Mary Durack, *The Rock and the Sand*, 1969:183–4.

60 Interview with Theresa Puertollano, Derby, 29.8.1994. She believes the other Filipinos found their wives in Broome. Her mother, Agnes O'Brien was the daughter of Irishman Patrick O'Brien and Helina. Helina's mother was Aboriginal, but her paternal descent is uncertain. Theresa was told that her grandmother was 'coloured', perhaps from an Asian father. Helina must have been born between 1865 and 1885.

61 Durack, *The Rock and the Sand*, 1969:218.

62 Ibid., 79.

63 Margaret Zucker, *From Patrons to Partners: A History of the Catholic Church in the Kimberley, 1884–1984*, 1994:43.

64 Durack, *The Rock and the Sand*, 1969:128.

65 Ibid., 96.

66 Elizabeth Salter, *Daisy Bates*, 1971:86, 223.

67 Zucker, *From Patrons to Partners*, 1994:50, citing *Morning Herald*, 31.1.1901.

68 CPA Neville to Colonial Secretary, 11.10.1917, in Zucker, *From Patrons to Partners*, 1994:76.

69 Ibid., 48.

70 Ibid., 60.

71 Ibid., 77.

72 Perez, *Kalumburu*, 1977.

73 Durack, *The Rock and the Sand*, 1969:190.

74 Ibid., 182–4.

75 Ibid., 189.

76 Zucker, *From Patrons to Partners*, 1994:61.

77 Ibid., 77.

78 Anna Haebich, *For Their Own Good*, 1988:166ff.

79 Prinsep, CPA report to June 1907.

80 Gale, CPA report to June 1909.

81 Isdell, travelling inspector, in Gale, CPA report to June 1909.

82 Gale, CPA report to 1908.

83 Gale, CPA report to June 1911.

84 R.D. Moseley, Report of the Royal Commissioner Appointed to Investigate, Report and Advise upon Matters in Relation to the Condition and Treatment of Aborigines, WAPP 1935.

85 Haebich, *For Their Own Good*, 1988:148ff.

86 Ibid., 258.

87 Ibid., 315. Haebich sees the *Native Administration Act 1936* as a 'direct result' of the Moseley commission, although 'its provisions showed the stamp of Neville rather than Moseley'. Predictably, Neville disagreed with Moseley on the question of the curtailment of his own powers, and on his critique of Moore River settlement, but overall Neville thought the report was a 'vindication' of his policies. Haebich, *For Their Own Good*, 1988:342–3.

88 Moseley Report, 1935:1, 9, 13.

89 Ibid., 7.

90 Ibid., 14.

91 Ibid., 8, 9, 19.

92 The Aboriginal evidence is described by Haebich, *For Their Own Good*, 1988:335.

93 Neville, CPA report to June 1936, WAPP 1936, 1st session, vol. 2.

94 Zucker, *From Patrons to Partners*, 1994:100–13.

95 Durack, *The Rock and the Sand*, 1969:229.

96 Interview with Theresa Puertollano, Derby, 29.8.1994.

97 Neville, Annual Report of the Commissioner of Native Affairs , WAPP 1938, vol. 1.

[98] Haebich, *For Their Own Good*, 1988:344. Excepted from the definition of 'native' were: 1) quadroons under twenty-one years who did not habitually associate, unless so classed by order of a magistrate; 2) quadroons over twenty-one years, unless so classed by a magistrate or who requested to be included, 3) persons of less than quadroon blood born before 1937.

[99] Mary Albertus Bain, *Full Fathom Five*, 1982:208, 219.

[100] Interview with (name withheld), Minjilang, Croker Island, 3.6.1995.

[101] Ian McIntosh, *The Whale and the Cross—Conversations with David Burrumarra MBE*, 1994:21.

[102] He was first recruited for the *Tubu Maru* (Tubumaro) at Galiwin'ku in the 1930s. In 1938 he joined Fred Gray's station at Umbakumba, Groote Eylandt, and in the 1950s he acquired a lugger with federal government assistance. McIntosh, *The Whale and the Cross*, 1994:10, 13, 85.

[103] *Northern Territory Dictionary of Biography*, vol. I:222–5; Ted Egan, *A Justice All Their Own—The Caledon Bay and Woodah Island Killings 1932–1933*, 1996:22.

[104] Daly River Police Journals, 1906–34, NT Archives, courtesy Darrel Lewis.

[105] Egan, *A Justice All Their Own*, 1996:98.

[106] Ibid.

[107] Interview with Fred Gray, Howard Springs, 4.6.1994.

[108] Egan, *A Justice All Their Own*, 1996:38.

[109] Ibid., 38; Fred Gray interview; McIntosh, *The Whale and the Cross*, 1994:passim.

[110] C. D. Rowley, *The Destruction of Aboriginal Societies*, 1970:295.

[111] Ibid., 314, 305.

[112] Neville, CPA report to June 1936 WAPP 1936; and Rowley, *The Destruction of Aboriginal Societies*, 1970:298.

[113] Interview with Tex and Nellie Camfoo, Bulman, 14.5.1995. For other sources on Tex Camfoo, cf. Gillian Cowlishaw, 'Talking history', 1995:30–1; and Gillian Cowlishaw, *Love Against the Law*, 2000.

[114] Rosalind Kidd, *The Way We Civilize*, 1997:109, 346.

[115] Timothy Jones, *The Chinese in the Northern Territory*, 1990:109.

CHAPTER 5: ETHNIC POLICY AND PRACTICE IN DARWIN *by Julia Martinez*

[1] Alan Powell, *Far Country—A Short History of the Northern Territory*, 1982:83.

[2] Douglas Lockwood, *The Front Door, Darwin, 1869–1969*, 1969:93.

[3] Ibid., 64.

[4] Margaret Rendell, 'The Chinese in South Australia and the Northern Territory in the nineteenth century', 1952:47–9.

[5] William Sowden, *The Northern Territory As It Is*, 1882:124.

[6] Lockwood, *The Front Door*, 1969:125.

[7] M. Stanley, Inspector of Fisheries and Chief Pearling Inspector, Report on the Administration of the Northern Territory for the Year Ended 30th of July 1932, CPP 1932.

[8] Powell, *Far Country*, 1982:105.

[9] Eric Rolls, *Sojourners: The Epic Story of China's Centuries-Old Relationship with Australia: Flowers and the Wide Sea*, 1992:28.

[10] Inez Cubillo Carter, 'Cubillo, Delfin Antonio (1913–1986)', in *Northern Territory Dictionary of Biography* (NTDB), vol. 2, 1992:43–4.

[11] Elsie Masson, *Untamed Territory: the Northern Territory of Australia*, 1915:51.

[12] Census figures for Darwin, five-mile radius, 1911 A1/15 11/16191, National Archives of Australia, Australian Capital Territory (hereafter NAA ACT).

[13] Powell, *Far Country*, 1982:161.

[14] *Aboriginals Ordinance 1911*, No. 16 of 1911, *Commonwealth of Australia Gazette* no. 2, Melbourne, 8.1.1912.

[15] J. T. Beckett to Dr H. Basedow, Chief Protector and Chief Medical Inspector, 29.7.1911, A1/1 1912/10964, NAA ACT.

[16] For a more detailed account of Spencer's activities in Darwin see D. J. Mulvaney & J. H. Calaby, 'So much that is new', 1985:278–84; Baldwin Spencer, *Wanderings in Wild Australia*, 1928, vol. 2:602–10.

[17] Baldwin Spencer to Atlee Hunt, 15.4.1912, Atlee Hunt Papers, MS 52/1042, NLA; Spencer in Annual Report of the Northern Territory, CPP 1912:42.

[18] Tony Austin, *I Can Picture the Old Home So Clearly: The Commonwealth and 'Half-Caste' Youth in the Northern Territory, 1911–1939*, 1993:45; see also Russell McGregor, *Imagined Destinies, Aboriginal Australians and the Doomed Race Theory, 1880–1939*, 1997:79.

[19] Cited in Powell, *Far Country*, 1982:163.

[20] Ibid.

[21] 'The Larrakeyah tribe, deputation to visit Col. Weddell', *Northern Standard*, 24.3.1936.

[22] Report on Northern Territory, 1922, A1/15 1927/7835; Customs Form, Darwin, 14.4. 1916, Statutory Declaration signed by Ah Sing, born Canton, Minute Paper, Department of Home and Territories, 4.6.1919, A1/15 19/8168, NAA ACT.

[23] Diana Giese, *Beyond Chinatown: Changing Perspectives on the Top End Chinese Experience*, 1995:43; Suzi Hutchings, 'The Darwin Chinese 1874–1983, transformations in ethnic identity and its situation', 1983:37.

[24] Giese, *Beyond Chinatown*, 1995:10–11.

[25] Eric Sager, *Discovering Darwin: the 1930s in Memory and History*, 1993:6.

[26] Giese, *Beyond Chinatown*, 1995:11.

[27] Lorraine Philipps, 'Plenty more little brown man! Pearlshelling and White Australia in Queensland 1901–1918', 1980:58.

[28] Ibid., 73–5.

[29] Bamford, Final Report, 1916, cited in Regina Ganter, *The Pearl-Shellers of Torres Strait, Resource Use, Development and Decline, 1860s–1960s*, 1994:114; see also 'Pearling Conditions', A1/15 1914/12612, NAA ACT; Philipps, 'Plenty more little brown man!', 1980:62–73.

[30] J. H. Kelly and J. T. Beckett, Report to the Chief Protector of Aborigines, 11.8.1911, A1/1 1912/10964, NAA ACT.

[31] S. Mitchell to the Minister for External Affairs, 1911:4, A1/1 1912/2937, NAA ACT.

[32] Powell, *Far Country*, 1982:161.

[33] Annual report for the Northern Territory, CPP 1911:5, 1912:42.

[34] Acting Administrator, S. Mitchell to External Affairs, 7.9.1911, A1/1 1912.2937, NAA ACT.

[35] Chinese storekeepers to Justice Mitchell, Government Resident, 22.3.1911, A1/1 1912/10547, NAA ACT.

[36] J. Symes, Solicitor, to Baldwin Spencer, 14.2.1912, A1/1 1912/6611, NAA ACT.

37 Petition from residents to Josiah Thomas, Minister for External Affairs; Atlee Hunt to Administrator of Northern Territory, 30.5.1912, A/1 1912/6611, NAA ACT.

38 H. E. Carey, Chief Protector of Aboriginals, Annual Report of the Northern Territory, 1917–18:44.

39 MacDonald, Superintendent of Kahlin Compound, Annual Report, 1917–18:45.

40 Bleakley Report, Curfew imposed by Protector Robert Macdonald, *Government Gazette, Northern Territory Times,* 14.10.1920:12.

41 W. L. Fothergill, Acting Chief Protector of Aboriginals, Report on the Administration, 1930.

42 *Northern Standard*, *Government Gazette*, 3.1.1936.

43 Aboriginals Ordinance, Section 30:941.

44 Report of the Chief Protector, in Report on the Administration of the Northern Territory for Year Ended 30.6.1936.

45 C. L. A. Abbott, Report on the Administration of the Northern Territory for the Year ended 1937.

46 Abbott, Report on the Administration of the Northern Territory, 1938.

47 Andrew Markus, *Governing Savages*, 1990:14–15.

48 In this document he gave permission for two marriages, one to a man from Chile and another to a man from the Philippines. 'Northern Territory. Marriage with Aboriginals', A1/1 1912/3519, NAA ACT.

49 J. T. Beckett in Commonwealth of Australia, Royal Commission on the Northern Territory, Minutes of Evidence, 1920:177.

50 In 1888 there had been five Japanese brothels with twenty-five prostitutes. D. C. S. Sissons, '*Karayuki-San*: Japanese Prostitutes in Australia, 1887–1916', 1976–77:328.

51 Ordinance No. 9 of 1918, *Government Gazette*, 26.10.1918.

52 For further discussion of Aboriginal women and sexual relations with white men, see Ann McGrath, '"Black Velvet"', 1987:68–94.

53 Owen Rowe, 'Aboriginal employment and conditions in the Northern Territory', 16.3.1932, ACTU Papers, N21/48 ACTU WA and Darwin.

54 Gordon Reid, *A Picnic with the Natives, Aboriginal–European Relations in the Northern Territory to 1910*, 1990:195.

55 'Return of Halfcastes and Quadroons in the Northern Territory', A1/1 1926/5350, NAA ACT.

56 Jessie Litchfield, 'Press collect', unpublished manuscript, p. 107, MS 132, NLA.

57 Cook, Chief Protector of Aboriginals, to the Administrator, 23.7.1932, A1/1 33/479, NAA ACT.

58 Report on the Administration of the Northern Territory, 1931.

59 Cook to Administrator, 8.7.1936, A1/1 37/70, NAA ACT

60 F. J. Quinlan to Sub-Collector of Customs, Darwin, 31.8.1925, A1/15 30/880, NAA ACT.

61 Clifford Pierce, Sub-Collector of Customs, Memo to Home and Territories Department, 29.10.1928, A1/15 30/880, NAA ACT.

62 *Northern Standard*, 7.1.1936.

63 Gregory & Company for Darwin Pearlers' Committee to Administrator, 28.10.1936, F1 1937/600, NAA Northern Territory (hereafter NAA NT).

64 Julia Martinez, 'The "Malay" community in pre-war Darwin', 1999:45.

65 A. E. Koop, Sgt, to Superintendent of Police, Stretton, Darwin, 18.10.1936, F1 1936/220, NAA NT.

66 Nylander to Crown Law Officer, Darwin, 30.10.1936, F1 1936/220, NAA NT.

67 'VD epidemic scandal', *Northern Standard*, 2.3.1937.

68 Memo, Department of the Interior, 1.9.1936, A1/1 36/9564, NAA ACT.

69 Report of Constable Don, Darwin, 9.10.1936, F1 1937/600, NAA NT.

70 Report by G. T. Goldsmith, Missionary in Charge, Goulburn Island, 5.12.1936, F1 37/600, NAA NT.

71 *Northern Standard*, 8.2.1938. The same issue gives the office-bearers of the Japanese Society as: President, I. Okada; Vice-President, M. Kusumoto; Treasurer, K. Mise; Auditors, Y. Saito and G. Naga; Committee, S. Imae, G. Murakami, S. Hakiyama, S. Kojima, R. Takahara, C. Tano, K. Hoshikawa, T. Ano.

72 'Round about', *Northern Standard*, 16.4.1937.

73 John Magripilis, transcript of interview by Helen Wilson, 1994, TS 802, NTRS 266, Northern Territory Archive Service; see Xavier Herbert, *Capricornia*, 1938:17–18.

74 Deputation from Residents of Darwin, 6.5.1912, A1/15 1912/10548, NAA ACT.

75 Fannie Bell to Nelson, 5.6.1926, A1/15 38/10188, NAA ACT.

76 T. W. Glasgow, to H. G. Nelson, MP Parliament House, 30.7.1926, A1/15 38/10188, NAA ACT.

77 Maude Allwright to Head Teacher, Mr Lampe, 28.8.1925, A1/15 38/10188, NAA ACT.

78 Giese, *Beyond Chinatown*, 1995:43–4.

79 *Northern Standard*, 12.1.1926, 17.4.1931.

80 Annual Convention, 1914:35, AWU Papers, Noel Butlin Archives Centre, ANU.

81 Verity Burgmann, *Revolutionary Industrial Unionism, The Industrial Workers of the World in Australia*, Melbourne, 1995:90.

82 North Australian Workers Union, 'Constitution and General Rules', Rule 6, Mitchell Library, NSW; Andrew Markus, "Talka longa mouth", Aborigines and the Labour Movement, 1890–1970', 1978:149.

83 'NAWU', *Northern Standard*, 28.8.1928.

84 'Australian Chinese Reception for Mr Nelson', *Northern Standard*, 25.9.1928.

85 *Workers' Weekly,* 13.4.1928; Markus, "Talka longa mouth", 1978:149.

86 *Workers' Weekly*, 30.5.1930:2.

87 *Workers' Weekly*, 6.11.1931:4.

88 *Workers' Weekly*, 24.9.1931:2.

89 Mahoney was leader of the Unemployed Workers' Movement in Darwin and was arrested during their 1931 protests. See A1/1 31/4202, *NT Times*, 30.1.1931, 21.3.1931; 24.4.1931 NAA ACT; Lockwood, *The Front Door*, 1969: 242–7.

90 Letter of protest by F. Martin, Secretary of the Unemployed Workers' Movement, *Northern Standard*, 25.8.1931.

91 Val McGinness, transcript of interview by Janet Dickinson, tape 4, p. 1, TS 532, NTRS 226, 1984, NTAS.

92 *Northern Standard*, 12.6.1936.

93 McDonald, 'Indentured labor in Darwin, White Australian policy flouted', *Northern Standard*, 24.1.1936, 'Union Notes', *Northern Standard*, 28.2.1936.

94 Abbott to the Department of the Interior, 10.11.1937, F1 1939/68, NAA NT.

95 R. H. Weddell to Department of the Interior, 10.12.1934, 654/1, 40/1/2189, NAA ACT.

96 Interview by author with Frank Ah Mat, Darwin, 13.6.1997; *Northern Standard*, 8.7.1932.

97 Carter, 'Cubillo, Delphin Antonio', 1992: 43–4.

98 'Carry on executive', *Northern Standard*, 9.1.1940.

99 The discriminatory membership rules were officially changed in 1948. Markus, "Talka longa mouth", 1978:152.

100 Ibid., 72.

101 Richard Broome, 'Enduring moments of Aboriginal dominance: Aboriginal performers, boxers and runners', 1995:171; SBS documentary, *As it Happened: Buffalo Legends*, screened 25.9.1997.

102 Anne Briggs, 'Cooper, Reuben John (1898–ca.1942), in *Northern Territory Dictionary of Biography*, vol. 1, 1990:62.

103 'Football', *Northern Territory Times*, 24.1.1920; 20.4.1920.

104 The Buffaloes team was formed in 1916 by Reuben Cooper after some members of a combined team had objected to playing with a 'half-caste'. Nevertheless, Cooper went on to play for Vesteys as their only 'coloured' player. He still played for the Buffaloes in 1937. *Northern Standard*, 13.11.1936, 5.1.1937; *Northern Territory Times*, 16.3.1916, 29.9.1916.

105 Robert Ah Mat previously played for Collingwood. See *Sydney Morning Herald*, 30.4.1997:45.

106 'NT Football League', suggesting the oval be restricted to 'whites', *Northern Standard*, 12.11.1926.

107 'Football', *Northern Standard*, 28.1.1927.

108 *Northern Standard*, 29.3.1927.

109 *Northern Standard*, 7.1.1927.

110 Memorandum and Articles of Association of the Chinese Nationalist Party of Australasia, 1921, in C. F. Yong, *The New Gold Mountain: The Chinese in Australia 1901–1921,* 1977:268.

111 Giese, *Beyond Chinatown*, 1995:35.

112 *Northern Standard*, 4.2.1927.

113 The Chinese players were: W. Lee, A. Jan, P. Jan, W. Jan, J. Ket, J. Lee, T. Lee, A. Fong, C. Fong, Kim Chack, See Pon, Loong Pack, H. Hing, and S. Jan. 'Soccer football', *Northern Standard*, 4.2.1927.

114 'Readmittance of coloured players', *Northern Standard*, 11.12.1928.

115 'Football', *Northern Standard*, 13.1.1933, 17.1.1933 and 20.1.1933; 'Juvenile football', *Northern Standard*, 6.3.1931

116 *Northern Standard*, 22.1.1937.

CHAPTER 6: THE POLYETHNIC NORTH

1 Marcia Langton, 'Urbanizing Aborigines: the social scientists' great deception', 1981:21.

2 Henry Chan has recently raised this as an issue for further detailed research. Pers. comm.

3 *Kwong Sue Duk—A Man of Family*, 1995.

4 Taam Sz Pui, *My Life and Work*, 1925.

5 Interview with Herbert See Poy (Jnr), Innisfail, June 1997.

6 Interviews with Albert Que Noy, June 1994, Marjorie Foster, Knuckey's Lagoon, 6.6.1994, Joan Kenyon, Humpty Doo, June 1994.

7 Diana Giese, *Astronauts, Lost Souls and Dragons—Voices of Today's Chinese Australians in Conversation with Diana Giese*, 1997:43–5. See also Diana Giese, *Beyond Chinatown: Changing Perspectives on the Top End Chinese Experience*, 1995.

8 Sarah Yu and Carol Tang Wei, 'The story of the Chinese in Broome', ca. 1998.

9 Interview with George Wah Day, Pine Creek, Gordonvale, 26.7.1997.

10 O'Leary, protector at Thursday Island, to CPA 10 December 1924, QSA A/58735. This application was granted. A 1921 application by Tommy Ah Fat from Normanton, submitted with deleterious comments by Protector Holmes at Thursday Island, and supported by union representative Walter Filewood, had been unsuccessful.

11 A. Corran, mayor of Thursday Island, to Protector, Thursday Island, 13.7.1920, and statements by Glamor Garr and Licoura Boota, QSA A/69414.

12 Ellen Cramond, unpublished MS held by Lily Ah Toy, Darwin.

13 Notes by Lily Ah Toy, Darwin, 19.7.1994. Ellen Cramond was her sister-in-law. Their clan name was Cheong.

14 Interview by Ann McGrath with Lily Ah Toy, Northern Territory Archives Oral History Project.

15 Entry 130/07 in Police Letterbook 1906–11, QSA 485/1.

16 J. Davis, Burketown protector, annual report for 1934. QSA A/58650.

17 Police Inspector Kennedy, Burketown, 'Report on murders of deceased Aboriginal Gin Lucy and her Chinese half-caste child Topsy' to Commissioner of Police, 2.5.1895, QSA A/45277.

18 Protector at Burketown wire to CPA, 13.11.1908, QSA A/58765.

19 George Farwell, *Ghost Towns of Australia*, 1976:152.

20 Paul Savage, *Christie Palmerston, Explorer*, 1992:71.

21 Hector Holthouse, *River of Gold—The Wild Days of the Palmer River Gold Rush*, 1967:106–8.

22 Ibid., 108.

23 Michael Pickering, 'Cannibalism among Aborigines', 1985.

24 Interviews with Billy Burchell (age eighty-eight) at Wonga Beach, Mossman, 3.7.1997, George Kulka, China Camp, 5.7.1997, Peter Fischer (age seventy-eight), China Camp, 4.7.1997.

25 Interview with Peter Costello, Hopevale, 8.8.1997.

26 Sz Pui, *My Life and Work*, 1925.

27 Interview with Moody Leon, Mt Isa, 9.8.1997.

28 Tim Jones, *The Chinese in the Northern Territory*, 1997:72.

29 J. Bourke, police inspector Normanton, to CPA, 20.11.1912, QSA A/69433.

30 Interview with Moody and Albert Leon and Ethel Clark, Mt Isa, 9.8.1997.

31 Interview with Steven Alberts, Broome, 3.9.1994.

32 List of aliens resident at Thursday Island, 29.5.1941, AA Qld BP 242/1#Q30511.

33 Interview with Hagiga bin Doraho, Thursday Island, 20.7.1997.

34 Yuriko Nagata, 'Japanese–Australians in the postwar Thursday Island community', 1999:33.

35 Yuriko Nagata, *Unwanted Aliens*, 1996:30, 54, 58; AA BP 242/1 Q2403, interview with Arthur and Kate Yamaguchi, Mt Isa, 6.8.1997.

36 Interview with Narelle Brown, Mackay, 6.8.1997.

37 Interview with Starchy Ahwang, Mackay, 26.6.1997.

38 W. Saville-Kent, 1890:730 cited in Yoshiharu Abe, 'The trepang industry in the Pacific and Southeast Asia: an anthropological and historical study', 1995:40.

39 Interview with Peter Costello, Hopevale, 8.7.1997.
40 Sub-Collector of Customs, Mackay, 24.5.1926, AA J2773/1, 670/26.
41 Peter Forrest, *The Spirit of the Daly*, 1994:66–7.
42 Elena Govor, *My Dark Brother*, 2000:126ff.
43 W. L. Clough, Lands Branch officer, 1947 in Forrest, *The Spirit of the Daly*, 1994:54.
44 The song appears in the *Ted Egan Songbook*, on the back cover of Forrest's history of the Daly, and in the Malak Malak land claim.
45 *Northern Territory Times and Gazette*, 5.10.1906, 3.8.1906, 1.11.1907, 6.11.1908, 31.12.1914. Courtesy Darrell Lewis.
46 Daly River Police Journals 1906–34, NT Archives, courtesy Darrell Lewis.
47 Interview with Lily Ah Toy, Darwin, June 1994.
48 Interview with Joan Kenyon, Humpty Doo, June 1994.
49 Interview with Marjorie Foster, Knuckey's Lagoon, 6.6.1994.
50 Interview with Arthur Que Noy, Winnellie, June 1994.
51 Interviews with Lily Ah Toy and Albert Que Noy, June 1994.
52 Forrest, *The Spirit of the Daly*, 1994:66.
53 Interview with Marjorie Foster, Knuckey's Lagoon, 6.6.1994.
54 Interview with Sunlight Bassini, Coen, July 1997.
55 Regina Ganter, 'The Japanese experience of the Great Barrier Reef', 1987.
56 Interview with Len Royee, Gordonvale, 26.7.1997. See also Robert Dixon, *Words of Our Country*, 1991, on Alick Morgan, Len's grandfather.
57 Sarah Yu, 'Broome Creole: Aboriginal and Asian partnerships along the Kimberley Coast', 1999:66–7.
58 Bray to Holy Child Orphanage, 18.12.1942, 113/45 Native Affairs file. By courtesy of Mary Ann Sahanna.
59 Sr Margaret to Bray, 25.2.1944. By courtesy of Mary Ann Sahanna.
60 F. Williams, Native Hospital Broome to Bray, 19.4.1944. By courtesy of Mary Ann Sahanna.
61 *Walkabout*, 1.10.1946:11–12.
62 *Cubillo v. Commonwealth of Australia*, Federal Court of Australia 1084, 11.8.2000. Usually referred to as the *Stolen Generations Case*.
63 Charlie McAdam, *Boundary Lines*, 1995:81.
64 Michael Cigler, *The Afghans in Australia*, 1986:2–3, 32ff.
65 Christine Stevens, *Tin Mosques and Ghantowns, A History of Afghan Cameldrivers in Australia*, 1989:22.
66 Legislative Assembly Hansard, 1892–93:401ff and 11.3.1892 p.847, WAPP.
67 Stevens, *Tin Mosques and Ghantowns*, 1989:140ff.
68 The order in council exempting Mahomet's shipment from new regulations was gazetted on 24.5.1901. It was cancelled by notice from Premier Throssel, who had taken office in March, on 1.6.1901.
69 Stevens, *Tin Mosques and Ghantowns*, 1989:24. This refers to 500 camels brought to Port Hedland on the *Century* by a syndicate associated with the Perth mosque, which sustained a huge debt as the animals were placed under quarantine.
70 Cigler, *The Afghans in Australia*, 1986:41.
71 Stevens, *Tin Mosques and Ghantowns*, 1989:5.
72 Gus Bottrill 'Sahanna—a precis of Gus Bottril's notes on Sahanna, "Afghan" squatter, cameleer and sandalwooder of Moonlight Valley, East Kimberely, WA', ca. 1993.
73 Stevens, *Tin Mosques and Ghantowns*, 1989:24–6.
74 Notes of the Wyndham Historical Society, based on an interview in August 1990. According to these notes the original shop-owner who devolved the shop to his father was a white man, but Billy remembers him as a Chinese. Interview with Billy Lee Tong, Wyndham.
75 Jeremy Hodes, 'Torres Strait Islander migration to Cairns before World War II', 1998, Appendix 6.
76 Interview with Kathleen Ketchell (née Lui), Cairns, 2.7.1997.
77 Interview with Lily Ah Toy, Darwin, June 1994.
78 Interview with Pedro Guivarra, Thursday Island, July 1997.
79 Vance Palmer, *Legend for Sanderson*, 1937.
80 Vance Palmer, 'People of the reef', 1935:25.
81 Ion Idriess, *One Wet Season*, 1967 (1949):31.
82 Hodes, 'Torres Strait Islander migration to Cairns', 1998:39.
83 Ibid., 27.
84 Cairns Historical Society library document, in Hodes, 'Torres Strait Islander migration to Cairns', 1989:32.
85 Hodes, 'Torres Strait Islander migration to Cairns', 1989:28–9.
86 Lee Bryce to CPA, 29.11.1916, in Hodes, 'Torres Strait Islander migration to Cairns', 1989:46.
87 Hodes, 'Torres Strait Islander migration to Cairns', 1989:45.
88 Ibid., 36, 10–11.
89 Ibid., 38.
90 Ibid., 37–9.
91 Ibid., 24, 21.
92 Ibid., 30–1.
93 Ibid., 31.
94 Interview with Starchy Ahwang, Mackay, 26.6.1997.
95 Interview with Pedro Guivarra, Thursday Island, July 1997.
96 Peter Dalton, 'Broome, a multiracial community', 1964:97.
97 Mary Albertus Bain, *Full Fathom Five*, 1982:320.
98 *Nor'West Echo*, 8.1.1921, in Michael Schaper, 'The Broome race riots of 1920', 1995.
99 *The Queenslander*, 23.6.1888, 7.7.1888:21.
100 Sarah Yu and Carol Tang Wei, 'The story of the Chinese in Broome', ca. 1998.
101 Interview with Pedro and Gloria Guivarra, Gladstone, 1994 and Thursday Island, July 1997.

CHAPTER 7: THE DECLINE OF THE POLYETHNIC NORTH

1 Alan Powell, *Far Country—A Short History of the Northern Territory*, 1982:203.
2 Yuriko Nagata, *Unwanted Aliens*, 1996:64.
3 List of aliens resident at Thursday Island, 29.5.1941, AA Qld BP 242/1#Q30511.
4 Nagata, *Unwanted Aliens*, passim, and Mary Albertus Bain, *Full Fathom Five*, 1982:320.
5 Robert Hall, *The Black Diggers*, 1997:27.
6 Powell, *Far Country*, 1982:190–200.
7 Bain, *Full Fathom Five*, 1982:320–40.
8 Hugh Edwards, *Port of Pearls: A History of Broome*, 1983:155, 157.
9 Bain, *Full Fathom Five*, 1982:340.
10 Powell, *Far Country*, 1982:204.
11 W. Prime, *Western Australia's Pearl Harbour: The Japanese Raid on Broome*, 1985:22; Bain, *Full Fathom*

Five, 1982:341. Hugh Edwards claims that in Broome a second air attack followed on 20 March on the township itself, causing only minor structural damage, but a number of casualties. W. Prime records four air-raids over Broome in March and August 1942. Bain, working from a 'list of raids on the Australian mainland' held in the Australian Archives, reports only one attack on Broome. She also refers to one on Thursday Island, while the general consensus is that Thursday Island was spared from attack. Beckett refers to only one air-raid in the Torres Strait. Neither the report of a second raid on Broome nor the one on Thursday Island fits the pattern of precision with which military installations were targeted by the Japanese forces.

12 Bain, *Full Fathom Five*, 1982:329.

13 Jeremy Beckett, *Torres Strait Islanders—Custom and Colonialism*, 1987:63.

14 Maurice Yonge, *A Year on the Great Barrier Reef*, 1930:168.

15 Internment policy document, 17.2.1941, in Nagata, *Unwanted Aliens*, 1996:47.

16 Regina Ganter, *The Pearl-Shellers of Torres Strait*, 1994:135–7.

17 Interview with Ogawa Taira (age seventy-four), 21.10.1987, Tanabe, Wakayama. See also his *Arafura-kai no Shinjo*, 1976. Former diver Wabuka Kyomi said that his uncle Horimoto marked the mines that were placed in Torres Strait on his charts. Horimoto Shinichi mentioned these mines in his interview, however, he was being interned at the time. Interview with Wabuka Kyomi, age sixty-seven, 20.10.1987, Susami, and interview with Horimoto Shinichi, Susami, 20.10.1987.

18 Bishop of Carpentaria to Atlee Hunt, 20.5.1909, AA ACT CRS AI 09-13685 and AA.ACT CRS AI 11/1594.

19 Peter Costello said that the mission had the *Pearl Queen*, and had friendly relations with the Japanese who would anchor at Cape Bedford Bay 'and they are really friendly people', though they didn't know much about getting trochus shell. Mission crews and the Japanese used to meet at Williamson Reef out of Port Douglas in the 1930s. Interview with Peter Costello, Hopevale, 8.7.1997.

20 Hall, *The Black Diggers*, 1997:116; see also Howard Pohlner, *Gangurru*, 1986.

21 A. Naylor, former superintendent of Yarrabah and Warangesda (Riverina, NSW), resident of Mantaka near Cairns, to the Commandant of Military Forces, Townsville, 28.1.1942, Australian War Memorial (AWM) 60 66/1/88.

22 Northern Command memo, 12.2.1942, AWM 60, 66/1/88.

23 Hall, *The Black Diggers*, 1997:10, 60.

24 Comments by the commanding officer of the RAAF unit at Karumba, in Hall, *The Black Diggers*, 1997:131.

25 Ibid., 140; see also P. Biskup, *Not Slaves, Not Citizens: The Aboriginal Problem in Western Australia, 1898–1954*, 1973:197.

26 Hall, *The Black Diggers*, 1997:116.

27 Ibid., 86, 95.

28 Ibid., 116–77, 120 note 27.

29 Ibid., 123.

30 Ibid., 125–7.

31 Powell, *Far Country*, 1982:214.

32 It is not clear when the evacuations referred to took place. Memo by Major General Brown at Queensland Headquarters, C Area, 14.6.1942, AWM 60, 91/1/4.

33 Stephen H. Davies, Bishop of Carpentaria, Townsville, to Deputy DNA O'Leary, 10.6.1942, QSA QS/505/IE/18.

34 Hall, *The Black Diggers*, 1997:119 note 23.

35 W. MacKenzie, Aurukun, to Mr Brown, 6.1.1942, QSA QS/505/IE/18.

36 David Garraway, moderator of the Presbyterian Church of Queensland to Minister of National Security, 20.1.1943, QSA QS/505/IE/18.

37 Hall, *The Black Diggers*, 1997:122.

38 O'Leary, Deputy Director of Native Affairs, to Public Service Commissioner, 29.9.1942, QSA QS/505/IE/18.

39 O'Leary to Acting Under Secretary, Health and Home Affairs, 17.3.1942, QSA A/4443.

40 Ibid.

41 Prime Minister to Queensland Premier, 21.2.1942; copy at Health and Home Affairs QSA A/4443.

42 O'Leary to Foote, Palm Island, 14.4.1942, QSA QS/505/ID/49.

43 Their homes were in Bunda Street, Draper Street, Florence Street, Buchan Street, Jubilee Lane, Aumuller Street, Spence Street, and a few in Shields Street, Lumley Lane and Maranoa Street.

44 Foote, Protector at Cairns and Acting Superintendent, Palm Island, to DNA, 1.5.1942, QSA QS/505/ID/49.

45 Powell, *Far Country*, 1982:210.

46 Hall, *The Black Diggers*, 1997:137ff.

47 Powell, *Far Country*, 1982:204, 216, 215.

48 Hall, *The Black Diggers*, 1997:86.

49 Powell, *Far Country*, 1982:215.

50 Hall, *The Black Diggers*, 1997:28.

51 Ibid., 111ff.

52 Powell, *Far Country*, 1982:208.

53 Hall, *The Black Diggers*, 1997:89, 99–104.

54 O'Leary to Foote, Palm Island, 17.4.1942, QSA QS 505/ID/49; Hall, *The Black Diggers*, 1997:38.

55 Beckett, *Torres Strait Islanders*, 1987:63; Hall, *The Black Diggers*, 1997:30.

56 Hall, *The Black Diggers*,1997:47, 66.

57 Beckett, *Torres Strait Islanders*, 1987:63.

58 Hall, *The Black Diggers*, 1997:47–52.

59 Ibid., 105.

60 Ibid., 106, 109.

61 Ibid., 130.

62 Ibid., 30.

63 Annual Report of the Commissioner of Native Affairs, to June 1945, WAPP 1947 vol. 2:9

64 Hall, *The Black Diggers*, 1997:30.

65 Ibid., 112.

66 Ian Welch, pers. comm., 2003.

67 Hall, *The Black Diggers*, 1997:59.

68 List of aliens resident at Thursday Island, 29.5.1941, AA Qld BP 242/1#Q30511.

69 Secret, n.d., 'Particulars of Anima Ahmat', NAA A367/1 C69559.

70 'Internments for Month of February 1943', AA Qld BP 242/1 Q39910, show the names of six women and their children. However, Nagata, *Unwanted Aliens*, mentions only four women by name. It is possible that the other two do not wish to be named.

71 Secret. n.d., 'Particulars of Anima Ahmat', NAA A367/1 C69559.

72 Ibid.

73 'Summary of Dossier and Precis of Case 4 December 1942', in BP 242/1 Q 24780, AA Qld.

74 Interview with Billy Shibasaki and Sariba (née bin Garape), Thursday Island, 19.7.1997.
75 Nagata, *Unwanted Aliens*, 1996:90–1.
76 Ibid., xi.
77 'General Headquarters Intelligence Summary 172', 10.4.1942, BP242/1/0 Q30579, AA Qld, in Kay Saunders & Helen Taylor, 'The enemy within? The process of internment of enemy aliens 1939–45', 1993:53.
78 Bain refers to a mimeographed manuscript, 'Aliens Control in Australia, 1939–46', written in 1971 by Noel Lamidey, former secretary of the Aliens Classification and Advisory Committee. He gives the total number of interned as 587, of which 247 were from Queensland and 251 from Western Australia. Bain 1982: 321. This is roughly half the number listed by Nagata.
79 Interview with Tatsuno Ryuhichi, age sixty-seven, 23.10.1987, Honai, Ehime.
80 Nagata, *Unwanted Aliens*, 1996:70.
81 Interview with Unoue Ushimatsu, age seventy-two, 18.10.1987, Miwazaki, Wakayama.
82 Nagata, *Unwanted Aliens*, 1996:68–71.
83 Interview with Horimoto Shinichi, age seventy-five, 20.10.1987, Susami, Wakayama.
84 Nagata, *Unwanted Aliens*, 1996:71.
85 Bain, *Full Fathom Five*, 1982:320, Nagata, *Unwanted Aliens*, 1996:71–4.
86 Nagata, *Unwanted Aliens*, 1996:117.
87 Interview with Phyllis Ah Loy, 19.7.1997, Thursday Island.
88 After sighting this evidence once in the Queensland branch of Australian Archives with my research assistant, and requesting a photocopy, we have been unable to retrieve the same set of documents for further perusal and referencing.
89 Nagata in Regina Ganter, 'Letters from Mapoon: colonising Aboriginal gender', 1999:36.
90 Interview with Billy Shibasaki, Thursday Island, 19.7.1997.
91 Nagata in Ganter, 'Letters from Mapoon', 1999:35–6.
92 Nagata, *Unwanted Aliens*, 1996:195, 227.
93 Ibid., 228.
94 Bain, *Full Fathom Five*, 1982:342.
95 Nagata in Ganter, 'Letters from Mapoon', 1999:33, 36.
96 Evelyn Suzuki, née Yamashita, in Nagata, *Unwanted Aliens*, 1996:230.
97 Interview with Billy Shibasaki, Thursday Island, 19.7.1997.
98 Bill Wong in Diana Giese, *Beyond Chinatown*, 1995:31.
99 Agnes Hannan, 'All out! The effects of evacuation and land acquisition on the Darwin Chinese 1941–1954', 1985:48, 74.
100 Giese, *Beyond Chinatown*, 1995:31.
101 Ibid., 31.
102 Ibid., 32.
103 Ibid.
104 Nagata, *Unwanted Aliens,* 1996: 138, 149.
105 A11797 WP 8258 NAA; and D1901/0#C974 James Chi, Loveday AA Qld.
106 Ibid.
107 Nagata, *Unwanted Aliens*, 1996:118.
108 A11797 WP 8258, NAA.
109 Hannan, 'All out!', 1985:48.
110 Bain, *Full Fathom Five*, 1982:343–4.
111 Giese, *Beyond Chinatown*, 1995:7, 31.
112 Nagata, *Unwanted Aliens*, 1996:73.
113 Giese, *Beyond Chinatown*, 1995:32.
114 Ibid., 33.
115 A. Coles, Member for Henty, in Hannan, 'All out!', 1985:36.
116 Abbott to Carrodus, 15.12.1943, NT NAA, AAD Series 46/159/1.
117 A. R. Miller, Chief Surveyor in the Northern Territory quoted in Hannan, 'All out!', 1985:47.
118 From the minutes of the Town Management Board, September 1941, in Hannan, 'All out!', 1985:41.
119 Hannan, 'All out!', 1985:42–3.
120 Ibid., 44, 50, 57.
121 Ibid., 53, 57.
122 Ibid., 54, 56.
123 Ibid., 32.
124 Christine Inglis, 'The Darwin Chinese: A Study of Assimilation', 1967:82.
125 Hannan, 'All out!', 1985:58–9.
126 Ibid., 43.
127 Bain, *Full Fathom Five*, 1982:343; Hugh Edwards, *Port of Pearls*, 1983: 157.
128 Ganter, *The Pearl-Shellers of Torres Strait*, 1994:125ff.
129 Bain, *Full Fathom Five*, 1982:347.
130 Interview with Oku Saioshi, age fifty-six, 15.10.1987, Taiji, Wakayama.
131 Nagata, *Unwanted Aliens*, 1996:238.
132 Statement of 13.12.1948, quoted in A. Palfreeman, *The Administration of the White Australia Policy*, 1967:44.
133 Keiko Tamura, *Michi's Memories: The Story of a Japanese War Bride*, 2001.

CHAPTER 8: MIXED HISTORY AND INDIGENOUS IDENTITY

1 See, for example, Gordon Grimwade, *Lit Sung Goong: Chinese Religious Practices in Cairns*, 1985; Shirley Fitzgerald, *Red Tape, Gold Scissors: The Story of Sydney's Chinese*, 1997.
2 See, for example, the account of Daisy Corunna in Sally Morgan's *My Place*, 1987:343.
3 UN working group, Merkle J, Federal Court.
4 Tony Koch, 'Aboriginal blood feud', *Courier Mail*, 16.12.2000:1.
5 Gordon Matthews, *An Australian Son*, 1996.
6 Morgan, *My Place*, 1987.
7 Mudrooroo, cited in Victoria Laurie, 'Identity crisis', 1996.
8 Laurie, 'Identity crisis', 1996.
9 Fiona Noble, 'Who do we think we are? People who are learning about their Aboriginality', 1996:2.
10 Isabel Tarrago, 'Response to Sally Morgan and the construction of Aboriginality', 1993:469.
11 Bain Attwood, 'Portrait of an Aboriginal as an artist: Sally Morgan and the construction of Aboriginality', 1993:302–18.
12 Noble, 'Who do we think we are?', 1996.
13 Henry Chan, 'The identity of the Chinese in Australian history', 1999:3.
14 Ibid.
15 Ibid., 7.
16 John McCorquodale, 'The legal classification of race in Australia', 1986:7–24.
17 Carol Gistitin, *Quite a Colony: South Sea Islanders in Central Queensland 1867–1993*, 1995.

[18] Interview with Len Royee, Gordonvale, 26.7.1997.

[19] From 1991 to 1996 the indigenous population increased by 33 per cent against a non-indigenous population increase of only 5 per cent. This has also been observed in New Zealand and Canada. In Queensland, there was an 18 per cent increase between 1996 and 2001, of which only 13 per cent can be accounted for through natural increase. The remainder indicates a greater propensity to identify as indigenous. Still, 3.7 per cent of the census population failed to complete the 'identity' question altogether, suggesting that the indigenous population may still rise more than its natural increase. ABS, National Centre for Aboriginal and Torres Strait Islander Statistics, 'Population and Identification Plain English Summary 7/97'; ABS, *Year Book Australia 2002*, Special Article: 'Aboriginal and Torres Strait Islander Australians: A statistical profile from the 1996 Census', ABS Catalogue No 1301.0. OESR Bulletin #2 Census 2001, 'Aboriginal and Torres Strait Islander Queenslanders'.

[20] John Darling, *Below the Wind*, ABC TV, 13.1.1994.

[21] 'Makassar and northeast Arnhem Land—missing links and living bridges', compiled by Michael Cooke, July 1987.

[22] Murray Garde, 'The Marayarr Murrukundja ceremony goes to Makassar', 1993:2.

[23] Ibid., 1.

[24] Ibid., 2.

[25] Ibid. The group consisted of: Johnny Bulunbulun as group leader and songman; Terry Mangapal as didjeridu player; Laurie Marburru, Charlie Djinmalala, Roselyn Gundijiriyardji, Philip Morris, Alfie Cooper, Tommy Steele and Laurie Guraylayla as dancers; and a support team of David Bond from Bawinanga, Diane Moon from Maningrida Arts and Culture, Simon Peart as interpreter, Murray Garde from Bawinanga, and Merv Bishop as photographer.

[26] Interview with Peter Danaja, Maningrida, 6.6.1995. *Abrus precatorius*, or jequirity bean, is a tropical plant whose decorative red and black seeds are used for necklaces and rosary beads.

[27] Rachel Morgan, 'Weavers of Biboki—Weavers of Maningrida', 1995.

[28] Marcus Breen et al., *Our Place, Our Music*, 1989:55.

[29] Ibid., 57.

[30] L. Thompson, 'Jimmy Chi: musician and songwriter', 1990.

[31] Sarah Yu, 'Broome Creole: Aboriginal and Asian partnerships along the Kimberley coast', 1999:69.

[32] Ibid.

[33] Professor Franz Kuna, Klagenfurt, pers. comm.

[34] Hannah McGlade, 'Grandmother Ethel Woyung McGlade: a history of the Nyungar, Chinese and pastoralists of the south-west of Western Australia'.

[35] Jeremy Beckett (ed.), *Past and Present Construction of Aboriginality*, 1988:6.

[36] Kevin Keeffe, 'Aboriginality: resistance and persistence', 1988.

[37] Beverley Ormerod, 'The Martinican concept of "creoleness": a multiracial redefinition of culture', 1998. Jean Bernabé, Patrick Chamoiseau & Raphaël Confiant, 'In praise of creoleness', in *Callaloo* 13, 1990:891–2. Raphaël Confiant, *Ravines du devant-jour*, Paris, Gallimard, 1993.

[38] Ormerod, 'The Martinican concept of "creoleness"', 1998.

Bibliography

Abe, Yoshiharu, 'The trepang industry in the Pacific and Southeast Asia: an anthropological and historical study', MA thesis, University of Melbourne, May 1995.

Atkinson, Anne, *Asian Immigrants to Western Australia, 1829–1901*, Nedlands, University of Western Australia Press, 1988.

Attwood, Bain, 'Portrait of an Aboriginal as an artist: Sally Morgan and the construction of Aboriginality', *Australian Historical Studies*, vol. 25, April 1992 – October 1993:302–18.

Austin, Tony, *I Can Picture the Old Home So Clearly: The Commonwealth and 'Half-Caste' Youth in the Northern Territory, 1911–1939*, Canberra, Aboriginal Studies Press, 1993.

Australian Bureau of Statistics, 'National Centre for Aboriginal and Torres Strait Islander Statistics, Population and Identification Plain English Summary' 7/97.

Australian Bureau of Statistics, *Year Book Australia 2002*, Special Article: 'Aboriginal and Torres Strait Islander Australians: A statistical profile from the 1996 Census', ABS Catalogue no. 1301.0.

Australian Customs Service, 'Coastwatch improvement program strengthens detect and deter capacity', *Manifest Magazine*, November 1999.

Bach, J. P. S., 'The pearling industry of Australia: an account of its social and economic development', prepared for Department of Commerce and Agriculture, University College, Newcastle, 1956.

Bain, Mary Albertus, *Full Fathom Five*, Perth, Artlook Books, 1982.

Bamford, F. W., 'Royal Commission on the Pearl-Shelling Industry Report and Recommendations', CPP 1914–17, vol. 5:831–41.

Bamford, F. W., (Chair) 'Royal Commission on the Pearl-Shelling Industry, Progress Report', Commonwealth Parliamentary Papers, 1913.

Bartlett, Senator Andrew, 'Parliamentary Speech' on 25.11.1999, www.democrats.org.au/parliament/bartlett/19991125border.htm

Beckett, Jeremy, *Torres Strait Islanders—Custom and Colonialism*, Cambridge University Press, 1987.

Beckett, Jeremy (ed.), *Past and Present Construction of Aboriginality*, Canberra, Aboriginal Studies Press, 1988.

Belich, James, *Making Peoples: A History of the New Zealanders from Polynesian Settlement to the End of the Nineteenth Century*, Auckland, 1996.

Berndt, Ronald & Catherine Berndt, *Arnhem Land—Its History and Its People*, Melbourne, Cheshire, 1954.

Biskup, P., *Not Slaves, Not Citizens: The Aboriginal Problem in Western Australia, 1898–1954*, St Lucia, University of Queensland Press, 1973.

Bopaniwung, *Dhäwu Dhuwal Gopiyawuywainguwuy. Ga Mangatharrawainguwuy*, Milingimbi Literature Centre, 1988.

Bottrill, Gus, 'Sahanna—a precis of Gus Bottril's notes on Sahanna, "Afghan" squatter, cameleer and sandalwooder of Moonlight Valley, East Kimberley, WA', ca. 1993.

Boxer, Charles, *Francisco Vieira de Figueiredo: A Portuguese Merchant Adventurer in South East Asia 1624–1667*, M. Nijhoff, Den Haag, 1967.

Breen, Marcus et al., *Our Place, Our Music*, Canberra, Aboriginal Studies Press, 1989.

Broome, Richard, 'Enduring moments of Aboriginal dominance: Aboriginal performers, boxers and runners', *Aboriginal Workers*, special issue of *Labour History*, no. 69, November 1995.

Burgmann, Verity, *Revolutionary Industrial Unionism, The Industrial Workers of the World in Australia*, Melbourne, Cambridge University Press, 1995.

Campbell, Bruce & Bu Wilson, 'Indonesian fishing off Australia: crime or tradition?', *Inside Indonesia*, December 1992: 2–4.

Campbell, Major, 'Geographical memoir of Melville Island and Port Essington on the Cobourg Peninsula, Northern Australia, with some observations on the settlements which have been established on the North Coast of New Holland, etc.', *Royal Geographical Society Journal*, vol. IV, London, 1834.

Carment, David et al., *Northern Territory Dictionary of Biography*, 2 vols, Northern Territory University Press, 1990.

Cawte, John, *The Universe of the Warramiri: Art, Medicine and Religion in Arnhem Land*, Kensington, University of New South Wales Press, 1993.

Cense, A. A., 'Makassaars-Boeginese Prauwvaart op Noord-Australie' *Bijdragen tot de Taal-, Land- en Volkenkunde van Nederlandsch-Indie*, Deel 108, 1952:248–65.

Chan, Henry, 'The identity of the Chinese in Australian history', in R. Ganter (ed.), *Asians in Australian History—Queensland Review*, vol. 6, no. 2, 1999:1–10.

Chase, Athol, '"All kind of nation"—Aborigines and Asians in Cape York Peninsula', *Aboriginal History* 5 (1) 1981:7–19.

Choo, Christine, *Mission Girls: Aboriginal Women on Catholic Missions in the Kimberley, Western Australia, 1900–1950*, Nedlands, University of Western Australia Press, 2001.

Cigler, Michael, *The Afghans in Australia*, Melbourne, AE Press, 1986.

Clarke, Anne, 'The "Moormans Trowsers": Macassan and Aboriginal interactions and the changing fabric of indigenous social life', *Modern Quaternary Research in South East Asia*, vol. 16, 2000:315–35.

Combés, Francisco, 'The natives of the Southern Islands', in Emma Blair and James Robertson (eds), *The Philippine Islands, 1493–1898*, Cleveland: Clark, vol. 40, 1904:99–182.

Cooke, Michael, 'Makassar and Northeast Arnhem Land—missing links and living bridges', Batchelor College Report on a Makassan Field Study, June 1986, July 1987.

Cowlishaw, Gillian, *Love Against the Law*, Aboriginal Studies Press, 2000.

Cowlishaw, Gillian, 'Talking history', *Land Rights News*, July 1995:30–1.

Crawford, Ian, 'Late prehistoric changes in Aboriginal cultures in Kimberley, Western Australia', PhD, University of London, 1969.

Dalrymple, Alexander, *A Plan for Extending the Commerce of this Kingdom and of the East-India Company*, London, 1769.

Dalton, Bill, *Indonesia Handbook*, Vermont, Moon Publications, 1978.

Dalton, Peter, 'Broome, a multiracial community', University of Western Australia, MA thesis in Anthropology, 1964.

Darling, John, *Below the Wind*, The Big Picture, ABC TV, 13.1.1994.

Dashwood, W., 'Pearl-shelling industry in Port Darwin and Northern Territory', CCP 1902, vol. 2:21–91.

Denoon, Donald, Philippa Mein-Smith & Marivic Wyndham, *A History of Australia, New Zealand and the Pacific*, Oxford, Blackwell, 2000.

Dixon, Robert, *Words of Our Country*, University of Queensland Press, 1991.

Djäwawungu, *Dhä-Dhuditjpuy Mangatharra*, Milingimbi Literature Centre, 1979.

Duncan, Graham, 'Misadventures in the button trade', *Good Weekend*, 30.3.1991.

Durack, Mary, *The Rock and the Sand*, London, Constable, 1969.

Earl, G. W., *The Native Races of the Indian Archipelago: Papuans*, London, Hippolyte Bailliere, 1853.

Earl, G. W., *Observations on the Commercial and Agricultural Capabilities of the North Coast of New Holland and Advantages to be Derived from the Establishment of a Settlement in the Vicinity of Raffles Bay*, London, 1836.

Edwards, Hugh, *Port of Pearls: A History of Broome*, Adelaide, Rigby, 1983.

Egan, Ted, *A Justice All Their Own—The Caledon Bay and Woodah Island Killings 1932–1933*, Melbourne University Press, 1996.

Elkin, A. P., *The Australian Aborigines*, Sydney, Angus & Robertson, 1979.

Elliott, Jill, 'Fishing in Australian waters', *Inside Indonesia* no. 46, March 1996.

Elliott, Jill, 'Indonesian fishermen: a Western Australian perspective', MS, ca. 1994.

Erdmann, Mark, 'Leave Indonesia's fisheries to Indonesians!', *Inside Indonesia* no. 63, July 2000.

Erdmann, Mark, 'An ABC guide to coral reef fisheries in southwest Sulawesi, Indonesia' MS, submitted to NAGA, the *ICLARM Quarterly*, February 1995.

Evans, Nicholas, 'Makassan loanwords in Top End languages', *Australian Journal of Linguistics* 1992, vol. 12:45–91.

Farwell, George, *Ghost Towns of Australia*, Adelaide, Rigby, 1976.

Fitzgerald, Shirley, *Red Tape, Gold Scissors: The Story of Sydney's Chinese*, NSW State Library, 1997.

Flinders, Matthew, *A Voyage to Terra Australis*, London, Bulmer, 1814.

Forrest, Peter, *The Spirit of the Daly*, Daly River Community Development Association, 1994.

Forrest, Thomas, *A Voyage from Calcutta*, London, 1792.

Forrest, Thomas, *A Voyage to New Guinea and the Moluccas from Balambangan*, London, Scott 1780.

Foster, W. (ed.), *Letters Received by the East India Company from Its Servants in the East*, vol. 3, London, 1899.

Fox, James, 'A report on eastern Indonesian fishermen in Darwin', *Illegal Entry*, Centre for Southeast Asian Studies, Northern Territory University Occasional Paper no. 1, 1992.

Fox, James, 'Notes on the southern voyages and settlements of the Sama-Bajau', *Anthropologica* XIX, 1977:459-65.

Fry H. T., 'Cathay and the way thither: the background to Botany Bay', *Historical Studies*, vol. 14, 1969–71:497–510.

Ganter, Regina, 'Letters from Mapoon: colonising Aboriginal gender', *Australian Historical Studies* no. 113, October 1999: 267–302.

Ganter, Regina, *The Pearl-Shellers of Torres Strait*, Melbourne University Press, 1992.

Ganter, Regina, 'The Japanese experience of the Great Barrier Reef' oral histories compiled for the Great Barrier Reef Marine Park Authority', 1987, MS held by AIATSIS Canberra and GBRMPA Townsville.

Ganter, Regina & Ros Kidd, 'The powers of protectors: conflicts surrounding Queensland's 1897 Aboriginal legislation', *Australian Historical Studies*, 25 1993:536–54.

Garde, Murray, 'The Marayarr Murrukundja ceremony goes to Makassar', Bawinanga Aboriginal Corporation, 1993.

Giese, Diana, *Astronauts, Lost Souls and Dragons—Voices of Today's Chinese Australians in Conversation with Diana Giese*, University of Queensland Press, 1997.

Giese, Diana, *Beyond Chinatown: Changing Perspectives on the Top End Chinese Experience*, Canberra, National Library of Australia, 1995.

Gistitin, Carol, *Quite a Colony: South Sea Islanders in Central Queensland 1867–1993*, Brisbane, AEBIS Publishing, 1995.

Govor, Elena, *My Dark Brother*, University of New South Wales Press, 2000.

Grimwade, Gordon, *Lit Sung Goong: Chinese Religious Practices in Cairns*, Cairns Museum, 1985.

Haebich, Anna, *For Their Own Good: Aborigines and Government in the South West of Western Australia, 1900–1940*, Nedlands, University of Western Australia Press, 1988.

Hall, Robert, *The Black Diggers*, Canberra, Aboriginal Studies Press, 1997.

Hannan, Agnes, 'All out! The effects of evacuation and land acquisition on the Darwin Chinese 1941–1954', BA Honours thesis, Monash University, 1985.

Hart, C. W. M. & Arnold Pilling, *The Tiwi of North Australia*, New York, Holt Rinehart & Winston, 1960.

Heeres, J. E., *The Part Borne by the Dutch in the Discovery of Australia 1606–1765*, London, Luzac & Company, 1899.

Hey, Nicholas, 'Report to the Colonial Secretary', 1.7.1897, Mf186, AIATSIS.

Hodes, Jeremy, 'Torres Strait Islander migration to Cairns before World War II', M. Letters, Central Queensland University, October 1998.

Holthouse, Hector, *River of Gold—The Wild Days of the Palmer River Gold Rush*, Angus & Robertson, 1967.

Hutchings, Suzi, 'The Darwin Chinese 1874–1983: transformations in ethnic identity and its situation', BA Honours thesis, Department of Anthropology, University of Adelaide, 1983.

Idriess, Ion, *One Wet Season*, Angus & Robertson, 1967 (1949).

Inglis, Christine, 'The Darwin Chinese: a study of assimilation', MA thesis, Australian National University, 1967.

Jones, Tim, *The Chinese in the Northern Territory*, Northern Territory University Press, 1997.

Keeffe, Kevin, 'Aboriginality: resistance and persistence', *Australian Aboriginal Studies*, no. 1, 1988.

Kidd, Rosalind, *The Way We Civilize*, University of Queensland Press, 1997.

King, Phillip Parker, *Narrative of a Survey of the Intertropical and Western Coasts of Australia*, London, 1827.

Kirmess, C. H., *The Australian Crisis*, Melbourne, Lothian, 1901.

Kolff, D. H., *Voyage of the Dutch Brig of War* Dourge, 1840.

Kwong Sue Duk—A Man of Family, video produced by the Kwong Sue Duk Foundation, 1995.
Langton, Marcia, 'Urbanizing Aborigines: the social scientists' great deception', *Social Alternatives* vol. 2, no. 2, 1981: 16–22.
Laurie, Victoria, 'Identity crisis', *Australian Magazine*, 20–1.7.1996.
Layman, Lenore, '"To keep up the Australian standard": regulating contract labour migration, 1901–50', *Labour History*, no. 70, May 1996:41.
Litchfield, Jessie, 'Press collect', unpublished MS, p. 107, MS 132, NLA.
Lockwood, Douglas, *The Front Door, Darwin, 1869–1969,* London, Angus & Robertson, 1969.
MacIntyre, K. G., *The Secret Discovery of Australia*, Menindie, Souvenir Press, 1977.
Mackay, John, (Chair) 'Report of the Royal Commission appointed to enquire into the working of the Pearl-shell and Bêche-de-Mer Industries, Queensland' VPP 1908, vol. 2:1–284.
Macknight, C. C., 'Journal of a voyage around Arnhem Land in 1875', *Aboriginal History*, vol. 5, no. 2, 1981:135–45.
Macknight, Charles Campbell, *A Voyage to Marege—Macassan Trepangers in Northern Australia*, Melbourne University Press, 1976.
Macknight, Charles Campbell, *The Farthest Coast*, Melbourne University Press, 1969.
Mander Jones, Phyllis, *The Tasman Map of 1644*, Sydney, Public Library of New South Wales, 1948.
Manderson, Desmond, *From Mr Sin to Mr Big*, Melbourne, Oxford University Press, 1993.
Markus, Andrew, *Australian Race Relations, 1788–1993*, Sydney, Allen & Unwin, 1994.
Markus, Andrew, *Governing Savages*, St Leonards, Allen & Unwin, 1990.
Markus, Andrew, '"Talka longa mouth"', Aborigines and the labour movement, 1890–1970', in Ann Curthoys & Andrew Markus (eds), *Who Are Our Enemies, Racism and the Australian Working Class*, Neutral Bay, Hale & Iremonger, 1978.
Martinez, Julia, 'The 'Malay' community in pre-war Darwin', in Regina Ganter (ed.), *Asians in Australian History*, *Queensland Review*, vol. 6, no. 2, November 1999.
Masson, Elsie, *Untamed Territory: the Northern Territory of Australia*, London, Macmillan, 1915.
Matthews, Gordon, *An Australian Son*, Melbourne, Heinemann, 1996.
May, Cathie, *Topsawyers: The Chinese in Cairns 1870 to 1920*, Townsville, James Cook University, 1984.
McAdam, Charlie, *Boundary Lines* as told to Elizabeth Tregenza, McPhee Gribble Publishers, 1995.
McCarthy, Michael & Lesley Silvester, 'Australian Contact Shipwrecks Program', MS, Curtin University, 1998.
McCorquodale, John, 'The legal classification of race in Australia', *Aboriginal History*, vol. 16, no. 1986:7–24.
McGlade, Hannah, 'Grandmother Ethel Woyung McGlade: a history of the Nyungar, Chinese and pastoralists of the south-west of Western Australia', paper at conference 'Lost in the Whitewash', Australian National University, December 2000.
McGrath, Ann, '"Black Velvet"', in *'Born in the Cattle', Aborigines in Cattle Country,* Sydney, Allen & Unwin, 1987.
McGregor, Russell, *Imagined Destinies, Aboriginal Australians and the Doomed Race Theory, 1880–1939*, Carlton, Melbourne University Press, 1997.
McIntosh, Ian, *The Whale and the Cross—Conversations with David Burrumarra MBE*, Darwin, Historical Society of the Northern Territory, 1994.
McIntosh, Ian, 'The bricoleur at work: Warang Dingo mythology in the Yirritja moiety of North-east Arnhem Land', M. Letters, University of New England, 1992.
Morgan, Rachel, 'Weavers of Biboki—Weavers of Maningrida', report of the Bawinanga Aboriginal Corporation, February 1995.
Morgan, Sally, *My Place*, Fremantle Arts Centre Press, 1987.
Morris, John, 'The coming of the Macassans to the Islands of the Tiwi', Northern Territory Reference Library MS, ca. 1960.
Moseley, R. D., 'Report of the Royal Commissioner appointed to investigate, report and advise upon matters in relation to the condition and treatment of Aborigines', WAPP 1935, paper 2.
Mulvaney, D. J. & J. H. Calaby, 'So much that is new', *Baldwin Spencer, 1860–1929*, Melbourne University Press, 1985.
Mulvaney, D. John, *The Prehistory of Australia*, Penguin, Ringwood, 1975 (1969).
Nagata, Yuriko, 'Japanese–Australians in the postwar Thursday Island community,' in Regina Ganter (ed.), *Asians in Australian History, Queensland Review* 6 (2) 1999:30–44.
Nagata, Yuriko, *Unwanted Aliens*, University of Queensland Press, 1996.
Noble, Fiona, 'Who do we think we are? People who are learning about their Aboriginality' MA thesis, Griffith University, 1996.
Office for Economic and Statistical Research Queensland, 'Census 2001 Bulletin #2, Aboriginal and Torres Strait Islander Queenslanders.'
Ogawa, Taira, *Arafura-kai no Shinjo*, Tokyo, Aiumi Press, 1976.
Ormerod, Beverley, 'The Martinican concept of "creoleness": a multiracial redefinition of culture', *Mots Pluriels* 7, 1998.
Palfreeman, Anthony, *The Administration of the White Australia Policy*, Melbourne, 1967.
Palmer, Vance, *Legend for Sanderson*, Sydney, Angus & Robertson, 1937.
Palmer, Vance, 'People of the reef', *Walkabout*, 1.3.1935.
Parry-Okeden, William, 'Report on the North Queensland Aborigines and the Native Police', QVP, vol. 2, 1897.
Patunru, Abdul Razak Daeng, *Sedjarah Goa*, Jajasan Kebudajan di Makassar, 1967.
Perez, Eugene, *Kalumburu*, Kalumburu, 1977.
Péron, F. & L. de Freycinet, *Voyage de découvertes aux terres australes*, vol. 2, Paris, 1816.
Philipps, Lorraine, 'Plenty more little brown man! Pearlshelling and White Australia in Queensland 1901–1918', in E. L. Wheelwright & K. Buckley (eds), *Essays in the Political Economy of Australian Capitalism*, vol. 4, Australia & New Zealand Book Company, Sydney, 1980.
Pickering, Michael, 'Cannibalism among Aborigines', PhD thesis, La Trobe University, 1985.
Pires, Tomé, *The Suma Oriental of Tomé Pires: An Account of the East, from the Red Sea to Japan, written in Malacca and India in 1512–1515*, translated by Armando Cortesao, 2 vols, London Hakluyt Society, 1944.
Pohlner, Howard, *Gangurru* Milton, Queensland, Hope Vale Mission Board, 1986.
Powell, Alan, *Far Country—A Short History of the Northern Territory*, Melbourne University Press, 1988 (1982).
Prime, W., *Western Australia's Pearl Harbour: The Japanese Raid on Broome*, Royal Australian Air Force Association, Perth, 1985.
Purcell, V., *The Chinese in Southeast Asia*, Oxford, 1951.
Ramerini, Marco, 'Timor Leste', www.geocities.com/Athens/Styx/6497/timor.html
Read, P. & J. Read, *Long Time, Olden Time*, 1991.
Reid, Anthony, 'Indonesian fishermen detained in Broome: a report on the social and economic back-

ground', in *Illegal Entry*, Centre for Southeast Asian Studies, Northern Territory University Occasional Paper no. 1, 1992.

Reid, Gordon, *A Picnic with the Natives, Aboriginal–European Relations in the Northern Territory to 1910*, Carlton, Melbourne University Press, 1990.

Rendell, Margaret, 'The Chinese in South Australia and the Northern Territory in the nineteenth century', MA thesis, University of Adelaide, 1952.

Reuter, Edward Byron, *The Mulatto in the United States*, New York Johnson Reprint Company, 1970 (1918).

Reynolds, Henry, *North of Capricorn: The Untold Story of Australia's North*, Sydney, Allen & Unwin, 2003.

Rich, Jenny, *Gum Leaf and Cowhide: William Voules Brown, South Australian Pioneer and his Family, 1809–1986*, Eastwood, Victoria, Rich, 1986.

Robert, Willem, *The Dutch Explorations, 1605–1756, of the North and Northwest Coast of Australia*, Amsterdam, 1973.

Rolls, Eric, *Sojourners: The Epic Story of China's Centuries Old Relationship with Australia: Flowers and the Wide Sea*, St Lucia, University of Queensland Press, 1992.

Rowe, Owen, 'Aboriginal employment and conditions in the Northern Territory', 16.3.1932, ACTU Papers, N21/48 ACTU WA and Darwin 1929–1940, Noel Butlin Archive Centre, Australian National University.

Rowley, C. D., *The Destruction of Aboriginal Societies*, Harmondsworth, Penguin, 1970.

Sachse, Rod, 'Indonesian fishermen—an overview', MS, ca. 1994.

Sager, Eric, *Discovering Darwin: The 1930s in Memory and History*, Historical Society of the Northern Territory, Darwin, 1993.

Salter, Elizabeth, *Daisy Bates*, Sydney, Angus & Robertson, 1979.

Sather, Clifford, *The Bajau Laut—Adaptation, History, and Fate in a Maritime Fishing Society of South-eastern Sabah*, Kuala Lumpur, Oxford University Press, 1997.

Saunders, Kay & Helen Taylor, 'The enemy within? The proces of internment of enemy aliens 1939–45', in Kay Saunders (ed.), *War on the Homefront: State Intervention in Queensland 1938–1948*, University of Queensland Press, 1993.

Savage, Paul, *Christie Palmerston, Explorer*, Records of North Queensland History no. 2, James Cook University, 1992.

Schaper, Michael, 'The Broome race riots of 1920', in Jan Gothard (ed.), *Asian Orientations: Studies in Western Australian History* no. 15, University of Western Australia, 1995.

Searcy, Alfred, *In Australian Tropics*, London & Carlisle, Hesperian Press, 1984 (1907).

Sharp, Nonie, 'Culture clash in the Torres Strait Islands: the maritime strike of 1936', *Journal of the Royal Historical Society of Queensland*, 11 (3):107–26.

Sholl, R. J., 'Journal', 29.4.1865 to 4.5.1865, Battye Library MS.

Sissons, David, 'The Japanese in the Australian pearling industry', *Queensland Heritage*, 3 (10) 1979:9–27.

Sissons, David, '*Karayuki-San*: Japanese Prostitutes in Australia, 1887–1916', *Historical Studies*, vol. 17, 1976–77.

Sissons, David, 'Immigration in Australian–Japanese relations, 1871–1971', in J. A. Stockwin (ed.), *Japan and Australia in the Seventies*, Sydney, Angus & Robertson, 1972.

Sowden, William, *The Northern Territory as It Is*, Darwin, Government Printer, 1984 (1882).

Spencer, Baldwin, *Wanderings in Wild Australia*, London, 1928.

Spillett, Peter, 'Dreamtime stories from Makassar and Marege', Darwin, Museum and Art Gallery of the Northern Territory, 1989.

Spillett, Peter (Daeng Makkulle), 'Gotong Royong: Hubungan Makassar–Marege', Paper Presented to the 2nd International Convention of the Indonesian Educational and Cultural Institute, Ujung Pandang, July 1987, MS.

Stevens, Christine, *Tin Mosques and Ghantowns, A History of Afghan Cameldrivers in Australia*, Oxford University Press, 1989.

Stokes, J. L., *Discoveries in Australia* … , vol. 2, London, 1846.

Szpui, Taam, 'My life and work', translated by and preface by Chan Wen Lung, 1925 (MS held by Seepoy Family, Innisfail).

Tamura, Keiko, *Michi's Memories: The Story of a Japanese War Bride*, Canberra, Australian National University, 2001.

Tarrago, Isabel, 'Response to Sally Morgan and the construction of Aboriginality', *Australian Historical Studies* vol. 25 (10), October 1993:496.

Thomas, Nicholas, *Entangled Objects: Exchange, Material Culture and Colonialism in the Pacific*, Cambridge, Harvard University Press, 1991.

Thompson, L., 'Jimmy Chi: musician and songwriter', in *Aboriginal Voices*, Simon & Schuster, 1990.

Thomson, D. F., *Economic Structure and the Ceremonial Exchange Cycle in Arnhem Land*, Melbourne, Macmillan, 1949.

Valentijin, F., *Oud en Nieuw Oost-Indien*, vol. 1, Dordrecht 1724–26.

Vosmaer, J. J., 'Korte beschrijving van het Z.O. schiereiland van Celebes', *Verhandeling van het Bataviaasche Genotenschap*, 1839.

Walker, Alan & R. David Zorc, 'Austronesian loanwords in Yolngu-Matha of Northeast Arnhem Land', *Aboriginal History* 1981, vol. 5, no. 2:107–34.

Warner, Lloyd, *A Black Civilization—A Social Study of an Australian Tribe*, Chicago, Harper & Roe, 1958.

Warren, Jim, *The Sulu Zone, 1786–1898*, Singapore University Press, 1981.

Watanabe, K., 'Sasude-to oyobi Toresu-Kaiko Tanken Hokoku', *Shokumin Kykokai Hokoku* 29, ca. 1894.

Weerasooria, W. S., *Links between Sri Lanka and Australia*, Colombo, Sri Lanka, Government Press, 1988.

Wildey, W. B., *Australasia and the Oceanic Region*, Melbourne, 1876.

Worsley, P. M., 'Early Asian contacts with Australia', *Past and Present* vol. 1, 1955:1–11.

Yarmir, Mary vs Northern Territory of Australia & Ors, Federal Court of Australia, 6.7.1998, Olney J presiding.

Yong, C. F., *The New Gold Mountain, The Chinese in Australia 1901–1921*, Richmond, South Australia, Raphael Arts, 1977.

Yonge, Maurice, *A Year on the Great Barrier Reef*, London, Putnam, 1930.

Yu, Sarah, 'Broome Creole: Aboriginal and Asian partnerships along the Kimberley Coast', in Regina Ganter (ed.), *Asians in Australian History—Queensland Review* 6(2) 1999: 49–73.

Yu, Sarah & Carol Tang Wei, 'The story of the Chinese in Broome', Broome, self-publication, ca. 1998.

Zorc, David Paul, 'Yolngu-Matha Dictionary—Macassan Loanwords Project', 29–30 May 1986, MS.

Zucker, Margaret, *From Patrons to Partners: A History of the Catholic Church in the Kimberley, 1884–1984*, Fremantle, University of Notre Dame Press, 1994.

Index of Places

Index of People

Subject Index